Stability and Security in the Baltic Sea Region

Stability and Security in the Baltic Sea Region

Russian, Nordic and European Aspects

Edited by

OLAV F. KNUDSEN

Norwegian Institute of International Affairs, Oslo

FRANK CASS
LONDON • PORTLAND, OR

First Published in 1999 in Great Britain by
FRANK CASS PUBLISHERS
Newbury House, 900 Eastern Avenue
London IG2 7HH

and in the United States of America by
FRANK CASS PUBLISHERS
c/o ISBS, 5804 N.E. Hassalo Street
Portland, Oregon 97213-3644

Website http://www.frankcass.com

British Library Cataloguing in Publication Data

Stability and security in the Baltic Sea region : Russian,
  Nordic and European aspects
  1. National security – Baltic States 2. National security –
  Russia (Federation) 3. National security – Government policy
  – Baltic States 4. National security – Government policy –
  Russia (Federation) 5. National security – Government policy
  – Europe 6. Baltic States – Foreign relations – Russia
  (Federation) 7. Russia (Federation) – Foreign relations –
  Baltic States
  I. Knudsen, Olav F.
  327.4'79'047

ISBN 0-7146-4932-5 (cloth)
ISBN 0-7146-4492-7 (paper)

Library of Congress Cataloging-in-Publication Data

Stability and security in the Baltic Sea region : Russian, Nordic and
  European aspects / edited by Olav F. Knudsen.
    p.   cm.
  Includes bibliographical references and index.
  ISBN 0-7146-4932-5 (cloth). – ISBN 0-7146-4492-7 (pbk.)
    1. National security–Baltic States. 2. National security–Russia
  (Federation) 3. Baltic States–Relations–Russia (Federation)
  4. Russia (Federation)–Relations–Baltic States. 5. Baltic States–
  Relations–Europe. 6. Europe–Relations–Baltic States.
  I. Knudsen, Olav.
  UA646.53.S73   1999
  355'.0330479–dc21   98-37435
                                                                 CIP

Typeset by Vitaset, Paddock Wood, Kent
Printed in Great Britain by
The Cromwell Press, Trowbridge, Wiltshire.

Contents

Introduction: A General Perspective on the Security of the Baltic Sea Region

OLAV F. KNUDSEN
Norwegian Institute of International Affairs, Oslo

By the end of the twentieth century the Baltic Sea was close to becoming a lake in the European Union (EU). The region had survived, yet not entirely shaken off, one of the most complicated transitions brought on by the end of the Cold War: liberation of the three Baltic states, the breakdown of the Soviet Union, and the transformation of the Baltic Sea area from a zone of confrontation into one of potential integration. Nevertheless, during the first half of the 1990s the Baltic Sea region experienced a range of conflictual encounters between the USSR and its successor state Russia on the one hand, and Estonia, Latvia and Lithuania on the other. Although instances of violence were fortunately brief, limited in scale and have not been recurring, conflictual relations and associated tension have continued to mark bilateral relations across these borders. At the same time, new cooperative relations have been established, which to varying extents encompass all the states in the region.

It must be taken for granted that conflict – in the form of diverging or incompatible interests or values – will always be present, in the Baltic Sea region as elsewhere. But new regional institutions and new, more equitable cooperative practices in the region indicate the possibility of overcoming traditional, destructive ways of dealing with conflict.[1]

The conceptual debates of the 1990s demand that some attention be paid to definitions and usage. *Security*, as the subject matter of this book, has to do with how one deals with conflict so as to limit the harm it brings to the physical and social well-being of individuals and the political and economic well-being of societies.[2] Overt conflict, whether involving just governments or also social groups,[3] is accelerated by fundamental social change such as the transition taking place in the east-central European area towards democracy and market economy. The maintenance of security in the region must therefore be linked analytically to the stresses brought about by such large-scale social change.

The transitions of societies to fundamentally different modes of governance and economic relations take time. However, external influences may speed up the rate of change. In the Baltic Sea case, impulses from regional Nordic and EU members stimulate the processes of change within the neighbouring transitional societies. There can be little doubt that the daily contacts established across the Baltic Sea in large and growing numbers since 1990 in themselves have spurred a reform-oriented outlook, especially in Estonia, Latvia and Lithuania.

Still, it needs to be recognized that even a decade after the dissolution of the USSR the changes brought about by this momentous event are only beginning. New economic systems depend also on changes of attitudes in the population, which in turn require generational change. New political habits, providing a new framework for the functioning of a society and its economic system, take shape only through repetition by successive political elites. Thus, the first decades of the twenty-first century, like the last of the twentieth, are likely to continue to struggle with the legacy of Soviet Russian rule. The fringes of Russia – east, south and west – will therefore continue to have a complex relationship with their great neighbour.

It is for this reason that the present volume emphasizes the long-term perspective. The book sets out to explore the prospects of security in the Baltic Sea region for the coming decades, to assess – on the basis of present trends and developments – the probability, as we enter the twenty-first century, that the governments and groups of this area will be able to resolve their differences without recourse to the threat or use of violence.

The Baltic Sea region's history in the twentieth century, marked by unprecedented levels of violence, has set the stage for such an inquiry. These upheavals were both preceded and followed by ideological confrontation, going back as far as the early part of the century. In the second half of the century the militarized and industrial evolution of communist rule in Eastern and Central Europe brought on the now-familiar environmental, economic and health-related disasters, spurred by the bipolar contest.

Many observers at the end of the Cold War saw in these trends a need to redefine security in a broader way to tone down the military aspects and increase the attention paid to non-military threats. The present volume emphasizes the links between the military and non-military aspects. One should not overlook the connections between the long-term convulsions of European social conflict and the excesses of the Soviet system as it fought for its survival. Before 1989 the contrast between the systems East and West was most visible in Germany. By the 1990s the Baltic Sea became a shuttle route connecting widely disparate sections of the social, environmental and economic spectrum at the two ends.

In the cooperative and conciliatory spirit of the 1990s, the discordant differences between the old 'East' and 'West' have been downplayed and muted. Nevertheless, significant discrepancies persist, even as some parts of the former Soviet Union proceed through fundamental economic change to get ready for membership in the European Union. Remaining disparities in social standards, life-style and political culture – not to mention living standards – are likely to continue to spur discord and trigger processes of regional conflict. Hopefully, such conflict will gradually be replaced by the conflicts of ordinary international[4] economic exchange, in which growing interdependence transforms the nature of conflict from a zero-sum to more of a positive-sum relationship. By the mid-1990s such trends were already underway, but in the short run their ameliorating effects would only be noticeable on the surface. In the meantime, one may observe that the processes of change in the region represent such a *mélange* of transnational and transregional factors that they cannot sensibly be captured within the old dichotomy of international vs. domestic.

Thus, the conceptual perspective on security underlying this book is a broad one, in which conflict in the Baltic Sea region is seen as a late consequence of the large-scale socio-political conflict that unfolded in nineteenth- and twentieth-century Europe and is continuing – in Central and Eastern Europe, at least – into the twenty-first. Though the outlook is broad, the book does not focus on the non-traditional aspects of security, but rather on the narrower, classical dimensions of insecurity which continue to be present during the process of transition.

The Baltic Sea region is to some extent arbitrarily defined. It has never been marked by a distinct regional culture, or been under a uniform system of law or authority, even if the memory of the Hanseatic system provides some indication to the contrary. The powers surrounding the Baltic Sea have more often been brought together in conflict than in cooperation.[5] Many, maybe even most of them, have long been used to regarding themselves as parts of other regions: Poland of Central Europe; Germany of Central and later Western Europe; Denmark, Finland and Sweden of the Nordic region. The delineation of a Baltic Sea region is therefore partly a matter of analytical convenience, partly done in recognition of the preferences of the governments in the area – led by Denmark, Germany and Poland. Those were the ones who started using the term as they prepared, from 1989 on, to establish the Council of the Baltic Sea States (CBSS) which was formally instituted in 1992.[6]

Our starting point implies that even the term 'region' is somewhat arbitrary. This is entirely in keeping with standard usage in the field of international relations. In the large literature on international regions, terminological precision has no great importance, despite the efforts of a classic such as Cantori and Spiegel's 'The International Politics of Regions' (1970) to introduce order. There is no conventional way to define a region, except to the effect that we are dealing with a group of countries geographically clustered together, in this case with the Baltic Sea as a crucial link. The most significant aspect of a region in security terms may be that it is a *security complex* (Buzan, 1991), that is, that its governments consider that their '… primary security concerns link together sufficiently closely that their national securities cannot realistically be considered apart from one another'. (Buzan, 1991: 192) The Baltic Sea region of the littoral states plus Belarus and Norway seem to conform to such a definition.

On the other hand, individual countries may (as already indicated) simultaneously be part of several regional clusters which only partly overlap, the most pronounced case being Russia. Some of the Nordic countries (Denmark, Finland, Sweden) are obviously also part of the Baltic Sea region, others – such as Iceland and Norway – are Baltic Sea states more by invitation[7] than by geography. In the eastern Baltic hinterland, Belarus is another non-littoral state whose geopolitical presence both inside and beyond the narrower region needs to be taken into account.

To the extent that these regional definitions correlate with feelings of loyalty in the populations involved, they are politically salient. It is normally assumed that political loyalties are multiple. Nevertheless, in some of the societies involved here, notably the ex-sovietized areas, the recognition in political life of multiple loyalties may be problematic, since political loyalty often continues to be thought of in binary terms.

At the same time countries are part of regions on different levels of inclusiveness. All countries in the Baltic Sea region are also part of the broader European geographic configuration, some are part of the political configuration 'the European Union,' some are part of the intermediate region conventionally called Central and Eastern Europe, others of Western Europe. Inevitably, this fact has some bearing on the outlook of the governments concerned.

Then there are regional sub-groups. The three Baltic states Estonia, Latvia and Lithuania are often designated as a subregion within the Baltic Sea region, while Scandinavia (Denmark–Norway–Sweden) and Fenno-Scandinavia (adding Finland) are other subgroups. We shall mostly be using the term *Nordic* to designate collectively Denmark, Finland, and Sweden (with or without Iceland and Norway), and *Baltic* to collectively designate Estonia, Latvia and Lithuania. The Baltic Sea region, in short, ordinarily embraces the Baltics, the Nordics, Germany, Poland and Russia, and in some respects even Belarus.

However, our design is not to go country by country, but primarily to try to see the security of the whole region from several broader angles. Chapters on individual states such as Germany, Poland, Russia and Sweden have been constrained to focus on the regional aspects of policy, more than on the nation.[8]

In the most general terms, the book deals with the following problems of regional security, which are typical of – but notably not specific to – the Baltic Sea region:

- the issue of spheres of influence and the balancing of power,
- the question of the role of organizational solutions to the region's security problems,
- the doctrine of the indivisibility of security,
- the popular notion of soft security,
- the question of security guarantees.

The questions of spheres of influence and of balancing power are related to that of linkages between subregional and regional security – or establishing regional security at different levels of geographic inclusiveness. Is the security of, for example, the Baltic Sea region best served by establishing arrangements at that level or by involving the broader, European-wide organizations such as the Organization for Security and Cooperation in Europe (OSCE) or NATO's EAPC? This touches the dilemma of weighing organizational efficiency against political equity: Local solutions may be more functional because the local actors are those who know the issues and are at the same time those who are directly concerned, who have interests in the disputes. But political equity may not be served if one actor is locally dominant; the result may be the emergence of a sphere of influence. To counteract that, local, 'subregional' solutions must either be anchored (to the extent that is possible) in more inclusive regional arrangements where countervailing power can somehow be brought to bear, or the entire issue must be dealt with on a more inclusive level. These are challenges which need to be met for stability to be maintained. They are discussed from different angles in individual chapters.

The book is divided into three main parts, the first of which provides a framework of general insights and theories relevant to the region, about asymmetric power relations, historical and geopolitical factors, worldviews and political culture. The second part analyzes the region in the perspective of the policies of key governmental actors. The third part focuses on intergovernmental cooperation and the role of regional institutions, in particular those of the Nordic countries and the

European Union, along with the WEU. The concluding chapter examines the issues dealt with in the light of three philosophical traditions in the study of international politics.

The 'Russian, Nordic and European Aspects' referred to in the title should be interpreted broadly.[9] The book focuses on aspects which link those actors in the Baltic Sea region who have a foot outside it – like Russians, some Nordics and other Europeans – to the region and therefore add an extra-regional dimension to it. For this reason, the three Baltic states as such may be seen to occupy a smaller place between these covers than could otherwise have been expected. Moreover, the first part – the general one – is held to serve a vital function in connecting the regionally specific subject matter with the more general and global.

This emphasis also expresses the intention of the editor in shaping the volume as such, with its general outline, the emphasis within chapters on the region as a whole and the longer-term perspective. Beyond this, each contributing author brings his or her unique approach to the subject, which can only be fully appreciated by going directly to the source.

In introducing the reader to the volume, the editor also wants to express the gratitude of his co-authors and himself to several less visible participants in our project. In addition to the supporting staff of NUPI[10] four colleagues – Pavel Baev, Klaus Carsten Pedersen, Ingemar Dörfer and Guido Lenzi – participated as discussants at our preparatory workshop and provided valuable feedback.

NOTES

The present volume is part of the 1996–97 project 'Conflict Resolution and Regional Security in the Baltic Sea Area' undertaken and completed at the Norwegian Institute of International Affairs (NUPI). The project was funded by the Norwegian Ministry of Defence, as proposed and conceived by the editor.

1 The book does not address the debate on whether regional security should be studied comparatively. While the editor tends to agree with such a position, his co-authors may not necessarily take the same view. It follows from this also that the book does not represent a unified view on the extent to which the security concerns of this region may be unique. On a theoretical level such issues are well handled in Lake and Morgan (1997), a book which systematically utilizes Buzan's (1983, 1991) concept of regional security complexes, taking a consciously comparative approach and presenting comparisons of selected regional security complexes.

2 This is a conception in the classical tradition of security studies which indicates that the 'new' security thinking of the 1990s may not be that new after all, as shown e.g. in Holst (1967) or Andrén (1972). On the thinking of the 1990s, see (e.g.) Buzan, 1997.

3 The perspective of this book is that states – represented by their governments – are still the major actors of international politics, though they are far from being the only ones that count.

4 'Transjurisdictional' may be a more precise and appropriate term.

5 Among recent works which have contributed to our understanding of the region are van Ham's collection of contributions from the region (van Ham, 1995); Joenniemi's anthology (Joenniemi, 1997) with sociological conceptualizations of regional politics, and the collection by Tunander, Baev and Einagel (Tunander *et al.*, 1997) with innovative geopolitical perspectives (though not confined to Northern Europe), as well as two works in the classical security studies tradition: Dörfer, 1997 – a pointed analysis with a Nordic focus, and Krohn's volume (Krohn, 1996) with a broad survey of the regional security situation.

6 'Formally', however, is not very formal: The Council of Baltic Sea States was instituted by a mere declaration on the part of the governments participating. Its existence is therefore fragile indeed in the formal sense.

7 These two states were not originally considered natural candidates for membership in the Council of the Baltic Sea States, but were subsequently invited to take part.

8 For a recent study of this region with a greater emphasis on individual state policies see Krohn, 1996.

9 Specifically, they should not be taken to mean (e.g.) that Russian authors provide the Russian aspects, Nordic authors the Nordic aspects, and so on.

10 The completion of this volume also owes much to the supporting staff of NUPI – not least Hilde T. Harket and Vibeke L. Sand – as well as assistants Knut Magne Sundal and Jolanda Wijnsma.

Part I

General Perspectives

Security on the Great Power Fringe: Dilemmas Old and New

OLAV F. KNUDSEN
Norwegian Institute of International Affairs, Oslo

INTRODUCTION

As implied in the title, this chapter argues that despite all the changes which have taken place since 1990, the classical security puzzles are still with us. They affect, as before, the future of small states, even as new threats and challenges have provided additional complexities.

The subject of small states is easily romanticized. Thus, it bears keeping a long-term perspective in mind. In the long run, the continuity of any smaller unit formally recognized as a 'state' can hardly be taken for granted.[1] Relevant experiences in the twentieth century are found – among others – in Afghanistan, Belgium, Cuba, Czechoslovakia, Denmark, Estonia, Finland, Hungary, Korea, Latvia, Lithuania, the Netherlands, Norway and Tibet. There is also the experience of the Kurds, Palestinians and other jurisdictionally fragmented nationality groups. For areas weak in power resources, independent statehood itself is in most cases discontinuous in the longer trends of time. At the beginning of the twenty-first century small-state governments find themselves repeatedly poised between the caprice of great powers and the effacing embrace of regional integration. The preservation of small, independent states[2] under such geopolitical circumstances may therefore safely be regarded as a hazardous undertaking. In historical perspective their existence at any given time is a stochastic phenomenon, broadly documented *inter alia* by Bozeman (1960) and by Hall and associates (Hall, 1986).

NEW PROBLEMS AND OLD

To what extent are the new security agendas really 'new'? We may take as a starting point the observation that great-power relations at this turn of the century are, if not fundamentally altered, at least in a phase of marked compatibility. The question is where that leaves *other* inter-collectivity relations. Events during the 1990s in Eurasian settings – ranging from the Caucasus and the former Yugoslavia to Moldavia and the Baltics – indicate that existential challenges to states are no less frequent than before 1990, and that these challenges derive as much from new transborder phenomena as from the classical state-to-state threats. Clearly, therefore, the new problems represent a fundamental challenge to the survival of smaller states, especially of weakly organized states. A vast increase in border-transcending activities and relationships has put great pressure on the border-management capabilities of ex-Soviet areas. The Baltic Sea region has faced particularly the new challenges of international crime, transjurisdictional resource management and displaced minority groups, which have posed unfamiliar, fundamental problems for the region's governments as they were designing new policies.

These new Eurasian circumstances altered, in other words, the working conditions of governments in the security field, and they may well be undermining the ability of individual states to function as such, but they have not invalidated the applicability of models focused on states and their mutual relations. The issues of security still concern how collectivities cope in deliberated ways with trans-collectivity problems.

What is different is that the new dimensions accentuate the need to focus on a broader range of responses by states to the challenges they face. The new transborder phenomena represent a 'second-generation' security dilemma, because if the way out of the old security trap is the opening of borders to international interdependence, then the new threats are precisely the potential undermining of the state by that same, new interdependence.

In the case of the small-state problematique I will now bring the argument one step further by claiming that what I have so far described as two different kinds of security challenges are actually largely overlapping. Security dilemmas (Glaser, 1997) are usually examined from the perspective of equals. Yet it is argued here that security dilemmas are no less relevant in conflicts between unequals, just the way they often occur along the fringes of great powers. When the classical notion of security dilemmas is brought into an analysis which assumes a wide disparity of power between the antagonists, the relevant security threats broaden dramatically in range from the classical confrontation of equals to the manipulation and penetration possible in relations of inequality. For this reason it is my contention that during the last decade, the topicality of security dilemmas on the great-power fringe has, if anything, increased.

Admittedly, along the way it did not always look like that. As the

Soviet Union struggled through its last difficult months, its utter pulverization was considered quite possible. That was long seen to apply even to its successor, the Russian Federation. However, Russia then began regaining at least its core strength. During the winter of 1997–98 Russian diplomacy *vis-à-vis* Estonia, Latvia and Lithuania showed a marked ability to draw on the role of russophone minorities to undermine the bargaining position of its Baltic neighbours (analyzed in the Vares chapter in this volume). These and other East-Central European states were squeezed between the old and the new. The European Union intruded from the west; Russia remained in the east. State capacities were challenged from two sides.[3]

At the same time, the debate over NATO's eastern enlargement, and that process itself, have in any case extended the preoccupation with classical security issues.[4] What all of this boils down to is that for old as well as new reasons the stability of regions located along the fringes of great powers is still in question. That applies not least when those great powers are inwardly disorganized and outwardly restive, when their governments and major social groups are not coping adequately with affairs within their jurisdiction and are at the same time dissatisfied with their country's international standing.

Is transjurisdictional integration the solution? To what extent can organized regional security cooperation provide an answer? How does one draw the line between the instrumental benefits of multilateral solutions and the costs of rigid institutional frameworks? In security affairs more narrowly conceived, is there a case for avoiding institutions in favour of some kind of implicit regional balancing of alignments? Finding workable solutions requires an adequate diagnosis of the nature of the problem. This and subsequent chapters explore the challenges and the possibilities for great power fringes.

TWO THEORIES

There are several plausible theories to explain the major ills in great-power/small-state relations. Here I shall concentrate on two which seem especially pertinent to the Baltic Sea region. One is that of great-power rivalry, another is the familiar theory of imperialism.[5] The former interprets the great power's motives in pressuring the small state as reasonable given its interaction with other great powers and thus in a sense unavoidable. The theory of imperialism, on the contrary, sees whatever pressure is applied to small neighbours as an inherent tendency in most great powers, a tendency which in turn is caused by economic, political or cultural factors.[6]

During the Cold War the USSR was frequently held to be

imperialistic, but its behaviour also fitted the pattern of great-power rivalry. So did that of the United States, otherwise also often charged with imperialism during the 1960s and 1970s.

With the Cold War gone and the great-power rivalry at a minimum, Russia could be seen as an intriguing test case. Pressure applied by Moscow under the new circumstances might be seen to justify the old charges of imperialism. Russia's best counterargument would be that NATO's enlargement has necessitated renewed vigilance and efforts to keep the Western alliance at bay, particularly within the area of the former USSR. In short, in our terms Russia (to the extent its government has been making such an argument) may be acting within the great-power model, whereas some of its Western neighbours are convinced that imperialism is back in the driver's seat in Moscow – and the US and its allies keep their fingers crossed, playing two horses – betting on two theories – at once. (More on the Russian perspective in the Moshes chapter below.)

Developments in North European security relations over the past few years illustrate this ambiguity. Between the governments in the region a subtle debate has been taking place. Prudence in many cases has dictated less than complete transparency in the statement of positions. The United States apparently has wanted the emergence of a separate, subordinate security arrangement in which Estonia, Latvia and Lithuania could be encapsulated and secured without NATO membership. With the exception of Denmark and Iceland, the Nordic states seem to have shared with Washington the sentiment – which has not, however, been officially expressed – that Baltic NATO memberships may not be the ideal solution in a broader perspective. At the same time, there are signs of internal division of view in several of these capitals. In any case, the Nordic states have all as one rejected the notion of a Nordic–Baltic solution. These aspects are further analyzed by Værnø in her chapter below.

The position of Russia on these issues is amply clear as far as Baltic NATO memberships go, but despite an active elaboration of Russia's Baltic policy after February 1997, its ultimate position remains vague (see the Moshes chapter and Knudsen, 1998a, 1998b). Russia has both launched new cooperative concepts for the region and revealed a clear preference for retaining within it an exclusive sphere of influence, what the Russian government called a 'bloc-free zone'. Nordic views on Russia's role in this context also continue to be vague, except for *obbligato* statements to the effect that Russia must not be 'excluded'. Thus, as will also be elaborated below, there are elements present both of implicit balancing behaviour and of multilateralist, institutionalist approaches.

The terms 'balancing behaviour' or 'balancing moves' refer to the adjustment of a country's alignment *vis-à-vis* major powers. It should be noted that balancing moves in the new circumstances of the 1990s (and beyond) are less clearly discernible than they were before. The overwhelming weight of the blocs at the time of the Cold War solidified the East/West balance of global power and made even subtle balancing moves by non-bloc participants easily perceptible. By 1996–97 clarity has turned to diffuseness. The complicating alternative interpretations are spelled out by Heisler and Quester in their chapter below. In the crowded stream of signals between states, balancing moves – for example, the shifting of informal or indirect ties between states,[7] or statements made, or statements anticipated and yet not made – such moves are much more difficult to read under the present circumstances. Communication between governments also has to cross other barriers, and the North European area cannot be regarded as homogeneous in this respect. The Leeds chapter in this volume shows how patterns of thinking and behaving are likely to vary between different geocultural domains, with the North-European region evidently straddling two such areas.

An analysis of life on the great-power fringe under post-Cold War conditions must sort out the relative salience of the circumstantial and the structurally determined, of the intra-regional specifics and the cross-regional generics (see also the discussion in Lake and Morgan, 1997). Great powers are not necessarily interested in the maintenance of independent neighbours. Yet, the point of creating an explicit security system between a great power and its neighbours would presumably be to preserve the units of sovereign government concerned. There are two further rationales for such a regional security system (if we take the preservation of the existing states as an objective): to prevent the system from turning violent, and to prevent it from becoming a sphere of influence. The two are linked. If one were to focus only on tackling violence, this might at the same time encourage the development of a sphere of influence.

GENERAL EXPLANATORY FACTORS

Let me first try to sort out the general from the circumstantial. The generic aspects of security in a great-power neighbourhood are a combination of a) inequality, or power disparity, and b) contiguity, implying a marked exposure in security terms, of the weaker[8] to the stronger. As already pointed out, there are at least two competing models to account for this problem, great-power rivalry and imperialism.

Great-power rivalry and regional neighbourhoods

Given a condition of great-power rivalry, relations between two contiguous powers, one small[9] and one great, tend to be unstable, because they are largely determined by factors outside the bilateral relationship.[10] A model to represent the relationship may include the following three causal variables (Knudsen, 1988):

1. the degree of tension between the great power A (the neighbouring great power) and its main opponent B;
2. the degree of extroversion in A's foreign policy;
3. the small state's foreign policy orientation; that is, the degree of its alignment with A or B, or with neither.

The model seeks to capture the probability of the application of pressure by the great power[11] – whether diplomatic, political (by manipulation and penetration) or military – against its smaller neighbour. Pressure is thought to be triggered by increased threat perceptions in the great power. Threats to the great power's security are in turn related to rival great powers. In this context a small neighbour's importance is secondary, but rarely insignificant. This is due to the possible harm the small state is thought to be able to bring to the strategic relationship. Hence its significance to both (or all) great-power sides: The greater the tension between the great powers, the greater the strategic importance of the small neighbour to its great-power neighbour; the greater the strategic importance of the small neighbour to the neighbour's great-power enemy.

This translates into a propensity to action on the part of the great power: As tension increases between the great power (A) and other states, and the greater the sensitivity to threat on the part of the great power's elites, the greater the great power's propensity to put pressure on the small neighbour for reassurances by various acts of compliance or self-denial on the part of the small power, so as to guarantee its non-hostile intentions (Jakobson, 1968).

The hypotheses imply that in one respect the small state's policies are likely to be uninteresting: It often does not matter much what the small state does to ameliorate neighbourly relations, because its role in the great-power competition is given by its location alone as potentially threatening. The territory of the small neighbour may be used as a stepping stone or a gateway in an attack on the big neighbour by its great-power rival. Such events may occur even against the will of the small neighbour, as its forces may be too weak to resist a major assault. The small neighbour cannot easily alter this by political moves, short of drastic accommodation or amalgamation with its bigger neighbour.

Even in the post-Cold War détente, however, Russian expectations of Baltic states' policies in the late 1990s, inspired by the anticipated threat of NATO expansion, often seemed to conform to this pattern of reasoning.

An early case from US foreign policy tells openly about the complexities involved. In 1915, Mexico was the object of considerable US attention during the ongoing international crisis. US relations with belligerents at the time were tense. The United States government was seriously concerned over German efforts to exploit domestic turmoil in Mexico, which might divert US attention from events in Europe (Link, 1963: 134; Blasier, 1976: 106–15). Here is how Secretary of State Lansing summarized the situation in October 1915:

> Looking at the general situation I have come to the following conclusions: Germany desires to keep up the turmoil in Mexico until the United States is forced to intervene; therefore, we must not intervene. Germany does not wish to have any one faction dominant in Mexico; therefore, we must recognize one faction as dominant in Mexico. When we recognize a faction as the government, Germany will undoubtedly seek to cause a quarrel between that government and ours; therefore, we must avoid a quarrel regardless of criticism and complaint in Congress and the press. It comes down to this: Our possible relations with Germany must be our first consideration; and all our intercourse with Mexico must be regulated accordingly (Link, 1963: 134n).

Blasier relates how the US–Germany–Mexico sequence was repeated during the crisis years of 1938–39 (Blasier, 1976: 126f).

Counterbalancing and *extended deterrence* are concepts dealing with the responses by a remote great power in favour of a threatened small state. Counterbalancing is here used as the broader concept, covering any move by the remote great power to support the threatened small state, from the most innocuous verbal declarations up to and including military measures.[12] Extended deterrence is a type of counterbalancing and refers to the use of explicit threats and military posturing on behalf of the threatened small state, such as the US policy during the Cold War.[13] Note that there was no question of extended deterrence in the Mexican case just cited, inasmuch as Germany was rather unlikely to engage itself more seriously in defence of Mexican sovereignty *vis-à-vis* the United States.

Provided the major states prefer the status quo, mutual deterrence and other inhibiting factors will start appearing in the great-power relationship as tension increases further towards the highest levels, inducing restraint. Beyond a certain, rather high level of tension between the great powers, the danger of a major war will keep them from maximum effort in seeking to control the small powers, nor will they have sufficient resources or attention to spare from a potential confrontation with their rival for an attempt to do so.

When tension is very high, counterbalancing by an opposing, remote great power may disappear altogether, on the reasoning that that in itself might precipitate the dreaded event. If, in a crisis or war situation, a remote great power fears that the opposing great power will intervene in the small power, the remote great power may well refrain from trying to draw the small power towards its own side (Riste, 1965: 50 and 126–7; also Fox, 1959: 175). Something like this may have been working against the diplomacy of Estonia, Latvia and Lithuania even under the more relaxed post-Cold War circumstances, as they sought to register the support of the United States. It seems likely that in US policy calculations the danger of precipitating a hardening of Russian policy could follow from a too-involved US policy in the Baltics.

During the First World War the British government, which – true to its traditional policy – was taking a highly restrictive stand on neutral rights, was quite lenient with Denmark and Holland when they were pressured by Germany to practise their neutrality in a pro-German manner. The same process was at work in the Norwegian case during the 1914–18 period, only turned around. Germany may well have wanted to intervene in Norway to stop patently pro-British practices, but was afraid to do so because of Britain's superior power at sea (Riste, 1965, Fure, 1996).

Thus, according to this model a great power's urge to control its neighbours derives primarily from tension with other great powers. When great-power elites perceive increasing external danger, they become wary of the small neighbour for possible deviant policy; hence there is an increase in the great power's propensity to put pressure on the small neighbour and demand compliance from its leaders (Jakobson, 1968: 38). If the cooperative patterns which emerged between the great powers in the 1990s can serve to reduce the likelihood of future great power tension, relations in the Baltic Sea area will benefit – provided the theory is right. If the other theory applies, it will be a different matter.

Imperialism and the power cycle

The alternative theory involves the familiar idea of imperialism. In this case, the reasoning is that the great power is simply out to add to its territory or its area of control, whether to satisfy dreams of political and cultural aggrandizement, or because of more pedestrian economic rationales. The main thing in this case is that the theory does not refer to direct politico-diplomatic interaction as explaining the great power's behaviour. The urge to expand is seen as simply arising internally and craving satisfaction. In the conventional wisdom of small-state policy-making, the expansionist urge will always be there and is not likely to subside easily.

Power-cycle theories argue that great powers go through cycles or phases proceeding from internal growth to external expansion to overextension and subsequent decline (Modelski, 1978, Gilpin, 1981, Kennedy, 1987). Population growth and resource needs also lead to lateral pressures (Choucri and North, 1975). The great power's power cycles manifest themselves as shifts between extroversion and introversion. Pressure on the small neighbours will rise and ebb as cycles change. In extrovert phases, not only are small neighbours squeezed, tension is also likely to rise between the great power and its rivals, further exacerbating the neighbourly pressures.

The primary stimulus to either phase of the power cycle is likely to be the state of affairs internally in the great power. Is the power elite fresh on the scene or long established; secure in power or on the verge of losing hold? A great power in the extrovert phase may bring out reactions from other great powers and easily raise international tensions just for this reason. Hence the two kinds of theory overlap to some extent. Assuming counterbalancing to be a feature of the system, great-power extroversion directed against its margins leads to great-power tension, leading to further great-power pressure on the small neighbour.

The absence of counterbalancing pressure between the great powers opens a broader leeway for one of them to further extend its influence. Absent counterbalancing may be simply a matter of how a great power's elite chooses to play the great power role, and whether they want to play at all. Regardless of the reason, a great power can by its mere presence in or absence from interstate relations affect the affairs of the system, and the amount of room for expansion on the part of others. By so doing it may also give other great powers the incentive to engage in, or refrain from, solo adventures, cf. Rothstein's ironic comment on how Britain sometimes chose to play its role: 'Note the correspondence between Britain's concentration on internal affairs and the partition of Poland (1772–95), the tribulations of Denmark in the 1860s, and the disappearance of Austria in 1938.' (Rothstein, 1968: 187n). The US isolationist period in the 1920s and 1930s, along with the long absence of Russia and Germany from the international system after the First World War, permitted destabilizing great-power activities to take place in East/Central Europe and in the Far East.

Expansionism may also be opportunistic, coming as a consequence of unforeseen changes in the international system. For example, if capability shifts dramatically to one great-power side, there will be increasing great-power pressures on a small state to lean to that side, as in the process of bandwagoning described by Fox (1959: 187) ('anti-balance of power' in her terms), theorized by Waltz (1979) and further developed by Walt (1987). If the ascendant power is a neighbour, the squeeze may be irresistible, as we had occasion to see with the power shift of 1935–39. If the closest great power is on its way down, however, the consequences may not be as obvious, as we can see from the unfolding of the equally monumental power shift after 1989.

The small state is not willy-nilly the object of external forces. Its governing elites have their own interpretations of the realities facing them abroad. They have their own aspirations for their nation, and their own experiences to build upon in choosing a foreign policy for the future. The small neighbour's chosen foreign-policy orientation serves as a signal to the great neighbour of the extent to which the latter has succeeded or failed in its influence attempts. An alliance between the two may pacify neighbourly relations entirely. A neutral stance by the smaller party may be grudgingly accepted by the neighbouring great power, but might also arouse its suspicion and vigilance. Were the small state to call for counteralliance – acts of global balancing – this may be perceived not merely as a deliberate insult, but as a direct challenge, as the cases of the three Baltic states and Russia demonstrated during the 1990s. There are earlier cases, perhaps most prominently Cuba after 1959. This – the ultimate move of lining up with the big neighbour's enemy – will be taken as a direct threat. Responding in such cases, the big neighbour has sought to counter the move, sometimes with threats, sometimes with persuasion. In most of these cases the small state has decided, sooner or later, to make concessions.

Part of the calculation here has to do with what the small state's foreign-policy orientation conveys to the great powers about effective territorial control. Mathisen (1971) offers a formulation that encapsulates the essence of an exposed small state's circumstances: 'When the small neighbour's strategic importance is great and the authority exercised over the small neighbour's territory is insignificant, the likelihood increases that one of the great powers will intervene.' (Mathisen, 1971: 49). As illustrations may be offered Belgium and Luxembourg in 1914; the Netherlands, Belgium, Luxembourg, Norway and Denmark in 1939–40, Afghanistan in 1979. This applies even when the small neighbour in question has long been within an established great-power sphere of influence. The anxiety of the USSR over Poland in 1956 and 1980 (cf. Kaminski's chapter below) and its interventions in Hungary (1956) and Czechoslovakia (1968) demonstrate the strength of this political logic.

The phenomenon is the subject of what is often referred to as the power-vacuum hypothesis. Conventionally, 'nature abhors a vacuum'. In this case, 'nature' is a great power. In traditional diplomatic relations, any demonstration that small-state territorial control was inadequate would ring a bell in great-power foreign offices; it raised the spectre of a power vacuum. An uncontrolled area was thought to be ripe for intervention, because if it was important to one great power it was *ipso facto* important to that power's chief rival and so ultimately to them all. In a case like this, given the appropriate circumstances, intervention became a pre-emptive affair.

Great Britain and Germany were both planning to intervene in Norway in 1939–40. In the end the danger of being pre-empted by the other side helped trigger the attack (Fure, 1996). While the moral burden ended up pretty squarely on Germany's shoulders, at least in the public eye, in actual fact Britain had maintained plans for such eventualities ever since Norway became independent in 1905 (Riste, 1965: 34n). Britain refused to guarantee Norway's neutrality in 1907, due to such contingency plans; it arrogated to itself, in other words, the right to intervene in Norway. In Germany, however, the idea apparently did not take hold until the interwar years. What made Germany's Danish–Norwegian campaign a more realistic proposition were other developments – above all technological – that increased these countries' presumed strategic importance, including the role of Danish airfields and the idea of using the Norwegian coast as a string of bases from which to achieve control of shipping lanes – with submarines and aircraft – in the oceans surrounding Britain and beyond.

The question for the twenty-first century according to this theory is whether Russian – or for that matter German – imperialist or expansionist impulses will regain their former significance as inputs for policy in the Baltic Sea region.

BACK TO THE CIRCUMSTANTIAL

By circumstantial aspects I am referring to transient phenomena like the characteristic working modes of the day; in other words, the subtler and more time-bound ways in which states deal with each other from day to day, in particular as such habits affect regional relationships. The collapse of the Cold War system brought significant changes in the way states relate to each other. It altered especially the amount of unofficial contact between former communist societies and other

countries, not least in Europe. It expanded the propensity of governments to use official, multilateral working arrangements. Regional
cooperative ventures rebounded in popularity, and a great number of
proposals were launched in the first few years of European post-Cold
War euphoria. Only some of them have survived, but the enthusiasm
continues.

In the long term the continuation of these new trends will in large
part be dependent on a combination of (a) a continuing political will
to maintain open borders for intersocietal transactions, (b) a continuing
acceptance of multilateral working modes in foreign affairs, and (c) the
continuing absence of tension. Historical experience with small-state
cooperation in strategically sensitive areas has shown such projects to
decline and falter as tension among the great powers increased
(Brundtland 1971: 132). Of these three factors, the possible interaction
of (b) and (c) would seem to offer the key to a more fundamental change
of relationships in the future, to the extent that the use of multilateral
diplomacy may overcome a return of great-power tension, thus
continuing to serve a problem-solving function, and perhaps by so
doing even to reduce the tension.

But tension is also dependent on concrete historical developments
beyond the great powers' control. In the long run it is difficult to
play the role of a great power without occasionally disagreeing – or
even getting involved in conflict – with other great powers. The 1990s
diplomacy in the UN Security Council and the Contact Group
regarding former Yugoslavia and sanctions on Iraq has demonstrated
that great-power discord is not just a thing of the past. Other examples
are in evidence on a smaller scale. Russia has given a number of
indications that its low-tension profile is selectively adapted. *Vis-à-vis*
the Baltic states there is little to be seen of the cooperative spirit of
Moscow's relations with EU members. Russian relations with Latvia in
the late winter of 1998 were marked by a return of tension over the
conditions for russophone speakers, apparently deliberately exag-
gerating the issue sparked off by a non-citizen pensioners' demonstration in Riga and allowing it for some time to severely disrupt
diplomatic relations. The chapter by Moshes clearly points to NATO's
expansion as the cause, in Russian eyes, of this return of tension.

In short, as is already well established, the achievement of a certain
level of mutually beneficial transactions does not – despite the
conclusion built into the term 'interdependence' – in itself guarantee
continued cooperation and certainly cannot prevent the wilful
disruption of international relations. The decisive matter after 1990 is
therefore whether the Bush–Gorbachev legacy of multilateralism can
survive – and even help to abate – the onset of renewed tension. That
is in the end a matter of political will and leadership.

CONCLUDING REMARKS

The state of North European security relations at the turn of the century is marked by the ensemble of these tendencies. On the one hand interdependence has grown by the day and integration has moved ahead. On the other hand, bilateral diplomacy between Russia and its neighbours has continued to stumble and fall. In the West, no responsible actor is ready to diagnose the Russian pattern of behaviour and intentions for sure. Russians themselves have been reluctant to do so. Ambiguity reigns. Options have been kept open. Yet the flows of trade, investments, information and people between East and West in Northern Europe have grown dramatically. The Council of the Baltic Sea States has symbolized continuing cooperation in all civilian fields. On the security side the Conventional Forces in Europe (CFE) agreement provides a formidable bulwark against a renewed military build-up.

Within this general framework of cooperative security we have seen little or no headway made in the area of security organization. NATO's Partnerships for Peace and the Euro-Atlantic Partnership Council have not made much headway in the face of Russian scepticism. The OSCE roundtable for the Baltic region has survived merely as a ghost. Diplomatic preference in the region has been for some, as yet undefined, sort of counterbalancing. The Baltic Charter, agreed between the United States and Estonia, Latvia and Lithuania in January 1998, was an important political document reflecting a strong US interest in the future of these states, but it was less than a security guarantee. In October 1997 the Russian Federation offered security guarantees to the Baltic states, and simultaneously offered to accept guarantees made by others – even NATO guarantees provided they did not involve membership. These offers were rejected by Estonia, Latvia and Lithuania, in joint as well as separate declarations (Knudsen, 1998b). The result left Russo-Baltic relations in limbo.

It was characteristic of Russian policy behaviour during most of the 1990s that it was devoid of any perception that Russia's neighbours needed to be reassured. With the Clinton–Yeltsin Summit in Helsinki 1997 there came a signal of change.[14] Still, Russian policy continued its ambiguous course, with soft and hard moves *vis-à-vis* its three Baltic neighbours alternating fairly regularly.[15] The consequently remaining uncertainty has strengthened the attraction of NATO membership, thus serving to enhance the overall ambiguity of the situation, whether seen from Moscow, Washington or any of the regional capitals.[16] On NATO expansion, Russia clearly felt entitled to more reassurance than it was getting, while NATO felt it had done enough by entering the Founding Act with Russia that set up the Russia–NATO Cooperation Council.

Under such circumstances regional balancing of alignments have been preferred to regional security organization in the day-to-day processes of interstate interaction (Knudsen and Neumann, 1995). In the *overall* pattern of power relations it is pretty evident that a strong bandwagoning trend has been underway in favour of the United States since the early 1990s. But the United States is not always responding the way its suitors are expecting. Washington has apparently not been eager in the case of Estonia, Latvia and Lithuania to play the game of extended deterrence. It has preferred milder forms of counter-balancing, supplemented by local 'subcontracting' in the shape of some kind of subregional security arrangement. The Nordics, clearly potential subcontractors for the Baltic Sea area, have not, however, been willing to enter any serious commitments, essentially hedging their positions for the time being, preferring instead to export their modes of thinking to the Baltic states, as shown in the Archer and Jones chapter below.

At the same time the German government has conducted a cautious diplomacy, presumably keeping its own priority for Polish–NATO membership and the pacification of Russia as its predominant considerations (see the Krohn chapter below). Hence the NATO aspirations of the Baltic states and their more enthusiastic backers in 1997 were coolly received in Bonn.

The nervous ballet of the 1990s to secure the independence of Estonia, Latvia and Lithuania while avoiding commitments on behalf of their security may therefore be seen as a *regional* balancing act in Northern Europe which in large part is conditioned by a wish to preserve, yet postpone, for certain states the option of higher-level (supraregional) bandwagoning as long as possible. It is balancing, but on a lower, regional level. This has come out in the small but intense NATO debates in Finland and Sweden during 1996–98, which more than most other signals have revealed the tensions and undercurrents at work beneath the surface of the so-called post-Cold War world.

In the opinion of the governments in both of these countries (excepting some intragovernmental dissension in Finland), to *organize* regional security would be to introduce regularities and inflexibilities in the relationships that would entail a preclusion of options which would otherwise be open to states like Sweden and Finland (cf. the chapter by Dahl on Sweden). Insisting to the last on their 'military non-alignment,' even as members of the European Union, there is little doubt what their main option is. Their assumption seems to be that if they were to take that step first, it would risk unleashing a series of complementary and/or compensatory moves and countermoves by other leading actors in the area. The perceived need to balance alignments regionally amounts to holding a push for regional organization in abeyance.[17]

Their loyal oppositions have taken a different view. There has been a small but vocal collection of prominent individuals in Finland and Sweden who have been arguing insistently that the time to make the shift and go for NATO membership is 'now,' sooner rather than later. Max Jakobson, the old Finnish diplomat and scholar, is perhaps the most eminent of this small group of dissenters.

Yet, for the time being, the governing side in Sweden and Finland play the balancing strategy. So, although the old Nordic balance is gone, a new North European balance has emerged, like it or not. It appears to serve a function, as long as the uncertainty of any Russian diagnosis remains. Given these facts, it may be prudent of the United States government to maintain its own little balancing act on the fence regarding North European security, neither directly accepting nor overtly rejecting a role in the regional power game.

For Estonia, Latvia and Lithuania – as well as Poland – a major consequence of the blossoming of new intersocietal relationships and the continuing uncertainties of Baltic regional security has been the strengthening of state institutions. Paradoxically, the state survives through the intermediaries of the European Union and NATO. Such may be the fruits of the second-generation security dilemma.

NOTES

1 Thanks are due to Jolanda Wijnsma for research assistance and to Pavel Baev, Klaus Carsten Pedersen, Martin Heisler, Guido Lenzi, Arkady Moshes and Viktor Sergeyev for comments on an earlier version. The classic in the literature on confrontations between small states and great powers is Fox (1959). See also Vital (1967 and 1971), Handel (1981) and Mouritzen (1988). The general small state literature is usefully surveyed in Amstrup (1976), Handel (1981) and Väyrynen (1984). The subject of small states and alliances is especially well covered by Rothstein (1968), Suhrke (1973) and van Staden (1995), with important material also in Glenn Snyder (1984). The significance of contiguity and proximity is focused by Fox in a later work (Fox, 1977) and by Riekhoff and Neuhold (1993). Definitions of 'smallness' are usefully discussed in several of the works cited, as well as in Baehr (1975), Väyrynen (1971) and Thakur (1991). Essentially, the adjective 'small' is here used as a shorthand reference to the nature of the capabilities of the less powerful party in a bilateral relationship of marked power disparity.

2 The intensity of the current debate on fundamentals of the field of international studies – reaching well into the field of security studies (witness, e.g., Buzan, 1997 and Katzenstein, 1996) – necessitates at least some statement of conceptual choice. The theoretical perspective of this chapter is minimalist, which is to say that it is geared to the subject of the occasion: the relations of security between great powers and small states in a regional context. It assumes that we may for analytical purposes approach the social collectivities we call 'states'

as if they were individuals acting in pursuit of goals, without thereby making any claim to the effect that they 'really' are such actors. The ongoing interaction between state-organized societies is analytically conceived to continually produce distributive effects between them, with consequences for their relative power. The focus on states does not exclude that other social groups partake in the interaction and affect its course. But the primary actors in the present analysis are the 'great powers' and their 'small-state' neighbours.

3   At the early stage of their EU membership quests, the Czech Republic, Poland and Hungary were in this situation.

4   In many ways an all-absorbing debate, despite its containment within a rather narrow circle of policy analysts and policy-makers. The absence of a broader debate in most Western countries may nevertheless be deplored. As for the trends in the region and the place of Russia in it, the chapters by Sergeyev and Godzimirski in this volume give a broad and varied survey of what Sergeyev calls the 'ponto-baltic system' over time. Russian interests and viewpoints are clearly profiled in the chapter by Moshes, also in this volume.

5   For a more broad-based set of theories in which to interpret the events of the region, see the closing chapter by Hubel in this volume.

6   There are also the theories of power cycles and lateral pressure. These provide considerable overlap with both the rivalry theory and the imperialist theory. See Gilpin (1981), Choucri and North (1975).

7   I.e., short of explicit political agreements or revisions in declarations of security or foreign policy.

8   The reference to weakness/strength here is the same as that in the concept of power disparity, unequal capabilities (as indicated in n. 1). That leaves aside the various other distinctions between 'strong' and 'weak' states, where in one conception the strength in question refers to the capacity of the governmental apparatus to manage affairs within its jurisdiction (industrialized countries being mostly strong, developing countries mostly weak), while in another it refers to the power of the state in relation to its own society (the United States being a weak state, Sweden and Austria strong states). For the latter conception, see Krasner (1977 and 1978), also Katzenstein (1977, 1984 and 1985).

9   Rothstein (1968) sensibly rejects the stance that only the major powers are 'real powers'.

10 It is assumed that other great powers are not contiguous to the small state. The geopolitically singular cases of buffer states are too volatile to be covered by the model, which thus only covers triangular cases in which one great power is located close to the small state while the other great power is located further away. On buffer states, see Partem (1983), Chay and Ross (1986).

11 As extensively argued elsewhere (Knudsen, 1988), a great power's propensity to apply pressure or intervene directly against a smaller neighbouring state is usually the other side of the coin of the small state's sense of freedom of action (freedom of alignment), a more subjective and narrowly defined conception.

12 Counterbalancing is not necessarily tantamount to extended deterrence, which may be unrealistic in the case of a small state contiguous to a threatening great power. The possibility must be kept in mind that other (non-military) ways of counterbalancing could have a significant political effect.

13 Somewhat curiously, the models of extended deterrence tend not to include as actors the small states which are being defended, nor to make any particular assumptions about their role. See in particular Huth and Russett (1984, also Huth, 1988), which have made important contributions to this subject by studying historical cases of extended deterrence. A good survey of the literature and summary of the reasoning are found in Achen and Snidal (1989). A recent

contribution by Lebow (1998) – drawing on new material on the Cuban missile crisis – emphasizes the need to accept models which are more complex in order to adequately understand the dynamics of extended deterrence.

14 At the final press conference with Finland's President Martti Ahtisaari after the Helsinki summit of March 1997 Boris Yeltsin demonstrated recognition of this consideration when he said that the Baltic states could not join NATO but have no reason to fear Russian intentions. OMRI Daily Digest No. 58, Part I, 24 March 1997. During the summit Russia also declared that it was necessary to deal with this factor of fear on the part of Estonia, Latvia and Lithuania.

15 Paul Goble pointed out in early 1998 that 'Conflicting statements by Russian President Boris Yeltsin and his foreign minister, Yevgenii Primakov, on the state of relations between Moscow and the West raise some questions about Russian foreign policy intentions in 1998.' (Goble, 1998) My own assessment of the policy moves of Russia during 1997 is that soft and tough moves and stances were alternating fairly regularly. See also Knudsen (1998b).

16 Evident in interviews by the author during 1996–97 with policy-makers and parliamentarians in most of the capitals of Baltic Sea littoral states and in Washington, DC, and earlier interviews (1993–94) in all of these capitals. See also Dörfer (1997).

17 The chapter by van Ham in the present volume sets out the role of the European Union and the WEU in the pattern of security structures encompassing the Baltic Sea region.

2

The Historical Structure of Conflicts in the Baltic Area and the Long-term National Interests of Russia

VIKTOR M. SERGEYEV

Centre for International Studies, Moscow State University of International Relations (MGIMO), Moscow

INTRODUCTION

A consideration of long-term security issues in the Baltic area is hardly possible without reference to the history of the problem. For centuries, Baltic issues were interwoven with the crucial interests of Russia. Undoubtedly, this is true of the present situation as well. However, the very nature of those interests seems to be changing now, due, first, to the general transformation of the situation in Europe, the termination of ideological antagonisms between the East and the West, the collapse of Communism in Eastern Europe, and the processes of European integration. Of no less importance for the changes are, naturally, the internal political and economic transformations within Russia itself. At the same time, I admit, one should be very cautious about projecting current internal changes in various states on to their foreign policy interests, which, in fact, are amazingly stable. Foreign policy conservatism stems from extraordinary difficulties in changing established views, both internal and external, on a state's place in the international system. Foreign policy priorities, fears, and expectations, deeply rooted in professional traditions of politicians, diplomats, and the military, in fact, form part of the cultural background, and their change is a very arduous task. One might recall the history over the last two centuries of Franco-German relations and the enormous effort both sides made in the 1950s and 1960s to break the tradition of hostility and rivalry.

At the same time, getting rid of traditional conflicts requires not only diplomatic effort but a good deal of theoretical understanding of their roots as well. This, in turn, presupposes that further research efforts be made within a theory of international relations, namely, while modelling a transformation of long-term interests of conflicting parties.

Such a development, I think, would inevitably involve the rejection of the concept of the international relations' system as a set of interactions based upon Kenneth Waltz's 'single actor model' (Waltz, 1979). An emphasis on interdependence in the spirit of R. Keohane and J. Nye's approaches (Keohane and Nye, 1977) also seems insufficient. What is urgently needed is a hierarchical multi-actor model taking into consideration the greater role of international organizations, on the one hand, and the lesser role of the nation-state, on the other, as well as the growing influence of territorial financial and industrial agglomerations (see, for example, Ohmae, 1995).

Therefore, I think, any inquiry into possible transformations within the interrelated structures of foreign policy interests is inconceivable without some kind of bilateral analysis. On the one hand, such analysis presupposes an explication of the traditional, long-established structure of interests, fears, and expectations. On the other hand, it includes an investigation of factors able to bring changes into the above structure. This is the research scheme that I shall follow in this paper.

In the first part, I make an attempt to explain the nature of the Baltic area conflict system which started taking shape some 600–700 years ago, beginning with the crusades to the South Baltic. In the second part, I am going to analyze the factors which, to my mind, can change our understanding of the structure of international relations within the Baltic area which has been formed and nourished by its cultural tradition and historical experience.

THE PONTO-BALTIC CONFLICT SYSTEM

Even a superficial analysis of historical data shows that political events and various conflicts in the Baltic area cannot be isolated from those occurring along the traditional separating line between Eastern and Central Europe. This line goes from the Gulf of Riga through the swamps of Belarus and farther south along the Carpathian foothills down to the Black Sea. Properly speaking, this line is a boundary between four different cultural and religious traditions: Catholicism to the west of it, Orthodox Christianity to the east, Protestantism to the north, and Islam to the south. The structure of ideological and religious clashes in the region had taken shape approximately by the beginning of the sixteenth century and was superimposed on the structure of national interests of the largest powers of Northern, Central, and Eastern Europe of those days, namely Sweden, Denmark, Poland, Russia, and the Ottoman Empire. A bit later Prussia and the Habsburg Empire also became elements in this system. (On the formation of the system of international relations in medieval Eastern Europe and the Baltic area, see Grekov, 1975.)

For centuries, the above-mentioned boundary acted as a nerve centre for the whole system of international relations in Central and Eastern Europe and in the Balkan area. Any serious political change at any point of this line produced a quick response elsewhere. Suffice it to mention the parallelism of Swedish–Polish and Russian–Polish conflicts, Russian–Swedish and Russian–Turkish wars, the Ukrainian campaign of Charles XII, or the interconnection between the Livonian war of Ivan IV and the Crimean Tartars' raid on Moscow. As late as the twentieth century, analogous events occurred several times. Closely interconnected were the secession of the Baltic states and the Ukraine from Russia in 1918, as well as the developments in the Baltic states, the division of Poland, and the Soviet occupation of the Trans-carpathians and Bessarabia in 1939–40. It is worth noting that the same type of causality was also essential for the developments of 1989–91: the new secession of the Baltic States from the USSR stimulated a break-away of the Ukraine and Moldova and, as a consequence, disintegration of the USSR as a whole.

It is just this system of permanently reproducing conflicts along the dividing line between Central and Eastern Europe that I call here the *Ponto-Baltic Conflict System*. In other words, I suggest that conflicts at any point within this system be analyzed paying due attention to conflict factors of the whole system.

The stability of this conflict system through time is remarkable indeed. After Yalta and Helsinki, the issue of the Ponto-Baltic Conflict System seemed to have faded for a long time, if not forever, but this point of view, which became almost an axiom for the Soviet political and military establishment, proved completely untenable by 1989–91.

It might be quite easy to treat the phenomenon of the Ponto-Baltic Conflict System in the spirit of Huntington's schemes, thus making reference to the notion of inter-civilizational conflict (Huntington, 1993 and 1996). In my view, however, such an approach implies an unjustified simplification of the real situation.

I think that the existence of stable conflict systems like the Ponto-Baltic one should be explained by a complex combination of geo-graphical, geostrategic, ethnic, economic, and cultural factors. Strictly speaking, it is only through this kind of multi-factored analysis that one can get an idea of the development of a conflict system in a new environment.

A purely civilizational account might lead to nothing more than stating the inevitably conflictual nature of the system which can be changed only through the destruction of at least one of its constituent civilizations. Historical evidence, however, proves that even a destruc-tion of civilizations within a conflict system may be not enough to challenge its stability. For example, the Near East Conflict System with its own boundary which goes approximately along the line connecting Trebizond and Basrah successfully outlived the Islamization of Iran and the collapse of the Byzantine Empire, and currently shows no signs of disappearance. On the other hand, as we shall see below, the existence of an inter-civilizational border does not necessarily entail deadly conflicts. Therefore, I see no grounds for explaining the existence and stability of conflict systems solely by reference to civilizational cleavages.

So, the question is: How did the Ponto-Baltic Conflict System evolve, and how did it maintain its stability through such diverse historical conditions? Without a doubt, the role of geographical factors was really important. The southern coast of the Baltic Sea is a typical Scandinavian landscape; starting from the middle of the first millennium AD this territory came under the ethnic and cultural influence of Scandinavia. Vast plains of what later became Central Russia were progressively settled by Eastern Slavs strongly influenced by Byzantium. The Western Slavs of what would become Poland and the Czech lands, and the Magyars inhabiting the Danube plains were under the influence of Western Europe, whereas the steppes to the north of the Black Sea were in the hands of the Islamized nomads, and later of the Ottoman Empire.

At first glance, the Ponto-Baltic zone clearly formed a border between religions and civilizations. But to mention this is definitely not enough to explain the conflict system's functioning. There are numerous examples of inter-civilizational borders which did not actually give rise to permanent conflict systems. For example, the co-existence of Islamic and Hindu civilizations in India was relatively peaceful for centuries.

Conflict systems are born, I suggest, through specific combinations of different factors, and such a combination did exist in the Ponto-Baltic area. The civilizational factor was complemented and reinforced by the economic one, namely, the existence of such things as the trade route connecting Scandinavia and Byzantium (in Russia it was called 'the way from the Varangians to the Greeks'). Considerable amounts of money and goods circulated along the route (virtually coinciding with the line of inter-civilizational cleavage) as early as the tenth to eleventh centuries AD. The Middle Ages witnessed a struggle for the possession of key points along this route; later on, with the rise of the Russian state, the control over trade with remote parts of Russia also became of great importance. For anyone who strove to exert such control, the Black Sea and Baltic coasts were crucial strategic areas. It is from this point of view that the foreign policy programmes of Russian tsars were formulated, from Ivan IV to Nicholas II (from the Livonian War to the aspiration to take control of the Bosporus during the First World War).

But while for Russia the existence of the Ponto-Baltic Conflict System stemmed, to a great extent, from the necessity to have 'a window on Europe', for countries contiguous to Russia in this area the existence of the conflict system ensued from the very existence of Russia, which was considered as a powerful, menacing, and inherently aggressive state, striving to suppress its neighbours and bring them under its control. The fear of Russia-USSR in the Baltic Region and Central Europe reached its peak between the First and Second World Wars when, within the framework of the Versailles Treaty, numerous small and feeble states appeared in the region after the disintegration of the Austro-Hungarian and Russian Empires. Those fears were not entirely unreasonable as after the Yalta Conference the USSR managed to take control of a considerable part of Central Europe and the whole of the southern Baltic. The collapse of the USSR in 1991 re-created a situation resembling that of the years 1918–40. Again we see an emergence of new states whose foreign policy is largely dictated by the fear of Russia, and Russia, albeit very much weakened, is still felt as a source of great danger. This entrenched fear underlies such foreign policy activities and developments as the material and diplomatic support rendered by Lithuania to Chechnya; the Ukrainian–Georgian and Ukrainian–Azerbaijanian contacts aimed at obtaining an alternative to Russian oil supply; the agreement between Ukraine and Latvia on training the Latvian military in the Ukraine; the smouldering conflict in the Trans-dniestrian region; the discrimination against the Russian-speaking population in Latvia and Estonia; and a deepening conflict in Belarus. We see the Ponto-Baltic Conflict System at work again, after a lull of about forty years.

Are there any chances of positive shifts here in the very near future? How can the activity of the Ponto-Baltic Conflict System be terminated? This system is fed by the fears felt by the Baltic and Central European States. The nature and character of those fears are more or less obvious. Therefore, to understand the current situation we now have to turn to an analysis of Russia's interests in the Baltic area and the forces forming Russia's foreign policy towards the Baltic and Central Europe.

FOREIGN POLICY OF A GREAT POWER IN CRISIS

An assessment of the possible future policy of Russia is of key importance for any understanding of long-term development in the Baltic area. From the viewpoint of international relations' theory, this one is a classical problem of analyzing a conflict of interests at the periphery of a great power (cf. O. Knudsen's paper presented in this volume). I would like to stress here the necessity to supplement

Knudsen's scheme with another model that seems to be relevant not only in the medium-term, but also in the long-term (10–15 years) perspective.

What I mean by this is a model of foreign policy behaviour of a great power in a state of crisis. If a crisis, in its essential features, is of an internal nature, the issue of peripheral conflicts – especially those which affect interests of the groups within the 'imperial nation' that became minorities in newly-born states after the collapse of the empire – turns into an important instrument of manipulation of national self-consciousness. Suffice it to mention the problem of *Volksdeutsche* after the Versailles Peace Treaty. Sometimes political parties and groups striving for influence in a crisis-gripped great power have simply no other choice than to utilize the factor of peripheral conflicts in an internal political struggle. Thereby international relations in a conflict area acquire a 'multi-factor' nature, and political parties of the great power in crisis transform into 'actors' at the international scene. The most objectionable peculiarity of this situation is that the *real* interests of these actors lie on the plane of domestic policy, and therefore are hardly accessible to any impact from outside. In fact, the situation becomes uncontrollable due to the lack of interdependence between principal actors within the former empire and foreign states involved in the conflict. Any attempt to exert external influence on the forces that destabilize the international situation may bring only negative results, because they would be immediately treated as an interference in the internal affairs of the great power in crisis, and hence it would cause no other effect than an intensification of xenophobic, imperialistic and nationalistic sentiments. At the same time, the government of the great power in crisis, even being under strong pressure from various interdependent factors, faces a very uncomfortable dilemma. Any concessions in foreign policy cost it a loss of influence within the state and may, in the case of serious discontent at further concessions, lead to a complete loss of power.

If one accounts for this situation in terms of the game theory, with the international community and the government of a great power in crisis as two principal players, and Kantian 'Eternal Peace' (A) and '*Realpolitik*' in the style of Otto von Bismarck (B) as the two main game strategies available, the matrix of the game would obviously be that of the 'Prisoner's Dilemma' (due, in the first place, to internal pressure placed upon the government of the power in crisis), as represented below as Fig. 2.1.

In other words, the equilibrium point (A, A) is unstable. It has been proved (Axelrod, 1984) that when a game of this kind is played repeatedly, the most successful strategy is Tit for Tat, that is, the mere repetition of the partner's moves. In such a case, to demand cooperative

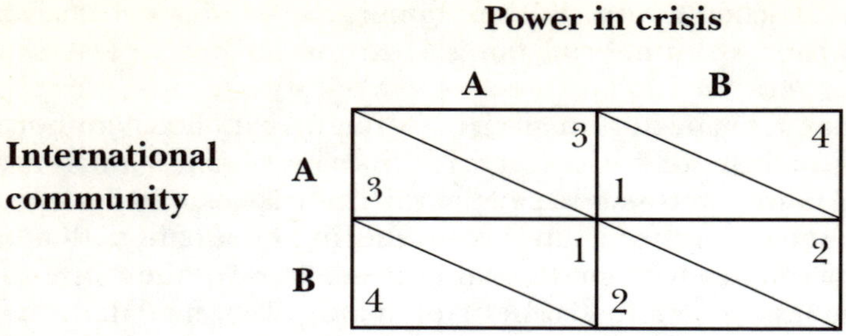

Power in crisis

A   B

Fig. 2.1. Prisoner's Dilemma Matrix

behaviour from the government of a power in crisis without *permanent external support* for cooperation is equivalent to demanding irrational behaviour.

At the same time, *on the surface* (without taking into account external violations of cooperation principles) the foreign policy of a power in crisis may look extremely chaotic, mostly because of its forced reactivity. Turning to historical precedents, one can easily see the distinctive features of such reactivity in the foreign policy behaviour of the Weimar Republic in the 1920s and Russia after 1991. In my opinion, the considerations that have been suggested above account for the actual lack of a long-term Russian policy in the Baltic area. Reactivity in the present situation means rationality.

However, the structure of interrelations that has evolved in the Baltic area is rather dangerous, and every possible effort must be made to change it.

RUSSIA'S INTERESTS

A formal look at Russia's national interests in the Baltic area immediately reveals a number of rather obvious problems: the position of the Russian-speaking population in Latvia and Estonia (in Lithuania the situation in this respect is much better); transport access to Kaliningrad province (in this case Russia's relations with Lithuania are at stake); the need to demarcate a mutually recognized border with Latvia and Estonia; ensuring the free transportation of oil and gas from Northern Russia. Admittedly, all these problems contain seeds of conflicts, and moreover, self-supporting conflicts. The more active Russia is in protecting the rights of the Russian-speaking populations in the Baltic states, the more dangerous these minorities look in the eyes of nationalistic movements there. The activism of nationalists in the Baltic states would probably contribute to the consolidation and political radicalization of Russian minorities. This, in turn, would give nationalistic and imperialistic movements in Russia better opportunities for capitalizing on the problem of Russian-speaking minorities and using it as a factor for strengthening their political influence and Russia's involvement in interethnic tensions in the Baltic states. The circle will thus start to close and the conflict escalate to a higher level.

The same is approximately true of the other problems listed above. Paradoxically, every time Russia pays more attention to defending its (traditionally understood) national interests in this area, these efforts only intensify the conflict with former republics of the USSR, while disregarding the national interests (in the vein of 1991–95 foreign policy) Russia does not contribute to problem resolution at all because such policy is immediately treated by nationalists in the newly independent Baltic states as a sign of weakness and a reason to put even more pressure upon Russia.

All in all, we see that problems associated with Russia's interests in the Baltic area cannot be solved unilaterally, without reciprocal co-operative steps being made by the Baltic states. However, such action is hindered by the distrust and suspicion borne out of historical experience. To break away from traditional views on foreign policy problems is an extremely difficult task.

The continuation of conflicts in the Baltic area gives strong impulses to the Ponto-Baltic Conflict System as a whole, translating into the Russian–Ukrainian conflict, tensions in the Transdniestrian region, and so on. It is hardly possible to escape from this vicious circle without a radical transformation of the participants' view on the situation. Otherwise, if one understands it entirely in terms of traditional 'national interests', the conflict in the Baltic area is virtually inevitable.

PROSPECTS FOR THE ELIMINATION OF CONFLICTS

Fortunately, the overall political situation in the Baltic area, as well as in Europe as a whole, is much more complicated and cannot be reduced to the system of 'balance of national interests'. On the one hand, there are *supranational* structures, such as the Council of Europe, European Union, Organization for Security and Cooperation in Europe (OSCE), and CIS, whose influence is considerable and whose structure of preferences and interests do not necessarily coincide with those of conflicting parties. On the other hand, there are *subnational* interests, that is, interests of regions and organizations *within* countries involved in a situation of potential conflict. In today's Russia such interests, especially those of Russia's regions, turn out to be a very considerable political factor.

Russia's North-West is very interested now in developing economic cooperation with the Baltic and Northern European states, first of all in obtaining investments for regional economic development. For the region, 'national' interests are gradually becoming of secondary value. This means that the regional interests of the members of the Russian Federation are *inhibiting* the emergence of conflicts in the Baltic area. It seems quite likely that with the development of market economies in Estonia, Latvia and Lithuania, the craving for mutually profitable economic cooperation will outweigh populist nationalistic trends.

On the other hand, in the context of the newly emerging understanding of state sovereignty in Europe, maintaining proper standards of civil and political rights is no longer treated as the internal affair of this or that state. From this standpoint, the position of the Russian-speaking populations in the Baltic must be considered, to a greater extent, as part of an all-European concern to maintain high standards of civil and political rights. A natural foreign policy implication of this new reality is that an emphasis on Russia's responsibility for its compatriots' conditions abroad should be laid not on attempting to influence policies of the Baltic states directly, but rather on creating initiatives at the European level, in the Council of Europe and OSCE. This approach can help to break the above-mentioned vicious circle of conflict escalation.

Thus, I see no grounds for assuming that conflict in the Baltic area is unavoidable. In the last decades, Europe has witnessed instances of successful elimination of inveterate conflicts due to mobilization of interests at subnational and supranational levels; suffice it to mention the postwar development of relations between France and Germany or between the USSR (and later Russia) and Finland. But this is only possible if all conflicting parties stop looking at the situation through the prism of narrowly understood 'national interests'.

3

Soviet Legacy and Baltic Security: The Case of Kaliningrad

JAKUB M. GODZIMIRSKI

Norwegian Institute of International Affairs, Oslo

INTRODUCTION[1]

One of the most difficult problems that Russia is still burdened with today is that of the Soviet legacy. This Soviet legacy has many dimensions, but two of these may be described as crucial for Russia's ability to get through the period of transition from the Soviet period to the system based on the principles of the market economy and compatible with Western-style democracy. The first has to do with the political, economic and social arbitrariness of the Soviet period that contributed largely to the shaping of the country's political, economic and social map, and that today's Russian leaders have to tackle and deal with (for more on Soviet arbitrariness see Friedrich and Brzezinski, 1956). The second has to do with the ability of the Russian leaders to reject their Soviet mental heritage by which, at least in the earlier stages of their political careers, they were formed and that may be an important obstacle to their approaching the post-Soviet problems in an innovative way. Since the collapse of the Soviet Union one of the areas where the two layers of the Soviet legacy has obviously played an important and often decisive role is the Russian enclave on the Baltic coast – Kaliningrad. The area can be treated in many respects as a perfect case study revealing how the Russian political elites have dealt with the problems resulting directly from the Soviet past, how they are adapting to the new realities of the post-Cold War order in Europe and how they are managing relations of different types that will determine the shape of the Russian state and its future priorities in domestic and international politics.

This study will consist of two parts. The first part will contain a look at the history of the Kaliningrad issue and show how this issue is directly linked to the Soviet legacy and the emergence of a new political conjuncture[2] in the Baltic region resulting directly from the Second

World War. This conjunctural setting had lasted until the collapse of the Soviet Union in 1991, when the entire region underwent a crucial change and the problem of the Russian exclave of Kaliningrad became an international issue due to the 'reconstruction' of the political map of the region. The second part will focus on the 'geo-realistic'[3] perceptions of Kaliningrad, on how the Kaliningrad issue was 'played' and the Russian security debate challenged, among other things, by NATO's plans to enlarge and how the debate on Kaliningrad in those countries in closest proximity, i.e., Poland and Lithuania, has also been dominated by security concerns.

SOVIET ARBITRARINESS AND THE EMERGENCE OF A NEW BALTIC CONJUNCTURE

The Soviet period in the history of Kaliningrad began at the Potsdam Conference, where the Western powers agreed to a Soviet proposal

> ... that pending the final determination of territorial questions at the peace settlement, the section of the western frontier of the USSR which is adjacent to the Baltic Sea should pass from a point on the eastern shore of the Bay of Danzig to the east, north of Braunsberg-Goldap, to the meeting point of the frontiers of Lithuania, the Polish Republic and East Prussia (Grenville, 1974: 234).

Kaliningrad or Königsberg, as the city was called at that time, was indeed handed over to Russia at this conference and the fate of the area was sealed by the agreement reached by the allies in Potsdam. But it is important to see the problem in a broader historical perspective, because it is precisely this historical perspective that is one of the most important reasons why Russia, in spite of the ongoing process of democratization, is still perceived as a possible source of instability and insecurity in the region. The handing over of Kaliningrad was a part of the deal settling the fate of Germany after the war, but it was first of all a symbolic and practical manifestation of Russian ability to organize postwar Eastern Europe in a way that would facilitate Soviet control of the area.[4]

One of the hidden goals of the Soviet political agenda in the inter-war period was to get rid of the results of the period of weakness of the Soviet state at the moment of its birth. This weakness was symbolized by the Brest-Litovsk Treaty with Germany. This treaty, on the one hand, made possible the victory of the Revolution in Russia, but on the other hand resulted in the creation of a belt of independent national states which formed a *cordon sanitaire* isolating Soviet Russia from the rest of Europe. This belt of states delayed the march of the

Revolution to the west and forced Stalin to invent the concept of revolution in one country. An attempt to export revolution was stopped at the outskirts of Warsaw in August 1920. The very existence of an independent Poland was perceived as one of the greatest obstacles to the realization of Soviet strategic plans.[5] The isolated Soviet Russia found another European outsider also vitally interested in rejecting the Versailles order. The Rapallo Agreement with Germany was the first sign of a political *rapprochement*, that only seventeen years later ended in the liquidation of all independent states separating Soviet Russia from, by then, Nazi Germany and in a complete redrawing of the political and ethnic map of Eastern Europe in 1945. The Ribbentrop–Molotov Agreement, signed on 23 August 1939, opened the way for the German and Russian invasions of Poland, and indeed started the Second World War. This Agreement opened the way for Soviet occupation of the eastern part of Poland (1939), Bessarabia (1940) and the Baltic states (1940). It marked the real beginning of the export of the Soviet revolution and of the Soviet domination of this part of Europe that was later confirmed and extended in Teheran, Yalta and Potsdam. The political game that Stalin began by signing the German–Soviet Pact in 1939 bore fruit six years later, when Stalin became one of the main winners of and profiteers from the war. Although Stalin ended up with allies other than those with whom he started this war, he proved able to realize his primary goal of getting rid of the consequences of the Brest-Litovsk Treaty and, not only restored Soviet/Russian hegemony in the areas that until the First World War had been under Russian control, but also widened substantially the sphere of Soviet influence.

One of the most important acquisitions from the strategic point of view was the Königsberg area, giving the Soviets an ice-free port[6] located much closer to the region of potential confrontation with the West than the Soviet bases before the war and that was much less vulnerable than Soviet facilities in the Finnish Gulf. Stalin also regarded Königsberg/Kaliningrad as a just compensation for the Soviet contribution to the final victory over Nazi Germany and Soviet losses during the war, although it was very difficult to find any historical or demographic reasons justifying Soviet control over an area that, unlike other territories claimed by Stalin, had never been a part of Russia.[7] In making a bid for Königsberg Stalin was motivated not by any historical or legal reasons, but first of all by purely strategic concerns. Rational as it was from the Soviet perspective, his decision on Königsberg was also a typical example of Soviet-style arbitrariness. The importance of this acquisition became more obvious when relations between the Soviet Union and its Western allies deteriorated and the Cold War broke out.

By forming a belt of dependent states whose human and natural resources were almost totally controlled by the real centre of power in Moscow, the Soviet Union also gained control over territory that could serve either as a kind of strategic protection zone in the case of aggression against the Soviet Union (defensive variant) or as a practical springboard for a possible invasion of Western Europe (offensive variant) (Davydov, 1997). In both cases the newly gained Kaliningrad area had an important role to play as a Soviet outpost on the Baltic Sea coast, but its role became even more crucial with the development of Soviet global strategy and the increased significance of the Soviet Navy.[8]

The fact that the Kaliningrad area was neither given to Poland as originally planned, nor to Lithuania, as discussed immediately after the war (as was the case with the Memel/Klaipeda region), but has since 1946 been incorporated, as an *oblast*, into the Russian FSR and thus subordinated directly to Moscow, underscored the strategic importance of the region. The very fact of its strategic importance influenced also to a great extent Soviet policy towards the region in the postwar period. One of the most visible results of this policy was a complete change in the ethnic structure of the Kaliningrad *oblast* (see Table 3.1). The rest of its German population, those people who hadn't fled before the Red Army occupied the area in April 1945, were forced to leave for Germany in 1947.

The fate of the region for at least five decades was sealed by at least three Soviet arbitrary decisions. The most crucial one was the Soviet claim on the area after the Second World War. This decision was followed by two others of great importance. The first had to do with the fate of the original population of the area, while the second transformed the whole area into a military superbase inaccessible until 1991 not only to foreigners, but also to many 'normal' Soviet citizens. An immediate consequence of those three arbitrary decisions was the de-Germanization of the area, its Sovietization and its development as a

Table 3.1. Ethnic composition of the area of the Kaliningrad *oblast* (based on Eberhardt, 1996 and statistical data provided by the local Statistics Office)

	1933	*1959*	*1989*
Total population	1,058,200	610,900	871,200
Germans (%)	97.7	0.1	0.2
Lithuanians (%)	0.9	3.5	2.1
Poles (%)	0.5	0.5	0.5
Jews (%)	0.9	0.7	0.4
Russians (%)	–	77.6	78.5
Belarusians (%)	–	9.4	8.5
Ukrainians (%)	–	5.8	7.2
Others (%)	–	2.4	2.6

unit separated to a large degree from its natural cooperation partners. De-Germanization and Sovietization were manifested most visibly by the region's new toponomy. All German place names were changed and replaced first of all by Soviet ones rather than purely Russian ones. Königsberg became Kaliningrad to celebrate Mikhail Kalinin, the former president of the Soviet Union who died in 1946, the old and historical city of Tilsit became Sovietsk, and the same was the fate of all the cities, villages, streets and places of the region. Sovietization of Kaliningrad city itself was made easier by the destruction of its historical centre by the RAF's intensive bombings in 1944 and by the fact that its new residents had no personal attachment to the city or its history. Sovietization of Kaliningrad had also a human dimension – very early on Kaliningrad became a kind of Soviet microcosm or mirror-image, due to its multi-ethnic composition, professional structure, local Soviet identity and 'overmilitarization'. It was therefore not totally unexpected that forty years after Kaliningrad's incorporation into the Soviet Union the region was facing the same types of challenges as the Soviet Union as a whole and that the same responses were used there in order to get rid of the same problems. But the problems did not want to disappear and five years later the Soviet Union became a historical issue. The collapse of the Soviet Union and division of the country into 15 more or less independent republics also generated totally new types of challenges in and for Kaliningrad. Incorporation of the Kaliningrad area into the Russian Federation was a non-issue in the period when the Soviet Union existed and sovereignty of its 15 republics had but a decorative and declaratory character. Once the full sovereignty of some of them was claimed and obtained, Kaliningrad turned out to be one of the 'hot spots' on the map of the former Soviet Union. The Soviet Union, with its internal borders – more 'paper' than real – and with its unifying party apparatus and centralized system of management was the sole guarantor of the relatively non-problematical development of the Kaliningrad *oblast*. Once the Soviet Union disappeared from the scene on 25 December 1991 the problems linked specifically with Kaliningrad emerged and proved very difficult to deal with.

LONG-LASTING STRUCTURES OR THE GEO-REALISTIC 'READING' OF KALININGRAD

First of all it is important to explain the title of this part. The term 'long-lasting structures' is borrowed from Braudel and it means only that the focus in this part will be put on what Braudel called the 'geographical time of history'. We are not going to analyze here the current developments in Kaliningrad because it has already been done many times (Lange, 1993, Oldberg, 1995, Wellmann, 1996, Joenniemi, 1996) and it would only mean repeating others' conclusions and accounts. Instead of doing so, I would like to pay attention to some central axes of the Russian debate on the shape of the Russian state and see what roles, often shifting, have been assigned to Kaliningrad in this state-building process. This approach also explains the two other concepts 'hidden' in the title. The term 'geo-realistic' means in this context that our reading of Kaliningrad will be based on some ideas that have dominated the Russian debate on Kaliningrad as well as the perception of Kaliningrad by its closest neighbours. 'Geo' stems from the 'geo-political' school of thought, because geographic, spatial thinking still seems to dominate Russian thinking about security, especially where the situation of Kaliningrad is concerned, with all the geographic barriers and determinants of development that have played an impor-tant role after the 1991 collapse of the Soviet Union. The geopolitical approach, based on spatial perception and interpretation of security and politics (Gray, 1996, Neumann, 1996, Sergounin, 1997a) can also be relatively easily combined with the Braudelian concept of lasting structures, geography being a common denominator and main deter-minant of both. The term 'realistic' requires a more detailed explana-tion, because it can be approached from two directions. On the one hand it refers to the 'realistic' and 'neo-realistic' approach to the study of international relations with its focus on the role of state and balance of power in international politics. On the other hand, this term refers also to a specific Russian 'realistic' approach which has dominated Russian debate on the main goals of Russia's foreign and security policy after rejection of the 'idealistic' atlanticist course in 1993 (Rahr and Krause, 1995, Bazhenov, 1996, Sergounin, 1997a). Common to both 'scientific' and 'political' realism is the focusing on the role of the state as the main actor in international relations and power as the main 'subject' of these relations. All three factors mentioned above – geography, state and power – have also been very central themes in the ongoing debates on Kaliningrad, both in Russia and in Europe.

The Russian perception of Kaliningrad can be described as fourfold. Since 1991 Kaliningrad has been perceived as:

1. a regional/political issue when the scope of regionalism and the region's political 'image' were discussed;

2. an economic issue, where the scope of local economic freedom and reforms implemented in the area were concerned;

3. a historical issue as the last and sole real Russian gain from the Second World War and symbol of past imperial glory and,

4. a security and military issue in the ongoing debate on Russian foreign and security policy, that has since 1993 been increasingly challenged by NATO plans to expand into Eastern Europe.[9]

Shifts in the Russian debate on Kaliningrad and decisions on which policy should be implemented in the region were caused mainly by shifts in the Russian debates on maybe the four most important issues of the Russian political agenda at the beginning of 1990s. The four issues were:

(a) the attitude towards market reforms in the economy,

(b) the form of Russian statehood and in consequence relations between the centre of power in Moscow and Russia's 89 regions,

(c) the attitude towards the Soviet period of Russian history

(d) the outcome of the Russian debate on the new foreign and security policy of the country.

1992 was marked by an 'outburst' of liberal economic thinking and practice in Russia symbolized by Gaydar's economic reforms and the ground was prepared for the further liberalization and marketization of the Russian economy. 1993 was very apparently 'coloured' by the debate on the form of the new Russian state system and by that on the scope of 'regionalism' and both of them were symbolized by the split of the country into pro- and anti-Yeltsin camps during the confrontation between the president and the parliament that resulted in the October 1993 bloodshed. The splitting into two camps was reconfirmed by the unexpected results of the first really democratic elections in Russia in December 1993, but at the same time the new state form proposed by Yeltsin's new constitution only won support by a slight majority of Russian voters, the two facts being maybe the most important events that have since 1993 been shaping the Russian political scene. The two opposing camps had also quite different views on the Soviet and Russian past.

1993 was also marked by an obvious shift in Russian foreign policy that in many ways rejected the idealist atlanticist, pro-Western approach and embarked on a more Russia-focused 'realism'. This shift was symbolized by a new foreign policy doctrine worked out by the Ministry of Foreign Affairs and presented publicly in January 1993, in Primakov's report on the possible negative consequences of NATO enlargement that was made public in November 1993, by the tough Russian stance during different phases of the conflict in former Yugoslavia, by the Russian focus on the 'near abroad', by the search for new

strategic partners in Asia (India, Iran, China) and, on the personal
level, by the replacement of Kozyrev by Primakov as the Russian
Minister of Foreign Affairs in January 1996.

The combination of the four aspects of specific policies towards
Kaliningrad with the general trends in Russian politics as presented
above allows us to identify some scenarios for the area that have been
discussed and in different ways tried out in Kaliningrad.

The problem of Kaliningrad has to a great extent been linked to
the different perceptions of this piece of land and its role in post-Soviet
space by both its closest neighbours and by Russian policy-makers. Most
often, Russian policy- and decision-makers, and their counterparts in
the Baltic region, have focused their debates on the new international
position of Kaliningrad. This was a natural and understandable trend
in a time of transformation, when one had to find a new way of approaching this complex problem, when Kaliningrad became an open zone
and one had to define its new place both in the Russian Federation and
in its new international environment. The two most important
scenarios, in a way alternative and to a great extent conflicting that
have been discussed and partly realized at the same time in the region
– the 'military base' scenario and the 'marketplace' scenario – have been
the most visible manifestations of the new thinking. The first – the
'military base scenario'[10] – was deeply rooted in the area's past and in
its past 'functions', while the latter – the 'marketplace scenario'[11] – was
more a choice of a possible future role for the area than an *ad hoc*
survival strategy for today.

KALININGRAD AND RUSSIA'S SECURITY DILEMMAS

In the early 1990s two issues seemed to be defined as the most
important goals of Russian security and foreign policy. The two were
the maintenance of the territorial integrity of the Russian Federation
and maintenance of the country's status as a great power on the
international arena.[12] The two issues have been also of great relevance
for the Russian debate on Kaliningrad, since Kaliningrad was by many
perceived as 'predestined' to play an important role in the shaping of
a new Russia. The separation of the region from 'mainland Russia', its
self-sufficiency as far as the 'defensive potential' is concerned, its
obvious lack of adequate economic support from the centre of power
in Moscow and conflicting scenarios of development partly imposed
on the region have made Kaliningrad probably more vulnerable to
'separatist' ideas than any other Russian region without an ethnic-based
status. It could lead either to attempts to upgrade its status within the
Russian Federation or even to the creation of a new 'quasi-state', similar

to Nagorno-Karabakh, Transdniestria or Chechnya on the perimeter of Russia's external 'line of defence'. Kaliningrad's history and its 'fresh' Russian status has made it also, in the eyes of Russian policy-makers, more vulnerable to the foreign powers' attempts to weaken the links between Kaliningrad and Moscow and then eventually replace Moscow in the region. No matter which of the 'separation' scenarios – internal, involving local political forces, or external, with the participation of 'foreign powers' – might be realized it would mean problems for Russia, as it could start a new wave of separatism within the Russian Federation, be interpreted as a sign of Russia's weakness on the international level, and, in the worst case, deprive Russia of its military outpost in the West perceived rather mistakenly, as very important for Russia's military and political security. In all cases, it would be very damaging to Russia's image as a great power (Sorokin, 1997).

As far as the steps needed to maintain Russia's great power status are concerned, the minimum programme had already been formulated in 1992 by the then Commander of the General Staff Academy I. Rodionov (Rodionov, 1992 and Brusstar, 1994). He listed some conditions for the successful transformation of the Soviet superpower into the Russian great power, and his ideas served probably as a model for most of the foreign and security policy programmes formulated later by Russian 'realists'. Rodionov's list included the following postulates:

1. The neutrality of the Central and East European countries or their friendly relations with Russia.

2. Free Russian access to seaports in the Baltic states.

3. Excluding 'third-country' military forces from the Baltic states and non-membership of the Baltic states in military blocs directed at Russia.

4. Preventing Commonwealth of Independent States (CIS) countries from becoming part of a buffer zone separating Russia from the west, south, or east.

5. Maintaining the CIS states under Russia's exclusive influence.

6. Preserving good-neighbourly relations with states of the Middle and Far East.

Three (1–3) of Rodionov's six 'points' could be related directly to Kaliningrad and Kaliningrad could be used as a leverage in achievement of at least these three 'minimal goals'. If one takes into account that the Baltic states are not a part of the CIS-project *formally*, but are, nevertheless, perceived, sometimes even *with* Poland, as a part of the 'natural' Russian sphere of influence or Russian 'security zone' (as clearly shown during the debate on NATO enlargement) the importance of Kaliningrad in the realization of the Russian grand strategy cannot be exaggerated.

Russia's efforts to maintain its great power status on the regional, Baltic level should be seen against the background of the historical developments and trends that for at least three hundred years have been decisive for the balance of power in the region.

From a historical perspective one of the main trends in the Baltic region was a series of attempts by the leading regional power to gain control over the largest possible portion of the Baltic coast. It was for many centuries a local variant of the 'Great Game', in which the main prize was hegemonic position in the region and, consequently, greater influence on European and global affairs. The Russian drive towards the Baltic coast has been one of the historical manifestations of what can without any doubt be treated as a long-lasting structure in the Baltic context. Russia replaced Sweden as the local Baltic hegemon at the beginning of the eighteenth century and managed over time to get control over a large part of the Baltic coast. Soviet/Russian control of the whole eastern and southern Baltic rim from Viborg in the east to the outskirts of Lübeck in the west, combined with the 'Finlandization' of Finland and 'neutralization' of Sweden was a direct result of the Soviet victory in the Second World War. But it also crowned some hundred years of Russian efforts to achieve one of its most important strategic goals: to get the widest possible access to an ice-free waterway. This waterway was meant to be used to export Russian goods and 'import' Western ideas (Petrine project) or export Soviet ideas and in the case of a global or local conflict, project Soviet military power (Soviet project).[13] The achievement of this goal in the wake of the Second World War seemed to strengthen the Russian position in the region and made Russia an apparently uncontested hegemon of the Baltic Sea. Kaliningrad *oblast* was transformed into a pivotal point of Soviet strategy in the region, into a kind of 'unsinkable aircraft carrier'. This strategic and military importance of the *oblast* was symbolized during the whole Soviet period by its closure to foreigners and by a continuous Soviet military build-up in the region. By the end of the 1980s it proved nevertheless that Soviet leaders had been preparing the country for a war that never came, and at the same time were unable to understand the nature of the real threats to the country. After five years of attempts to reform the Soviet system, it had proved unreformable and fell like a house of cards. It resulted in the Soviet and then Russian strategic retreat from the Baltic coast, the most direct and dire consequence being the separation of Kaliningrad from the rest of the country, its exclavic character[14] and its specific strategic and geopolitical location. Kaliningrad, more maybe than any other subject of the Russian

Federation (with the exception of Chechnya-Ichkeria, whose status within/outside the Russian Federation is still very undefined) is today, both geographically and politically, a land 'in between'.

The strategic importance of Kaliningrad to Russia is directly linked with the new strategic and geopolitical realities that Russia is confronted with today. The most important change that has occurred is that concerning the character of the state Moscow has to rule. The process of building first the Russian and then the Soviet empire resulted in the creation of a typical *hegemonic empire*, consisting, at least since 1945, of three zones and three types of relations between the hegemon and its clients. These three zones were in Luttwak's classic work on the strategy of the Roman Empire (Luttwak, 1976) described as:

1. a zone of direct control – in the case of the Soviet Empire the Soviet core or the Inner Empire;
2. an inner zone of diplomatic control – consisting of a group of client states directly dependent on the hegemon; in the Soviet Empire this group was identical with Soviet European clients that formed the Outer Empire and were 'glued' together by the ideological 'binder', with Warsaw Pact and COMECON (the Soviet-era instrument of East European economic cooperation) being the two most important instruments of hegemonic control;
3. an outer zone of influence that could be described as a system of Soviet client states in the Third World that was, according to

Figure 3.1. Kaliningrad and the hegemonic Soviet Empire in a bipolar world

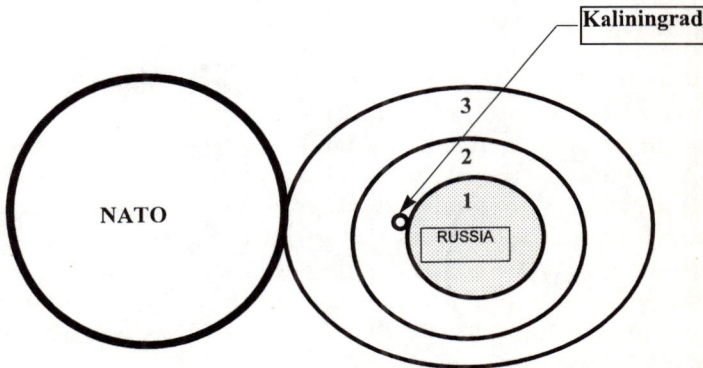

the official ideology, seen as the arena of competition with the capitalist world.

For almost fifty years it seemed that this model was able to satisfy Soviet strategic needs on both the regional and global level (more on changes in Soviet grand strategy in Rice, 1991). However, after coming to power Gorbachev realized very soon that the real costs of the imperial overexpansion/overstretch and confrontation with the West were too high and that a modernization of the Empire and its foreign policy was needed in order to ensure its survival (Jack Snyder, 1991). This modernization attempt, however, did not end in the improvement of the hegemonic model but in its collapse, in total Russian military withdrawal from Eastern Europe, in a partial retreat from the former Soviet Union (Baev, 1996b and 1997) and in the emergence of the Russian *territorial empire* confined within the limits existing at the end of seventeenth century. In consequence Kaliningrad was no longer a base on the perimeter of the zone of direct control. It became an exclave separated from the 'mainland' by the territories of at least two newly independent countries (Lithuania and Belarus). Not only that, it bordered a third country (Poland) that very soon applied for membership in the military organization that for almost 50 years was presented, perceived and believed to be the most important external threat to the Soviet fatherland. This new challenge and new quality had to be met by a new strategy. This strategy had to ensure Russian interests in the region and Russia's strategic interests as a great power that had at its disposal very limited political and economic leverage. At the same time this strategy could not be detrimental to Russia's improving relations with the West defined as perhaps the most important strategic goal by the new leadership believing that Western assistance and investment

Figure 3.2. Kaliningrad and the Russian territorial empire in the post-Soviet setting

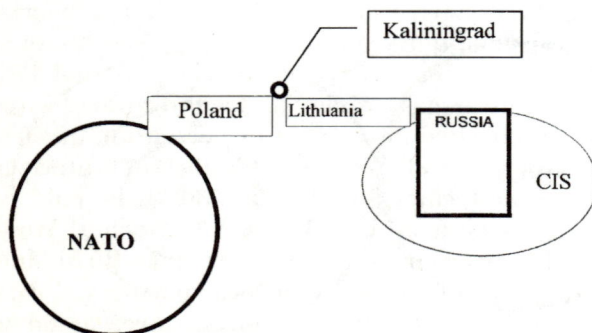

were crucial for a successful transformation and modernization of the Russian state.

This dramatic change had generated three new geopolitical challenges that both Kaliningrad itself and Russia as a whole had to cope with. These three challenges were:

1. The need to secure communication lines between mainland Russia and the Kaliningrad exclave.
2. The need to limit and, if possible, repair strategic damage caused by the collapse of the Soviet Union in the region.
3. The maintenance of the status quo, because changes could, under given circumstances, be detrimental to Russia's national interests in the region. One should also try, where and when possible to first stop and then reverse negative trends threatening Russia's position not only on the regional, but also on the continental and global level.

Translated into the realities of the 1990s it meant the need to find a working solution to the problem of transit to and from Kaliningrad, the need to 'invent' some new and efficient political and/or economic leverage in relations with the former parts of the hegemonic empire and, last but not least, the need to prevent the West from gaining lasting strategic advantage. The West was seen as poised to include into its widened sphere of influence the parts of the former Soviet empire, that were still perceived as vital to first of all 'spatially' defined Russian national interests but at the same time rather forgotten in the ongoing debate on the new shape of Russian foreign policy (Lamentowicz, 1997). While the first problem was a practical one, the other two were seen as very important from the strategic perspective, as on the one hand damage-limitation measures and, on the other hand, symbolic steps on the way towards regaining parity and equality in Russia's relations with the West.

These three goals have also a spatial dimension. *Lithuania* has been 'chosen' as a transit land in communication with Kaliningrad and has been seen, because of the obvious disparity of potential and economic dependence on Russia (gas supplies and withdrawal of Russian troops were used as an effective instrument of persuasion in Russian policy towards Lithuania), as well as the more reluctant attitude of the West (being a part of the former Soviet Union, all three Baltic states were perceived in the West as a special political case, and Western policy towards them has been marked by a more 'take-Russia-into-account' attitude) as the most vulnerable of the local 'partners'. *Poland* has been perceived as probably the most important area as far as Russia's national interests and national security in Central Europe were concerned, because of its potential and size, its status as an important actor in the region, because it was for over the last two hundred years a part of the Russian sphere of influence, and because after 1990 it very soon became an important area of competition for influence between the West and Russia.

In this new post-Soviet setting in the immediate vicinity of Kaliningrad the most important priority was therefore the need to work out a new range of relations with Poland that could secure Russia's interests and influence in the region, but that could no longer be based either on the hegemonic approach or on ideological ties. Until the reunification of Germany and the final settlement of potential problems between Germany and Poland – first of all the final recognition of the Polish–German border – the Soviet and then Russian leadership could hope that Stalin's 'strategic' decision to give Poland control over the former German territories in the west and north (among others, the southern part of the former Eastern Prussia) as compensation for Polish territorial losses in the east was a guarantee of a Polish pro-Russian stance even after the disappearance of the artificial 'ideological' link and the Brezhnev doctrine. The situation changed dramatically when it became obvious that democratic Poland and Germany had embarked on a policy of reconciliation, when Germany became one of the most important advocates of Polish integration with Western institutions and when this integration was at a very early stage defined as the most important strategic goal of Polish foreign policy, supported by almost all the political forces within the country. This pro-Western trend and manifest lack of interest in strengthening relations with the new Russia were strengthened also by some other factors. The most important of these were the apparent lack of stability in Russia, that was plagued by different, often bloody conflicts (the August 1991 putsch, the 1993 conflict between Yeltsin and the Parliament, the 1994 intervention in Chechnya), the more or less successful Russian attempts to regain control of and reintegrate the post-Soviet space accompanied by a great dose of assertiveness and coercion, and a visible decrease in trade between the two countries and Russia's diminishing role in the Polish economy. The actual absence of a pro-Russian political lobby in Poland, the political consensus on the pro-Western course and the relatively quick economic integration into the Western economic system have left Russia without any workable leverage in its relations with Poland.[15] At the same time Russia defined halting the planned NATO enlargement as the most important goal of its foreign policy in the period 1993–97. Since Poland was believed to be one of the candidates with a big chance of becoming a member of the alliance as early as the first round of enlargement, Kaliningrad, as the sole piece of Russian territory bordering on it, was to play a relatively important role in this process.

The Russian debate on NATO enlargement has been through different phases and various arguments have been used to halt the process. In the beginning, at the 'idealistic' stage of the Russian debate on the priorities of the country's foreign and security policy many policy-makers believed that the best option for Russia was simply to join Western institutions, NATO included (Sergounin, 1997a: 8–10). After the 'realistic' turn in 1993 it was hoped that the West and NATO could be stopped by Russian tough rhetoric, and good relations with Russia were from the Western perspective much more important than filling the so-called security vacuum in Central Europe. The American 'Russia First' policy, realized in the first place by 'early' Strobe Talbott and an attempt by Les Aspin to slow down the push for enlargement by proposing Partnership for Peace were perceived as obvious signs of the effectiveness of this approach. At this stage the argument of the negative effects of NATO enlargement on domestic developments in Russia was often used. NATO enlargement, if realized, could result in growing support for Russian extremists (argument no. 1 – 'democratic'). This argument was especially useful after the 1993 elections, won unexpectedly by Zhirinovsky's Liberal Democratic Party of Russia (LDPR). It was also argued that NATO enlargement would result in the isolation of Russia and in the creation of new dividing lines in Europe (argument no. 2 – 'civilizational'), that the Western leaders promised Gorbachev not to enlarge NATO during talks on reunification of Germany (argument no. 3 – 'gentlemen's agreement') and that NATO enlargement will affect Russia's military and strategic security (argument no. 4 – 'geopolitical').

One can also try to sketch some of the principal lines of the Russian 'deep defence' concept in the discussion on NATO enlargement. The first line of 'political fortification' was constructed mainly from a mixture of 'democratic', 'civilizational' and 'gentlemen's agreement' arguments and the main task was to prevent NATO enlargement from taking place at all, to 'freeze' the situation in Eastern Europe and base the new security architecture in Europe on the 'softer' and less 'defined' OSCE. Having realized already in 1994 that the decision on NATO enlargement was probably irreversible, Russian policy-makers withdrew to the 'second line of defence' and tried to find a new formula that could possibly limit the negative consequences of this plan to Russia's strategic interests in the region and provide Russia with a bargaining chip. The proposed formula could be described as the *'unacceptability of NATO enlargement to Russia's borders'*, and the main argument used was the 'geopolitical' one. The concept was for the first time discussed in a serious way by Primakov in SVR's (Foreign Intelligence

Service) report on the consequences of NATO enlargement presented in November 1993 and has since been repeated by almost all central Russian policy-makers, in the strongest manner by President Yeltsin in September 1995 when he denounced the NATO engagement in the former Yugoslavia and said that NATO's expansion to the 'borders of Russia would light the fires of war all over Europe' (*OMRI Daily Digest* 11.09.95).

This modified policy of trying to halt not NATO enlargement itself, but NATO approaching Russian borders was a clear sign of a new, more flexible, more realistic and more sophisticated approach to the problem. If NATO could not stop its enlargement, because it would cast a slur on its reputation, a face-saving solution should be found. The formula of not enlarging to Russia's borders was probably an attempt to suggest to the NATO leadership what this face-saving 'enlargement' could look like. Kaliningrad was seemingly assigned the role as the Russian border area, that could serve as an excuse for not accepting Poland and Lithuania as the alliance's new members. This type of 'limited' enlargement, that would include only countries of marginal importance to Russia's national interests (Hungary, the Czech Republic and even Slovakia)[16] could be presented as only a prestige defeat, but in terms of *Realpolitik* it would mean maintaining the status quo in the area perceived by Russians as crucial for their national security. It could also help the Russian leadership to limit the negative consequences of the enlargement both on the strategic level and in domestic politics. Excluding Poland and the Baltic states from the process of enlargement would mean keeping open the possibility of an imperial comeback to Central Europe later on, after recovery from the current crisis, while letting Poland and the Baltic countries join the enlarged alliance would mean a strategic defeat and the eventual end of the imperial dream in Central Europe. In this pre-enlargement argument with the West, Kaliningrad has played a role both as a military base, and as the sole piece of Russian territory bordering on the potentially enlarged NATO.[17] In the political phase of the conflict with NATO on the alliance's plans to enlarge this 'spatial' dimension of Kaliningrad was as important as its military potential, because it could be used to back the Russian claim for not enlarging NATO towards Russia's borders.

When it turned out that the West was not willing to listen to Russia's geopolitical arguments and that NATO would enlarge, notwithstanding Russian protests, the Russians withdrew to the 'third line of defence'. It was still 'geopolitical' concerns that played a central role in Russian argumentation, and the Russian proposal was that new members be granted a 'second class' membership (no nuclear weapons, no foreign troops and bases on their territory), while Russia would obtain a say in NATO matters. It was also clear that Russia's willingness to accept enlargement had its limits. The unthinkable for Russians at this stage was to let any of the Baltic states into the alliance (Maslov, 1997), the main argument being that it would mean NATO troops would be deployed only about 100km from St Petersburg. It also clearly showed that Rodionov's ideas from 1992 and the supposed inclusion of the Baltic states into a 'mental, geopolitical CIS' were still realities that all sides had to take into account.

At the same time Russia, paradoxically enough, launched a 'political counterattack' and took some offensive steps towards enlarging its zone of contact with the potentially expanded NATO. Political *rapprochement* with Belarus was dictated by both domestic and international political concerns. The signing of a treaty with President A. Lukashenko in April 1996, only two weeks after the State Duma's denouncement of the Belovezha Agreement,[18] was to show voters with a more nationalistic and 'Soviet-friendly' leaning that Yeltsin realized in fact the policy of reintegration of the post-Soviet space proposed by his political opponents. This move was, however, also dictated by security concerns and it was not surprising that D. Ryurikov, who was at that time one of President Yeltsin's closest aides and his adviser on international issues,[19] was actually one of the main advocates of this *rapprochement*. *Rapprochement* with Belarus was clearly meant as a warning to the West that Russia would not wait for a deterioration of its strategic position, that the country's leadership was determined to take appropriate steps in order to improve Russia's bargaining position in negotiations with the West and was willing to 'enlarge' its domain to limit negative geopolitical consequences of potential NATO enlargement. If the Russian–Belarus *rapprochement* leads to a closer strategic and military cooperation, the strategic role of Kaliningrad would probably be diminished, because the main zone of potential confrontation would be located again on the traditional East–West strategic axis. This *rapprochement* will also mean a new strategic situation for Kaliningrad's closest neighbours.

KALININGRAD AND POLISH/LITHUANIAN SECURITY DILEMMAS

What for Russia has been first of all a great-power status game has in Poland and Lithuania been perceived not as a 'status dilemma', but almost as a question of national survival. These two countries' strategic choices in the post-Soviet period of their history have been dictated not by the search for 'international status', but by the necessity of securing conditions for the sovereign existence of their respective nations. The security dilemma of both countries is closely related to their past experiences of history and to their present perceptions of the obvious disparity of potentials in the region. Kaliningrad is perceived not only as a military threat, but also as a reminder of the Soviet-style political arbitrariness, that, unfortunately, can still be detected in today's Russia,[20] handling of the two most important crises. In the past, both countries fell victim to Russian hegemonism, both regained their independence after the fall of the tsarist regime in Russia and both saw the loss of their sovereignty in the wake of the German–Russian *rapprochement* in 1939 and as a result of the Soviet Union's victory in the Second World War.

Polish and Lithuanian relations with Russia have been very strongly influenced by the perception of the Russian Federation as a direct heir of the Russian and Soviet Empires. Since the seventeenth century, historical relations between Poland/Lithuania and Russia have been marked first by the rivalry of the two local powers in Eastern Europe, and then by the domination of Poland and Lithuania by their more powerful Eastern neighbour, lasting practically until 1989. The record of the Russian and then Soviet domination of Poland and Lithuania is perhaps the most weighty factor influencing the perception of the Russian Federation after the dissolution of the Soviet Union.

Russian opposition to the NATO enlargement, reiterated many times by almost all the Russian leaders, has been met by Warsaw with an understandable nervousness as a confirmation of Russian plans to keep open the possibility of regaining control over Eastern Europe. The shortest and maybe most revealing description of the Polish perception of Russian policy towards Poland in this period can be found in a statement made by one of the leaders of the Polish opposition after his visit to NATO Headquarters in the spring of 1997, where he commented on his talks with the Russian envoy to NATO, V. Churkin. He said, paraphrasing von Clausewitz, that for the Russians 'politics is the continuation of war by other means'. This perception of Russia as the power that uses all means to counter the sovereign decision of neighbouring states to join an international organization unfortunately fits the historically determined image of Russia produced by the Polish and Lithuanian 'historical narration' and, in combination with the recent and obviously excessive use of force in solving internal problems and the inability to reform the system in an effective way, makes Russia a main point of concern for countries' political elites and for Poles and Lithuanians generally.[21]

Poland's geopolitical location in the heart of Europe, the Polish historical experience of being dominated by stronger regional powers and the obvious lack of resources to 'invest' in the country's security and to become a self-sufficient security provider and guarantor of the inviolability of the country's borders have led to the formulation of the strategic goals of Polish foreign policy of becoming a full-fledged member of EU and NATO.[22] The very experience of being located between two more powerful states is shared also by Lithuania, although Lithuanian leaders seem to have understood that the main threat to the country lies in the east, and that the Western neighbour will rather play a role of a bridge to the West.[23] The 'hidden' – realistic – objectives to be achieved by realization of the strategic goals of Polish and Lithuanian foreign policy are very similar and can be summed up as:

a) an attempt to internationalize security and economic relations with all historical hegemons of the region (Germany and Russia in the case of Poland; Russia, Poland and to a lesser degree Germany in the case of Lithuania);

b) the countries' attachment to the most effective and most democratic security alliance of the region, combined with American security guarantees;

c) full-fledged participation in economic cooperation in Europe and a boost in the development of the countries' economies resulting in the narrowing of the civilizational gap between the West and the East (Portuguese, Spanish and Irish 'patterns of EU-membership' based on transfer of economic resources to the underdeveloped areas).

In the Polish political tradition of the last two centuries, in which geopolitics has played quite naturally a very central role, the worst-case scenario has always been based on the fear of cooperation between the two powerful neighbours – Germany in the West and Russia or the Soviet Union in the East. The last Polish leader, who tried to pursue a policy of 'secure navigation' between the German Scylla and the Russian Charybdis, without joining one of them against the other, was J. Pilsudski, who had managed to conclude non-aggression treaties with both neighbours before he died in 1935. His views and attempts proved fatal to Polish independence in August 1939, when the two totalitarian neighbours reached an agreement on the future of Poland over Polish heads and only one week later waged war on their weaker neighbour. 1939 put an end to the Polish dreams of a balance of power in Central Europe. It became obvious that Polish independence was in many respects a 'hostage of geopolitics' and Poland was in a way doomed to live in the shadow of one of the local hegemons. The Soviet victory in the Second World War was fundamental for the creation of a new order in this part of the continent based on Soviet hegemony, and Poland and Lithuania, albeit in diverse conditions, had to wait until the totally unexpected end of the Cold War to see their dreams of freedom come true.

In 1991 Poland and Lithuania faced a new strategic choice, and the choice was made in favour of the West, whose institutions could provide in the foreseeable future a direct access to democracy, security and a market economy. It had also been hoped that joining the West could 'offer' the internationalization of relations with Germany and protection against the potential revival of Russian 'hegemonism'. The end of the Cold War, the collapse of the Soviet Empire, the 'Europeanization' of Germany and to some extent the 'Americanization' of Europe have opened a window of opportunity for Poland – it was maybe the first time in Poland's recent history (after 1918), that the country was given an opportunity to liberate itself from this until now fatal 'logic of geopolitics'. The choice was no longer between joining Germany against Russia, or Russia against Germany – the choice was between joining a stable Europe that could 'dissolve' in a way the German problem, staying in the Central European 'political and security vacuum' or finding a new formula for relations with the apparently unstable Russia.

The debate on Kaliningrad in Poland and Lithuania has therefore focused, quite understandably, almost exclusively on security matters and was dominated by geopolitical concerns.[24] This perception of Kaliningrad is to a great extent due to the obvious disparity of military potential concentrated in the area. Even if one compares the quantity of military hardware deployed on the *whole territory of Poland* with what is concentrated *only in the Kaliningrad oblast*, the situation is rather disadvantageous to Poland.

Table 3.2. Local balance of power: military 'hardware' in Kaliningrad and Poland, 1995/96
(Data on numbers from IISS *Military Balance 1995/96*, p. 105 for Kaliningrad and *Military Balance 1996/97* for Poland)

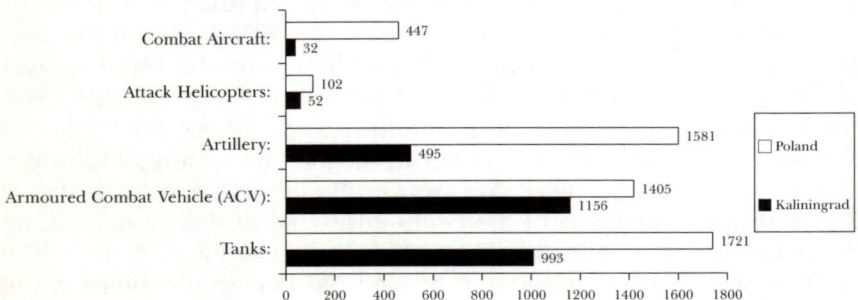

This difficult geostrategic situation of both Poland and Lithuania deteriorated dramatically as a consequence of the Russian–Belarus union. Both countries today face a situation in which they feel threatened on both flanks by a potential enemy, which has at its disposal an overwhelming military power that has many times in the past been effectively used to achieve political goals. The Russian–Belarus *rapprochement* means not only 'diversification' of threat compared with the situation where both countries bordered only on Kaliningrad. It also means the 'multiplication' of the threat and its further 'immediatization'.

Table 3.3. The strategic balance of power: Poland, Russia, Belarus and Kaliningrad in the light of CFE limits (per cent).
(Data on CFE limits from *SIPRI Yearbook and Military Balance*, on Kaliningrad holdings in 1995 from *IISS Military Balance 1995/96*, p. 105)

Category:	Poland's CFE limits as a percentage of Russia's CFE limits	Poland's CFE limits as a percentage of Belarus's CFE limits	Kaliningrad 1995 holdings to Poland's CFE limits
ACV	19	15	54
Artillery	25	20	31
Attack helicopters	15	13	40
Combat aircraft	13	12	7
Manpower	16	15	?
Tanks	27	21	57

In the case of Poland, and in purely military strategic terms, the situation today is in a way a mirror-image of the situation in 1938,[25] although the international mood, the real chances of becoming a member of a working military alliance, the apparent lack of a strategic German–Russian partnership, the German recognition of Poland's western borders guaranteed in a way by the American presence in Europe and the institutional Europeanization of Germany all seem to give hope that the lesson of Munich has in fact been learned, that, at least in this case *historia* is really *magistra vitae*.

For both Poland and Lithuania the Russian presence in Kaliningrad is a reminder of the past – both past simple and past perfect, if we can use these fitting 'grammatical' categories. Past simple – because it is an obvious and continuous manifestation of the Yalta order, that had been shaping the political map of the region and to a large extent the very 'asymmetric' relations among all its actors until the Soviet Union collapsed in 1991, the result being, among other things, the independence of the two countries. Past perfect – because Russian presence in Kaliningrad is the manifestation of one of the most lasting trends in Russian and then Soviet 'national grand strategy', that is, Russia's drive to the Baltic coast. This drive is symbolized on the one hand by the establishment of the new imperial capital on the banks of the Neva river by Peter the Great, and on the other hand by the Soviet 'territorial demands' formulated in the secret chapter of the Ribbentrop–Molotov Pact. What is at stake today is therefore whether Russia's withdrawal from the Baltic coast has a lasting character, whether Russia will from now on perceive its greatness and its security not in territorial terms but as a function of its economic strength and participation in international decision-making based on democratic principles, or whether Russia will in the near future re-embark on its imperial policy and become anew a source of insecurity and instability. Cooperation with the eventually enlarged NATO could be treated as a real litmus test of Russia's true intentions in the region. If Russia's commitment to democracy and a market economy is serious, accepting new NATO members, Baltic countries included, should not be perceived as a threat to Russia's security and its great-power status. Greatness, also political greatness is best manifested not by assertiveness, but by generosity. Thinking in geopolitical categories of control, power and territory should be perceived as obsolete in this time of building a new, common Europe, with democratic Russia as an important and equal partner. Today Russia faces a real strategic choice – it can either get rid of its imperial past or still deceive itself and build its future on mythical and dangerous illusions. Today's Russia reminds one to a certain degree of an owner of the greatest supermarket in the city, who loudly declares his commitment to the principles of a free-market economy, but whose store is full of outdated and outmoded products, and who, instead of renewing his offer in order to attract customers, threatens them with sanctions if they refuse to do their shopping in his store offering only products that can hardly be perceived as attractive. It seems that in today's world in which the rule of the market is overwhelming, the only effective way to 'buy' influence with neighbours and potential 'political customers' is through cooperation and/or attraction. It appears, fortunately, that the signing of the NATO–Russia agreement may pave the way for cooperation at a time when Russia's 'attraction potential' still needs some time to develop.

NEWSPAPERS, ELECTRONIC SOURCES:

Biuletyn Kaliningradzki, Osrodek Studiów Wschodnich (*Kaliningrad Review*, Centre for Eastern Studies OSW) all 1993–97 issues.
Kaliningradskaya Pravda
Krasnaya Zvezda
Nezavisimaya Gazeta
Open Media Research Institute Daily Digest, 1995–97 (internet version)
Radio Free Europe/Radio Liberty Daily Report, 1991–94 (internet version)

RFE/RL NewsLine, 1997 – (internet)
RIA–Novosti – *HotLine, Daily Review, Military Bulletin* (internet service)
Rossiyskaya Gazeta
Segodnya
Strazh Baltiki

NOTES

1 I would like to express here my gratitude to all those who have helped me in shaping this paper, especially to Ewa Jastrun from the Centre for Eastern Studies in Warsaw, who provided me with a substantial part of the data on Kaliningrad and to Bartolomiej Sienkiewicz, who made it possible. I would like to thank also my colleagues, Iver B. Neumann, Geir Flikke and Helge Blakkisrud for their moral support and inspiring discussions, as well as Pertti Joenniemi and Christian Wellmann for inspiring discussions on Kaliningrad in Travemünde. This article also owes a lot to my interviewees in Kaliningrad in Oct. 1996, where I had the opportunity to exchange views with amongst others A. Songal, S. Ginzburg, S. Tseplonkov and A. Kuznetsov, who all tried to help me understand the specifics of Kaliningrad. I would also like to thank A. Aasland and E. Hansen from the Institute for Applied Social Science, Oslo (FAFO), who helped me practically in organizing my stay in Kaliningrad, as well as all those more or less anonymous 'forces' in the Norwegian Ministry of Defence and Ministry of Foreign Affairs, who made the realization of this project possible by providing financial resources.

2 By 'conjuncture' we understand here a relatively lasting political, social, and economic regional setting in the Braudelian understanding of the term. Braudel (Braudel 1975: 20–21) defined it as a manifestation of history with 'slow but perceptible rhythms', 'the history of groups and groupings'.

3 The term 'geo-realistic' will be explained in the introduction to the relevant chapter.

4 Stalin's generosity towards Poland, that had been given control of the former eastern part of Germany and as Churchill said had been commanded to move 150 miles westward, was not motivated by feelings of guilt caused by the capture of eastern Poland in 1939. It was a calculated move that on the one hand would give political support to a Polish government controlled by Stalin's marionettes and on the other hand – and this reason was maybe even more important – was caused by a hope that by giving Poland a substantial part of German territory he could put an effective end to the Polish strategic dilemma, and force Poland into an 'eternal' alliance with the Soviet Union/Russia that became a sole guarantor of Poland's territorial integrity (more on that in Davies, 1981).

5 Soviet Minister of Foreign Affairs V. Molotov later described Poland as 'the grotesque bastard of the Versailles Treaty'. It was probably an opinion shared by his political master Stalin, who had personal reasons to have no love for Poland, as he was made partly responsible for the defeat of the Soviet Army in the Warsaw Battle in 1920.

6 The need to have access to an ice-free port in the Baltic was one of the main official reasons the Soviets used to persuade the West to hand over Königsberg to them, although they had already, by getting control over Liepaya, Klaipeda and indirectly over Polish ports such as Gdansk and Szczecin, had a broad access to open, non-freezing sea.

7 In the earlier phase of negotiations on the new borders in Europe it was proposed that the entire, undivided eastern Prussia had to be handed over to Poland as a compensation for territorial losses in the East (Eberhardt, 1993: 98; 111).

8 One of the best accounts on the development of Soviet naval strategy is still to be found in Polmar (1983: 37–9).

9 Many of the Russian policy-makers have linked, quite naturally, NATO expansion directly to Kaliningrad *oblast* – maybe the most explicit of them was Minister of Defence I. Rodionov, who said: 'NATO enlargement would reanimate a situation similar to the Cold War era, when the bloc's military groupings would directly confront Russian troops, in particular in the Kaliningrad region. The putting of a ramified network of airfields under the command of NATO (even hypothetically) would considerably expand its possibilities, allowing its planes to reach targets along the Smolensk–Bryansk–Kursk and Petrozavodsk–Yaroslavl–Belgorod lines. As a result the Europe-based tactical nuclear weapons would actually become strategic weapons, which would jeopardize the START-1 and START-2 treaties and call in question the possibility of concluding the START-3 treaty. In addition, the admission of the Baltic states would give NATO strategically important naval bases and uni-lateral military advantage, while the activities of the Russian Baltic fleet would be largely restricted.' (Rodionov, 1996a). See also Rodionov, 1996b, Barynkin, 1996, Maslov, 1997.

10 S. Shakhrai's article on the future role of the Kaliningrad area (Shakhrai, 1994), his stubborn opposition against giving Kaliningrad a special treatment (his article in *Nezavisimaya Gazeta* 26.10.94, where he accuses the local adminis-tration of focusing on local interests and neglecting the interests of Russia in the region) and the creation of the Special Defence Region in the area by Minister of Defence Grachev in March 1994 are the best known examples of this old-type thinking. Military aspects of developments in Kaliningrad have also often been underscored by Russian policy-makers during discussion on how to halt NATO enlargement.

11 The best manifestation of this type of thinking about the future role of the area have been the numerous attempts to create a free or special economic zone in the Kaliningrad *oblast* that could attract foreign investments and then lead to improvement of the situation in the region.

12 Sergounin (1997a: 51–2) formulates the 12 most important points of concern of Russian foreign policy. Great-power status and territorial integrity of the country seem to be very central issues in almost all the 'schools' of political thinking he analyses in his brilliant article. The same minimum programme can also be found in almost all main texts on Russian foreign policy published in Russia – it seems that the two issues form a hard core of Russian political thinking, although the cost of defending the two ideas can be very high, both in political and human terms, the Chechen war being maybe the most visible example of this.

13 More on the importance of the Baltic region in Soviet military plans – *The Voroshilov Lectures*, 1989: 104–18. For the Western view on the Baltic Sea's strategic importance, see Tunander, 1992 and Visuri, 1992.

14 There are only four classical exclaves in today's world – Kabinda, Walvis Bay in Africa, Kaliningrad in Europe and Nakhichevan (separated from Azerbaijan by Armenian territory) in Transcaucasus. To these four one can also add a handful of 'quasi-exclaves' such as Gibraltar, Macau, Spanish dependencies in Morocco (Ceuta and Melilla) and the special case of Nagorno-Karabakh, an Armenian area in Azerbaijan that has in fact become a part of Armenia as a

result of one of the bloodiest conflicts in the post-Soviet space. This 'collection' of exclaves may be supplemented by the best known historical example – East Prussia (Ostpreussen), that is a direct historical 'ancestor' of Kaliningrad.

15 The use of natural gas deliveries as a political leverage in relations with Poland was ruled out, because it would damage Russia's credibility in the West as a potential supplier of gas to the West and deprive Russia of desperately needed export incomes. Russians knew also that they could be relatively easily out-manoeuvred by their Western rivals, as happened later in the Czech Republic where Ryabov's attempt to 'politicize' the gas supplies ended with the Czechs signing a contract on gas deliveries with the Norwegians.

16 The Russian military tried, however, to blackmail both the alliance and potential members by saying that Russia would react to enlargement by deploying nuclear weapons in Kaliningrad and/or by targeting new members. One of the best specialists in military matters among Russian journalists Pavel Felgengauer said in his article published in *Moscow News* on 1 June 1995, that the Russian military may plan to deploy nuclear weapons in Kaliningrad if NATO enlarges, the same ideas were discussed also in *Życie Warszawy*, 23 Sept. 1995, *Komsomolskaya Pravda*, 28 Sept. 1995, *OMRI*, 10 Oct. 1995. On 26 March 1996 the Russian Minister of Atomic Energy Mikhailov said during his talks with J. Rotenblat from Pugwash (the international movement of scientists against nuclear weapons) that Russia may punish countries applying for membership by directing its nuclear warheads on them – *OMRI Daily Digest*, 27 March 1996. The Russian Institute of Defence Studies also prepared a recommendation to President Yeltsin in which he was advised to deploy nuclear weapons closer to the enlarged NATO borders – amongst others also in Kaliningrad (Richard Staar in *Wall Street Journal*, 12 June 1996).

17 In an interview with Pavel Felgengauer published by *Gazeta Wyborcza*, 2 June 1995, this Russian expert said that Russia may only accept the Czech Republic as a new member of NATO, while opening the alliance to one of the Baltic countries would be treated by Moscow as a *casus belli*.

18 The agreement made in Minsk in December 1991 to dissolve the USSR.

19 Enthusiastic support for the idea of closer ties between Belarus and Russia eventually led to Ryurikov's fall, when in March 1997 the 'pro-integrationist' group within the Russian establishment lost to 'economic realists' led by Chubays and Nemtsov and integration with Belarus became more decorative than real.

20 The handling of the two most important crises in the short history of democratic Russia – the conflict between President Yeltsin and the Supreme Soviet in 1993 and the Chechen war in 1994–96 – combined with Russia's attitude towards these countries' choice of strategic partners (NATO enlargement), Russia manifested assertiveness in its relations with some CIS countries (the Abkhaz war in 1993, Russia's partiality in the conflict between Azerbaijan and Armenia) and Russia's enlargement to the West (the reintegration with Belarus) are in these countries interpreted as visible signs of the 'reversibility' of the political processes in Russia and as a source of instability and insecurity on the local level.

21 Two public opinion polls – one from June 1990 and the second one from Oct. 1993 confirm a dynamic of the Polish 'fears'. In Oct. 1990, 32 per cent of respondents said they believed that Germany was the most important threat to Polish security, while only five per cent pointed at Russia. In Oct. 1993 the results were completely different – 31 per cent feared Russia, while only five per cent pointed at Germany. Also when asked who may pose a threat to Poland's security in the future the respondents answered similarly – in June 1990 30

per cent pointed at Germany and five per cent at Russia, while in Oct. 1993 – only 11 per cent pointed at Germany, while 26 per cent pointed at Russia.

22 After the collapse of the Soviet hegemonic system Central European decision-makers could choose one of four options for securing the region's security. The options were: (a) zero variant – e.g. continuing cooperation with Russia; (b) armed neutrality (the very costly – and not yet proved effective – Swedish or Swiss model, that in the case of a conflict and taking into consideration Poland's location on the European crossroad would probably end as did the Belgian version of neutrality in being violated twice in this century by its powerful neighbour); (c) creation of a local security structure securing the countries of the region against the potential revival of Russian or German hegemonism (the best known attempt was President Kravchuk's proposal of 1994 to create a Baltic–Black Seas Union); (d) joining working Western institutions.

23 President Landsbergis's emotional speech at the Polish Parliament in Feb. 1997 and his 'invitation' to increase more substantial cooperation between Poland and Lithuania are signs of a new, more pragmatic and realistic attitude towards Poland in Lithuania.

24 Marczak and Pawlowski, 1995: 49–51 and 72 define the Kaliningrad area as one of the five most important 'operational directions' in the case of a potential conflict.

25 This association is justified by many facts, the most important being (1) the separation of Kaliningrad from Russia resembling the situation of East Prussia (Ostpreussen) in the interwar period, and neighbour's claim for a 'corridor' to link the enclave with the mainland; (2) the political mood in Russia reminiscent of the Weimar Republic syndrome, with civilizational, economic and 'status' depression; (3) Russian political assertiveness and Russian political use of the 'Russian diaspora question'; (4) strategic encirclement – in 1996 Russia's union with Belarus and in 1938 German occupation of Czechoslovakia; (5) the apparently 'correct' relations with all neighbours – in 1938 Poland had non-aggression treaties with both Soviet Russia and Nazi Germany and was allied directly with one of the European great powers, France, and cooperated with Great Britain; (6) a large part of Poland consists of territories that have been for many years seen by one of the powerful neighbours as Polish war loot – in 1938 it was the case with eastern Poland, today it's still to a certain degree, a problem of the so-called 'Regained Territories' in the west and north.

4

International Security Structures and the Baltic Region: The Implications of Alternative Worldviews

MARTIN HEISLER
AND GEORGE QUESTER
Department of Government and Politics, University of Maryland

The United States and the other Western democracies are having difficulty in determining what they will want and need in international structures for the post-Cold War world. Debates persist about the expansion of NATO, and even about whether NATO should be maintained. Concepts of collective security and regional security are juxtaposed against the question of 'security against what?', while formerly 'neutral' countries like Sweden pose the same question as 'neutral against whom?'

Some of the confusion here stems from the surprise caused by the sudden ending of the Cold War and the collapse of the Warsaw Pact and of the Soviet Union itself. Very few Western analysts would have dared to predict such a happy ending to the Cold War conflict, or would have looked ahead to sorting out what the ideal arrangements of international structure would then be.

But a deeper source of confusion stems now from alternative versions of what will drive the international tensions and foreign policy motives of this world. The purpose of this paper will be to sort out these analytical perspectives on what international political conflict will be all about, focusing on the example of the Baltic region, showing how alternative predictions of international conflict can produce very different implications for what kind of international treaties and organizational structure are needed.

There are at least five different sorts of patterns for international interactions in the near- to medium-term future; and, we argue, international relations are likely to reflect one of these or some combination of them. After outlining these patterns, we shall turn to sorting out their implications for international security arrangements.[1]

GEOPOLITICS

One view could be described as basic geopolitics. In this view, the outside world must be concerned about *any* power which dominates the centre of Eurasia, no matter how it is governed, by tsars, commissars, or democratically-elected presidents. This view hails back to Mackinder and, even earlier, to the British nineteenth-century concern about the 'great game' in Asia. In this view, whoever has the central position in the largest continent on earth has the military advantage of being able to move outward in all directions from that centre, and, thus, soon to dominate the periphery of the continent as well. From that stance, such a power might pose the threat of militarily dominating the entire globe (Glassner, 1993: 226ff.; Neumann, 1997).

This is a perspective by which 'little has changed' since the end of the Cold War, except that the central Eurasian power has been pushed back somewhat. In 1998, Russia still threatens to dominate Belarus and Ukraine and Kazakhstan, and from there Poland and Mongolia, and so on, just as in 1958 or in 1898. Britain and the United States, and the Scandinavian countries, according to this view, will still have to mount lines of confrontation and containment, since geography can not be changed, since the central position enhances the military power of whoever is holding it. Russia will have to be opposed and painted in as the potential 'enemy', regardless of how it is governed.

From this perspective, retaining the existing alliances, or even expanding and reinforcing them, is hardly a self-confirming prediction of hostility. It was the inherent dictate of the shape of the continents that set up the Cold War, just as it set up earlier tensions between Britain and tsarist Russia. A Russia governed by Kerensky and his successors might, by this view, have been just as difficult for London and Washington (and Warsaw and Riga) to deal with.

NUCLEAR POLITICS

A second kind of analysis would fasten onto a post-1945 factor which seemed to offer some counters to the geopolitical threat, but which is of course very double-edged, the introduction of nuclear weapons. Rather than expending enormous economic and human energy in trying to contain the Soviet geopolitical threat by matching ground forces with ground forces, the United States after 1945 tried to deter any exploitation of Moscow's geopolitical advantages by the threat of escalations to nuclear warfare, a threat which might well have worked for all the years of the Cold War. While the Cold War was underway, the West might thus have welcomed the existence of nuclear weapons, as a 'great equalizer'. But the Soviet Union had acquired its own nuclear weapons by 1949, and, with the end of the Cold War, it may now be more appropriate for the West to regret the existence of nuclear weapons, and for Russia to welcome them. This is an interpretation which plays down the geopolitical threat of Russian conventional forces and their central position in the post-1989 world, but which sees Russia as having to be accorded various kinds of special, most probably positive treatment, in the Baltic region and anywhere else, because it retains the ability to destroy the cities of the world in less than an hour.

If nuclear weapons did not exist, by this interpretation, Russian interests could be ignored much more safely, as the Western democracies sort out what kind of treaty and alliance agreements or collective security arrangements they might wish to pursue. But since the nuclear weapons do exist, since even the most democratic leaders in Moscow are aware of the possible advantages they offer to an otherwise under-endowed Russia, such weapons of mass destruction will play an important role in shaping what international security structure is now developed.

This is a view by which it is not so much of an accident that the five permanent members of the United Nations Security Council just happen to be the five states openly possessing nuclear weapons. This is a view by which a total elimination of nuclear weapons is very unlikely, not just because of the difficulties inherent in verifying such disarmament, but because Moscow, as well as Paris and London and Beijing, has realized that the retention of such weapons conveys benefits, and offers leverage over the future of international alliances and organizational changes.

CULTURAL CONFLICT

A third interpretation of the world would emphasize the surprising resurgence of ethnic conflict that we have seen since 1989, in the former Yugoslavia and the former Soviet Union, and possibly around the rest of Eastern Europe.

Samuel Huntington has captured a great deal of attention with his provocative 'clash of civilizations' argument, by which the end of the Cold War will see a wide variety of political conflicts emerging along the fault lines of contact between differing religious and ethnic traditions (Huntington, 1996).

If Yugoslavs can kill each other about something so seemingly trivial as the alphabet they use for the language they otherwise share, one might then expect similar conflict wherever the Orthodox Christian tradition confronts the Western Roman Catholic and Protestant traditions, which of course brings us directly back again to Eastern Europe and the Baltics.

Outsiders, by this kind of argument, might be predicted to choose sides then based on their own ethnicity, and/or might be well-advised to do so, since these will be the conflicts that affect their own future life-style. If some Scandinavians feel culturally less distant from Russia than most Americans do, and if differences in religious denominations may not be as important for them, it might be more difficult for their leaders to mobilize support for the 'people more like us'. Nonetheless, both they and their counterparts elsewhere in the West would have a difficult time justifying international arrangements that did not protect Poles or Estonians against Russians.

It has to be noted that any endorsement, or prediction, of such ethnically-based conflict would have had difficulty getting a hearing *during* the Cold War. One of the few points on which the Marxist and liberal perspectives agreed was that disputes about religion or language were foolish; these were the kinds of disputes the Nazis had exploited, the kinds of disputes that reflected the unenlightened thinking of the past.

Anyone preaching a message of ethnic conflict in Eastern Europe in the days of Communist rule would have been imprisoned, and someone advocating the same message in the West would have been ridiculed as sounding like a neo-Fascist. This is not to say that ethnicity or, in Soviet terminology, 'nationality', did not matter. But such 'identity' issues were regulated from above, whether in the form of official classification, policies of Russification and Russian preference, or other means. And both sides in the Cold War exploited ethnic differences in surrogate conflicts, especially in the Third World. But the post-1989 resurgence of such conflict nonetheless came as a shock and surprise to all concerned.

One of the 'advantages' of the ideological conflict of the Cold War years was that both sides at least pretended to be altruistically involved with the welfare of all mankind. The Nazis had, by contrast, preached a doctrine of outright selfishness, where Germans should benefit at the expense of other ethnic groups that would either be enslaved or annihilated. The return of the explicit selfishness and the 'them versus us' thinking of ethnic conflict is thus ugly, as well as surprising, after the Nazis demonstrated what it could lead to. Some would argue that this shows all the more how real such issues are, since there were so many good reasons to hide and repress them (see, e.g., Van Horne, 1997). Others, in contrast, would continue to champion the causes of 'historically disadvantaged' minorities. Human rights arguments are being progressively extended to collectivities, not just individuals (Van Dyke, 1985; Sniderman *et al.*, 1996, esp. chap. 7).

LIBERAL POLITICS

A still very different interpretation of the future of international politics, in the Baltic region and everywhere else, would attach primary importance to the spread of democracy. Rather than asking who holds the central strategic position, or who has nuclear weapons, or who uses the Cyrillic alphabet, this would ask whether people are being governed by their consent, whether governments have to face opposition in fair election contests, with freedom of the press and speech, and so on.

Democracies, in this liberal democratic view, are the most likely to produce domestic success. And, by the same view, such political democracies are very unlikely ever to get into wars with each other, or even to have arms races and crises with each other (see, e.g., Russett, 1993; Brown, Lynn-Jones and Miller, 1996).

The United States and the other existing democracies thus would have both altruistic and selfish reasons to assist the spread of democracy around the world, because this helps other peoples solve their problems and achieve a greater happiness, and because it makes wars less likely, the wars that can draw in peace-loving states involuntarily, the wars that could inflict horrendous destruction on the entire globe.

Democracies, in this view, could be expected to side with any new democracy against any country which was more autocratically ruled, on both grounds. Supporting the democracy would increase the portion of the world's population that was governed by its own will. Supporting the democracy would most probably also be supporting the side that was the victim rather than the perpetrator of aggression, since democracies are not inclined to be warlike.

Some scenarios in the Baltic Sea and East European regions can be used to illustrate some elementary sources of confusion and tension here, for Scandinavians and other westerners. What if Russia now becomes more of a democracy politically than either Belarus or Ukraine? What if Estonia is seen to fall short of basic democratic standards and exclude from citizenship a substantial minority of the people born and living within its territory, or Latvia denies a large number of those born and living there the right to vote? And what if the voters of a politically democratic Russia become exercised about discrimination being practised against their ethnic kinsmen across some border and call for action, including perhaps, as a last resort, military action, to protect them?

It has to be remembered that the three Baltic states were not very successful in preserving political democracy in the years between the two World Wars; under the pressures of the worldwide economic depression and without well-institutionalized democratic traditions, they succumbed to a form of Fascist rule even before Germany fell to the Nazis. If one or another of these states were to wander away from democratic processes, while Russia stuck more closely to them, a conflict here might cut across every dimension we have noted, with very confusing implications for the shape and role of international structures.

A system of 'collective security', as envisaged by Woodrow Wilson in the designing of the League of Nations at the end of the First World War (and as envisaged again by President George Bush when he spoke of a 'new world order' in response to Saddam Hussein's aggression towards Kuwait), is closely connected to a liberal faith in political democracy. Wilson spoke of making 'the world safe for democracy', but he also meant making it safe by democracy.

Collective security systems reflect a liberal self-confidence that the system of law-and-order governing domestic life can be transplanted to international dealings as well, as violence is outlawed, as the first state to use violence is always at fault, as all of this is underscored by the rule of law and by government by consent of the governed. Believers in power politics, or believers in the power of ethnic drives, will scoff as to whether this liberal view of the future of world politics can ever prevail.

CHAOTIC POLITICS

Our fifth perspective would see problems not in Russian military strength, but in political weakness, exacerbated by the ethnic considerations noted above, but without much cohesion or central authority on the Slavic or non-Slavic side of the line. If governability and economic viability prove elusive in the Russian Federation, Russia's neighbours will face some very different, and not necessarily lesser, threats.

As the chaos that has characterized a growing number of countries in Africa in the 1990s shows, effective governance and social and economic order cannot be taken for granted. The presumption of what Robert Jackson has called 'positive sovereignty' is questionable for an increasing portion of the world's states, including Russia and a number of the other successor states to the Soviet Union (Jackson, 1990).

Even if nuclear weapons had never been invented, there are still some other reasons why the neighbours of today's Russia might have second thoughts about any greater fractionation and division of the former Soviet Union. The risk is that the population or populations of the fragments will prove uncontainable, fighting their way across the borders of the Russian littoral, to escape warfare or economic misery. Conflicts among armed factions might spill across borders; or richer neighbours might become attractive targets for organized brigands.

Economic and social, as well as political, order is thus now a major concern for the West in general and for Russia's western neighbours in particular. Such order will be essential for forestalling an exodus of large numbers of Russians, and perhaps people from other such European parts of the former Soviet Union as Belarus and Ukraine, an exodus caused by disorder, conflict or economic collapse. We do not have to look to Africa for illustrations of massive human dislocation in the wake of the breakdown of governance, violence and privation: Bosnia and, more recently, Albania, provide more direct examples.

It was easy to keep Russians out when the Soviet Union kept them – and Poles, Ukrainians, Hungarians, and others – in. For 40 years, the West harangued the Warsaw Pact states to accord their populations 'the right of exit'. Those who managed to get out were greeted as heroes; their crossing was evidence of the superiority of our political and economic values and achievements. Such migration was not just devalued by the end of the Cold War and the evanescence of familiar dangers, it was converted into a threat.

Now that the countries of the old Warsaw Pact permit their citizens to leave, we are loath to accord them entrance. This is so for many reasons, most of them related to the prevailing political and economic climates in what students of migration now call 'the target states'. While there may be sufficient military and paramilitary means for closing borders, ethical compunctions and other factors in Western societies militate against using force to repel large numbers of uninvited guests. There may even be a time-tattered invitation in the minds, if not the pockets, of some potential migrants: the self-congratulatory advertisements and encouraging rhetoric of the Cold War. The West can no longer count on Russia to keep Russians and other would-be travellers in.

Europe's geopolitical stability during the Cold War owed much to the effectiveness of mutual nuclear deterrence; but in an important sense, it was made possible by the demarcation of spheres of influence in the Yalta agreement and Stalin's use of the Red Army and political intrigue to effectuate it through repression and intimidation. Relatively clear lines of demarcation provided an important part of the certitude in the mix of clarity and ambiguity that effective deterrence requires. Those lines remained virtually unchanged between the late 1940s and the late 1980s, at least in Europe. Thus, the master strategy of containment could be implemented through the confrontation of two alliances across relatively non-porous frontiers and without unmanageable fuzziness between them. Nothing exemplified that enforced clarity more than the inner-German border and, most specifically, after August 1961, the Berlin Wall.

The post-Cold War world has no counterpart to Yalta. There are no general agreements on spheres of influence; nor does effective

military control demarcate zones of mutual defence in as unambiguous
a fashion as in the past. Boundaries are increasingly permeable; and
there are many areas of overlap or interpenetration. Some of these are
discussed below; suffice it here to note a novel consequence for classic
geopolitical thinking of the current circumstances of Russia and its
neighbours. While, as in the past, those neighbours must be attentive
to any hegemonic power in the heart of Eurasia, now they must also
be concerned about the ramifications of the absence of such power. If
managing potential threats from a powerful and centralized Russian
or Soviet state was difficult, managing potential threats from a fragmented, imploding, or isolated Russia armed with nuclear weapons,
wary of the fate of its ethnic kin in a vast diaspora where it has little
influence, facing severe and protracted economic problems, and
encountering difficulties in establishing the rule of law or maintaining
domestic order, is hardly easier. In any event, the derived conclusions
for the shape of international organizational arrangements will surely
differ from one worldview to another.

IMPLICATIONS FOR SECURITY ORGANIZATION

We will consider a range of as many as six or seven international
political/military institutions here. Very important and vigorous, economically and politically, is the European Union (EU), formerly
the European Community. Second, but less important or active so far,
has been its 'military component', the Western European Union
(WEU).

Third, inevitably very central to our discussion, is the North Atlantic
Treaty Organization (NATO). Discussions by analysts tend to focus on
five options: expanding NATO; eliminating it; extending its scope to
some states in some qualified fashion, short of full membership;
continuing NATO basically as it has been; or some combination of these
alternatives.

Fourth, far less tangible and meaningful, is the (PFP) programme
– Partnership for Peace established in 1993, basically continuing the
North Atlantic Cooperation Council (NACC) founded in 1991. Both
of these sought to allow former Warsaw Pact members and former
Republics of the Soviet Union to have a modicum of interaction with
NATO, as is the Euro-Atlantic Partnership Council (EAPC), currently
extending to 29 countries, aiming to lessen Russian anxiety in the face
of NATO's expansion eastward. The conclusion in January of 1998 of
a 'Charter of Partnership' between the United States and the Baltic
states is at once intended to launch at least a symbolic security relationship, one that would not increase Russia's sense of encirclement in a

fashion that even discussions of future NATO membership for those three countries might do.

Fifth, a very different 'relic of the Cold War', is the Organization for Security and Cooperation in Europe (OSCE), intended to be a confidence-building measure when the Cold War was still in place, and when it looked as if it might remain so indefinitely into the future. Sixth, we may also find an enhanced role, of course, for the United Nations, an organization intended for global purposes and not just for a particular region, intended to settle political disputes and prevent military conflict.

Seventh, and finally, it is conceivable that the Council of the Baltic Sea States (CBSS) may come to play important security-related roles, especially along the non-military dimensions of security (cf. Knudsen and Neumann, 1995: 7ff.; and also see Wellmann, 1992). Many of the political (especially human-rights focused), economic, transportation and communications-related aspects of the CBSS's expanding mission have at least indirect security ramifications. The CBSS's neo-functional approach to linking various policy universes and technical and bureaucratic staff across the former East–West divide may have more important implications for future security relationships in the region than any explicit preoccupation with more conventionally cast security issues.

We shall see that these structures, and the options for activating, expanding, altering or combining them, will fit very differently into the varying versions of international conflict that may emerge. But one generality will certainly loom up, a version of 'nothing ventured, nothing gained': the greatest help in solving any version of the future security problem will come most probably where a greater sacrifice is made in terms of existing military, political or economic impact. That is, much more will be at stake in what one envisions as changes in the 'going concerns' of international structure, NATO and the EU, and correspondingly less impact is likely to be derived from some of the other structures (cf. Zelikow, 1996).

Having outlined these alternative perspectives on how the world will now interact in conflicts of interest, we turn to the implications of each for the particular case of the Baltic region, and for Eastern Europe in general, in part because it is the focus of this volume, but in larger part because this region provides good illustrations of the possible confusions and tensions flowing from these alternative guesses about the future. The possibility surely remains that these analytic perspectives will not sort themselves out so well that one predominates over and eliminates all the others. If the future were then to remain uncertain and confusing, with differing theories seemingly coming and going in their immediate relevance, it remains possible that the

structures built on such theories may also have to be left less clear and
defined, also coming and going in relevance. Finally, we recognize that
combinations of elements of these perspectives may animate *practice* in
world politics; but our aim here is to project analytically discrete views.
Such exaggerated clarity or neatness is useful at an early juncture in
thinking about the problems at hand; other papers in this volume
reflect more faithfulness to the more complex 'realities'.

IMPLICATIONS OF THE PRIMACY OF THE GEOPOLITICS VIEW

From the classic geopolitics perspective, the Cold War's end and the
Soviet Union's demise are reasons for rejoicing, but also for continuing
vigilance. The core power on the Eurasian land mass has been rolled
back substantially, from Finland and the Baltics in the north, through
Poland and the former East Germany, to Ukraine, the Caucasus and
the Balkans in the southwest; and an increasingly self-confident and
rich China looms on its southeast. But, while Russia is clearly smaller,
weaker and less coherent than the Soviet Union was, these geopolitical
setbacks may have made it more dangerous, if either of the most obvious
possibilities comes about: if it succeeds in re-establishing effective
central control and direction, or if it fails to do so.

If these reversals do not signal Russia's terminal decline or
disintegration, then we can expect it to push against its frontiers in the
future much as it has during the past three centuries. In this scenario,
Russia will seek strength through consolidation, by reasserting central
authority within its borders, increasing its links to some or most of the
former Soviet republics in the 'near abroad', and by trying to recon-
struct buffers of friendly, or at least neutral, states on its borders. It is
difficult to imagine a successful effort to re-establish the ties of nation-
hood and patriotism without recourse to chauvinism or projections of
hostile encirclement or both. These are the means that were used to
cement Russia's cultural and political components in the past. The re-
establishment of central control is accompanied by at least symbolic
demonstrations of power and high expectations of respect from others.
In this view, it is not a question of whether it will return to its quest for
openings in the west, resources in the south, and security around its
perimeter in general, but when and how.

Such traditional concerns of geopolitics make Poland, Ukraine and
the Baltic states eager for membership in NATO. As before, they would
fear Russian armoured divisions crossing their border, or merely
posing the threat of doing so, in a new version of 'Finlandization'.

There was a time when 'Finlandization' was perhaps the best that
one could hope for, in Poland or in Estonia, as a nation might be freed

from having to adopt Marxist political and economic systems domestically, while still having to adjust all pronouncements about world politics to the wishes of the regime in Moscow. Westerners therefore regarded the situation in Norway or Denmark as much superior to that of Finland, and used the NATO alliance and other projections of commitment to guard against any similar shadows of threat being cast over the Western European countries. But the same Westerners would have regarded the situation in Finland as far, far, superior to that of Estonia or Poland, or any of the other countries subjected to Communist rule, even Hungary (Quester, 1990).

Having now achieved a national and personal freedom greater than had been allowed under 'Finlandization', the formerly Communist countries are concerned to preclude any reversion to such political intimidation by the latent threat of force. To head off this kind of threat, an extension of NATO membership may thus seem attractive, if the surrogate alternative of an extension of European Union membership, the solution for Sweden and Finland, cannot be easily negotiated.

The Russian political leadership has expressed itself as being particularly sensitive to a NATO expansion 'to its borders', despite the fact that Norway is already contiguous with the Russian Federation, and that Turkey was contiguous with the old Soviet Union. Hungary and the Czech Republic do not touch this touchy Russia, and Poland does so only at the Kaliningrad *oblast*, Russia's half of the old German territory of East Prussia (Ostpreussen). But with the process of integration into NATO having been launched for these three countries, it is most likely that the three Baltic states, the most immediate focus of our attention here, will want the same, as will most probably Ukraine (see Carr and Ifantis, 1996: chap. 6).

To summarize, a broad NATO expansion might well then be the appropriate solution, if the traditional geopolitical considerations noted above prove paramount, with Russian objections being shrugged off or arrogated to the domain of the EAPC. Rather than worrying about Russian democratic processes, or political cohesion, the concern will simply be a matter of deterring Russian military aggression and neutralizing the threats of such aggression. It is when nuclear considerations are introduced, however, that the issue of NATO expansion may take a very different turn.

IMPLICATIONS OF NUCLEAR POLITICS

Despite widely reported decay in its military forces and the thinning of its nuclear arsenal, massive strategic resources remain in Russia. Weakened political authority makes civilian control – for that matter, coherent control of any sort – over those resources problematic. Even if we discount alarmist scenarios in which ethnic, regional, or factional warlords gain control of nuclear weapons, domestic political instability weakens the reliability of classic deterrence. While the problem can be summed up neatly in analytic terms as one of reliable command and control, in practical terms it is one of effective and coherent governance. It is difficult to specify the degrees and forms of threat that may follow from such problems in governance, but they are no less real for that. It is even more difficult to develop means for dealing with such threats than for conventional military or classical nuclear confrontations. Thus, the West's most significant and direct goal might have to be a fostering of political development in Russia that is at once moderate and stable.

The advent of nuclear weapons, and the financially and politically seductive qualities of stable security through mutual deterrence, have thus become very much a double-edged sword. While the West relied on them to deter conventional as well as nuclear threats over the course of 40 years, it also struggled with ways in which it might respond to encroachments more ambiguous or piece-meal than a frontal attack or nuclear salvo. The clear lines of demarcation institutionalized in the bipolar security relationship, coupled with periodic efforts to give substance to some sort of 'flexible response', helped to give credence to the notion of 'massive retaliation:' a strategic nuclear answer to (virtually) any aggression. Today, the danger of large-scale nuclear attack continues, although in somewhat different form; and the challenges of responding to conventional, or not directly military, threats grow more daunting.

Although mutual reductions in nuclear warheads are under way, the numbers that will remain, even after the dismantling agreed to, are much more than sufficient to present serious threats to all major population centres. For Russia, strategic nuclear weapons have thus taken on added significance, as currency with which it can pay its dues in the most selective club of major powers. They assure it a place at many or most tables in international discussions, no matter how tenuous the country's political order or threadbare its economy may become.

Where the Soviet Union was previously thought to hold the advantage in conventional forces, today's Russia sees itself outnumbered and outclassed in these terms, especially after the American capabilities were demonstrated in, or at least associated in most minds with, Desert Storm.[2] Just as NATO used to see nuclear weapons as a beneficial 'great equalizer', so some Russian military planners will see nuclear weapons now and in the future.

The seats Russia claims in various security and even economic fora by virtue of its nuclear power status doubtless provide tangible benefits for it; but another significant consideration is that they also bring Russia into those fora. In short, membership in the nuclear club may serve to engage it. Such engagement has sometimes led to co-optation in other arenas. While for Russia the consultation agreement it signed with NATO in May 1997 was perhaps a distant second choice to a role in the Western alliance's decision-making that it had initially sought as a security compensation for NATO expansion, from the West's stand-point, it can be viewed as a step to engage it. It remains to be seen how, if at all, Russia might be co-opted into at least informal security relationships.

Various Russian spokesmen have at times commented that they have no objection to NATO expansion, as long as Russia itself is allowed to become a member. This is often then brushed off, in the West, as nothing more than a resurrection of the old Soviet proposals, in Cold War days, that the Warsaw Pact and NATO somehow should be merged, with the result of gutting NATO of all its ability to reassure the democracies against aggression. Snickers have been directed at the notion that the 'North Atlantic' would extend to the Ussuri River frontier with China, and indeed to Vladivostok. The serious problem might indeed emerge that Beijing would see such a NATO extension as part of an American effort to 'contain' and encircle China.

But if one were to take the risks of nuclear civil war or insub-ordination, or another such disaster, very seriously the policy impli-cation is that the West should be devoting substantially more resources to heading off such problems, and perhaps even committing the precious resource of NATO.

The United States and other Western countries are probably less concerned about the command and control of former Soviet nuclear weapons than they should be. The mere possibilities of what could happen are so awful that we turn our attention elsewhere, for example, directing far less aid to Russia, just a fraction of America's economic resources in comparison with what was mustered 50 years ago for the Marshall Plan.

Perhaps it would therefore not be so foolish to call the Russians' bluff on the proposal that Russia be made a NATO member as well, including all the co-ordination and interaction of military commands that have reassured the world about West Germany or Italy, or Greece and Turkey.

Because Russia has nuclear weapons, it commands much more respect than it would otherwise. Because it has nuclear weapons, it might similarly be urgent for the outside world to reassure itself about the reliability of the controls on such weapons. If NATO has become such a symbolically important issue for Russians, as some of them claim, and if NATO is not nearly as crucial to protecting states like Germany or Norway against a conventional attack (and against intimidation by the mere threat of such an attack), then perhaps NATO could be adapted instead to co-ordinate the Russian military, in particular its nuclear military.

Defenders of the current status of NATO, or of the possibility of expanding it up to, but not across, the Russian border, will argue that there must surely be other ways of getting to know and interact with (that is, to 'engage') the Russian nuclear command and control authorities, so that the world would be no more worried about them than about the British and French nuclear commands. But it may be difficult to develop a sense of importance and infra-structural muscle for any of the alternatives, including the OSCE or the Partnership for Peace, or even the WEU, as long as they sit in the shadow of NATO, as long as they seem dwarfed in importance by that alliance.

For the Nordic countries, nuclear politics has always been much more than solely a matter of nuclear weapons. The generation of energy by nuclear reactors, with a risk of accidents – particularly in the wake of Chernobyl, and problems in the disposal of radioactive material – such as in the Soviet submarines abandoned in the waters off the Kola peninsula, are highly politicized and emotion-charged concerns.

Russia has apparently continued the Soviet tendency to cloak all matters nuclear under the rubric of military security. This does not augur well for decoupling issues related to nuclear safety, disposal, and the like from the military dimensions of nuclear politics. Such de-coupling is essential if the Nordic states' interest in developing peaceful, constructive links with Russia, the Baltic states, and several Eastern European countries, through technical cooperation aimed at managing problems in nuclear energy, safety and disposal, is to bear fruit.

Extending NATO membership to Russia might thus not suffice to relieve the Nordic countries, or anyone else, of concerns about the safety of Russian nuclear power plants, or about the propulsion systems of Russian submarines. Perhaps one would have to contemplate the even more fantastic, and difficult to achieve, extension of European Union membership to Russia.

But extending such EU membership even to Poland seems a difficult process. In the case of NATO, many might argue that the end of the Cold War has at least diminished some of the traditional importance of the military alliance, so that it might be adapted to a very different, now perhaps more urgent purpose. But the importance of the pre-existing economic and political functions of the European Union has indeed increased in the past decade, so that the Western states could hardly write this off simply as an important contribution to easing concerns about the Russian civilian or military nuclear establishment.

We would return then to the argument that NATO, or perhaps some other more military and less political or economic integrative structures, might be mustered for the problem of nuclear politics, for use to prevent the destruction of any cities or ecological basins by what was developed in the nuclear sphere by the old Soviet Union.

The importance of whatever helps to hold the Russian state together is very much increased, for the policy choices of Scandinavians and other Westerners, by the nuclear factor. Anyone scoffing at the contemporary importance of nuclear weapons indeed must confront such factors here, as they may drastically alter how outsiders react to developments inside Russia, and how such outsiders contemplate the future of NATO.

Sceptics may question whether nuclear politics are as determining as suggested here. But it would take only one close call, for example, where terrorists actually made threats to exploit a Russian reactor or a Russian nuclear warhead, to focus our attention, and to substantially readjust our priorities.

IMPLICATIONS OF CULTURAL CONFLICT

Cultural conflict can lead to international security concerns as well as to threats to the coherence of the Russian state. (For reasons alluded to earlier, internal chaos or disintegration may have adverse affects on international security.) The Soviet state was markedly multinational, as well as ethnically extraordinarily heterogeneous. Until the late 1980s it was strong enough to stifle demands for the recognition of cultural distinctiveness, and even more so, autonomy or independence. The venerable tsarist policy of Russification was continued, perhaps with more subtlety. Self-interest propelled many non-Russians towards the dominant cultural and political centre; and it served the regime well to leave those not attracted to that centre in the marginalized, apolitical peripheries. But with the dismantling of the Soviet Union, many instances of what had been ethnic diversity or frustrated aspirations for national autonomy have become international concerns (Chinn and Kaiser, 1996; Kolstoe, 1995).

The attractions of the peripheries have become much greater and those of Russia substantially less in the post-Soviet era, especially for non-Russians in the former Soviet Union, but even for many with Russian 'nationality' who established themselves in the republics. An important source of such attraction for some successor states, and for most of the Eastern European countries that had been members of the Warsaw Pact, is acceptance by the West. Some illustrations of what constitutes acceptance, in the minds of elites and populations with new-found autonomy in international relations, are membership in such Western institutions as the EU and NATO, foreign investments from multilateral institutions and corporations, bilateral state aid, and increasing cultural and technical links. There is some evidence that such concern with acceptance can stimulate peaceful relations among culturally distinct segments of populations and attentiveness to liberal democratic norms (see, for example, Breckinridge, 1991; Heisler, 1992).

There are several sorting processes taking place simultaneously. Within Russia, there is strong resistance to secession, or even to any loudly asserted claims to limited autonomy by culturally distinct populations. One argument is that the coherence of the (diminished) state must be maintained, an argument apparently supported by most Western governments in the case of Chechnya, if the rhetoric aimed to some extent at the domestic audience is pushed aside. Another calls attention to the need to avoid a slippery slope, where the magnitude of the minorities or the rightness of their cause cannot be stipulated before the onset of conflict. Without such boundaries, with more than 120 'recognized' cultural groups in Russia, there is virtually no limit to potential demands for complete or partial autonomy.

The West is less than eager to champion the causes of autonomy-seeking minorities in Russia, in part because their success would make it more difficult to govern the country. But there is another, perhaps more immediately important, reason for acquiescing in Russia's effort to maintain its territorial integrity, even by means of force. Justifying secession based on cultural distinctiveness might well undermine the integrity of many states, including most of the Soviet successor states.

We have already noted the concern of littoral states lest they be inundated with refugees from a militarily or economically chaotic Russia. Such concerns would be somewhat different if these refugees were ethnically grounded in a clearly aligned 'clash of civilizations' or 'imagined community', with refugees in the future perhaps moving in both directions, as ethnic Russians fled Estonia, even while ethnic Estonians were being punished and forced to flee from the Russian side of the boundary.

Will outside states simply be torn by an elementary human sympathy for all the people suffering inside Russia, set against a concern that these states themselves not be swamped by refugees who would bring much of the misery with them? Or will the outside states (and will the Russians and their government as well) instead be distinguishing between the peoples involved, on the basis of who is an ethnic cousin and who is not?

The situation is of course never symmetrical. There are definitely more Russians in the Baltic states, than there are Baltic peoples inside

Russia. And Russia will always be more militarily powerful than Estonia or Latvia. And, finally and perhaps a little less definitely, Americans or Swedes may always be more ready to identify with Estonians than with Russians.

If ethnic considerations take a great deal of priority, the case for a *particular* expansion of NATO is all the stronger, for the most 'Western' of the states formerly in Moscow's sphere, that is, for the Poles and the always 'Western' Czechs and Hungarians. Arguably, this sort of consideration, buttressed by domestic political considerations,[3] underlie the American position that only these three countries should be included in the first round of NATO expansion. After that might come the turn of somewhat less proximate or evident 'members of our civilization', such as the Estonians, Latvians, and Lithuanians, the Baltic peoples who, when asked to describe themselves, always claim to be 'Western Europeans' rather than 'East Europeans' or even 'Central Europeans' (see Vares and Zurjari, 1992: 106ff.). By this ethnic logic, these peoples are culturally qualified for admission to membership in Western institutions, including the EU, while perhaps Ukrainians and Russians are not.

Even if one thus bases identification on culture and treats ethnic issues as serious, however, it would presumably be preferable to head off rioting and other abuses of individuals, to try to avoid what an outsider might regard as an elementary violation of human rights. The same Finn or Swede, or American, who regarded it a travesty that large numbers of Russians had moved into Tallinn under Soviet rule would never, today, countenance any forced ouster of such Russians, or any other brutalities and harassment that seemed to be a punishment of the innocent to get even with Stalin.

A more worldly and liberal Westerner, whose viewpoint is discussed in the next section, would go further. He or she would avoid taking any sides in any 'clash of civilizations', arguing that all suffering peoples should be treated alike, and that wars should be ended and misery alleviated, and human rights should be protected, regardless of which alphabet anyone uses.

IMPLICATIONS OF LIBERAL POLITICS

The liberal-politics interpretation of the motives of the current democracies would treat all ethnic groups alike, and would attach primary concern to fostering government by consent of the governed. But, as noted at the outset, this presents a number of paradoxes and difficult choices for the United States and for the West European democracies. It will be important to support democracy where it has just been established, as in the Russian Federation, and as in the former members of the Warsaw Pact. Admitting Poland or Hungary to NATO has often been defended as a means to solidifying democracy in these places, just as it may have done in Greece, and more recently in Spain. But what if such a limited expansion of NATO were to undercut the appeal of democracy in Boris Yeltsin's Russia? Will the NATO–Russian agreement concluded in the Spring of 1997 suffice to undergird democracy's attractiveness?

In addition to supporting democracy where it has already been implanted, moreover, the expressed goal of the United States, fully consistent with the Wilsonian worldview of Americans in general, and probably of liberals around the world, is that the democratically-governed world should be expanded. But can this always be done peacefully? Or is the spread of democracy to be a military challenge to every regime, in the former Warsaw Pact or former Soviet Union, that relapses into harassments of political opposition, the closing down of a free press, and so on?

As noted, a belief in domestic political democracy is closely tied to a belief in collective security for the international arena, where whoever initiates a war is at fault, and where the outside world should ignore cultural affinities, or prearranged alliances, to rally behind the victim of the first military blow.

If there were to be a conflict between two countries, therefore, one of which was a democracy and the other a dictatorship, the prejudice of a liberal worldview would be that it was the democracy that was most probably the innocent, injured, party, and that the world should thus rally to its side. But this, in any future conflict between a democratizing Russia and a less 'reconstructed' former republic, would produce a very different action-rule from what we discussed earlier, since the political and economic reforms in a number of the other SSRs of the former Soviet Union have not matched those of the Russian Federation. Rather than siding with the smaller power against the larger, as part of a balance-of-power response to geopolitics, the general rule for a system of collective security, for a democratic world, would thus be to side with the more completed democracy, most probably the victim of aggression.

Even tougher questions emerge, as noted, where the majority of people in a smaller territory, claiming the rights of democracy and self-determination, want to secede from a larger country. The democratic majority of the entire country would vote against letting them secede, while the democratic majority of the smaller portion would vote for independence. And what if the two sides were ready to go to war over the issue?

This comes very close to offering a disproof to one article of liberal faith, that democracies will never go to war against each other. The United States under President Lincoln would not let South Carolina, or the rest of the Southern Confederacy, secede. President Yeltsin's Russia has used major military force in an attempt to keep Chechnya from seceding, and Canada is debating whether Quebec has the right to secede.

A defender of a liberal worldview can try to brush aside the problems here by noting that African-Americans were not allowed to vote in South Carolina or the rest of the Confederacy, were indeed held in the bonds of slavery. Had they been allowed to vote, a majority of all the voters in South Carolina might well have opposed secession. Supporters of President Yeltsin would similarly have argued that the opposition in Chechnya actually consisted of a group of criminals and warlords, not reflecting the majority view of the population in the region, so that no local democracy would be overridden if Russia were held together.

Yet the abstract problem here cannot be ignored by the world, as it contemplates what it wants from various forms of military alliance, for there surely will be some cases, in Russia or the rest of the former Soviet Union, or elsewhere in Europe, where the local majority truly disagrees with the overall majority about whether a union should be maintained or broken up.

If the local independence movements then grind things up finer and finer, taxing the attention-span and the memories of the voters of the outside world, undermining economic efficiency and political manageability, demanding complicated boundaries and lines of partition such as we see in the truces of Bosnia, it will become more difficult to support democracy as a good in itself, and as a means to producing international peace. It will be much more difficult to make collective security work, through the UN or any such global structure.

Much thus depends on how strong the commitment of the outside world, the democratically-governed world, will be to collective security, and to the protection of human rights and democratic processes in any such region as the Baltic. At the minimum, this outside world-concern for democracy already produces a major challenge to the absolute prerogatives of sovereignty which many remember as having emerged at Westphalia.[4] The world may, much more than in 1861, apply pressures to intervene where self-government seems in danger. Even where the issues are complicated as above, it may feel driven to intervene, not on the basis of ethnic identification, but on an argument where even Christian Americans could rally behind Bosnian Muslims, against Christian Serbs.

The role of overarching political and military structures for this kind of worldview becomes as complicated as the problems themselves.

The extension of virtually any of the political, economic and military memberships, EU, WEU, PFP, OSCE, NATO, or, for that matter, even CBSS – and perhaps even the 'Charter of Partnership' noted earlier – may play a helpful role here, offering a way to split the difference between respecting sovereignty and supporting self-determination, a way to establish some rough-and-ready federalisms, backed by the prospect of honest-broker or peacekeeping police and military forces. And this is the kind of political worldview where an enhanced role for the United Nations, rather than particular military alliance, becomes all the more appropriate (cf. Sperling and Kirchner, 1997, esp. chap. 8).

As was noted above, the impact of an extension of membership is almost directly proportional to the substance and strength of the organization already, i.e. to how much might be sacrificed in existing purposes as a means to supporting newer purposes. If NATO were eventually but prematurely – before Russia could reasonably be considered a member of a security community formed by the alliance – expanded to include Russia itself, it would lose some or all of its ability to guard Western Europe against Russian attack. But it might, in the process, establish a means by which democracy could thrive in the ethnically non-Russian portions of the Russian Federation, even while it thrives in the Russian.

The European Union, were it to be similarly expanded, might lose or delay much of its contribution to West European prosperity and economic integration, as it cannot become deeper while it is becoming so much wider. But it might in the process again work as a tool for protecting and spreading democracy, and for sorting out the nuances of federalism and centralization and local autonomy.

The less costly expansions of membership have already been undertaken, as in the OSCE and PFP, but with less impact. Most important perhaps, but entailing enormous questions going beyond the focus of this paper, would be enhancing the stature and role of the United Nations, which seemed at hand at the time of Desert Storm, but which slipped away again in the frustrations of Somalia.

IMPLICATIONS OF CHAOTIC POLITICS

If we see relatively few new attempts at secession from the Russian Federation, the complications of extending democracy will not create huge problems. But, if such secession movements proliferate, the world may give priority to harnessing its existing international structures, to prevent the violent conflicts such movements can produce – and especially the possibility that they may spill over borders.

Just as the countries bordering Russia do not want to be invaded, or struck with nuclear weapons, all these countries will also not want to confront the threat of hordes of refugees seeking to cross their borders. Perhaps this is the threat that would be the most likely to be realized, if real chaos struck in Russia, or even under conditions well short of such chaos.

The derived policy choices for the Western countries, on the application of existing international organizations and alliances, might thus be very much the same as for the nuclear politics or liberal politics viewpoints noted above, dismissing identifications with particular nationalities, dismissing worries about Russia's central geopolitical position, and assigning the highest priority instead to enhancing the effectiveness and moderation of Russia's governing processes.

If the issue is serious, Poles can let down their guard against Russian armoured divisions or even approve NATO's extension to Russia, all to avoid the greater risks of uncontrolled population movements or other social unrest that might produce expansive conflict. If the issue is serious enough, even the EU could be harnessed to the task, postponing some of its contributions to prosperity in Western Europe, to provide a safety net for the former Soviet Union. And, if this issue is serious, all of the power of PFP and OSCE, and the United Nations, may need to be brought to bear.

CONCLUSION

There is no reliable way to predict the future of Baltic security, of course. But the five worldviews we sketched here do suggest some limits to a future that is likely to remain uncertain – and to some degree changeable – for some time. Elements of those perspectives point to potential dangers, as well as the means for managing them.

Thus, geopolitical realities change little in the short to medium term. The Soviet Union no longer exists; but Russia remains by far the largest, militarily most powerful, neighbour in the Baltic region. The Soviet Union contained all too well tensions arising within its borders from national or ethnic divisions and economic malaise. This was not pleasant for many of its inhabitants, and it was an ideological goad to Western states. However, the closed order and borders of the Soviet regime did contain the potential triggers for instability associated with these and other factors. The states in the region must now be attentive to developments inside Russia and in its northwestern 'near abroad'. Russia's relationships with the Baltic states, Poland, Ukraine and some of its other neighbours present more complex problem for security and stability.

The end of the Soviet Union has blurred lines of demarcation. The independence of the Baltic states and the other SSRs has not mitigated the threats inherent in Russia's still massive nuclear arsenal; but, rather, it has decreased the functions of nuclear weapons as keepers of the peace, at least locally and regionally. The states in the region need, and are likely to continue to need broader security frameworks for containing Russia's military nuclear resources, perhaps less for strategic reasons than to cope with lapses in command and control, for the continued dismantling of nuclear weapons, and for ameliorating dangers posed to the immediate environment by the decay of fissionable material.

We are in the midst of redrawing the boundaries of cultural solidarity in the region. It is not yet clear how far and in what degrees and forms the 'we' will be extended, to include newly autonomous states and populations in Western security, economic and political institutions. This is clearly a dynamic process, with Western domestic politics playing important roles. It is also a negotiated process, evident in the US–Baltic 'Charter of Partnership' as a confidence-building move, to reassure Russia that NATO's boundaries are not likely to be extended to include the Baltic states in the near future. Thus, the Charter is intended to extend the boundaries of 'we' without extending formal institutionalized security commitments that might pose a security dilemma for Russia.

All the while, the encouragement of the consolidation of democratic regimes of governance in all of the Soviet successor-states continues on several fronts. Bilateral and multilateral assistance and (not always solicited) advice are directed towards that goal, in part for its intrinsic value and in part in the hope that the notion of the 'democratic peace' will become a self-fulfilling prophesy. The prospect of membership in Western institutions, especially NATO and EU, constitute incentives for 'good behaviour' for some of those states, but, significantly, not for those facing the most difficult challenges. Neither NATO nor the EU can include all; membership is valued in part because it is not universal. The tasks of defining what remains outside, more for the long term than the near future, must be addressed not only by those who speak on behalf of such institutions but, perhaps more important, by those not likely to be included. What will being on the other side of the borders of Western institutions mean to them? What kinds of relationships do they envision with those institutions and their members?

The uncertainties of the future and the possibilities of what we termed chaos in Russia and many of the other successor-states and former Soviet allies carry the most diffuse, but by no means the most remote, grounds for concern about the security and stability of the region. The previous four perspectives – geopolitics, nuclear politics, cultural conflict, and liberal politics – highlight some of the reasons. Russia is too large and powerful, and in some respects, too weak to ignore; but, it is also too large to transform from the outside. Fostering effective governance inside it and its European successor-states while preparing for the consequences of its failure have been, and should remain, the posture of Western states and institutions.

Finally, we must bear in mind that many of the political meanings of the security relationships that defined the mission of such institutions as NATO during the Cold War have changed. Thus, what remains of the Soviet nuclear submarines adjacent to the Kola Peninsula now represent more of a hazard to Nordic environments due to the decay of their radioactive powerplants than a strategic threat to the Western alliance; and Fulda has come to represent a controversial Roman Catholic bishop in German church politics, rather than the site where Warsaw Pact tanks might break through. Even where our institutional frameworks remain constant, interpretations of interest and the political will that gives it meaning may be changing.

NOTES

1 We are concerned here with analytic worldviews or perspectives, not those of policy-makers. We stand on a higher rung of the ladder of abstraction than do most actors. The question of which of these or other conceivable perspectives underlie the actions of the latter is at least one rung lower on that ladder.

2 Cf. the report on actual effectiveness of high technology weapons in that war, *Washington Post*, 27 July 1997.

3 The great number of Polish-American voters is sometimes put forward, by American cynics, as a primary explanation for President Clinton's 1994 commitment to expanding NATO to include Poland.

4 The Peace of Westphalia, 1648, which is widely regarded as the birth of the modern system of international politics.

5

Worldframes and Cultural Perspectives with Specific Focus on Scandinavia and Russia

CHRISTOPHER A. LEEDS
University of Nancy 2, France

1. INTRODUCTION: CULTURE, LEVELS OF ANALYSIS AND WORLDFRAMES

Culture enters as a comparatively new area of inquiry into the field of International Relations and Conflict Resolution but remains an elusive element.[1] Norms influence the generally accepted pattern of values, attitudes and assumptions of a group, as reflected in habits, customs and laws. Hsu (1981) defines culture as 'the accepted pattern of behaviour in every society'. Hofstede (1991) refers to culture as 'the collective programming of the mind' which distinguishes the members of one group from another. Norton (1991) defines a worldview as the 'constellation of beliefs, values and concepts that give shape to the world a person experiences and acts within'. This study covers certain aspects of culture which might cause difficulty in communications, official and informal, between Scandinavians and Russians. Overarching organizations, such as the OSCE and the Council of the Baltic Sea States, Germany and Russia being members of both, provide fluidity and overlapping membership which counteract the growth of rigid blocs (Kolankiewicz, 1994). The joint Russia–NATO Council reinforces this trend.

Hofstede (1991) refers to various layers of mental programming carried by individuals as a result of the different levels to which they may belong. Ten levels of analysis could be envisaged as possibilities for research on culture: the universal or global; the bipolar; worldframes; the civilizational; major supranational/regional groupings; the national; the subnational; the community; the family (nuclear or extended); the individual/personal.

Some scholars concentrate on the bipolar, the contrast, largely coterminous with the East–West divide, between individualist and collectivist societies. Huntington (1996) focuses on six or seven major civilizations as the significant level of analysis.[2] Frequently researchers highlight differences or similarities at the level of national culture. The aim of promoting peace provides an incentive to collect data on cultural factors separating or uniting nations (Hofstede, 1991). This study focuses primarily on four macrocultures or worldframes, situated between the binary East–West divide, and Huntington's civilizational level. The various values or traits associated with each of the four world-frames are based on research findings discussed in this article and the end notes. *See* Table 5.3.

2. THE BINARY DIVIDE

For various reasons, outside the scope of this paper, Europeans gradually distanced themselves from the rest of the world from at least the seventh century, and noticeably from the fifteenth century onwards, in terms of religious and broad cultural differences. The modern European worldview emerged as one based on rational and empirical faculties, associated with the search for scientific truth, fairness and process. Other aspects of human nature of an affective, intuitive, emotive, romantic, or mystic nature were rejected as irrelevant for a proper study of the world. Scholars have applied various terms to the contrasting worldframes or ways of thinking of the west and non-west. These include objectivism and subjectivism (Lakoff and Johnson, 1980), rational and intuitive (Capra, 1992), sensate materialism and ideational spiritualism (Smoker and Groff, 1996), and the distinction between low context, individualist and high context, collectivist societies (Gudykunst and Ting-Toomey, 1988).

High context societies follow an integrationalist or wholistic approach to life. They communicate in an indirect, circular manner, adopting a flexible approach to time commitments. People frequently do many things at a time (called polychronic behaviour). While involved in meetings they may tolerate interruptions of a personal or family nature. High context societies are committed to a people-based view of life, and consider that the fostering of personal relationships forms the basis of all activity. Much information derives from social networks.

Low context societies, notably North Americans and northern Europeans, including Scandinavians, tend to work in a linear, incremental manner (monochronic behaviour). They communicate or negotiate in a direct, explicit manner, valuing conciseness, accuracy and verity. Such people appreciate punctuality and adherence to deadlines. They tend to operate in a task-based, impersonal manner, appreciating information in 'objective' concrete form – facts, statistics, documents (Hall, 1976; Hall and Hall, 1990). In future LC, HC, I and C will sometimes be used to denote low context, high context, individualist and collectivist societies. *See* Table 5.1 for the position of countries and groups along these dimensions.

How differences in LC and HC behaviour may cause serious misunderstandings in diplomacy, notably in American–Egyptian and Israeli–Palestinian relations, has already been amply demonstrated (Cohen, 1987) (Cohen, 1991). Examples include problems related to being direct or indirect (blunt or tactful) in communication.[3]

Talcott Parsons, the most prominent American sociologist of the early postwar period, made a major contribution to functionalism. Functionalists believed that it was important to discover how various 'parts' or institutions combined to give a society continuity. Parsons proposed five pattern variables, indicating how individuals and cultures could find their own particular solutions to universal problems. A variable, dimension or continuum, demonstrates how individuals or groups differ with respect to particular values. These five pairs are as follows: (a) specificity–diffuseness; (b) neutrality–affectivity; (c) universalism–particularism; (d) achievement–ascription; (c) self-orientation (individualism)–collective orientation (Parsons, 1951).[4]

Specificity denoted a 'parts' emphasis in an encounter, focus on the task at hand rather than the relationship. Diffuseness denotes linking up the parts and basing a decision upon a sense of the whole picture. HC people usually wish to know all about a person (diffuseness) and to establish a relationship of trust before discussing seriously any transaction. Neutrality implies control of feelings and a detached approach to relationships, whereas affectivity suggests that the whole gamut of emotions may also be legitimately involved. Universalism indicates consistent application of laws, rules and procedures. Particularism involves making exceptions, deciding where and when not to adhere to rules, laws or codes of behaviour, depending on the situation or circumstances, the ingroup–outgroup distinction being important (Hofstede, 1991). Subsequent research has confirmed that, very broadly, the first in the series of pairs above corresponds with the value orientations of most of the Western world, and the second relates more noticeably to the value orientations of cultures outside North America and Europe.[5]

The second dimension, mentioned above, provides an exception. Asians disguise their emotions publicly while many Americans tend to exhibit emotion, although Euro-Americans separate it from objective, rational decisions (Trompenaars, 1993).[6]

In an achieving society people appreciate what a person succeeds in 'doing' himself. Failure is the fault of the individuals. Achievers are optimistic, believing in action and progress. The focus of control is internalized within the individual, who can conquer the forces of nature, the latter viewed as mechanistic and controllable. Ascription denotes a society that attributes status by virtue of birth, age, seniority, qualifications and connections ('whom one knows'). The focus of control is externalized, the individual adjusting to the forces he encounters. Fisher (1988) observes that fate represents a central theme in Latin American literature, art, cinema and television.[7] Inner-directedness versus outer-directedness (externalized control) has also been tested as a separate dimension.[8]

3. WORLDFRAMES, ORIGINS AND FEATURES

Closely related terms such as worldviews, ontologies (Cox, 1997), mindsets (Fisher, 1988), worlds and frames (Nudler, 1990) have been used metaphorically to refer to different versions or interpretations of reality held by different peoples, or to various sets of beliefs, assumptions, and habits of reasoning for rendering the external environment coherent and meaningful.

This study proposes four major clusters of countries which might be called, metaphorically, worldviews or macrocultures. However, the term worldframe is used as the preferred metaphor. Various forms of the keyword 'frame', such as 'framework' and 'framing', have been applied by scholars for understanding processes related to communication, conflict and problem-solving. 'Frame' suggests malleability, flexibility and lack of finality, in terms of content or size. It may also be compared, metaphorically, to a lens. If a lens becomes cloudy as a result of the appearance of opacities, new cultural predicaments or experiences, adjustments can be made to make the vision transparent.

Huntington argues that a major divide separates the West (defined in terms of primarily Catholic and Protestant communities) from Orthodox Christian and Muslim peoples. The line passes south between Finland and Russia, and cuts across Belarus, the Ukraine, Romania and former Yugoslavia. This places Greece, cradle of European classical civilization and member of the European Community, in the non-west (Huntington, 1996). Huntington stresses that Russia belongs to a different civilization along with the remainder of Orthodox Europe. This study finds evidence to support the Huntington thesis to the extent that Russia, culturally, falls primarily in different worldframes from northern European countries. However emphasis is also placed first, on important overlaps between worldframes, in terms of shared values, second, on the fact that all countries are situated to a degree in all four and third, on methods of reconciling different cultural perspectives. These worldframes emerge as a result very largely of the division of both LC and HC societies into two clusters.

Jung (1921) provided inspiration for the conceptualization of four possible worldframes, and also the clue as to their main components. He proposed four functions in relation to the brain, each supplying a means by which people process information and render the external world meaningful and coherent. These four consist of two opposing pairs thinking–feeling and sensation–intuition. While sensing uses the five senses to identify on a practical basis concrete facts, experiences and details, thinking focuses on logical and rational analysis, stressing an intellectual foundation of planning and organization in the search for universal truths. Values such as fairness, honour and trust preoccupy the feeling function, while intuition searches for links between patterns, and for visualizing the wider picture (Ralph Lewis, 1993).

Parsons and Shils (1951) highlight the first two pairs of the pattern variables, discussed earlier as specificity–diffuseness and neutrality–affectivity. As discussed above, Trompenaars associates specificity and diffuseness with low and high context societies. The former tend to be task-based in negotiations and the latter people-oriented; a distinction which resembles the neutrality–affectivity distinction. Peabody (1985) applies similar terms, impulse-control and impulse-expression, contrasting North and South Europe. Hampden-Turner and Trompenaars (1993) note that machine and organism are two chief ways globally by which managers conceive their organizations. In addition they rename the specificity–diffusity dimension as analyzing (parts-focus) and synthesizing (big picture).

A group of scholars, acknowledging Jung's influence, develop a four-part model associating management styles with core philosophical ideas, and delineate four clusters. The west–east pair are pragmatism–wholism, the north–south pair rationalism–humanism. Pragmatism, chiefly sense-based, refers notably to English-speaking countries. Wholism/idealism, chiefly intuition, is attributed to Russia, Asia and partly to Germany. Rationalism, primarily thinking, applies to France, parts of Germany and northern Europe, and humanism, chiefly feeling, to Latin America, Mediterranean Europe and Africa (Lessem and Neubauer, 1994; Gatley, Lessem and Altman, 1996).[9]

Gatley, Lessem and Altman (1996) situate the four worldframes along the individualism(I)–collectivism(C) continuum in the following order: west (individualist), north (moderately individualist), south (moderately collectivist) and east (collectivist). This ordering coincides with the findings of Hofstede, Trompenaars and Hampden-Turner. However, although Hofstede (1991) places the low context–high context dimension as a subcategory of I–C respectively, these two dimensions do not coincide completely. For example, in various listings of countries along the low context–high context scale, the Germans, Swiss, Scandinavians and Euro-Americans are conceived as low context, with the British as medium context (Hall and Hall, 1990) (Usunier, 1992). Nevertheless Hofstede (1991), Gatley, Lessem and Altman (1996) place Scandinavians as moderately individualist.

Table 5.1 summarises the ideas discussed above within a four-fold model of worldframes which includes the model of Lewis (1996) (see p. 84). Notice that the four terms associated with Jung, Parsons, Lessem and Neubauer, Peabody, Hampden-Turner and Trompenaars fit together, the terms under west, north, south and east representing synonymous, alternative ways of describing the same basic idea, whether applied to management, communication or cognitive style.

Table 5.1

West	*North*	*South*	*East*
Individualist	Moderately individualist	Moderately collectivist	Collectivist
Sensing	Thinking	Feeling	Intuition
Specificity	Neutrality	Affectivity	Diffusity
Pragmatism	Rationalism	Humanism	Wholism
Analysis (parts-focused)	Impersonalism (task-focused)	Personalism (Relationship-focused)	Synthesis (big picture)
Low/Medium Context	Low/Medium Context	Medium/High Context	High Context
Linear-active	Linear-active	Multi-active	Reactive
North America (primarily people of northern European origin, anglo-phonic (English-speaking) countries).	Northern Europe	Southern Europe, Eastern Europe, Latin America, Arab world, Africa, Afro and Hispanic Americans, most of the Indian sub-continent.	Asia and the Pacific. (To a degree certain northern European countries share reactive attributes.)

Wendy Hall argues that for understanding the origins of conflicts and misunderstandings in interpersonal relations or business negotiations between companies, attention should be given to a model formed by the assertivity and responsiveness dimensions. This fourpart model applies both to national and corporate cultures. However companies based in one country may have a style different from the national style for various reasons, such as change of ownership. In a similar manner to that of Lessem and Neubauer, Hall describes four different styles or options as metaphorically west, north, south and east, and also acknowledges Jung's influence. The four styles are as follows: (a) high assertivity, low responsiveness, USA/Germany (W); (b) low assertivity, low responsiveness, Great Britain, The Netherlands, (N); (c) high assertivity, high responsiveness, France, (S); (d) low assertivity, high responsiveness, Japan and Italy, (E). The findings on national styles of seven countries are included.

A link can be made between these two fourpart models, both forming elements of the worldframes. Low context cultures, task-oriented or impersonal, are low responsive in the phraseology of Wendy Hall. In contrast, the high context societies tend to be people-oriented, or in effect high responsive. With respect to the Lessem and Neubauer model, pragmatism, associated with action, adherence to deadlines, short-termism, and entrepreneurial risk-taking, suggests high assertion. Humanism (S), the most emotionally charged of the four values, can also be linked to high assertion. In contrast, attributes associated with Scandinavians (north style) caution, consensus, and non-confrontational behaviour, and with Asians (east style) harmony and indirectness, suggest low assertion.

Lewis (1996) prefers a threefold categorization to Edward Hall's twofold model, distinguishing between linear-active, multi-active and reactive societies. He describes these as data-oriented, dialogue-oriented and listening cultures respectively. Most low context societies are linear-active (west and north). Linear-active societies tend to be introvert, unemotional, analytical and to confront with logic.[10] Body language, an aspect of non-verbal communication (NVC) is limited. Reactive societies comprise essentially the high context societies of Asia and the Pacific Islands (east). Finland, and occasionally Sweden and Britain (north), according to Lewis, share attributes of Asian countries. Reactive societies tend to be introvert, quietly caring (emotions disguised), silent, nonconfrontational. They use subtle body language, see the whole picture, and prioritize courtesy and respect.

Multi-active societies cover Edward Hall's remaining high context societies. This large grouping (south) consists of a number of sub-categories, each with their own distinctive features. Mediterranean peoples, the Indian sub-continent, Latin Americans, Arabs, Africans and, to a lesser extent, Russians and Eastern European peoples are in this category.[11] In communication, these societies tend to be extrovert, talkative, to behave emotionally in confrontations, to interrelate everything, and to use unrestricted body language (see Table 5.3).[12]

Individualist and collectivist societies have been described as respectively guilt and shame cultures. In the former a person who infringes rules may be ridden by his own conscience, whereas in the latter a person feels ashamed if his infringement of the rules or norms of society are known to others. 'Face' is also important in collectivist societies, 'losing face' causing humiliation (Hofstede, 1991, 60–61). Values associated with honour (or reputation) are important in many parts of the south, including the Mediterranean area (Peristiany, 1965), the Arab world (Feghali, 1997) and Latin America.

Major negotiation styles correlate closely with the features associated with worldframes. One four-part classification, derived from Jungian categories, distinguishes between the following styles: factual/action-based (west), the analytical/process-based (north), the normative/people-based (south) and the intuitive/wholistic (east) (Casse and Deol, 1985).[13]

Other studies show considerable agreement as to the characteristics of negotiating styles, but not on where they apply. One study, based on UN Security Council discussions, associates the factual-inductive as the preferred method in the West, the axiomatic-deductive and affective-intuitive as the predominate forms in the former Soviet Union, and the affective-intuitive also with Arab countries (Glenn, Witmeyer, Stevenson, 1977). Russian diplomats applied the axiomatic-deductive method during the early sessions of the Disarmament Conference of 18 countries, March 1962–April 1963. They insisted that general principles be agreed before participants explored details. This deductive method clashed with the pragmatic, inductive approach of the Americans, used to reaching agreement on specific issues, incrementally, before establishing general principles (Wedge and Muromcew, 1963).

Walker (1990) identified three styles, based on the discourses at the Third United Nations Law of the Sea Conference, Caracas, Venezuela, 1974. He attributed the inductive/pragmatic to the West, the deductive/rational to the former communist block, except China, and stressed the emotive, moral, past-oriented nature of the third style adopted by the less-developed countries. However, the third world shared in common with the second world the tendency to stress principles over details, the general and the abstract over the specific and the concrete. A fourth study associated the inductive style with the Americans specifically, the deductive style with Europeans, and the intuitive concrete-based style with the Japanese, who attach meaning wholistically to immediately perceived events (Stewart and Bennett, 1991). This fourth, intuitive style focuses on interpersonal relationships. The Chinese and the Japanese, for example, aim in business negotiation to reach agreement initially on general principles, which derive from the nature of the relationship established (March 1988).

Basically four styles emerge from the work of the scholars discussed above. These are the factual-inductive, the axiomatic-deductive, the affective-intuitive (multi-active) and the intuitive-concrete (reactive), these four broadly corresponding to the model of Casse and Deol. Basically Europeans use both the inductive and the deductive methods of reasoning.

4. SCANDINAVIAN AND RUSSIAN VALUES, AND APPROACHES TO COMMUNICATING AND NEGOTIATING

In many respects the Russian model form of communicating and negotiation (or particular combinations of the four styles or world-frames) differs considerably from that of the Scandinavian. One scholar argues that the traditional Russian character contrasts in almost every respect with the Protestant ethic (Peabody, 1985).

Although all people are individualist and collectivist in different ways, the significance lies in the degree to which societies emphasize values associated with one rather than the other. The popular view stresses the group-orientedness of the Russians (Peabody, 1985). Emphasis has been placed both on the Russian child-rearing patterns during formative years (Triandis, 1995), and on the persistence of rural traditions associated with the *mir* and commune as elements contributing to the strength of Russian collectivism. Excessive emphasis on individual achievement at the expense of the group is not appreciated (Reisinger, Miller, Hesli and Maher, 1994). As in other collectivist societies they exhibit two different codes of behaviour. In public they may be hypocritical, passive, silent, and in private – honest, passionate, talkative, allowing their emotions to flow freely (Smith, 1976). This typifies particularistic behaviour, a feature of collectivist societies (Hofstede, 1991). Russians habitually use connections or personal contacts as a means of circumventing bureaucratic procedures and rules, and for surviving daily obstacles. People understand that favours rendered may be reciprocated later (Gannon, 1994).

The Russians approach business agreements in an all-embracing manner, in contrast to normal Western linear step-by-step methods, and preference for precise agreements. The Russians negotiate as they play chess, planning several moves ahead (Lewis, 1996). In diplomatic negotiations they accept broadly-worded rather than detailed agreements. Consequently the ambiguity of such agreements can be exploited, or adhered to in the manner seen as most advantageous (Sloss and Davis, 1987). In addition business contracts are not considered so binding as in the West. Like Orientals, Russians regard a contract as valid only if it continues to be mutually advantageous (Lewis, 1996).

Two of Hofstede's dimensions, low and high power distance (PD) and weak and strong uncertainty avoidance (UA), reveal important information for understanding cultural differences. High PD denotes inequalities and hierarchies within organizations, and formality, respect for status, and adherence to rules of etiquette in negotiations. Strong UA denotes the need for many rules, and dislike of unfamiliar risks. His worldwide survey revealed that collectivist societies tend to be high PD, and strong UA. This category comprises the largest number of regions and countries in Hofstede's sample, southern Europe including former Yugoslavia, Latin America, the Middle East and parts of Asia.

Highly individualist countries and regions fall within the category of low PD (flat hierarchies, informality and egalitarian relationships) and weak UA (few rules), including North America, Australasia, Britain, Sweden, Norway and Denmark. Hofstede describes these as pragmatic countries which rely often on *ad hoc* solutions to problems. The low PD and weak UA countries in Hofstede's survey are those predominantly in the west and north, while medium to high PD and medium to strong UA characterizes most of the countries in the east and south. Hofstede argues, on various grounds, that Russians, not involved in the original survey, share with the Serbs and Greeks the common mental programming of large PD, strong UA, and collectivism (the south style) (Hofstede, 1996).

Another interpretation defends the view that Russia de-emphasizes social class distinctions, indicating low PD, since Russians have for a long time lived with uncertainty and ambiguity. Stephan and Abalakina-Paap (1996) cite, in support of their argument, a study revealing that 87 per cent of decisions approved at Russian meetings were abstract, not specifying when recommendations were to be implemented. Probably Russians oscillate between the extremes on both dimensions, depending on the context or circumstances, and that on average they are both medium PD and medium UA.

One study describes the Russians as basically characterized by impulse-expression rather than impulse-control, as a people exhibiting a high degree of expressiveness and emotionality (Peabody, 1985). The Russians, noted for their mystic nature and intense feelings, combine emotion, sentiment and sensitivity (Gannon, 1994). In business negotiations they are often 'theatrical and emotional', conveying clearly their intent and requests (Lewis, 1996). The diplomatic style of Russian leaders, such as Stalin and Khruschev, alternated between hot–cold emotional shifts. Stalin, during Second World War negotiations with the Americans and the British, combined friendly and cordial discussions with hostile and adversarial outbursts, a strategy intended both to confuse others and to strengthen a weak negotiating position (Griffin and Daggart, 1990). Low context societies tend to interpret verbal language literally without paying attention to the nature of the communication taking place. Examples were the response of the West to Khruschev's announcement 'We will bury you', and the way Scandinavians reacted to public announcements in the early 1990s of ultranationalists such as Zhirinovsky, who advocated that Russia should re-annex Finland. Observations reflecting rhetoric and passion serve to project a strong image. Russians, when questioned about their country, do not normally focus on problems, as Americans or Scandinavians might do, but rather on espousing virtues (Carbaugh, 1994).

The Russians are noted for an 'intense personalness', rather than impersonalness typical of universalistic cultures (Peabody, 1985). What really matters is a person's spirit, his relationship to others (Smith, 1976). Russians try to nurture personal relationships as a means of 'oiling the wheels', rather than focusing exclusively on task-based, substantive issues. Consequently they appreciate small talk, particularly during the preliminaries. According to one view, the development of personal relationships during business negotiations with Russians may facilitate remarkable progress in the case of apparent official deadlock (Lewis, 1996).

Another interpretation is that the Russian attempt in diplomatic negotiations to go for a personal relationship, probing for flexibility, represents a pressure tactic (Sloss and Davis, 1987). Glenn, Witmeyer and Stevenson (1977) stress that the Russians are not particularly responsive to an opponent's concessions in negotiations, interpreted as weakness, and that they rarely reciprocate. Further they do not seek a continuing relationship.

Russian diplomatic negotiators have been described as 'confrontational' or combative, aiming to put the other side on the defensive (Sloss and Davis, 1987). In business they communicate in a blunt, direct manner, talk tough if in a strong position, and push forward vigorously if the other side seems to retreat. Russians make as few concessions as possible, remaining opportunistic and averse to risk-taking (Lewis, 1996) (Ghauri and Usunier, 1996).

Russians have been judged, on average as medium to moderately high context (Lewis, 1996) (Stephen and Abalakina-Paap, 1996). *See* Table 5.1. For example they may adopt a direct, spontaneous, low context approach to communicating. Their directness, combined with assertiveness, resembles in this respect the West. However Russians, in common with other cultures, can be both direct and indirect, depending on whom they are dealing with.

In a 1970s survey, Scandinavian countries clustered closely in terms of degree of individualism. Denmark ranked 9th, Sweden 10th equal, Norway 13th, and Finland 17th.[14] These countries have been described as moderately individualist (Gatley, Lessem and Altman, 1996). Communitarian affiliations tend to be directed towards the local community and voluntary associations rather than the family. Strong identification with the State, as a level of solidarity, has been noted in relation to the Swedish (Fant, 1992). Individualist societies tend to rank high on universalism. The basic norm is that a person should treat everyone alike (Hofstede, 1991) (Trompenaars, 1993). As a result particularistic and personalistic practices are not appreciated.[15] The Russians, on the other hand, incline to particularism. Scandinavians tend to value egalitarianism and informality. Horizontal individualism, attributed as an important feature of Sweden (Triandis, 1995), applies to Scandinavians generally.

Scandinavians, even if direct in communication, are judged generally unassertive (Peabody, 1985). The Swedish appreciate values such as being modest and a good listener rather than values tied to dominance (Fant, 1992). Scandinavians look for equitable or just solutions, and view making compromises positively. With reference to handling problems at work, Norwegians and Swedish search for solutions acceptable to both sides (Rognes, 1994) (Fant, 1992). They stress keeping calm, and the adoption of a non-confrontational style.[16] Arguments are based on logic, reason, interests and facts (Rognes, 1994). Rhetoric is seen as manipulative behaviour.

Jenkins (1968) notes that the Swedes exhibit a pronounced devotion to unemotional practicality, and possess a talent for organization. They believe problems can be solved calmly and satisfactorily through the proper application of reason. Fant (1992) observes that, in business negotiations, the Swedes are seen as closed, distant and strongly impersonal. One drawback of Scandinavian negotiating is that the failure to empathize with others may result in emotional signals communicated by the other party being missed (Griffin and Daggart, 1990).

Masculinity–femininity comprised one of the four original dimensions that Hofstede developed as a result of his worldwide survey. The Scandinavian countries registered the lowest scores on masculinity. Traits associated with masculinity include dominance and assertiveness, and with femininity, being soft spoken, caring and sensitive to the needs of others (Bem, 1974; Hofstede, 1991).

As discussed above, the Scandinavians generally adopt a non-confrontational approach when negotiating, and search for equitable solutions acceptable to both sides. Their style basically incorporates features of LC and Western behaviour to the extent that they focus on task-orientedness, minimum rules and concrete facts, and especially the north style, to the extent that their approach is characterized by deductive reasoning, egalitarianism and informality.

Lewis (1996) stresses that the Finnish, and occasionally the Swedes are reactives, traits of which include being quietly caring, and having flexibility. Scandinavian countries did not feature in Wendy Hall's study. It would seem feasible to predict that they could best be characterized by the north and east styles in terms of the Hall model, and also by certain features of the overall west worldframe.

Based on the above discussion, in this section, the Russian style appears less predictable than the Scandinavian, likely to move more rapidly between extremes. Kimura (1996) points out that, though the Russians normally view compromise negatively as a solution to a stalemate, they can be flexible. In diplomatic negotiations, once they realize that the hard line does not work, a volte-face may occur.

The Russians value principles, ideas, form and style, but may not necessarily be people-oriented and responsive. They use emotion and intuition in argument and decision-making, and adopt a wholistic approach to decision-making, interrelating all elements. In contrast to the Scandinavians, the Russian modal style is likely to incorporate greater formality, more respect for status, hierarchy and greater deference to rules and instructions from superiors.

Russia, a Euro-Asian power, has been associated in negotiation with both the rational, axiomatic-deductive (N) and the affective-intuitive (S) styles (Glenn, Witmeyer and Stevenson, 1977), discussed above. In terms of many traits Russia, and many East European countries have also been placed in the south, associated with multiactives (Lewis, 1996). However the assertiveness attributed to Russians in negotiations, discussed earlier, allied to low responsiveness places Russia in the west style. Gatley, Lessem and Altman (1996) categorize Russia as east. In terms of the Wendy Hall model, the Russians appear to fall into the south or west dimensions. A case can be made, as demonstrated especially in Sections 3–4 above, that the Russians overall typify the south style marginally more than the east.

5. STRATEGIES OF RECONCILIATION BETWEEN WORLDFRAMES

In summary, both in terms of the Hall fourfold model and of the worldframes generally, the Scandinavians and Russians tend to follow different communication styles. Empirical research provides the basis for estimating the positions attributed in Table 5.2 to countries and regions in the Baltic area.[17] A reasonable supposition would be that North Americans and North Europeans vary for the most part within the range of 50–75 per cent in predominantly left-brain orientation (sensing-thinking), while many southern Europeans and much of the rest of the world vary mainly between 50 per cent and 70 per cent in predominantly right-brain thinking (intuition-feeling). The Scandinavians and the North Atlantic area, including Iceland, exemplify the north style.

The letter (a) in Table 5.2 below indicates the particular worldview considered of major importance to each of the countries/regions enumerated, and the letters (b), (c) and (d) indicate in descending order the importance of other worldviews, styles or orientations.

Table 5.2. Worldframes/Communication Styles

	West	*North*	*South*	*East*
Sweden/Scandinavia	(b)	(a)	(d)	(c)
Germany	(b)	(a)	(d)	(c)
Russia	(d)	(c)	(a)	(b)

(Suggested ordering in terms of value orientations)

Regional differences and ethnic diversities are two of the factors which explain why countries can be placed in different worldframes.[18] Some evidence points to Germany oscillating in terms of worldframe orientation more obviously than the Scandinavians. With respect to two dimensions assertivity and responsiveness, Hall (1995) places Germany in the west style. Peabody (1985) found that overall the Germans tended to high assertion and impulse-control, which fits the west style most closely. In terms of low context behaviour, Germany also fits into the north and west styles. However Lessem and Neubauer (1994) place Germany in the east style, emphasizing Germany's wholist traditions, reflected in thinkers such as Hegel and Goethe, and certain quasi-Japanese business practices.

Research on negotiating and behavioural styles leads to the conclusion that in terms of worldframes and communication styles, Scandinavia can be placed first in the north, second in the west, and that Russians can be placed primarily in the south and east. The fact that important cultural differences characterize two adjacent regions of the world does not imply that relationships need be conflictual.[19] Russians and Scandinavians share to an extent similar climatic and geographical terrain. If they are both outer-directed this indicates a respect for nature and its forces. Scandinavians, moderately individualist, have similar consensual and egalitarian traditions to the Russians. Various overlaps, in terms of shared values, characterize adjacent worldframes, as explained in this study. *See* Table 5.3.

Cultural differences provide a means of mutual learning. The overt or relatively detectable values or traits of one party represent the hidden or buried side of another, basically the us–other problem of contrasting behavioural patterns and mirror images. Unidimensional continuums such as achievement-ascription do not necessarily indicate all the complex patterns underlying interpersonal or interstate relations. All countries ascribe and achieve in certain ways

Table 5.3. Worldframes

North

1. Rational/empirical
2. Low context/moderately
   individualistic
   (Direct communication, occasional
   indirectness)
3. Neutral/low emotive (feelings
   strongly hidden), low responsive
4. Introvert/low assertive
5. Nonconfrontational, harmonious,
   consensual
6. Universalistic
7. Inner and outer-directed.
   (Achievers)
8. Egalitarian/informal
   (Low power distance)
9. Weak to medium uncertainty
   avoidance
10. Caution, thoroughness
11. Guilt
12. Minimal NVC. (Non-contact society)

East

1. Wholistic/intuitive, people-focused
2. High context/collectivist
   (indirect communication, circular)
3. Affective/disguised emotive,
   sensitivity, high responsive
4. Introvert/low assertive
5. Nonconfrontational, harmonious,
   consensual
6. Particularistic
7. Outer-directed ('being'). (Ascribers)
8. Hierarchical, formal, status-
   conscious
   (High power distance)
9. Medium to strong uncertainty
   avoidance
10. Caution, thoroughness
11. Shame, 'Face'
12. Disguised NVC. (Non-contact
    society)

West

1. Empirical/rational
2. Low context/individualist
   (Direct communication,
   understatement)
3. Neutral, moderately emotive/low
   responsive
4. Extrovert/high assertive
5. Confrontational/competitive
6. Universalistic
7. Inner-directed ('doing'). (Achievers)
8. Egalitarian/Informal
   (Low power distance)
9. Weak uncertainty avoidance
10. Action, short-term thinking
11. Guilt
12. Minimal NVC. (Minimum contact
    society)

South

1. Humanistic/intuitive, people-focused
2. Medium to high context/collectivist
   (Indirect communication, imagery,
   rhetoric, exaggeration)
3. Affective, visibly emotive, high
   responsive
4. Extrovert/high assertive
5. Confrontational/cooperative
6. Particularistic
7. Outer-directed ('being'). (Ascribers)
8. Hierarchical, formal, status-
   conscious
   (High power distance)
9. Medium to strong uncertainty
   avoidance
10. Impulsive but long-term thinking
    ('*mañana*')
11. Honour, 'face'
12. Maximal NVC. (Contact society)

(Trompenaars, 1993). Universalism may not inevitably be opposed to particularism, or exceptionalism, as rules need the exception. Weak uncertainty avoidance cultures tend to have few rules, but these are generally obeyed, indicating universalism. In contrast strong uncertainty-avoidance countries tend to have many rules and laws. Some may be ignored, considered redundant or ambiguous, others modified or adapted according to circumstances prevailing.

Researchers generally accept that how disputants conceptualize or frame a communication, problem or situation shapes the process of a negotiation and its outcomes. When negotiations between disputants reach deadlock a mediator endeavours to reframe or reformulate the conflict as seen by the participants. Spector (1995) proposes techniques, such as the stimulation of new cognitive orientations, to encourage breakthroughs and reframing with respect to intractable negotiations.

Framing serves various purposes. It may involve, for example, the negotiating parties (and maybe a mediator) trying to narrow the differences on how both parties perceive the problem, or the solution, so that a commonly shared frame may materialize. This aspect relates to key problems or issues. Another aspect concerns cultural and communication differences.

Nudler (1990) looks at problems of deep culture, ways of knowing and of interpreting social reality, outlining the various processes involved in reframing. Through dialogue each party retains his/her own preferred metaphor (or way of building worlds and frames), and at the same time develops the capacity to adequately represent the other party's metaphor. Finally both parties cooperate in building a new frame. In practice this entails establishing a common meeting of minds, a synergy, the restructured frame serving as a practical device for resolving a particular conflict.

Wendy Hall (1995), Casse and Deol (1985) demonstrate how the gap or disparity between negotiators regarding cultural differences and communication styles can be reduced. For example, Russian and Scandinavian negotiations might find that cultural differences related to different degrees of assertivity employed by each party hindered their ability to find a solution to a diplomatic issue. Reframing in this instance involves one party decreasing its assertivity level and the other increasing it, so that both feel comfortable at some mid-point between the original behaviours.

6. CONCLUSION

Countries have been grouped into more than four categories, as exemplified by Huntington's model. The typology discussed in this study (the worldframes) highlights four different ways of interpreting reality, while demonstrating overlaps and commonalities. The categories or frames are not rigid, every individual and country sharing to a degree values associated with all four. The model moves beyond dichotomies associated with dimensions such as I–C, by emphasizing the presence of 'parts-whole' and 'impersonalism-personalism' dilemmas in joint problem-solving. Security problems in the Baltic can be interpreted in a narrow sense as confined within the territorial space of this region, or as intertwined with broader issues affecting NATO and the CIS.

This study has focused on the Scandinavians and the Russians, as a means of highlighting cultural problems that may occur in communicating. In practice each country contains micro-cultures and, in a postmodern world of instant communication and greater movement of people across frontiers, individuals are becoming more adaptable in acquiring multiple identities and perspectives. The Baltic region represents in itself a microculture, illustrated by the tradition of maritime trades and present-day touristic, educational and other forms of interaction. The two Baltic states, Poland and Germany, with their own distinctive cultures, have the potential for making important contributions to overall harmonization and reconciliation, culturally, within the region. The fact that Scandinavians and Russians are largely associated with different worldframes provides the opportunity for both to apply alternative means of perceiving reality that can facilitate problem-solving in the region.

NOTES

1 For a summary of the origins of concepts such as culture, belief systems and cognitive maps in the field of International Relations *see* Black and Avruch (1993).
2 Huntington (1996) defines a civilization as the broadest cultural entity with which people can identify, both through common objective elements, such as language, history, religion, customs, institutions, and by subjective self-identification.
3 Similar problems could occur in Russian–Scandinavian relations. Examples are discussed in Section 4.
4 The pattern variables stem in part from Parsons's dissatisfaction with Tönnies's *Gemeinschaft-Gesellschaft* dichotomy.
5 In other words they coincide largely with the distinction between low context, individualist and high context, collectivist societies respectively. *See*, for example, Trompenaars (1993) in which the Parsonian variables were tested among managers as part of a survey of seven dimensions.
6 The Americans have been placed near the centre of an emotional spectrum that includes the effervescent Latins at one extreme and the subdued Asians at the other (Harris and Moran, 1979). Peabody (1985) contrasts impulse control (northern Europe) with impulse expression societies (southern Europe plus Germany). For the purposes of this study the distinction made is between visibly emotive societies (south), moderately emotive societies (west), disguised emotive societies (east), and low emotive (north). *See* Table 5.3.
7 Results of two of the questions on achievement-ascription by Trompenaars in

his worldwide survey show northern Europe, North America and English-speaking countries as largely achievement-oriented, including Scandinavian countries, and Russia as more ascriptive (Trompenaars, 1993).

8   Sweden was found to be outer-directed in one survey. Managers preferred to adjust to signals and trends in the outside world rather than trust their own judgements and commitments (Hampden-Turner and Trompenaars, 1993). Many Russians are likely to be outer-directed and ascriptive, a feature generally of collectivist societies. Old people are venerated while, traditionally, individual achievement is not emphasized (Lewis, 1996) (Peabody, 1985).

9   Metaphorically the management styles described were as follows: commercial culture of the entrepreneur/pioneer (west); financial culture of the administrator/manager of change (north); technical culture of the industrialist/architect (east); service culture of the community leader/animator/visionary (south) (Lessem and Neubauer, 1994).

10 NVC also includes voice qualities such as tone, silence, and physical distance (proxemics). Watson (1970) distinguishes between contact and non-contact societies. The former covers the south, including the Russians, who converse quite closely. Non-contact societies (basically west and north), prefer a wider distance, and forms of touching, notably shaking hands, kissing, are less frequent publicly than in contact societies. Indians and Asians converse further away still.

11 Naturally the various regions just enumerated have other affiliations. For example, the Indian sub-continent, commonly known as South Asia, has historically retained close religious links with Asia (Nakamura, 1964).

12 The word 'style' reflects the meaning already imputed to worldframes, discussed earlier. They denote a distinct way of looking at life, or handling daily problems, including approach to communicating, problem-solving, and interpersonal behaviour. However no one style influences completely any one culture or individual. A negotiator or organization may adopt a variety of negotiating strategies and techniques associated with more than one style, during any one situation or at different times, depending on the circumstances or situation, and the nature of the interaction with the other party. *See* Walker (1990).

13 Patai (1973) enlarges on the normative idea as applied to the south by emphasizing the Arab preference for thoughts or ideality (wishes, ideas, ideals, aspirations) over factual reality. This covers not only religion but all other aspects of ideality.

14 Individualism-collectivism was one of four dimensions tested in a worldwide survey of IBM managers from over fifty countries (Hofstede, 1991).

15 Hofstede (1991) places universalism and particularism as characteristics of individualist and collectivist societies respectively. Trompenaars tested the dimension universalism-particularism in his worldwide survey among managers working for Shell. On one question relating to honesty and respect for the law, as opposed to protecting a friend, in relation to a car accident, countries in the north and west (as these terms are understood in this paper) came in the first twelve positions in terms of universalism, Sweden and Norway fourth and fifth. In contrast Russia came 36th out of 38, at the particularistic end of the dimension.

16 Assertiveness/dominance versus submission has been stressed as one of the main dimensions along which social behaviour varies. Americans are perceived as assertive in other parts of the world, while in the east, for example, China and parts of Indonesia, assertiveness and disagreement are avoided, or at least confined to members of the same group (Argyle, 1982). In the north and east,

in consequence, unassertiveness tends to be the norm.

17 For specific data on worldwide surveys *see* Hofstede (1991), Trompenaars (1993), Hampden-Turner (1994) and Gatley, Lessem and Altman (1996).

18 *See* also note 12.

19 Remnick (1997) stresses Russia's distinctive past compared to the West. However, he writes of Russia's embryonic 'alternative political culture', and of an electorate likely to reject a return 'to the maximalism of communism or the xenophobia of hard-line nationalism'.

Part II
Regional Policies of Key Actors

6

Russian Policy in the Baltic Region

ARKADY MOSHES

Institute of Europe, Russian Academy of Sciences, Moscow

The imperative to elaborate a comprehensive policy towards the Baltic region is not yet fully recognized in Russia. This topic has not thus far become and is unlikely to become a subject for national debate in the near future. This is partly due to the fact that amidst many political challenges facing Russia, the Baltic region as a whole is not perceived as reaching a level of high priority.

On the one hand, the Baltic area is a region 'in-the-making'; it has not existed as a well-established entity for at least several decades. In the policies of such countries of the Baltic rim as Germany, Poland and even Norway dimensions other than those of the Baltic have clearly prevailed.

On the other hand, Russia concentrates its attention on its uneasy relations with Lithuania, Latvia and Estonia. It is worth noting here that only these three newly-independent countries – in Russia as elsewhere – are identified as 'the Baltic states', as if other littoral states of the Baltic Sea were not. Russia's understandable focus first on bilateral aspects of its relations with Lithuania, Latvia and Estonia and second on the influence of European organizations on this relationship apparently decreased the significance of the regional dimension for Russian policy-making.

However, on the empirical level Russia has a policy towards, and in, the Baltic region.[1] The main tasks of this policy are more or less clear. They are largely connected with the sphere of security, if we understand the term not as a narrowly-defined military security for individual countries, but a cooperative multifaceted process aimed at preventing destabilizing developments in all areas. In the course of this process Russia should cease to be perceived as a security problem and should really become a security partner.

This chapter intends to analyze the importance of the Baltic region for Russian foreign policy in a changing security environment, to describe the Russian current position in the region and to characterize key problems of Russian security policy in the area.[2]

WHY THE BALTIC REGION

To pursue an active policy in the Baltic region is extremely important for Russia, basically for two sets of reasons. First, the region provides Russia with a number of unique opportunities which, if exploited, could bring Russia many political benefits. Second, Russia faces here unique political challenges which need to be responded to.

Opportunities for Russian policy in the region result from the following factors.

First, the Baltic region was on the periphery of the Cold War. When Central Europe and the German–German border were the focal points of East–West confrontation, the situation in the Baltic region was to a large extent a function of the 'Nordic Balance' with all its diversity and specifics, including the Norwegian model of NATO membership. As a result, the region as a whole has a good deal of immunity towards attempts to shape the security debate along ideology-dominated lines (oversimplified 'friend or foe' distinction) and, therefore, it is easier for Russia to get involved in pragmatic cooperation with other countries in regional security-building.

Secondly, traditions of neutrality play an autonomous role in the ongoing process of strengthening regional security. These traditions largely predetermine the fact that the Baltic region is so far the only *region* in Europe, where 'NATOmania' did not become a prevailing trend.

Thirdly, centuries-old traditions of good-neighbourliness between Russia and several countries of the region provide good chances of transferring positive bilateral experience to regional cooperation, proof of which can be found in the Visby process.[3] Progress in co-operation in the Barents/Euro-Arctic region where Russia and its Nordic neighbours establish patterns of partnership is at the same time a factor strengthening cooperation in the Baltic Sea area.

Fourthly, economic cooperation with Russia is vital for Lithuania, Latvia and Estonia and important for Finland, Poland and potentially for Sweden. This creates another factor of stability. In turn, Russia's economic interests in the region go far beyond volume of trade, although this, too, is an important consideration, taking into account the payments' reliability of countries of the Baltic rim (unlike, for example, Russia's leading economic transaction partners in the CIS). Only in the Baltic region does Russia have a border with the EU along the 1,200km long Russian–Finnish border. The significance of the Baltic Sea routes for the transit of Russian exports does not need to be emphasized, since Russia's ability to use another trade artery connecting it with Europe, the Black Sea, is limited due to the Turkish position with regard to the Dardanelles.

In general, in the Baltic region Russia has a large agenda for fruitful dialogue with other countries, including the security area. This dialogue, highly valuable in itself, also makes it possible to overcome or at least circumvent the deadlock over the issue of the gradual expansion of NATO eastward, if such a deadlock emerges in Russia's relations with other countries of Europe.

The political challenges Russia is facing in the Baltic region are also very specific and even unique.

1. Although there is no direct military threat coming from the Baltic Sea area – all the first-priority security threats and challenges are concentrated on Russia's own south and southward from its borders – a risk of destabilizing developments indirectly affecting Russia's security interests remains.

Already the first wave of NATO enlargement has worsened the military aspect of the situation around Kaliningrad; any further enlargement could make this exclave non-defendable by conventional weapons which could require Russia's reliance on tactical nuclear weapons, not necessarily land-based.

Russian-speaking residents of Estonia and Latvia without citizenship and/or a considerable number of citizens of the Russian Federation in these countries (120,000 in Estonia and 70,000 in Latvia) may under certain circumstances (for example, if deterioration of the living standards of people is coupled with the ethnic factor) demand 'protection' from Russia which could cause negative domestic implications for the democratic process in Russia and for its foreign policy.

Although already withdrawn, the territorial claims of Latvia and Estonia – the only territorial claims to Russia in its European part – created a nervous atmosphere at the border region of Pskov that in 1996 elected a nationalist Liberal-Democratic Party governor, again, the only one among 89 of Russia's regions; if the feeling of defencelessness among the regional population grows stronger for any reason (NATO enlargement, internationalized crime, etc.), stability may be threatened.

2. The relationship between Russia and the three Baltic states cannot be compared with any other that Russia has. First, this is due to the dual place these states occupy in Russian foreign policy considerations: on the one hand, for historical reasons, they constitute, together with the CIS, the post-Soviet space and virtually all bilateral problems are rooted in the common Soviet past; on the other hand, politically, Lithuania, Latvia and Estonia belong to the region which is properly named Central and Eastern Europe and the Baltic states. Second,

Russia's relations with Lithuania, Latvia and Estonia are recognized as a litmus test of Russia's maturity to be an equal member of the family of democratic nations. Third, the way Russia treats its citizens in Latvia and Estonia, quite probably the largest number in individual post-Soviet states, will be attentively followed by Russia's other neighbours and may affect the fate of the 25-million members of the Russian diaspora.

3. To ensure the security and economic prosperity of Kaliningrad means to determine the future of Russia's only exclave, the geopolitical point where Russia meets Central Europe.

THE RUSSIAN POSITION IN THE BALTIC REGION IN THE LATE 1990s

For Russia, the most significant security trend in the Baltic Sea area has been the decline of its own military potential (see Table 6.3).[4] Russia is no longer in a position to launch an offensive operation against its neighbours. Its military presence even in once heavily militarized Kaliningrad has been downsized considerably. Large arsenals were deployed in the *oblast* to a large extent due to shortcomings of the CFE regime with its flank principles (Kaliningrad belonged to the Central European zone). In fact, Russia is on the eve of a debate about whether it has sufficient defensive capabilities for Kaliningrad.

Continuing reductions of Russian forces should be considered as a stabilizing factor in regional security.

Among other developments in the security sphere one not so clear-cut trend deserves special mention. Perhaps, it is a perception rather than reality. But nevertheless, Russia is concerned with the growing regional activity of organizations of which it is neither a member nor yet a real, declared partner. These developments are not dominant, because Russia has compensatory possibilities (membership in the OSCE, the Council of the Baltic Sea States and bilateral relations), but they are still worrisome.

First, there is NATO's extended activity within the framework of the extended (PFP) programme – Partnership for Peace. Russia's rare participation or even prolonged non-participation in PFP exercises raises the justified concerns of other countries in the region. But the Russian approach can be logically explained. In spite of the Russia–NATO Founding Act, signed in May 1997 and establishing the non-inimical relationship between them, Moscow has maintained its opposition towards the enlargement of the Alliance. This attitude is unlikely to change before the declared Russia–NATO partnership

Table 6.1. The Kaliningrad Group of Forces and the Baltic Sea Fleet

	1993	*1995*	*1997*
Ground forces	103,000	24,000	19,000
Main battle tanks	750	870	850
Armoured combat vehicles	900	980	925
Artillery and mortars	600	410	426
Attack helicopters	48	52	50
Air Defence			
Fighters	35	28*	28*
Surface-to-air missiles	250	75	50
The Baltic Fleet			
Submarines	15	9	6
Cruisers	1	3	–
Destroyers	2	2	2
Frigates	24	18	23
Patrol and coastal comb.	140	65	42
Mine counter-measures	60	55	37
Amphibious	20	15	12
Support and miscellaneous	110	102	111
Naval Aviation			
Combat aircraft	200	195	93
Armed helicopters	45	35	25
Naval infantry			
Main battle tanks	40	25	25
Artillery	60	36	34
Coastal Defence			
Artillery	120	133	133

* Fighters belong to the Baltic Sea Fleet
Source: *The Military Balance, 1993–94, 1995–96, 1997–98.*

brings results (although the significance of the problem of enlargement in general could gradually decrease). The same refers to the rather negative approach of Moscow to the PFP which is being considered not as a vehicle of all-European security partnership, as was the case in the beginning, but as a NATO waiting-room, a tool to bring potential candidates and applicants closer to the Alliance. The military components of the Programme are assessed as a way to increase NATO activity in non-NATO areas. It would be logically incorrect to expect Russia's active participation in the Programme in this situation.

Second, the formally logical refusal of the Western European Union to consider the possibility of Russia's participation in its initiatives in the region (these initiatives are for members and partners) delays establishing a dialogue between Russia and the WEU.

An impression could be created in Russia that the two leading Western security organizations are orienting their activities at superseding Russia in the emerging regional security system, if not isolating it. Unfortunately, this interpretation can be strengthened by facts found in other spheres. For instance, the politically far-reaching concept of the Via Baltica initially did not include Russia that would only have access roads to this route from Kaliningrad and St Petersburg. Another example is the Western position *vis-à-vis* Russian relations with the Baltic states. It is practically impossible to convince Russians that this position is not biased in favour of the Balts.

Analysis of trends in the security sphere in the Baltic region leads to one important conclusion: the principal goal of Russian regional policy should be to prevent further weakening of its position. Hypothetically, this can be achieved either through a military build-up or through participation in working out the rules of the game with which Russia later will have to comply. Considerable reductions in the level of forces prove that Russia is interested in choosing the second option and counts on meeting a corresponding understanding on the part of other countries.

KEY PROBLEMS OF RUSSIAN SECURITY POLICY IN THE BALTIC REGION

In order to make Russia a security partner in strengthening regional security, Russia should be assisted in responding to the above-mentioned challenges. In other words, Russia's concerns should be carefully taken into account in a way that allows it to solve its problems in the interests of all. Pushing Russia towards unilateralism would not only be counter-productive but potentially dangerous.

The Russian–Baltic Relationship

The existing *modus vivendi* in Russia's relations with the Baltic states is a significant step forward as compared with the tense relations of the early 1990s. Nowadays mutual economic interests create a reliable safeguard not only against military conflict but also against the introduction of economic sanctions by Russia. This model is likely to work in the short- and medium-term perspective.

At the same time it appears that there are no influential political forces on either side advocating any further and dynamic improvement of the relations through mutual concessions. If this is the case, then some negative scenarios of destabilizing developments cannot be excluded. To stabilize the situation, Russia and the Baltic states should, mostly bilaterally, solve or at least reach progress in the solution of three problems.

The improvement of the situation concerning the Russian-speaking population in Estonia and especially Latvia is a critical issue. If progress is achieved here, compromises in other areas will quickly follow. Otherwise, possible positive developments will remain hostages to the stalemate over the citizenship issue.

The crisis emerged when, in accordance with the concept of restored independence, Latvia and Estonia put into force legislation, restoring citizenship rights for those who were citizens before these states were occupied in 1940 and guaranteeing these rights to their direct descendants. Only 120,000 Russians in Estonia (out of 475,000) and 280,000 in Latvia (out of 906,000) became citizens in this way. Those who had arrived in Latvia and Estonia after 1940 were required to speak the state language and to meet certain residency conditions in order to obtain citizenship.

The Estonian legislature was more liberal and this resulted in about 90,000 people obtaining citizenship by naturalization from 1992 to the first half of 1997. In the Latvian case which is more complex only 3,400 people were naturalized from February 1995, when the law was enforced, to February 1997.

The difference between the rights of citizens and non-citizens in Latvia and Estonia is pretty large. With regard to political rights the difference is natural – non-citizens may not vote or be elected to office (except for local elections in Estonia where they may vote). In the sphere of economics non-citizens are inferior too – they may not own property, they have unequal status in the privatization process, and so on. There are a number of other limitations also affecting non-citizens.

The Russian approach towards the issue of citizenship in Latvia and Estonia is that all those who were permanent residents at the moment when independence was 'proclaimed' (official documents use this word – A.M.) must have the right to citizenship as well as those born in these countries. In various official documents Russia expressed its concerns about the inequality of the rights of Russians and the Russian-speaking population resulting from the current legislature on citizenship, state language and education, and called for the elimination of residency requirements and a lowering of the language requirements. All these measures would facilitate the absorption of those loyal to their respective states which can be considered as one of the aims of Russian policy.

However, until now this policy has brought no significant results. Since, as it was mentioned, economic sanctions are unlikely, or rather totally excluded, prospects for the success of a Russian unilateral course in the Russophone issue should be assessed with a great deal of scepticism.

It appears also, that despite an officially declared interest in engaging the mechanisms of the UN, the EU, OSCE and the Council of Europe, Russia does not have much confidence in the abilities, or maybe the willingness, of international organizations to get deeply involved in the problem, because these organizations displayed their general satisfaction with the situation as shown by the following:

– European organizations criticized only minor items in the citizenship legislation, especially that of Latvia, not challenging the whole approach; these organizations, therefore, can be useful for monitoring the situation, perhaps, preventing abuses by local bureaucracy, but not for changing the whole picture;

– during the debate in the Council of Europe on the issue of Estonian admission, an argument was made that Russians in the Baltic countries were not a historic minority, but migrant workers who had arrived during the period when Latvia and Estonia could not control the process of immigration; the conclusion should supposedly follow that international law on minorities does not fully apply here;

– the fully democratic character of the statehoods of Estonia and Latvia was recognized when they were admitted to the Council of Europe in May 1993 and February 1995 despite the remaining problem of the Russian-speakers.

Therefore, improvement of the situation predominantly depends on changes in the Latvian approach and further liberalization of the Estonian one. A powerful factor here will be the prospects for joining the EU, already real in the Estonian case and potential in the Latvian one.

The border issue[5] *per se* is becoming less and less important for Russian–Baltic relations; in Russian–Latvian relations it has almost completely lost its political significance. Having withdrawn their territorial claims, Latvia and Estonia clearly demonstrated their acquiescence to the present model, resulting from the initially uncompromising stand by Russia on the issue which even led to the unilateral demarcation of the border with Estonia.

However, absence of the border treaties will continue to render direct negative impact on Russian–Estonian relations (and indirectly influence the Russian–Latvian dialogue) as long as Moscow relies on the 'package' principle in negotiations with Tallinn, linking the border issue and the problem of the Russophones and thus putting forward a demand for further concessions as a precondition for accepting earlier concessions.

In reality Russia has two options. One is to sign the border treaties (which will not necessarily be ratified by either parliament), trying to improve the general atmosphere of its relations with the Baltic states after they recognized *de facto* that the Russian approach had been justified. Another option is to continue the policy of 'no treaty', possibly based on the assumption that the absence of the border treaty will diminish the chances of the Baltic countries joining NATO.

In general, the second approach will most probably be rather disadvantageous for Russia. Absence of territorial claims is more important than absence of border treaties as far as further *rapprochement* between the Baltic countries and the West is concerned. At the same time the Russian position is likely to be found unconstructive which, in turn, will push Russia back to 'the Western bias' type of discussions, thus creating a vicious circle.

The start of an autonomous security dialogue between Russia and the three Baltic states seems to be useful. It is possible since 1) there is a precedent in the form of the Russian–Lithuanian agreement on military transit and 2) Lithuania, Latvia and Estonia successfully cooperate in the defence sphere which gives them a well-coordinated position towards Russia in this respect.

The main idea of this dialogue should be the introduction of additional confidence-building measures and transition from threat perception to threat assessment, preferably joint threat assessment. In the process of the dialogue the Baltic states would hopefully realize that Russia in the foreseeable future, for both military and political reasons, is unable to threaten them militarily. That could be a break-through, since now in the Baltic capitals threat assessment is too often dominated by negative historical experience.

A security dialogue between Russia and the Baltic states could also open the way to security cooperation within the framework of multi-lateral organizations and initiatives, which is especially important for the security of the Baltic region.

Further Demilitarization of Kaliningrad

It has to be admitted that Russia has done a lot unilaterally in reducing its military potential in the Kaliningrad area.

However, space for Russia's unilateral measures with regard to the demilitarization of Kaliningrad is limited, given the following considerations:

- the defence role for the Kaliningrad district concerning air- and sea-surveillance, air defence, missile defence potentially, and the fact that this is the only fully suitable naval base of the Baltic Fleet;

- the role of Kaliningrad in the discussion of the whole issue of arms control in Europe, above all – the flank problem;
- the uncertainty of the military outcomes of NATO enlargement (for example, how freedom of transit will be ensured in case 'the second wave' comes about) raising concerns about the defensibility of the area and long-term worries about the future of Kaliningrad as Russian territory.

In this context, it appears that a solution for the Kaliningrad problem could be found and the level of defence sufficiency could be determined within rather low limits if several preconditions could be met.

1. Without raising the issue of the present borders of Kaliningrad as part of the Russian Federation (which should be taken for granted), and outside the NATO enlargement paradigm, Russia should be guaranteed free and unhindered land, sea and air transit between its mainland and its exclave by means of treaties between Russia and all other interested countries, first of all Finland and Estonia. Passage through territorial waters of these two countries in the Finnish Gulf may become necessary, if problems emerge with land transit through Lithuania in case of further enlargement of NATO. Procedures for the international monitoring of the transit could be agreed upon.

2. Negotiations could be started with the agenda of introducing naval arms control measures, which *per se* would be a major step forward in the sphere of arms control.

3. Russia and Poland, preferably under the auspices of some regional forum, or even the OSCE, could hold consultations on confidence-building measures aimed at connecting a further lowering of Russian forces in the Kaliningrad district and the non-deployment of Polish forces in certain agreed areas.

The steps proposed could well be in line with the general goals of the Russian security policy in the Baltic area, discussed below, and could contribute to establishing a general climate of confidence in the region.

A Security Model for Russia

To ensure that the security model emerging in the Baltic region will be acceptable for Russia is, of course, a task for its own foreign policy. However, it seems that making Russia a security partner would be equally beneficial for every country. If Russia's interests are not taken into account these days, the same 'unpredictability' may grow in the medium-term future, and in the long run exclusion of Russia may push it towards the pursuance of a power-political course.

Now Russia's interests with regards to the security model in the Baltic region seem to be the following:

Firstly, making the Baltic Sea a zone of low military activity. That would be very stabilizing. There are no reasons why the military activity of the littoral countries should increase. There are no security challenges in the region to be adequately met this way. Russia itself contributes to the security of the region and does not understand the need for an increase there of NATO-centric activity. Russia accepts a certain, minimal amount of regional NATO activity, but will object as soon as it exceeds that low level;

Secondly, ensuring the security of Lithuania, Latvia and Estonia outside NATO. This is the issue where the position of Russia and that of the three Baltic states are mutually exclusive since while the former opposes NATO's expansion, the latter consider NATO as the leading European security organization and are afraid that if they show readiness to accept security guarantees other than NATO membership, they will surely never become members. That is why this problem is not suitable for the bilateral Russian–Baltic format, but may for several reasons be solved in the regional or wider international context.

It can be assumed that there are possibilities for ensuring the security of the Baltic states through the EU and especially through WEU membership. Although obtaining full status in these organizations will clearly take the Baltic states many years, presumably, even the associated partnership of today is a sufficient guarantee, since it cannot be imagined that current WEU members for political reasons would leave infringements of the security of partner countries unanswered.

Again, the same conclusion is fully applicable to the Scandinavian countries and the US. Although hard security guarantees in the form of alliances are virtually impossible, broadly interpreted soft security guarantees (including bilateral defence cooperation) will be a powerful factor for the security of the Baltic states. A specific precedent of the kind can be found in US and British security guarantees given to Ukraine when it decided to go non-nuclear.[6]

As for NATO, a precedent in the form of the Russia–NATO and Ukraine–NATO agreements, completely different in essence, constitutes a suit to follow. An agreement between NATO and the Baltic states could contain a lot of security guarantees, but not formal membership. This would still not be ideal from the Russian point of view but could be acceptable.

Presumably, the search for analogous security models for the Baltic countries has been started by Western countries (RAND report, the WEU Hanseatic Corps, the US–Baltic Charter, and so on). On the other hand, at least in Estonia there are shifts in favour of 'non-NATO' security, should it be a transitional model. Russia apparently is ready to contribute to this process by providing necessary guarantees, if those can be accepted;

Thirdly, a new phase of arms control. In addition to measures, proposed in other parts of this paper, highly valuable in themselves, evolution of the overall arms control regime should be seriously considered as necessary, especially in the long run. The adaptation of the CFE treaty of 1990, being an attempt to solve political problems by technical means, may prove to be insufficient, since it retains the shortcomings of the CFE regime, such as the limited number of parties. Later on new approaches may be required. In this context, negotiating a CFE-2 treaty for all OSCE member-states, free from any legacy of the bloc principle, would be especially beneficial for the Baltic region:

- considerably lower ceilings would be an important stability factor for all countries, including Russia;
- repeal of the flank principle would first and foremost allow Russia to redeploy forces to the South, thus greatly facilitating the solution of the Kaliningrad problem; Norway's concerns with regard to the level of forces in the Russian North and, probably, Russia's apprehensions with regard to evolution of the Norwegian security model should be a matter also for bilateral dialogue; perhaps, agreement on this issue can be made a precondition for an overall agreement;
- the Baltic states would join the system of European arms control that on the one hand would give them an equal say in the process, but on the other could calm down Russia's possible concerns regarding 'the free ride' that the Baltic states could get in an emerging regime of European conventional arms control.

Taking into account that negotiating such a treaty would take a long period of time, the countries of the Baltic region could start negotiations on a regional arms control agreement which later could either become an element of CFE-2 or continue to exist autonomously.

CONCLUSIONS

For a better understanding of Russia's interests and policies in the Baltic region, it is necessary to admit that Russia decreasingly deserves a mention in the category of first-priority security problems faced by other states in the region. The policies pursued by Russia in the 1990s (discounting rhetoric by the opposition or non-influential political forces of the radical wing) demonstrate that it rather wants to be a cooperative partner in regional developments. Russia drastically reduced its military capabilities in the Baltic region without being pressured in its relations with the Baltic states (which should not be put into the same basket as its rigid stand on some issues) and so on.

However, Russia is still too often expected to go much further along its part of the road towards cooperation. These expectations are by and large false. Ready to be cooperative in the region, Russia now is frequently concerned whether other countries are really prepared to see it as a full participant in the regional security process, or whether their policies are still aimed at neutralization of the potential 'Russian challenge' through isolation.

No doubt, making Russia a security partner is not an easy task, but this is within reach. To achieve it, Russian interests and apprehensions should be taken into account in the process of creating a security model for the Baltic region. By ensuring the security of the Baltic states in cooperation with the West but outside NATO, by defining acceptable parameters of defence sufficiency in Kaliningrad in an atmosphere of non-provocative development around it, by starting a new phase of European and regional arms control with a great deal of reliance on bilateral and multilateral confidence-building, Russia and the other countries of the Baltic region could open a large window of opportunities, the significance of which would go far beyond the regional dimension.

NOTES

1 Russian attention to the region is obviously growing. Although it may well be mere coincidence, the last visit abroad paid by the Russian President Boris Yeltsin, before a long interval caused by the election campaign of 1996 and his illness, was one to Norway. The first visit after he recovered was paid to Finland, and this was formally separated from the Russian–US summit.

2 The chapter draws on the following literature: Asmus and Nurick (1996), Castel (1996), 'Interesy Bezopasnosti ...' (1995), Joenniemi, Pertti (1997), Möttölä (1997), 'Noviy Oblik Baltiyskogo Flota' (1997), 'Rossiya i Pribaltika' (1997), Stranga (1996), Trenin (1997a), Trenin (1997b), Vushkarnik (1997). For complete citations, see the list of references at the back of the volume.

3 Summit of Baltic regional leaders at Visby in Gotland (Sweden) in May 1996.

4 Commander of the Baltic Fleet, Admiral Yegorov, pointed out in one of his interviews that in 1985–95 the number of servicemen (strength) in the Fleet had been reduced by half, the number of ships by two-thirds, naval aviation by 60 per cent. After the withdrawal from the Baltic states the Fleet lost 80 per cent of its bases (where 50 per cent of the ships and all the submarines used to be based beforehand), 30 per cent of the airfields (bases for up to 25 per cent of the Fleet's air force), 80 per cent of the system for shore surveillance, 64 per cent of the ship-repairing and ship-building facilities. ('Interesy bezopasnosti ...', 1995)

5 By border issues in Russian–Baltic relations one means territorial claims of

Estonia and Latvia on parts of Russian territory which during the inter-war period belonged to the Baltic states in accordance with the Tartu and Riga peace treaties of 1920. Estonia claimed several territories in the Leningrad and Pskov regions (2,300 square km altogether), Latvia – Pytalovo (Abrene) and Palkino districts of Pskov region (1,600 square km). The Balts made the argument that legally Latvia and Estonia continued to exist as independent states, though occupied, and they restored, not proclaimed independence in 1991; therefore, the Tartu and Riga treaties which were cornerstones of their statehood in the 1920s remained valid and, thus, the border between these states and Russia should be based on them.

6 The difference is that the Baltic states are not willing to accept such security guarantees from Russia as Ukraine did in 1994. On the other hand, this could establish an outstanding precedent if Russia were included in the mechanism of regional security cooperation.

7

Germany's Security Policy in the Baltic Sea Region

AXEL KROHN
Christian Albrechts Universität, Kiel

INTRODUCTION

Two assumptions describe the cornerstones of European and Baltic Sea Region security.

First, a 'tightly coupled security community' (Ruggie, 1997) exists among the nations of North America and the European Union (EU) visible for example in the North Atlantic Treaty Organization (NATO) and based so far on a wide range of common values and interest.

Second, the present political developments in Europe indicate a shift towards a further 'Europeanization of security', by developing a European security identity within an intensifying process of European integration and enlargement.

Both have considerable impact on German political affairs. Therefore, I will focus on German military security policy in the BSR by embedding the topic in a framework of European and transatlantic security developments.

For decades Germany's policy towards the Baltic Sea Region (BSR) could sooner have been described as 'non-policy'. Even though a special German Nordic or Baltic Sea Region policy still does not exist, the political changes in Europe have had their impact on German politics and brought the region more into the focus of Bonn. Germany is getting more involved in the Baltic Sea Region also by increasing military security cooperation with its neighbouring countries.

After the end of the bloc confrontation (i.e. the Cold War) Germany's security interests are basically directed towards two goals: first, to embed the unified Germany into the European order by an intensified integration process and, second, to strengthen the stabilization of the Central East European Countries (CEE) by enlarging the EU and NATO (Schmidt, 1996). The support of these simultaneous processes, integration and enlargement, create major tasks for German foreign and security policy.

Obviously, Germany's violent history and its developing profile as a middle power in the centre of Europe, give it a special responsibility. German policies have to adapt to the new political situation in the CEE countries and Russia as well as to the complex domestic situation in Germany. At the same time, Germany is faced with the Western countries' demands to assume greater obligations in accordance with its economic and political strength.

A lot will depend on the way in which Germany takes up its future responsibilities. In this context 'partnership in leadership' means first of all 'partnership in burden sharing'. Certainly Germany will have to play a bigger role within burden sharing – for example, sending out soldiers if required, which is a rather new role for Germany and continue to give a 'pay cheque' which is the 'traditional' German part. However, this pay cheque will have to be considerably higher in future, due to the rising costs of NATO and EU enlargement.

Additionally, a sensitive perception among its neighbouring countries is still alive; there is still a residual awareness of the potential danger that Germany might develop hegemonic capabilities in Europe. Germany's strong support for widening and deepening the European Union is not only to be seen as an instrument for enlarging the European region of political, economic and military stability, but is also understood as a means to minimize such perceptions. Obviously, these conditions create a difficult environment for German foreign and security policy.

So far, Germany's political priorities are fundamentally determined by the process of European integration, developments in Russia, and transatlantic relations with the United States, the emerging 'double enlargement' of NATO, that is, enlargement to the East by incorporating new members and enlargement to the West by the military reintegration of France. To support the transfer of West European stability to the new democracies in the East, is considered to be a key task for German foreign and security policy. In this context, the Baltic Sea Region and Northern Europe are located geographically and conceptually between Washington, Brussels and Moscow.[1]

GERMANY S 'LOW PROFILE'

While the Nordic countries have a somewhat 'traditional' foreign policy interest in the Baltic Sea Region and Northern Europe, the present developments also put the region more into the political focus of Germany as well, leading to a growing involvement. But Germany is still avoiding any action that might fuel the impression that Germany could take a leading role in Nordic/Baltic issues.

If we try to identify explanatory factors for Germany's rather low profile in the Baltic Sea region, there are basically six complementary factors that add up to the past German 'non-policy'.

First, German perspectives on the Baltic Sea Region were much in line with the general Central European view on Northern Europe, which was, until the beginning of the 1990s, that the region was hardly on the political and economic map of the political elites in Brussels and Bonn. While Nordic identity, Nordic integration and cooperation was a constant factor within Scandinavian politics, Germany's interests were not specifically directed towards Northern Europe.

Second, Germany's policy towards the Baltic Sea region is only part of and complementary to the 'new Ostpolitik' which is driven by security and economic logic (Kurth,1995: 384). Germany is a strong supporter of NATO's enlargement and the extension of the EU. However, the CEE region seems to be of incomparably greater importance than the Baltic region.

Third, Germany's primary interest was to support Poland in becoming one of the first new NATO members. Not to endanger the Polish integration was an overriding foreign policy goal, which was based on security logic and historical grounds. Therefore, Germany was careful not to irritate Russia, for example by giving stronger support to the Baltic states.

Fourth, there is the 'Moscow factor'. Obviously, one of the main factors for keeping a rather low profile concerning German foreign and security policy activity lies in the close and well-established German–Russian relations, which are of fundamental importance. To a certain extent Russian interests are anticipated within German politics. Without giving Russia a *droit de regard*, German politics have to fulfil the difficult task of reassuring the CEE countries and the Baltic states while not putting off Russia (Krohn, 1996: 102).

Fifth, Germany is reluctant to become more involved in the Kaliningrad *oblast* and the Baltic states, not only because of possible Russian irritation, but also to avoid any impression that there might be a special German interest in turning time back, that is, possibly claiming territorial interest in the region. Instead it has been officially made clear that there are no open territorial questions.

Sixth, there are also limits to Germany's financial engagement. Germany became the major provider of Western assistance to the CEE countries. So far, Germany is transferring almost 50 per cent of its financial aid to the CEE countries (Schmidt, 1996: 214). But the main task remains the reconstruction of the former German Democratic Republic (GDR), which is proving much more costly and complicated than anticipated.

As a result of these factors Germany does not wish or have the capacity to play 'great power politics' in European affairs or to take a leading role in Nordic/Baltic issues. Instead German foreign and security policy is focusing on multilateralism – making clear that Germany is one partner among others.

The following two examples might illustrate the German cautiousness towards the BSR. In March 1992, a new cooperative intergovernmental body was founded in Copenhagen, the Council of the Baltic Sea States (CBSS).[2] Germany was among the founding members, as were the other Baltic littoral states and Norway. This initiative gained considerable public recognition, particularly in northern Germany. Even though a general supporter of the CBSS, German politics remained somewhat inconsistent, as Germany was not supporting any further institutionalization, for example by establishing a permanent office. Additionally Germany saw to it that security was exempted from the agenda of the CBSS. Only in the field of 'soft security', that is, customs and border control and the build-up and training of police forces was Germany supporting a growing cooperation. This policy was probably fuelled by German anxieties of ending up with additional financial burdens in case the activities of the CBSS should be expanded and intensified.

The north German 'Länder' were much more supportive and positive. Schleswig-Holstein was always supporting the establishment of a permanent secretariat. As Gert Walter, the minister of Justice, Federal and European Affairs of Schleswig-Holstein stated, the final decision by the CBSS to establish a secretariat is an 'encouraging signal' for the future development of cooperation in the Baltic Sea region.[3]

Particularly in German politics towards the eastern part of the BSR, that is, the Baltic states and the Kaliningrad *oblast*,[4] the 'Moscow factor' in German politics becomes obvious.

During the early years after the Baltic states became independent, Germany was reluctant in offering any major military aid.[5] However, each of the Baltic states received assistance in the field of soft security, i.e. to develop police forces as well as support for the border control and coast guard of the Baltic states. Subsequently, the policy of reluctance on military aid slowly changed, as shown in the case of two German military advisers who served in Tallinn and the delivery of two German minesweepers to Estonia.

Beside possible Russian objections, the question arises, what would happen, if Germany should opt for a stronger build-up of its foreign policy engagement in the Eastern Baltic. It could happen that Germany might get into a competition with other Nordic countries. The relatively longer 'Nordic' engagement and their well-developed contacts in the region would have to compete with the substantial weight of the German economy. Denmark for example 'would therefore prefer Germany's energies to be directed towards other parts of Eastern Europe closer to home' (Petersen, 1994: 19).

If countries like Denmark together with Sweden and Finland would incorporate Germany in common activities in the eastern part of the Baltic Sea Region it could help to overcome the obvious German difficulties and avoid a possible German 'overweight'.

Today, the Baltic Sea Region as a link between the North European, the Central European and the East European countries becomes more important and recognized by Germany in the field of politics, economy and security policy. The stronger involvement in various common activities with the neighbouring countries in military security are indicating an increased German interest. But also in future, German foreign policy will have to anticipate possible Russian reactions and, in case of disagreement, might probably decide to be 'pro-Russian' at the expense of the Baltic states.

TRANSATLANTIC AND EUROPEAN SECURITY

The problems with NATO enlargement are in determining the German security discussion. Germanys position was and is in line with the general NATO view, that is, inclusion of the CEE countries, mainly Poland, Hungary and the Czech Republic, excluding the Baltic states. While other Baltic littoral countries like Denmark stressed that the Baltic states are to be among the first new members of NATO, Germany was not stressing any further extension to the East.

Russian objections to NATO's enlargement were very strong. They were and are among the pressing problems to be solved. Both NATO and Russia backed themselves into a corner from which it seemed difficult to get out without losing face – NATO because of setting a date for deciding on its extension and Russia by always and strictly objecting to any enlargement at all.

These objections cause problems also for a possible redefinition of the present German policy. The future will show whether the new NATO 16 plus 1 can ease Russian objections or whether the new consultation mechanisms between NATO and Russia will instead endanger quick decision-making. Still, even though NATO is constantly stressing that Russia has a voice but no veto, it seems rather obvious that the new founding act gives Russia a lot of say in NATO affairs. It is certainly not just a document to be put aside if both parties agree to differ on a vital subject. The fact that 17 heads of state signed the document and that it was ratified by the Russian duma gives it a substantial weight in international politics, even though it is 'only' a charter and not a treaty. One will have to consider this when talking about future prospects of Baltic membership in NATO.

When talking about NATO's enlargement it seems obvious to look eastward. However, I would also like to elaborate on NATO's enlargement to the west, i.e. the military reintegration of France.

The French policy goals are rather ambitious: Europe should not only develop military security capabilities to assure stability on the continent but also have in mind a certain kind of global power projection. This seems to create a dilemma, as most of the other European countries don't share that vision, but rather stick to the well-established transatlantic ties or try to follow neutralistic traditions.

In this context German–French relations are gaining in interest and the other countries are observing German politics *vis-à-vis* French security interests carefully. However, one should not underestimate the differences in German–French security interests. First, Germany's security interests are clearly directed towards the east, while France considers the Mediterranean and Africa to be vital areas, second, besides strongly supporting a European defence component with the WEU, German politics still remain transatlantic, and thirdly, Germany favours a Europe that is economically prosperous and politically stable but does not have ambitious visions regarding global politics.

The general weight of the German–French friendship and the growing German support for French positions in European security affairs could fuel suspicions that German politics might intensify German–French cooperation at the expense of the traditionally strong transatlantic ties. The countries in the BSR such as Denmark and Norway in particular, perceive the United States to be vital not only to European security, but also to 'counterweigh' the position of Germany. Additionally, it seems clear to most of the European countries that despite various political statements, a credible defence of Europe is, and will be, possible only with a substantial transatlantic link.

The future will show whether we get a 'NATO *à la française*' (B. Schmidt, 1997). But we should be cautious not to fuel those voices in the US that see the old common values and interests between Europe and the United States diminished and replaced by a US foreign policy orientation towards Asia at the expense of Europe.

Henry Kissinger wrote about the indivisible transatlantic security links: 'Without America, Europe turns into a peninsula at the tip of Eurasia, unable to find equilibrium, much less unity ... Without Europe, America will become an island off the shores of Eurasia condemned to a kind of pure balance of power politics ...'.[6] However, as the former

Chancellor Helmut Schmidt stated, the US must understand that in the next century Germany will not automatically take the side of the US in conflicts between Washington and Paris.[7] German–French relations seem too vital.

A viable European security structure would have considerable impact on the Baltic Sea Region as well, possibly offering a security alternative to those countries who did not want to or did not manage to reach the goal of NATO membership. However, such a European security structure is not yet visible.

Germany is a strong supporter of a closer integration and a further enlargement of the EU to the CEE and the Baltic states. The German government believes that the two goals of deepening and widening the EU can be achieved simultaneously. However, this will rather be an ongoing process within the EU for the next decades. Additionally also, German domestic support for 'grandiose visions of European integration is much weaker than some CDU leaders care to admit'.[8]

The costs to the EU for the inclusion of Hungary, the Czech Republic, Cyprus, Estonia, Slovenia and Poland are estimated to be approximately 150 billion DM for the years 2000 to 2006. Germany will probably have to finance about 29 per cent of this amount.[13]

The process of widening and deepening the European Union has fuelled a wide and sometimes controversial discussion in Germany on various topics, ranging from economic and monetary issues to security policy.

Despite their difficult starting positions, all the Baltic states have made considerable progress in transforming to and establishing a market economy. In all countries the Gross National Product (GNP) amounted to approximately four per cent in 1996.[9] However, among the Baltic states Estonia seems to perform the best from the viewpoint of economic development. Therefore, in 1997 the EU commission recommended negotiations on possible EU membership for Estonia.[10] Their successful privatization became visible by a share of approximately 70 per cent of private economy in the Estonian Gross Domestic Product (GDP) in 1996.[11] During the first half of 1997 the economic growth rate rose to 10.8 per cent, arousing fears that the economy could become 'overheated'.

The danger of a double rejection for the Baltic states, that is, non-membership in NATO and non-membership in the EU seems to be removed at least for one country. The future will show, whether Russia is willing to accept the closer politico-economic integration of the Baltic states, or whether a negative attitude similar to the objections against NATO enlargement will come up. The Russian diplomatic attitude towards Estonia give reasons for concern.[12] It is possible also that the EU might have to carry out their enlargement despite Russian objections.

During the 1997 conference on the Bundeswehr and society in Berlin, the German minister of defence Volker Rühe stated that the Baltic states have the opportunity to become members of the EU and therefore, also to become members of NATO. However he made clear that there is no necessary link between EU and NATO membership.[14]

As a step in the direction of stronger European efforts to develop a European security system, the WEU, the 'oldest' European defence partnership, was revived as a phoenix from the ashes. Germany is a strong supporter of increasing WEU activity and capability.

However, the present shortcomings of the WEU do not offer much credibility to the idea of becoming the 'European pillar' for military security, even though NATO accepted that the WEU can have access to NATO's military resources. In future, the new concept of Combined Joint Task Forces will allow peacekeeping and peace-enforcement activities without the US and within the WEU. But the NATO Council has still to give its approval, and the WEU's dependence on NATO continues. At present Germany is the only country in the Baltic Sea region which is a full member and strong supporter of the WEU. Probably because the French–German weight is rather heavy in the WEU, and the transatlantic relations are considered to be vital, the organization does not seem to gain much attraction in the region. Other countries like Denmark, Norway, Sweden and Finland, who could have joined the WEU, favour the status of 'observer' or 'associate partner' instead of member.[15]

Germany is confronted with the dilemma that it wishes to preserve NATO as an Atlantic security community and additionally wants to empower the EU's authority in foreign and security policy. 'In order not to undermine NATO cohesion and effectiveness, it has been decided to establish the WEU both as an inner-European co-ordinator within NATO and as a defence arm of the EU' (Haftendorn, 1996: 98).

But for the foreseeable future the United States possesses military capabilities that even a united Europe would have great difficulty in matching.[16] We should consider this fact when talking about 'European Security'. In this context 'Germany should ensure that the EU–WEU structure does not develop into an alternative to NATO but enhances the two-pillar concept on which European security rests' (Haftendorn, 1996: 111).

However, the bigger the zone of security in Europe and the more intensified the cooperation becomes, the less important it is who is a member or a negotiating member of EU. The security of the Baltic states is clearly connected with the whole of Europe.[17]

GROWING COOPERATION

German military policy can be simply described by quantitative reduction and qualitative cooperation. As it is outlined in the 'Bundeswehr-concept', the overall strength of the German armed forces will be not more than 338,000 men. Due to changing military scenarios and budgetary cuts the ongoing discussion indicates much lower figures. Figures ranging from 200,000 to 250,000 men are discussed, even though not officially. Probably after the next German election in September 1998 the government will have to decide how to adapt more drastically to its needs.

This is also true for another 'hot' issue, that is, the conscript system of the German Armed Forces, which is being heavily discussed within the armed forces and the political elites in Bonn as well.

The reduced service time for soldiers creates problems of major complexity for the German armed forces, that is, of whether and how a modern and highly sophisticated army can still be run with conscripts. A service period of ten months hardly provides enough time for the necessary training and exercise with modern electronic equipment and weapon systems.

The subject of giving up the conscript system for a professional army is widely discussed, not only among the political parties, particularly the liberals and the conservatives, but also in the armed forces. However, so far the present system is dealt with as a 'holy cow', not to be questioned in public, either by the leading politicians or by the Chief of the Federal Armed Forces Staff. Therefore it is hard to envision how the political and military elites will decide between technical needs and political wishful thinking. Obviously it is a difficult issue.[18]

Clearly, one of the major tasks will be shaping the armed forces according to future security tasks also outside the NATO area. As the European and international community is expecting a larger portion of German participation, German armed forces need to adapt according to future needs.

The ability of the German naval forces to participate in operations for crisis prevention and crisis management gains more weight.[19] The extended role of the German navy would mean to be deployable wherever the political interests of Germany require her. Besides continued operations in the North Sea and the Atlantic, the Mediterranean Sea gains more importance.

Still, the northern region retains its security importance. To my understanding this is also partly due to developments in the Baltic Region. They have created opportunities for permanent partnership with the other Baltic littoral states. 'More than any other maritime area the Baltic provides for the possibility of cooperating with navies of former Warsaw Pact countries within the framework of NATO's Partnership for Peace programme. (*Naval Forces Special Issue*, 1996: 16).

Even if we assume, that after the first round of NATO enlargement there is more to come, this would mean a rather lengthy process. The reasons are basically threefold. First, the whole process of enlargement might turn out to be more costly than even the present financial 'worst-case scenarios' indicate. Second, due to the different standards of military and political infrastructures the process of adaptation between the old and the three new members will require considerable time. Third, if Russian objections cannot be totally removed within the new NATO–Russia Council, further enlargements would burden European–Russian relations for the next decades, certainly postponing the incorporation of other members.

Because of such a time-frame, political and military cooperation will build the basic military security network among all countries in Europe, members and non-members. Cooperation will become an important tool to handle such a 'waiting period'. Here, also the German military cooperation in the BSR comes into perspective. Despite different approaches towards certain aspects in European security, there always was and still is a German interest in cooperation in the Baltic Sea region.

In the field of military security the BALTAP Command (Baltic Approaches Command in NATO)[20] serves as an old and good example. BALTAP has served in close cooperation with the Federal Republic and Denmark in the defence of land and sea approaches during recent decades. Meanwhile a great variety of different cooperation activities have taken place. Besides personnel and expert meetings in various specialized fields, great emphasis is placed on joint exercises which are conducted on a bilateral or multilateral basis. A great deal of search and rescue (SAR) exercises and exercises with mine counter-measures were conducted.

In 1995 Germany conducted 407 bilateral activities with different countries in the region. In 1996 the figure rose to 600 single projects in 13 countries of the CEE, CIS and the Baltic states. However, half of these were devoted to Poland, the Czech Republic and Hungary.

Obviously Germany is beginning to develop more military cooperation with and more military assistance to the Baltic states. The German and Latvian ministers of defence (Volker Rühe and Andrejs Krastins) agreed on cooperation in training and education among the navies of their countries.[21] The first cooperative task was that German minesweepers gave technical aid and assistance to the Latvian navy, starting with assistance in minesweeping in the bay of Riga on 26 August 1996. The German navy conducted the training with seven ships, and finished the activity on 20 September 1996.[22] This minehunting took place in connection with a similar minesweeping operation by the Swedish navy outside Estonia.

Additionally two German officers served as military advisors in Tallinn. Despite financial constraints the Estonian government decided not to incorporate the Estonian naval units into the coastguard (Piirivalve) but to maintain them as a maritime force and therefore 'alliance capable'. The German advisors prepared for the deployment of two German minesweepers, which were delivered in July and August 1997.

The advisory group proved to be a positive example for necessary and well-received cooperation with the newly independent countries in the BSR. Since the Baltic states will not be those who become members of NATO within the foreseeable future, it is important to make clear that they are not peripheral to European security interest. Military cooperation thus proves to be an important tool.

If we look at the ongoing military activities in the BSR, it is obvious that besides PFP activities, the area with the highest military profile in the BSR is at present training and involving the three Baltic states in peacekeeping operations within the United Nations. Denmark took quite a leading role in co-ordinating the efforts of the Nordic states – together with other NATO countries such as the United States and Great Britain – in the build-up of a Baltic Peacekeeping Battalion (BALTBAT).

Germany's involvement in international peacekeeping operations lacks the historical experiences of its Nordic neighbours, and is additionally complicated by a complex domestic struggle between the political elites in Bonn and the German public. Until recently German politics seemed to favour an 'IFOR type of security', where Germany could provide the logistics and keep NATO and the US involved. But things necessarily change, as the 1997 German military engagement in Albania seemed to prove. There was no public or political objection against this action after German soldiers got involved in sniper fire while evacuating civilian personnel.

In 1998 the idea of a maritime Baltic Squadron (BALTRON) under German co-ordination and in close cooperation with Sweden came up. The decision was taken by the German ministry of defence to co-ordinate the establishment of a common naval unit by Estonia, Latvia and Lithuania. From 1998 on, the naval units participate in PFP activities.[23] Tasks will be rather maritime border protection to prevent smuggling and illegal migration, and minesweeping in the Baltic Sea, instead of naval operations under a UN commitment.[24] The first training opportunity was the participation in the exercise OPEN SPIRIT in August 1998 led by Germany.

Summing up one can state, that besides the various PFP activities, there are basically three important military structures which allow the Baltic states to cooperate with Germany and other NATO or non-NATO countries.[25] The above-mentioned BALTBAT, with the task of training for UN peacekeeping, BALTRON, as a maritime Baltic naval squadron and the newly established BALTNET, an air control and surveillance network for the Baltic region.

At present Poland is still the primary focus for German assistance. Cooperation has expanded significantly, and a military cooperation agreement was already signed in January 1993. So far this constitutes the most intensive German cooperation with a CEE country. The various activities have ranged from military training to expert meetings. Since 1991, Polish officers have undergone their training in Germany. More are expected in the future.[26]

Two important trilateral agreements were concluded in 1997. The first is the trilateral partnership in military and security policy between Denmark, Germany and Poland. A further intensification of cooperation among German, Danish and Polish forces appears to be in the interest of all three states and is a means to generally strengthen the cooperation in the Baltic Sea Region.[27] Among other activities, a trilateral cooperation in peacekeeping is planned. An expert group was established under the topic 'Peacekeeping Cooperation' and is supposed to come up with the suggestion for a yearly programme.[28]

In this context also the future position of the Baltic states was discussed. It was suggested that it would be important to incorporate them in some way, for example by a regionalization of PFP with subregional headquarters. The regional HQs could co-ordinate the PFP activities and allow the Baltic states to cooperate. The three countries decided to establish a German/Danish/Polish corps. The corps is named 'Multinational Corps North-East' and is supposed to be ready by 1999 when Poland becomes a NATO member.

The second important trilateral agreement is the German–French–Polish initiative on security cooperation. The 4th trilateral meeting of the German, French and Polish ministers of defence took place in Warsaw on 2 and 3 February 1997. Besides agreement on closer military cooperation in training and exercises the question of intensified arms cooperation was also discussed. In particular, a possible trilateral defence cooperation on the French–German 'Euromissile' HOT 3 was considered.[29]

Obviously military cooperation among all Baltic littoral countries is increasing. Germany is also getting more involved in the intensified cooperation network among the different national services. However, it is voiced that the figure of 600 projects mentioned above, indicates the end of the line as far as German capabilities are concerned. Financial and personal resources in the German armed forces are limited.[30] Due to these restrictions the cooperation in various fields of military security will rather shift from quantitative activities to intensified qualitative cooperation. The present planning indicates a deepening but not a widening of cooperation.[31] The emphasis will be on support for future 'self reliance'.

SUMMING UP

German foreign and security policy remains located somewhere between its transatlantic responsibilities and an emerging European identity (Schmidt, 1996: 217). To maintain and further develop the Atlantic Alliance and the European Union as complementary bodies always was and still is a primary goal for German foreign and security policy. The fact, that France has different perceptions on the structure and goals of future European security policy and that it is beginning to articulate its special interests, might in the long run create a problem for German politics. One should not underestimate possible suspicions by the other Baltic littoral countries, that the traditionally strong German transatlantic ties might become weaker in future.

Thus far the whole CEE region remains a 'disputed area'. If one describes the CEE region as a corridor ranging from the Baltic Sea to the Black Sea, it appears to be both a new dividing line and a region of disputed political control between Russia on the one side and the European countries and the United States on the other.

It seems obvious that the present security problems cannot be solved in the short term. Differentiated security concepts and instruments are required; at present both are lacking. Neither Germany nor anyone else has a 'blueprint'. This is not just because of the 'Moscow-factor'; there is an understandable reluctance on the part of the US and the European allies to take on new security commitments. This is certainly also true for Germany. To support the ongoing integration process in NATO and the EU, cooperation is to become even more important in the future. As all Baltic littoral countries share the same interests in stabilizing the region, further intensified cooperation with Germany in the field of military security seems likely.

A German comprehensive security concept for the Baltic Sea Region or the whole of Northern Europe does not exist. So far, Germany has reduced and redeployed its armed forces in the Baltic, according to the new political landscape in Europe and as part of the ongoing co-operation process within the PFP and the framework of the Euro-Atlantic Partnership Council. Even though it has not taken a leading role in security in the region, Germany has started to recognize the importance of security developments there.

Certainly the new German 'Ostpolitik' will be continued in future. Even though the BSR receives more attention and cooperation from Germany, a German 'Nordpolitik' is not yet visible. Germany's Central European and East European policy focus, as well as financial and personal limits, leave limited energy to be directed towards the North.

As for Germany's future policy orientation, the ranking seems clear. The geographic cornerstones are still Washington, Paris and London and, last but not least, Moscow and the CEE countries. So far, German politics have not been very 'inventive', but Germany pragmatically increased its participation in military exercises and in military co-operation with countries in the region. As mentioned above, I would argue that highly integrated military cooperation could become the major future security network to provide stability and peace in this part of Europe.

NOTES

1 Werner, Jann, 'Common Security in the Baltic Sea Region: The View from the German Länder', Common Security in Northern Europe after the Cold War, a report from the Olof Palme International Centre Seminar, Stockholm, 18–20 Mar. 1994, p. 182.
2 See: Kukk (1994: 20–27). For a general view on cooperation in the Baltic Sea Region see: Joenniemi (1994).
3 Minister Walter quoted in: Koopmann,1997, p. 28.
4 Kaliningrad is still a highly sensitive issue for Russia and announcements to create a special defence region in the area to comprise large groupings of ground forces, military aviation, naval units and other military installations, prompted anxiety about Russia's plans regarding the role and task of such forces.
5 Besides rifle ammunition and other surplus matériel from former GDR stocks, no weaponry was delivered.
6 Kissinger, Henry, 'Expand NATO Now', *Washington Post*, 19 Dec. 1994, p. A27.
7 *International Herald Tribune*, 12 May 1997, p. 6.
8 The European Monetary Union (EMU), in particular, which means giving up control over the Deutschmark does not seem to be a done-deal in domestic German politics. See also Geipel (1995: 378).
9 Koopmann, Werner, Das Baltikum als Handelspartner und Investitionsstandort, Koopmann, p. 22.
10 In Estland könnte die Konjunktur heißlaufen', *Frankfurter Allgemeine Zeitung*, 5 Aug. 1997, p. 10.
11 Koopmann, p. 22.
12 See also: Lange (1997: 11).
13 'EU-Osterweiterung kostet rund 150 Milliarden DM', *Frankfurter Allgemeine Zeitung*, 17 July 1997, p. 13.
14 Neuntes Forum zu Bundeswehr und Gesellschaft der Welt am Sonntag, partial reprint in: *Welt am Sonntag*, Zeitgeschehen, 8 June 1997, pp. 33–40.
15 The WEU is not yet a viable alternative. In 1995 the organization came up with the plan to establish a 'Hanseatic Corps' in the Baltic Sea. This corps would protect the region's maritime safety and security. This standing Baltic Sea Force

should comprise Denmark, Estonia, Germany, Latvia, Lithuania and Poland as founding members. The tasks would include border control, monitoring of fishing and environmental rules, shipping control and last but not least search and rescue. However, the idea of a 'Hanseatic Corps' so far seems dead. No concrete steps to establish such a force were undertaken in 1997. See also: McEwan, Gavin, 'WEU sea force proposed', *The Baltic Independent*, 8–14 Dec. 1995, p. 5.

16   See also: Ruggie (1997: 113).

17   See report on the final conference on Baltic Security and Securing Democracy, Riga 25 and 26 July 1997, in: Neumann, Tanya, 'New security agenda – Common future destiny', *The Baltic Times*, vol. 2/70, 31 July–6 Aug. 1997, p. 1.

18   However it has relatively little to do with military reasoning or possible resentment from the public. Provocatively one could argue that it is much more about the fact, that in such a case the system of conscientious objectors would have to be removed as well, with the result, that the state would have to employ and pay people for their work in the social services, a rather costly undertaking. At present everything is being done to avoid raising the issue, as the government is trying to cut down on medical and social costs.

19   Bundesministerium der Verteidigung, *Weißbuch 1994*, Bonn 1994, para. 64, p. 120.

20   BALTAP is located in Denmark. Responsibility (not membership) of Denmark and Germany jointly under NATO authority.

21   BmVg, 'Bundesminister Volker Rühe vereinbart Ausbildungskooperation der deutschen und lettischen Marine mit dem lettischen Verteidigungsminister Andrejs Krastins'. BMVg online http://www.bmvg.government.de./PM-96082200.htm, 19 Sept. 1996.

22   BmVg, 'Ausbildungskooperation der deutschen und lettischen Marine', http://www.bmvg.government.de/presse/pressemappen/bi-multi/lettische-marine.htm

23   'Bundeswehr-Hilfe für die Baltischen Staaten', *Kieler Nachrichten*, No. 64, 17 March 1997, p. 4.

24   Eneberg, Kaa, 'Baltron fortfarande i sin linda', *Dagens Nyheter*, 23 Feb. 1997, p. 8.

25   Other ideas which came up, such as to establish a Baltic Treaty Organization (BALTO) incorporating all Baltic littoral countries, aiming at a stronger integration of Sweden and Finland with the goal of securing the Baltic states, were rather speculative and did not gain much recognition for the following reasons: First, the discussion on division of labour in security is already going on between the countries in the region and, second, Germany would certainly not be interested in playing a leading role within such a 'Baltic mini-NATO'. Such an idea was brought forward by Alten (1996). See for a critique: Zektri, Sonja, 'Wer wird Balto Generalsekretär?', *Frankfurter Allgemeine Zeitung*, 19 July 1996, no. 166, p. 11.

26   Bundesministerium der Verteidigung, Presseforum, 'Deutsch–dänisch–polnische Zusammenarbeit im militärpolitischen und militärischen Bereich'. BMVg online, 7/17/96, p. 1, internet, http://www.bmvg.government.de/Presseforum/Pressemappen/M2Q1.htm

27   The trilateral agreement is the result of meetings between the ministers of defence in August 1995 in Ærø (Denmark) and February 1996 in Krakow and Zakopane (Poland).

28   Bundesministerium der Verteidigung, Presseforum, 'Deutsch–dänisch–polnische Zusammenarbeit im militärpolitischen und militärischen Bereich'. BmVg online, 7/17/96, p. 2, internet, http://www.bmvg. government.de/

Presseforum/Pressemappen/M2Q1.htm
29 Particularly as Poland does not seem to be satisfied with the present perfor-
    mance of the system 'Spike' which they intend to buy in Israel. However, it
    might become difficult for Poland to get out of the contract.
30 The discussion on further cuts in the defence budget by 2 billion DM in 1997
    underlines the rather tight budgetary situation. Such a cut could have
    endangered the Eurofighter project as well as the prolongation of the SFOR
    commitment in former Yugoslavia.
31 BmVg, FüS III, July 1996, appendix 1.

8

Polish Perspectives on Baltic Security

ANTONI Z.KAMIŃSKI

Institute for Political Studies, Polish Academy of Sciences

The fundamental circumstance affecting the thinking of the Polish political elite is that over the last two hundred years Poland has only functioned as an independent state for 28 of them. Partitioned at the end of the eighteenth century, it re-emerged on the maps of Europe in 1918 only to succumb 21 years later to joint German–Soviet aggression. After the Second World War, Poland reappeared having lost an important part of its territory in the east for which it was compensated with a chunk of Germany. In addition, due to the joint efforts of Messrs Hitler and Stalin, it went through an ethnic cleansing that deprived it of most of its minorities.

The lesson drawn from this experience by the Polish political class is that every loss of independence has been the result of a Russian–German conspiracy against the existence of their country. Thus, from the nineteenth century on, all important treatises on the political future of Poland turned around the single topic: how to recover and preserve her independence in the area between Germany and Russia.

The key effect of the eighteenth-century partitions of the Polish–Lithuanian Commonwealth was that they helped Prussia and Russia to become European superpowers, and brought Russia territorially and politically closer to Europe. Re-emergence of Poland after the First World War was greeted by both countries as an insult to their national pride. The Ribbentrop–Molotov Pact was a direct consequence of this attitude.

After the War, the victorious USSR did not have to share Poland with Germany. In 1945 Joseph Stalin informed two Polish communist politicians that 'Russia views Poland as the main War trophy' – interesting treatment of a country which fought Nazi Germany on all fronts during the whole War assisting Soviet Russia, during her most difficult moments, with intelligence and sabotage of Nazi communication and transportation lines. This short historical outline may explain the propensity of Polish politicians for occasional hysterical outbursts, but also explains why Poland is so sensitive on the issue of its security.

Yet, it is evident that the situation that has evolved after the demise of communism exhibits features very different from those of earlier times. Germany does not need supremacy over Poland's territory to be a great power. All it needs instead is a stable and peaceful neighbour. Thus, as long as Germany's strategic interests consist in the desire to erect a stable democratic regime and dynamic market economies in the post-communist world, they will coincide with those of Poland. This affinity of interests is particularly manifest in German support for Poland's membership in the EU and NATO.

To the east of Poland, a string of former Soviet republics have turned into independent states. The three Baltic countries – Lithuania, Latvia, and Estonia, also victims of the Soviet–Nazi conspiracy, regained the sovereignty they had lost during the Second World War. Ukraine which has for centuries aspired to its own statehood saw her dream fulfilled, and Belarus joined in as a free-rider.

These geopolitical alterations imply that, with the exception of the enclave of Kaliningrad, Poland is separated from Russia by a belt of independent states, although this last attribute may no longer apply entirely to Belarus. These states, particularly Belarus and Ukraine, have strong cultural, economic, and historical ties to Russia. But they also have long-standing historical and cultural ties to Poland and to Lithuania. Their independent existence is an important factor contributing as it does to regional stability. Yet, the critical situation of their economies, the weakness of their state structures, and the sorry condition of their societies may cause anxiety as to their future prospects. Unlike the Visegrad Group and the three Baltic republics of the former USSR, Belarus and Ukraine have not yet been able to restructure their foreign trade. (See Kamiñski, Wang and Winters, 1996.) Nor were they able to establish viable political structures, although in this respect Ukraine is way ahead of Belarus.

Russia is in the middle of a deep economic, political, and demographic crisis. It still searches for a new definition of its national identity. For the next decade, at least, it poses no threat of aggression against East-Central Europe. Whatever the intentions of its political class, Russia's economy and population would not be able to sustain a major war. The real question is not whether Russia will engage in a military adventure against its neighbours or not, but rather whether it is ready to address its internal problems in a constructive and pragmatic way, and act as a constructive and reliable partner in regional and world affairs. Looking at Russia's behaviour from the Polish perspective, Moscow chooses at some moments to be a helpful partner, but more often than not it favours the path of a revisionist power keen on subverting all attempts oriented towards regional stabilization. It is only when such attempts are frustrated by external or internal opposition, that it returns to a more moderate strategy. (See, for instance, Rakowska-Harmstone, 1994; Goble, 1993).

Democratic and peaceful Russia will see in the sovereign Ukraine, Belarus, and the Baltic states useful and friendly collaborators; Russia driven by national-imperialist passions perceives them as territories which have once belonged to it and must be recovered, while their populations must be brought back into subjection. Thus, Russia's policies towards the ex-republics of the USSR is a litmus test of its true intentions and political priorities.

Poland's strategic interests in the West involve membership in NATO and the EU.[1] Poland's objectives in the East are similar to those of Germany towards East-Central Europe – the most desired state of affairs in Lithuania, Belarus, Ukraine, and in Russia is an effective democratic consolidation and economic development. A new division of Europe between spheres of influence of adversarial superpowers is definitely against her vital interests.

The Baltic Sea – along with the Mediterranean, the North Sea, and the Black Seas – is one of the water basins around which historically the military conflicts and the ties of cooperation systems of northern Europe evolved.

The countries of the Baltic Sea depend on it for their transportation and economic needs; it serves recreational purposes and, last but not least, it is important from the point of view of their security. And although, as mentioned earlier, a military conflict in the area is at present highly unlikely, such a threat must at least be considered. Thus, the Baltic Sea is an important common pooled resource and security problems of individual members of the 'Baltic community of nations' must be treated seriously by all the others. Some of the problems are acknowledged as such by all parties involved, including those that are highly technical and costly to remedy, like the state of the ecology. Controversies appear only when it comes to decide who is going to pay the bill.

On the other hand, there are also issues that are highly divisive or contain a high destabilization potential. These issues relate mainly to problems connected with the imperial disintegration of the USSR. To this category belongs the problem of the Russian minorities in Estonia, Latvia, and Lithuania – particularly in the first two.[2] Another potential problem with high destabilization potential is posed by the possible role of Kaliningrad in Russian policies towards the region. Both these problem areas are produced by and depend on Moscow's political priorities in the region. Last but not least, another potential threat may result from the failure of liberal-democratic transition efforts in the post-communist world, or in a part of it. This may not be probable in the case of Poland and the three Baltic Republics of the former USSR, but the prospect must not be entirely excluded in the case of Russia, Belarus, and Ukraine.

The reason Belarus is included in this discussion, although it is not a maritime country, is its strategic location between the Baltic Sea (it has common borders with Russia, Latvia, and Lithuania) and the Black Sea areas (Ukraine). Thus, Belarus is an important outpost both on the West–East, and the North–South axes of European politics. The priorities on which Russian–Belarusian cooperation are founded are also a relevant indicator for judging Moscow's intentions.

A lot of space in this paper is devoted to Russia. But, as Bertel Heurlin notices, 'all in all, Russia is the most important factor in the Baltic region – and also the most unpredictable and insecure factor'. I may also agree with his point that 'Russia seems first and foremost to be a threat to itself'. (Heurlin, 1995:73) But if and when the threat becomes a reality, it will affect all other countries in the region, and beyond it.

As to the question of the Russian minority rights in Estonia and Latvia, it is rooted in the history of post-Second World War Europe and Russian responsibility for the crimes of communism. According to the often-voiced Russian position, the population of Russia suffered the most under the communist system. Although, there is no doubt that there were many Russians among the victims of the regime, the first place on the list of victims may surely be disputed by other nationalities. If one accepts the Russian perspective, the whole issue of responsibility becomes blurred. There is some inconsistency, if not dishonesty, in the fact that where material property is concerned, the Russian Federation presents itself as the sole legal successor to the USSR, while it rejects all historical responsibility for the odious crimes of the regime. Yet, in large part, the Russian minority problem in Estonia, Latvia, and Lithuania is rooted in these very crimes. For millions of people conquered or subjected by the USSR, this has been associated with Russian domination, and for millions of Russians the USSR has been one of the most glorious moments in all Russian history. Are they, then, victims or unjustly defeated victors who deserve a special place among nations? This is one of the quagmires of the mental transition to democracy in Russia.

It is possible to take the view that the communist victory in Russia was a combination of circumstantial factors and of certain predilections that are part of the Russian tradition. Also the Ribbentrop–Molotov Pact may be seen as part of this political heritage. The deportations of Estonians and Latvians, the physical elimination of an important part of their intellectual elites, and their replacement by ethnic Russians who had enjoyed special privileges in the two countries had been part of a strategy to establish durable Russian domination in the region. Thus, the Russian Federation has good reason to show itself as more cooperative with and more understanding of the difficulties that the Russian minority poses to the Estonians and Latvians.

The several hundred thousand Russians in Estonia and Latvia cannot be held collectively responsible for the crimes of the USSR. The problem of their fate is a very complicated one. The great majority of them should be allowed to stay in the countries where they live possibly enjoying full legal rights. Also the interest shown by the Russian government in their fate seems natural. There is, however, the question of the motive.

If one assumes that these motives are honest and straightforward, which would be rather difficult in the case of the Latvians and Estonians, then the fate of Russians in the Baltic states, would be solved in a cooperative analytical way: the governments would try to understand each other's position and make an effort to find a compromise. The truth is that the Russian side has not shown much good-will in addressing the controversy. It has found recourse most often to threats and blackmail.

An alternative proposition assumes that the Russian government does not care much about the fate of these minorities. One reason why it must speak on its behalf is related to internal politics: the government wants to neutralize its opponents. Another explanation is that Russia may be treating the minority issue as a handy instrument for, apparently legitimate, interference in the internal matters of the two states of the 'near abroad'. There are grounds to assume that influential forces in Russia represent this approach, particularly when, while representatives of the Russian government complained about the treatment of the Russian minorities in the two states, thousands of ethnic Russians were perishing at the hands of Russian soldiers in Chechnya, and while in other places in Russia the rights of its citizens are brutally violated.

Among the elements of Russian presence in the Baltic region the role of Kaliningrad has been of particular relevance. Kaliningrad is the product of the division of Eastern Prussia between Poland and the RSFSR after the Second World War. The *oblast* was turned during the Cold War into a military fortress. Russia's designs in regard to the *oblast* were initially rather unclear. After 1989, it served as a transit point for the troops removed from Germany, Lithuania, and later Poland. Thus, the numbers of troops, amount and type of weapons and equipment stationed in Kaliningrad have varied. Moreover, there have been persistent rumours that Russia is storing tactical nuclear weapons in Kaliningrad.

The demise of the USSR, and the end of the Cold War started serious debates about the future of the area. One option, represented among others by the former chief of the *oblast* administration, Yurii Matochkin, saw the future of the region as a free-trade area, with much administrative autonomy, cooperating closely with its neighbours and Germany. Another orientation, represented chiefly by the military and nationalist forces, thought that the region should retain its primarily military character.

Poland, for obvious reasons, has showed from the beginning an interest in the economic development of Kaliningrad supporting, therefore, the first option. On 6 September 1992, the Polish–Kaliningrad Round Table was held to discuss prospects for economic, political, cultural, educational, and scientific cooperation. The Agreement was signed by the deputy prime ministers of Poland and Russia.[3] A strong expansion of trade between Poland and Kaliningrad *oblast*, and creation of a large number of joint ventures with Polish capital registered in Kaliningrad followed. Polish capital investments in the *oblast* remain, however, pretty insignificant. The main reason for unwillingness to invest is an inefficient institutional infrastructure: the legal status of the region has changed several times from one presidential decree to another, the level of taxes and custom duties is high, law enforcement is ineffective and criminality high, administration is arbitrary and unpredictable, and penetrated by the mafia. The militarization of the region is still very high. The defeat of the reform-minded Yuri Matochkin by the more conservative candidate, Leonid Gorbienko, has contributed to the uncertainty.

The economic and social problems of Kaliningrad are as critical as those existing in other regions of the Russian Federation. They are additionally amplified by the militarized character of the region. Officers stationed there have not been paid their salaries for months, the food that the soldiers receive is inadequate in quality and quantity, and the armed forces are demoralized. Wives of officers reallocated to the region stand no prospect of finding a job.

Finally, there is the psychological problem of life in an exclave. Until the end of 1991, the *oblast* had been part of the unified territory of the Soviet Union. The demise of the USSR means that to get from Kaliningrad to Russia by train or car a person must cross Lithuania (or Poland) and Belarus. The progressive integration of Belarus and Russia somewhat changes the situation. Yet, the region remains an enclave. At the end of 1996, Presidents Yeltsin and Lukashenka asked Poland to agree to the construction of an extraterritorial connection linking Belarus and Kaliningrad. The connection would consist of a highway, a railway, gas and oil pipelines. That would also mean that Poland would be deprived of a common border with Lithuania.[4] The request has been repeated several times by both governments. It also became a slogan in the May 1st parade in Kaliningrad. One of the members of the Russian Duma accused the Polish government during the meeting of the Council of Europe, held at the beginning of June 1997, of a 'gross violation of international law' for opposing the proposal. All this suggests that we do not know whether Kaliningrad may become in the future an important centre contributing to Baltic cooperation, or whether it will remain a constant source of instability and anxiety for its neighbours.

Belarus has no direct access to the Baltic, yet it has common borders with four states of the Baltic Sea basin: Poland, Lithuania, Latvia, and Russia. Unlike Ukraine, Belarus has not made any effort to achieve economic and political sustainability. It has been governed by the political circles of the *ancien régime*. Its first prime minister, Mr Kiebich, before he assumed his political function had been a director in an armaments factory. During the presidential elections in 1994 he lost to a former director of a *kolkhoz*, Mr Lukashenka. Already during the controversy over the signing of the Tashkent Agreement in 1993, the motives of the move were clearly specified. The Belarusian political class, dominated by the old nomenclature, which opposed all democratic and market reforms, intended to trade national sovereignty for Russia's political support and economic subsidies in the form of cheap fuel and energy. These designs were opposed by Moscow reformers who realized that a closer integration with Belarus would mean a heavy financial burden for Russia, and would strengthen forces opposed to the liberal-democratic reforms. Thus, when President Yeltsin decided to proceed with an integration of the two countries, Yegor Gaidar, deputy prime minister for economic policies in the FR government, resigned in December 1994, giving this change in policy as one of the most important reasons for the step.

Alexander Lukashenka's victory in the Belarusian presidential elections, and Yeltsin's efforts to present himself to the Russian public as a staunch nationalist, resulted in an intensification of the process. Lukashenka has become not only the closest ally of the Russian nationalists, but also the only ally of Yeltsin in Belarus. According to the report on corruption presented on 20 December 1994 by Serhey Antonchik, the deputy to the Supreme Soviet of Belarus, Russian companies contributed heavily to Lukashenka's electoral campaign. Meanwhile, the economy of Belarus has kept declining faster than the economies of its neighbours, Ukraine and Russia.

By unconditionally accepting Belarusian initiatives Russia has given support to the anti-reformist forces. In exchange for the support and subsidies, Moscow obtained the political military integration of the country with Russia. The first decisive steps towards this end were made at the beginning of January 1995 in the agreements signed by the deputy prime minister of Russia, Aleksey Bolshakov, and the prime minister of Belarus, Mihail Czahir. The agreement specified the conditions under which Russia could use the military facilities in Belarus for the next 25 years. The two countries established a customs union. Over a month later, in February 1995, Boris Yeltsin paid a visit to Minsk to sign a number of agreements on military collaboration between the two states. From then on the Russian army took over the task of guarding the borders of Belarus with Lithuania, Poland and Ukraine. The last step towards the integration of Belarus and Russia has been the Unification Agreement, which however does not imply full integration – they still remain as two separate, albeit closely interlinked, states.

Meanwhile, President Lukashenka has dissolved the Supreme Soviet creating a bogus parliament not different from that of the communist period. He dissolved the Electoral Committee, and the Constitutional Tribunal. The government of Belarus has been deprived of any real authority. All important decisions are made now at the President's Chancellery. The only independent medium of communication is through Russian TV programmes. All other media operate under close political control. The President's collaborators are involved in illegal operations. But this does not matter much when only the President decides what is legal and what is not. Human rights are not respected. That is the image projected by Belarus to the outside world.

From the point of view of Belarus's neighbours the fact of the Union between Russia and Belarus is less important than the circumstances under which it was established. The problem, widely noticed by the Russian liberal press, is that the integration may hamper the consolidation of democracy and the rule of law in Russia as well as slow down economic recovery. The priority given to military interest in the process of integration, which had in fact preceded the decision to enlarge NATO, as well as provocative moves by Mr Lukashenka both internationally and inside Belarus, suggests that Belarus can become an instrument of regional instability. Moreover, Alexander Lukashenka may have a stake in amplifying international tensions to justify the anti-democratic measures and brutal repression of the opposition in his country.

Finally, the weakness of political and economic institutions in Russia, Belarus, and also Ukraine poses another threat to their neighbours and, more generally, to European stability. It has been remarked that behind the formal façade of democratic institutions, there is the reality of informal connections and mafia-type conspiracies that determine the content of political life in Russia.[5] These informal structures have a tendency to spread undermining the process of political and economic consolidation in other post-communist states. (See Sherr, 1995). It is connected with the flow of crime and corruption coming from the East. Even official intergovernmental contacts are not free from it. This factor makes large-scale cooperation with Russia difficult and risky. There is the additional problem of the permeability of national borders to migrants from Asia and Africa. Thus, if these tendencies prove stronger than efforts to build democratic and market institutions, the key concern of the East-Central Europeans – the extension of political and economic stability eastward – may be thwarted.

The examples mentioned above show that the 'Russian threat' does exist, although its nature is not chiefly military. Some of the dominant circles in Russian politics are depressed by the loss of the empire and seek to regain it by opposing, through political pressure and internal subversion, direct integration of the former dependencies into the world economy. This is indicated by the above-mentioned support provided by Moscow to Alexander Lukashenka, the close relationship it maintains with Prime Minister Meciar's government in Slovakia and President Milosevic's regime in Serbia, as well as with Bulgarian communists until their defeat in the last parliamentary elections. It is also evident in Russian behaviour in the Caucasus and in Central Asia.[6]

The major objective for Russia's neighbours is to engage the country in constructive regional cooperation.[7] This may be possible only when Moscow decides to treat them as partners and not as objects of new imperial designs. Although some changes in the Russian approach to East-Central Europe may be noticed, by and large Moscow's position remains hard to decipher and predict.[8] The paranoid disjunction between internal democratization and market reforms in Russia accompanied by the support for anti-democratic and anti-market forces in other post-communist countries must cause anxiety among the ex-satellites and the ex-republics of the former Soviet Union in the Baltic region.

Although Russia remains the major security concern of Poland in the Baltic Sea region, it is not the sole one. The security concerns of contemporary governments go far beyond the danger of military aggression or political instability. The regional institution that covers the non-military security concerns of the Baltic states, although it also has implications for military security, is the Council of the Baltic Sea States.[9] Its interests involve: support for the new democratic institutions, economic and technical assistance, protection of the Baltic Sea ecosystem, transportation and communication, tourism and cultural contacts, and so on.

Poland, like other formerly communist states, has heavily contributed to the sorry ecological state of the Sea. The communist regimes had downgraded all such concerns. Nonetheless, awareness of the role and importance of the Baltic basin as a common pooled resource had preceded the fall of communism. Poland organized, in 1973, one of the first conferences on fisheries and the state of the Baltic Sea biosystem. Also, with Swedish support, she initiated the conference of prime ministers of the Baltic states in Ronneby, in 1990. Poland has been intensely engaged in regional cooperation and supported the establishment of the CBSS, in March 1992, in Copenhagen.[10]

There are many factors that make multilateral cooperation in the Baltic Sea Region relevant from the Polish perspective. Firstly, it provides a forum to discuss issues connected with the exploitation of the Baltic Sea. Secondly, it brings together EU member-states (Denmark, Germany, Finland, and Sweden), NATO members (Denmark, Germany, and Norway), with countries aspiring to join these organizations, or developing close ties but not showing a desire to join (Russia). Thus, it helps to build bridges across the lines of a potential European divide. Thirdly, it brings together in a multilateral setting the two sources of Polish worry of the last two centuries – Germany and Russia. If Germany is no longer such a source, and belongs to the group of countries with the biggest stake in the preservation of European stability – Russia continues to be a threat. Fourthly, the CBSS offers a platform for discussion of the problems arising between Russia and Estonia, Latvia, and Lithuania. Hence, some of the most serious bilateral tensions can be discussed within a multilateral setting.[11] Furthermore, it has been designed as a setting for cooperation which means that there is an emphasis on consensus, as defection of one or more participants can bring the whole system to a halt. Last but not least, the CBSS has proven to be a relatively effective working concern, unlike some other regional groupings of this kind.

In conclusion, the CBSS provides a platform for discussion, and possibly help to solve some of the key Polish security questions deriving from uncertainty concerning Russian regional policies. It offers the possibility of removing differences of view between Russia, on the one hand, and Estonia and Latvia, on the other, from the realm of bilateral relations, and addressing them within a multilateral setting. The problem of the future role of Kaliningrad, whether it is going to remain primarily a military stronghold or an important centre for regional co-operation, is of relevance not only to Poland but to all other actors in the area. Therefore, the CBSS offers a proper framework in which to discuss some of the controversies arising from this dilemma. It is also important to note, that functioning within a multilateral framework is a source of constraints upon the internal freedom of manoeuvre of governments. As the major problem for societies in transition is institutional weakness, that is, the weakness of constraints imposed on political actors, the supranational institutions, by giving additional support to internal constitutional constraints, help the transition.

NOTES

1 On the Polish position on NATO enlargement see Ananicz, Grudziński, Olechowski, Onyszkiewicz, Skubiszewski and Szlajfer (1995).

2 On Poland's relations with these three countries see Kolecka (1996).

3 The problem of the role of Kaliningrad became an issue even during the Roundtable. I participated in the sessions on educational and scientific co-operation. During the discussion on the future of the 'European Immanuel Kant University in Kaliningrad, the Rector of the University said that the main function of the 'European' University should be to support expansion of Russian cultural and political aspirations in Lithuania, Latvia and Estonia. He did not want to accept that such a narrowly nationalistic mission might not have been compatible with the 'European' status of his University, while being an insult to the memory of its patron.

4 An interesting solution to this problem has been presented by N. Koptiev. Poland and Lithuania could maintain contacts through tunnels or viaducts built under or over the 2km wide Russian linking system (*Kaliningradskaya Pravda*, 12 Dec. 1996).

5 See the appraisal of the Russian political scene by Anna Ostapchuk and Yevgenyi Krasnikov, 'The Time of Turmoil in the Kremlin', *Moskovskiye Novosti*, no. 77, 5–12 Nov. 1995; Thomas Graham, 'The New Russian Regime', *Niezavisimaya Gazeta*, no. 124, 23 Nov. 1995.

6 An excellent discussion of Russian policies in these areas has been provided by Blank (1995).

7 The position represented by the Polish government on this point does not differ from that of Blackwill, Braithwaite and Tanaka (1995).

8 One of the first such signs was the article by Sergey Kortunov, 'Russia Rediscovers Central Europe for Itself', *Nezavisimaya Gazeta*, no. 112, 2 Nov. 1995.

9 Pertti Joenniemi and Carl-Einar Stålvant remark that 'No reference is made to the subject (of security – AZK) in the statutes of the CBSS. On the other hand, the absence of institutional and formal recognition does not mean that such issues do not exist.' Joenniemi and Stålvant (1995: 30). They also give an interesting discussion on the ways the security concerns are expressed within the framework of the CBSS (pp. 30-31).

10 On the Polish government's policy towards Baltic cooperation in general and the Council of the Baltic Sea States in particular, see Bernatowicz (1995).

11 Joenniemi and Stålvant correctly remark that 'As a recently developed institution where direct cooperation with, and the participation of, Russia is a crucial element, the CBSS is valuable both as a token of Russia's commitment to regional development and as a vehicle for the promotion of stability. In addition, Baltic Sea transnational dynamism spills over into its western provinces, adding new dimensions to their path of development. In particular, the future of Kaliningrad *oblast* appears to depend on regional and joint efforts.' Joenniemi and Stålvant (1995: 37).

9

Sweden and the Baltic Sea Region – Activism on a New Arena or the End of Free-Riding?

ANN-SOFIE DAHL
The Swedish Atlantic Council

THE BALTIC SEA REGION AFTER THE COLD WAR

The Baltic Sea region rapidly attracted world attention when it became evident in the mid-1990s that an enlargement of NATO which excluded the three vulnerable Baltic states might place them in a strategically risky *grey zone* which could affect the stability of all of Europe. To Sweden, modern interest in the Baltic Sea region dates back to the final years of bipolarity but intensified as the end of the Cold War brought a sense of increased instability, rather than, as was the case on the Central Front, a dramatically improved sense of stability on the Northern Flank. But only as the possible consequences of NATO enlargement was debated did Nordic concern for developments on the eastern shore of the Baltic Sea become fully appreciated by actors outside the region such as NATO.

The Baltic Sea region also became the scene of a profound change of direction of Swedish security and foreign policy in the 1990s. After decades when foreign policy focus was quite exclusively set on the Third World, Swedish ambitions to play an active role as a regional power in the Baltic Sea region in the post-Cold War era are reminiscent of the country's glorious past as a European great power, only this time the means and goals are of a more peaceful nature. Swedish hopes to play the role of a regional leader were obvious in the 1996 creation of the *Baltic Sea Council*, assembling representatives of all the countries around the Sea in an effort to co-ordinate and discuss economic, social, environmental, and political assistance to the three Baltic countries. Relations with Sweden's neighbours were adjusted to fit the new policy. While Sweden aspires to co-ordinate policies with Finland, old sentiments of (this time friendly) rivalry have been evoked in relations with Denmark. In addition, Sweden has made some attempts to attract

Germany to a more active role in the region. However, concern about Russian reactions to developments in the region tends to influence every aspect of Swedish activity in the Baltic Sea region. As has historically been the perspective emanating from Stockholm, Russia continues in the late 1990s to be viewed as a neighbour with which it is urgent to uphold a constructive dialogue and involve in extensive forms of cooperation; criticism voiced against plans to enlarge NATO emanated from this uneasiness with anything which might be interpreted as even mildly provocative to Moscow.

How did this complete and highly significant turnabout of Swedish policy to a regional focus evolve in the post-Cold War era? What consequences could this policy have, for the region as well as for Sweden? How does the future look for this new and dynamic approach to regional security?

TWO TRADITIONS IN SWEDISH POLICY

During the many years of Social Democratic tenure in the government complex *Rosenbad* (but to a somewhat lesser extent during the non-Socialist governments in 1976–82, and in particular, 1991–94) modern Swedish foreign policy has relied on two, seemingly contradictory, traditions: international activism and isolationism. While an active stance has been applied to matters of foreign policy, security policy has traditionally been guided by an isolationist ambition to maintain a certain aloofness to the outside world. The modern version of the doctrine of neutrality was born of a desire to remain unattached to both power blocs which dominated and divided the world during close to fifty years. In reality, the credibility of the supposedly independent position has been severely tarnished by the pattern of close cooperation which the Swedish government has entertained with NATO and a number of its individual countries ever since the late 1940s, contacts which were officially documented in 1994 after years of suspicions (SOU, 1994: 11).

The official stance of neutrality, and the parallel policy of international activism in foreign affairs which accompanied it – primarily in the Third World – were closely connected, almost inseparable. While the activist foreign policy conceptually and ideologically arose from that independent third role between the superpowers which only neutrality could offer, the neutral security policy in turn required an active element for its moral and political justification (Nilsson, 1991).

The end of the Cold War brought an end to any claims to a third role, now that the superpower community had been reduced by one and no ideological conflict existed in which to maintain a neutral posture. Though the label on the Swedish doctrine was changed from 'neutrality' to 'nonalignment' (which was as a matter of fact always the legally correct terminology in peacetime) in the early 1990s, the ambition to provide an independent policy remains well and alive. The same can be said for the activist stance, though today it is implemented not in the jungles of the Third World but in the 'near abroad' in the Baltic region which has seen a dynamic Swedish performance since the end of the Cold War. In addition, the openness with which cooperation with NATO today is exercised is nothing short of unique in modern Swedish history. As a Partnership for Peace (PFP) country – and one of the first to sign up – and in Bosnia, Swedish contacts with NATO are carried out on such a cordial basis, and the importance of the transatlantic link is emphasized so regularly by the Swedish government, that the suspicion has been voiced that this may all be part of a grand scheme to gradually change Swedish security doctrine without provoking much attention.

Considering this apparent dichotomy of Swedish policy, it is necessary to ask whether the activist policy which we witness today in the Baltic Sea region is just activist business as usual, though performed on a new arena, or a new security doctrine in the making? And in that case, would such a change imply that the end of Swedish activism – in the Baltic and elsewhere – is approaching as rapidly? In other words, is the assumption correct that an activist policy can only be combined with a nonaligned security doctrine?

Activism is seen here as primarily a means to uphold and exercise an internationalist ambition, be it *universalist* or *particularist* in character; in other words, to aspire to better the world in an altruistic sense, or the efforts of a particular state to expose itself on the international scene in order to gain international recognition for its own country or its politicians (Goldmann and Boréus, 1990: 124–5).

THE APPLICATION OF TWO TRADITIONS IN THE BALTIC REGION

The Evolution of Swedish Policy in the Baltic Sea Region

After decades of concentrating on the Third World and development problems as they appeared there from the often anti-American perspective of a neutral country claiming to occupy the position of a third force between the superpowers, it took a few years after the fall of the Berlin Wall for Swedish policy to adjust to new realities. When the decision was taken to apply for membership in what was then the European Community (after years of arguing that this was inconceivable for a neutral country), and the actual application was handed in, in the summer of 1991, it was for example not the result of a redirection of Swedish foreign policy but the combination of economic necessities and domestic politics.

Though the Baltic region emerged as one which would increasingly be demanding the world's attention as the Cold War drew to a close, the then-Social Democratic government reacted quite hesitantly to developments in the neighbourhood. Only when the weekly solidarity demonstrations for Baltic freedom from Soviet oppression on *Norrmalmstorg* in central Stockholm had been organized every Monday for months by a group of activist non-Socialists did representatives of the then-government start to attend. Though this was a region with which it had little experience, the government quickly put the three vulnerable Baltic countries high on the list of priorities (*Svenska Dagbladet*, 28 January 1991). It remains at the top of the list as the end of the century approaches.

A difference in perspective was nevertheless evident between the non-Socialist opposition, which could present a long history of interest and engagement for the Baltic cause, and the government which still had to learn the vocabulary of the new trade. The statement by then-foreign minister Sten Andersson when visiting Estonia in 1989 that this Baltic country was not the victim of occupation was in a sense symbolic of the unfamiliar perspective with which the government was confronted in the region (Küng, 1990).

As the non-Socialist coalition replaced the Social Democrats in power after the 1991 election, the turn of focus to what could be seen as also a Swedish 'near abroad' was definite. Solidarity with the three small and vulnerable Baltic states was ideologically driven, as well as a logic of the new government's ambition to 'Europeanize' the content and direction of Swedish politics in anticipation of EU membership. The Bildt government received international praise when the Soviet Union pulled out of the Baltic countries as a result of direct Swedish involvement, which engaged the Prime Minister personally, proving in the process once again that activism was obviously not a solely Social Democratic phenomenon (Bildt, 1994).

A number of factors coincided in the decision of the Bildt government to remove the neutral label on Swedish security doctrine in favour of an expressly nonaligned one (Dahl, 1997a). Always the result of a slightly incorrect vocabulary, neutrality emerged as a somewhat outdated label in the new international system now dominated by only one superpower. Consequently, the new non-Socialist government abandoned the concept of neutrality in the 1991/1992 Defence Bill, which however subtly stated that 'no one else defends Sweden, and Sweden only defends itself' (*Defence Bill*, 1991/1992, p. 102). Apart from a consequence of unipolarity, the step to remove neutrality and instead use nonalignment as the official label also represented a desire by the new government to emphasize that Swedish nonalignment was only a matter of military, not ideological, non-cooperation. That Sweden now saw itself as part of Western Europe had been evident since the EU application was submitted in 1991, and even more so when membership was formally accepted by the Swedish population, although with a tiny margin, in the referendum three years later.

The new formulation in which nonalignment was emphasized and neutrality removed had particular relevance in the Baltic region, which in addition contributed to provoking the change in the first place by providing Sweden with a next-door security problem. Since Swedish nonalignment excluded any possibility of extending security guarantees across the Baltic Sea (or anywhere else), military support could only be extended indirectly, for example through delivery of surplus matériel and the training of military officers. Support to the Baltic countries was co-ordinated with the Nordic neighbours as Sweden signed up for the Partnership for Peace programme in 1994, which has ever since been utilized as the main instrument to serve national interests in the region and in which Sweden, with long-time peace-keeping expertize, prides itself on being a *security-producer* rather than consumer. Another important aspect of the package has been Swedish assistance to facilitate Baltic participation in joint Nordic–Baltic peace-keeping activities. Regardless of government, Sweden has from the very beginning been a strong and determined supporter of the joint peacekeeping ventures which multiplied during the 1990s, such as the joint battalion in Bosnia BALTBAT, or the various Nordic initiatives resulting in BALTRON, BALTSEA, and BALTNET.

In addition, even though Sweden still 'only defended Sweden' Prime Minister Bildt declared that he found it hard to believe that Sweden would just sit idly by as a passive observer if the three small and vulnerable countries to the east were attacked or seriously threatened. The new wording emphasizing nonalignment was an indication to Russia that Sweden should not be expected to quietly observe an unfavourable development in the region, though exactly which means the country would apply in a crisis remained highly uncertain. In a speech at the Swedish Institute of International Affairs Bildt provocatively stated that he had difficulty 'regarding neutrality as a likely choice for Sweden in the kind of conflicts in our neighbourhood which we might imagine today,' since 'neutrality sets very narrow terms on what we can do, primarily in political terms, to help neighbouring countries which need our support. And I do not believe that either our own interests or the views of the Swedish people on the requirements of common decency would favour such a narrow approach' (address on 17 November 1993).

The return of the Social Democrats to power in the election of 1994, preceding a national referendum on EC membership in November the same year, brought about a return of a more traditional approach to security. Assisted by the neutralist Centre Party, one of four parties in the previous non-Socialist government which now acted as support group to the Social Democrats, the new government abandoned the expressly nonaligned line which the country had adhered to during the past few years, in favour of a traditional policy of neutrality. During the rather brief tenure of then-Prime Minister Ingvar Carlsson, neutrality was for all practical purposes restored as the description of Swedish security doctrine.

Yet another change of guard in March of 1996, as Göran Persson ascended to prime ministerial power following Ingvar Carlsson's voluntary retirement, marks the beginning of another approach to security policy; this time again in a bolder and more independent direction compared to the one immediately preceding. The soft spot which Persson quickly developed for the Baltic Sea region as an arena where Sweden – and its prime minister – could play a role soon became apparent. Suffering from limited experience of the complex world of foreign and security policy, Göran Persson rapidly made headlines for his frank comments in support of Baltic membership in NATO (a declaration which caused the Foreign Ministry, which had successfully avoided the tricky issue of NATO enlargement thus far, some trouble to explain). Persson's declaration that he regarded Baltic security as 'a Swedish cause' constituted yet another exceptional statement for the prime minister of a nonaligned country which for a century and a half had based its security doctrine on a policy of noncommitment towards the surrounding world (the statement was cited for example in *Svenska Dagbladet*, 4 June 1996 and 28 August 1996).

Still, it was evident that Persson's attachment to the Baltic cause by nonaligned necessity only included a moral, political, and economic – but not a military – position. Instead, the government maintains a Swedish tradition by being a great believer and a strong advocate of the many opportunities offered by *soft security*. Proof of this adherence to a wide definition of security is a number of initiatives in the Baltic Sea region, such as efforts to provide environmental support and assistance to fight crime, aid to promote economic and democratic development, and so on, to the countries east of the Sea, investing a grand total of a billion Swedish kronor to this project (the so-called 'Baltic Sea billion'). Continuing the programme started by the non-Socialist government, assistance has thus been provided in a comprehensive package of various kinds of aid in order to assist the three vulnerable countries in their efforts to uphold their fragile sovereignty

With Persson, and following the Bildt legacy, the Baltic Sea region confirmed its key position in Swedish security and foreign policy. The

Baltic Sea region, and the security problems emanating from that region, became Sweden's number one priority in the early 1990s and maintains that position as solidly as ever at the end of the decade, century, and millennium. It seems highly unlikely that it would be removed from that central role in Swedish policy in the foreseeable future, as the region's position within the European security architecture, and its organizations, is being chiselled out.

Sweden shares this interest in the Baltic Sea region with its Nordic neighbours which all turned their attention east as Cold War stability was replaced by post-Cold War instability on the Northern flank. It is interesting to note the sense of rivalry which has developed within the community of Nordic countries, all yearning for international praise for their various activities in the region. Praise emanating from Washington, DC seemed particularly appreciated. In this pursuit, they were joined by the American ambassadors to Stockholm and Copenhagen who engaged in an intense competition to convince President Clinton that the particular country where they were stationed was the one worthy of a presidential visit following the Madrid summit in July 1997. In that intra-Nordic competition which Sweden eventually lost to Denmark, Sweden cherished the relative advantage granted by the initiative for a Baltic Sea Council, a result of the summer 1996 summit in Visby on the Baltic island of Gotland which attracted substantial international interest and attention (*Dagens Nyheter*, 3–5 May 1996). The friendly conversation which Prime Minister Persson had with President Clinton that same summer also added to the Swedish sense of a special role in the Baltic in spite of the President's choice of itinerary a year later (the visit by Persson was covered by the two main daily papers, *Svenska Dagbladet* and *Dagens Nyheter* on 7 August 1996).

The Baltic Region from the Perspective of Swedish Activism

Since it was first begun in a modern fashion in the 1960s as a result of the direct involvement and passionate engagement of then still-to-be Prime Minister Olof Palme, Swedish activism has primarily been directed at issues and arenas far from the Nordic region. With the notable exception of initiatives for nuclear-free zones in Europe, the activist perspective was mostly applied to Third World areas and problems. An extensive development aid programme, efforts and offers to mediate regional conflicts in Africa and Latin America, and disarmament proposals, were the main ingredients of Swedish activist policy performed through the Nonaligned Movement, multilaterally through the UN, or individually as a country. The activist ambitions of this small and nonaligned country had thus a decisively global perspective (Nilsson, 1991).

As the bipolar system disappeared almost overnight with the demise of the Soviet Union and the Warsaw Pact, the Swedish activist policy, based on an independent role between the competing blocs, immediately suffered. With only one surviving superpower – the introduction of a unipolar system – the claim to represent an ideological and economic 'Third Way' lost most, if not all, credibility, as did any attempts to continue a 'neutral' line of policy. 'Neutral between what?' critics repeatedly asked, gaining further support as Sweden definitely confirmed its position in the Western camp by joining the European Union in 1995.

At that point, the entire direction of Swedish policy had once and seemingly for all time moved away from far-away continents and conflicts. Instead, attention was turned towards Europe, where Sweden was now a proud – if, from the perspective of the popular view, at times somewhat reluctant – partner, and to the regional neighbourhood where instability on the eastern part of the Baltic had been on the rise since the end of the Cold War. The first few years after the collapse of the Berlin Wall may be characterized as the 'European' years in Swedish politics, a period when close to every part of the political process was somehow adjusted to the expected membership in the European Union. Interest in the Baltic region was already substantial before the actual demise of the Soviet Union but escalated from the mid-1990s onwards, coinciding more or less with the entrance into the Union (which apparently lost its attraction to the Swedish population once membership was gained).

Relatively little attention has since been paid to European matters; only when criticized – as it is quite frequently – does the EU make an appearance now in the Swedish media and debate. One telling example was the very scarce coverage received on questions related to the 1996 Intergovernmental Conference – the 'Maastricht II' process – and the Common Foreign and Security Policy (CFSP). The Swedish approach to the IGC was criticized for lacking preparedness and engagement (for example in *Sydsvenska Dagbladet*, 23 January 1997). Yet another reason for complaint among Sweden's partners on the continent surfaced when the government (following a debate within the Social Democratic Party) in May of 1997 chose to opt out of the process for membership in the European Monetary Union, a legally speaking complicated position for a country which had signed all parts of the Maastricht agreement.

A similar fate descended upon the WEU, which attracted a sudden surge of attention – most of it undoubtedly long overdue, considering the lack of interest paid and information accumulated during the Cold War – in the early 1990s, as Swedish EC membership was debated. Towards the mid-1990s, interest in the WEU dramatically faded, and was replaced to some extent by NATO whose plans to enlarge provoked more interest at that time. How the process of enlargement could affect Swedish security through the Baltic region was, however, an issue which primarily interested the community of security experts. Curious to note, considering this lack of interest in matters European, was the result of the survey conducted by the *National Board of Psychological Defence* in 1996 which showed the hitherto unseen numbers of 61 per cent of those polled in favour of Swedish participation in European defence, while 42 per cent responded favourably to the idea of closer contacts with NATO, and 68 per cent to Swedish participation in the PFP-programme (*Opinion- 96*).

PFP not only comes across as the most popular form of cooperation as judged by the Swedish public, but is also by far the government's preferred instrument in the area of security policy. This has been evident both in the Baltic Sea as well as in the part of Europe which dominated world attention in the 1990s: the former Yugoslavia, and Bosnia in particular. However, the transfer from UN to NATO command in Bosnia resulted in surprisingly limited interest in Sweden in spite of the wide-ranging practical and political consequences for its nonaligned forces which experienced a historical moment when donning NATO berets. Oddly enough, considering the sensitivity which accompanies all matters related to NATO in Sweden, that moment passed without creating any major reactions among the population or the media. Both extensive and intensive, Swedish involvement in the UN, IFOR and SFOR forces in the former Yugoslavia testified to the country's eagerness not to be left on the outside when the European map was being redrawn as well as to the realization of the significance of the transatlantic link, in practice as well as in theory.

Swedish awareness of the importance of that link for national and European security is evident in the regular emphasis which the Foreign Minister, Lena Hjelm-Wallén, places on relations across the Atlantic (Dahl, 1997b). An interesting aspect of the new activism, as performed in the Baltic region as well as in, for example, Bosnia, is how geared it is to meet American approval and support. For a country whose international image had a distinct anti-American tilt for a number of years, or even decades, this is truly a new ingredient to its policy. Swedish activism at the end of the decade is, thus, performed *with* the Americans, and in an effort to promote American interests, which is quite a dramatic change from previous years when the activist programme consisted mainly of opposition to American policy, though labelled as a 'Third Way' to the bipolar division.

The new transatlantic company that Sweden actively seeks when engaging in world affairs is therefore no minor step away from the content and direction which previously characterized the activist ambition. While Sweden may be a member of the EU, it is a reluctant one and a much more enthusiastic partner of the United States than of its neighbours on the Continent. As somebody cleverly put it during the EU campaign, it would indeed have been much easier to convince the in many ways highly Americanized Swedish population to join the United States than the EC, had that been at all possible. This is particularly novel policy for a Social Democratic government such as the one headed by Göran Persson (while much less enigmatic when performed by non-Socialist governments such as the one led by Carl Bildt in 1991–94). Also for the Prime Minister, whose party has a long tradition of anti-American rhetoric and criticism – as particularly evident during the Vietnam war – the United States occupies a very central position in Swedish policy in the late 1990s. No doubt, the conversation which Prime Minister Persson had with President Clinton in August of 1996 represented a cherished peak in the Prime Minister's career as well as in Swedish diplomacy. Just as the war in Vietnam provided former Prime Minister Olof Palme with an opportunity to enter the international scene, the sensitive situation in the Baltic Sea region offered an opening for Göran Persson to create an activist niche and an international role of his own.

The emphasis on transatlantic security which the Foreign Minister regularly puts in her speeches does, however, not exclude a continued concern about Nordic–Russian relations. In spite of the evident transatlantic interest, the security policy performed by the Social Democratic government is representative of a traditional 'Russia first' policy which has generally characterized Swedish policy over the past few centuries. The Social Democratic government eagerly anticipated the conclusion of the NATO–Russian Charter in Brussels in the summer of 1997, which was seen as indicating that Russian opposition to the enlargement process had been brought under control. The integration of a democratic, and economically stable, Russia into European structures as a means of facilitating peaceful cohabitation in the neighbourhood as well as generally in the international system, continues to be a very central Swedish ambition.

THE BALTIC REGION FROM THE PERSPECTIVE OF FUTURE SWEDISH SECURITY POLICY:

Activism and Non-alignment

Could all this be seen as proof of a new direction not only in Swedish activism but also in the country's security doctrine, away from nonalignment? If that is the case, then a basic underlying idea cherished and often voiced by the government is actually being challenged. Many high-ranking Social Democrats in particular (as well as politicians on the centre-left of the ideological spectra) are firm believers in the idea that only nonalignment enables a country to engage in an activist foreign policy. Thus, were Sweden to exchange its nonaligned security doctrine for alliance membership, the activist stance which has become a Swedish trademark – whether in the Third World or in the Baltic – would seriously suffer, it is argued, perhaps to the extent where it would have to be discontinued. Though this perception of allied life could quite easily be falsified – a quick glance at the foreign policies of activist, yet allied, European neighbours such as Denmark, Norway, and the Netherlands would suffice – it is indeed very firmly planted within the Social Democratic movement. Contrary to those neighbours, for whom NATO provides one of several fora for policy initiatives albeit undoubtedly the most effective one, Sweden has had to focus on the OSCE and the United Nations, which have in addition exerted a considerable amount of ideological attraction for Social Democratic governments (in particular the UN).

Crucial to this perception is the *particularist* concern that a no-longer nonaligned Sweden would lose that special niche, or role, which activism supposedly grants the country (Goldmann and Boréus, 1990). One prominent representative of this view is the Prime Minister himself, arguing on the very topic of Baltic security that only nonalignment would allow Sweden to play an independent, and thus, according to this view, effective role there and elsewhere. A similar argument was presented by the Foreign Minister when she met with NATO's secretary general, Javier Solana, during his official visit to Stockholm in October 1996 (for example in *Svenska Dagbladet* on 31 October 1996). Whether or not policy in the Baltic Sea is interpreted as indicating an emerging change of doctrine depends to some extent on the significance granted this particular perception of the linkage between security and foreign policies. Its importance as a very central Social Democratic belief should in any case not be underestimated, just as the immense pride surrounding the Swedish (and primarily Social Democratic) internationalist – and activist – tradition should not be.

Though indeed a strong one, this is, however, not the only current sign in support of a continued nonaligned policy. The Bildt declaration that 'Sweden only defends Sweden' (from which Bildt appears to be gradually distancing himself at the end of the 1990s) may not be altogether true in the time and age when Swedish soldiers carry NATO-helmets when upholding peace in Bosnia, but it is an accurate expression of what appears to be a national desire not to engage in any activities even remotely resembling an Article Five commitment. The many years of isolation, when Sweden was left in peace while war raged all around, did not create much of a sense of practical solidarity with its European neighbours within the Swedish population. A similar, slightly selfish, tendency may have been fed by the nonofficial defence agreements between the Swedish government and a number of NATO allies, effectively agreeing to come to the support of the country in case of an emergency but asking for – and receiving – much more limited favours in return.

A document from the US National Security Council warned in 1952 that it was of great importance that the allies not be given the impression that Sweden was granted for free all those favours that they themselves had to sign mutual defence contracts to get (*SOU*, 1994: 11, pp. 105 ff., plus appendices). Still, Sweden was allowed to enjoy its cherished – though secret – position under the nuclear umbrella all through the years, never challenged to seriously contemplate the possibility that the country itself would have to go to war to save the life of others. The effect of so many years of a protected existence became evident during the EC campaign, when the rather widespread fear that the country's sons and daughters would have to travel to faraway shores to sacrifice their lives if a common European defence arrangement were to materialize, was expertly exploited by the 'no' side. That membership in an alliance would also result in the opposite kind of commitment, from the outside world towards Sweden – whose strategic location in the Nordic–Baltic region may be among the most vulnerable ones in Europe in the post-Cold War era – was rarely brought up in the debate.

But oddly enough, while the idea of providing security guarantees apparently does not find strong support in Swedish society, sending soldiers to Bosnia to participate in robust peacekeeping under NATO command did not provoke much negative reaction, in spite of the consequences it really involved for the nonaligned country. And though the country has been lucky in not counting any casualties, the sight of wounded Swedish soldiers returning home did not result in any popular cries that the troops be brought back. The lack of any such reactions may indicate a more balanced approach among the population to the issue of military cooperation than most politicians would give it credit for. The discrepancy between popular reactions to the idea of defence commitments during the EC campaign and generally and the response with which practical military cooperation has been met comes across as truly intriguing.

The public vs. the 'elite'

For decades, the mere idea of polling the public mind on the subject of security policy was interpreted by the government as tantamount to unacceptable questioning of the policy of neutrality, a step which might challenge the credibility of this doctrine abroad if presenting a less than united population. The issue of popular views evoked, however, endless analysis and speculation within the security 'elite' once a series of polling studies began in the mid-1990s. The results tend to vary quite a bit depending on the way the questions are posed, but a general trend can be traced of increasing support for more open relations with NATO. Nevertheless, the seemingly indecisive public mind and the assumption fostered by some polls, suggesting a majority in favour of 'continued neutrality' that the population would be far from ready for a modernization of the official security doctrine (bringing official policy in line with practical policies), have caused Social Democrats in particular to hesitate. Thus, the public assurances – especially on occasions such as May 1st – that Sweden is bound to continue the nonaligned policy regardless of external (and supposedly domestic) circumstances. In spite of the rather astonishing developments of the last few years, the government goes to great lengths to avoid having to admit that the country's security doctrine has been subjected to any alterations.

An interesting contrast can be noted between declarations designed for public consumption, and statements – by the Foreign Minister and others – aimed at the security policy community in and outside the country, in which the significance of the transatlantic link is regularly emphasized and the point is being made that nonalignment should not be seen as an eternal or permanent policy for Sweden (*Svenska Dagbladet* on 15 February 1997 and 3 April 1997). It was on such an occasion at the end of 1995 and again in early 1996 that the former Prime Minister, Ingvar Carlsson, made his now famous statement that, as he saw it, Sweden 'could not join NATO for the next six to seven years'.[1] According to many analysts, Carlsson's statement should be interpreted as indirectly arguing that Sweden could indeed join once those years had passed and NATO had entered into its new, all-European identity.

Significant for this conclusion by the then Prime Minister – whose candid declaration became the target of intense analysis and speculation for quite some time – is the evolution of the Alliance into a 'new' NATO. The new identity of the Alliance, which could be presumed to gradually emerge in the next few years following the successful conclusion of the first round of enlargement and the creation at the 1997 Madrid Summit of the Euro-Atlantic Partnership Council, in which Sweden aspires to play an active role, has frequently been referred to by high-ranking officials and ministers alike as an organization of considerable attraction as well as relevance in Europe.[2] In particular, such a positive approach to the enlargement process has been articulated ever since Russia signed its bilateral treaty with NATO in the early summer of 1997. Before it became evident that Russia would not overreact to a first round of enlargement of the Alliance to include a number of former Warsaw Pact members, there seemed to have been quite some concern in government circles about the entire process. Not only did the former Defence Minister, Thage G. Peterson, maintain a critical attitude to the idea of an enlargement process, but the Supreme Commander, General Ove Wictorin, surprised the country when emerging as a staunch opponent in Sweden to NATO's plans (*Svenska Dagbladet* on 24 January 1997 and 18 February 1997).

Sweden, the Baltic Sea region, and the second round of NATO enlargement

The prospect of a second round of enlargement of NATO is approached with much greater anticipation in Sweden than discussions surrounding the first one ever managed to evoke. Within the community of security policy experts, there is quite a bit of speculation as to whether Sweden is likely to appear on the next list of candidate countries. If such a candidacy were to take place, it would most probably be in the company of Finland, which is seen as likely to precede its more cautious neighbour and thus, present a whole new meaning to the old 'Finnish argument', the idea that Finnish security plays a pivotal role for the Swedish choice of doctrine. While many on the Continent appear to group all former neutrals into the category of next-round countries, analysis in the Northern part of Europe is more focused on Sweden and Finland entering the Alliance jointly with the three Baltic countries in an attempt to avoid the much-feared grey zone from taking hold in the Baltic Sea region.

Already, years before such a development could possibly take place, the idea of a *regionalization* of security, in which the Nordic and Baltic countries would form a special subcategory within the greater security community, began to take shape. A host of proposals on such a regionalization of security in the North was presented in the course of 1996 by such respected practitioners as Max Jakobson, Douglas Hurd and Carl Bildt, and a series of articles emanated from the RAND Corporation (in particular Asmus and Nurick, 1996). However, any implication that such a regionalization would assign to the Nordic countries a special role of responsibility towards the Baltic region does not meet with approval in the still nonaligned Sweden. The Social Democratic government draws a distinct line at the point where any kind of security assistance or guarantees are attached to the activities which Sweden engages in through the PFP (such as educational programmes for military personnel, the provision of certain supplies, various kinds of joint peacekeeping efforts, and so on).

In spite of such reluctance, it is evident that the Baltic Sea region has been the scene of a gradual but greatly significant evolution of the

Swedish approach to security policy and cooperation. There are no signs that Swedish involvement and interest in developments in the region, which was launched in a more determined manner with the coming to power of the Bildt government and which has since remained the number one security priority of the country, would at all weaken in the foreseeable future; quite the contrary. Sweden fully agrees with US Secretary of State Madeleine Albright when she argues that Europe is not safe unless the Baltic region is safe (Asmus, 1997).

That developments in the Baltic Sea region might actually result in a change of security doctrine – for the first time in close to two centuries – and that the possibility of such a change is actually the subject of considerable discussion at the end of the 1990s, demonstrates the enormous significance of the region in Swedish policy. To return to the title of this chapter, Swedish involvement in the Baltic Sea region should perhaps not be defined as a matter either of 'activism in a new arena' or 'the end of free-riding', but the final convergence of two hitherto parallel aspects of Swedish policy.

NOTES

1 Ingvar Carlsson at Q&A-session following his speech at the Swedish Institute for International Affairs on 10 October 1995, and at a conference organized by Folk och Försvar as reported in *Svenska Dagbladet*, 31 January 1996.
2 Defence Minister Björn von Sydow on 'Studio Ett' (Swedish national radio) on 8 July 1997; Foreign Minister Lena Hjelm-Wallén on television in 'Åtta dagar' on 6 July 1997.

10

Estonia and Russia: Interethnic Relations and Regional Security

PEETER VARES
Estonian Academy of Sciences, Tallinn

ESTONIA'S SECURITY OPTIONS[1]

The security of the country came to the agenda soon after it was widely recognized on the international arena in the autumn of 1991. Both the politicians and public opinion, neither of them very much aware of what was to be done, debated various options.

Neutrality was just discarded – relying on their personal experience, Estonians did not have any specific illusions about it.

The Nordic direction which had become so popular in the perestroika years, although offering both material and moral support, did not promise any military assistance. Possible 'Estonianization' à la 'Finlandization' was unattractive: Estonian public opinion was psychologically not ready for a Finnish–Soviet-type relationship with Russia.

Creation of a New Hansa Union, of the kind which existed in the thirteenth to seventeenth centuries and which united the biggest towns of Germany, Scandinavia, the Baltic lands and Russia, just remained on paper. But even with the best outcome of the project it could not have provided security for Estonia.

The idea of creating a Baltic and Black Sea Commonwealth, nourished in more recent years by some Baltic and Ukrainian experts, was of little interest to Estonians. The US, promoter of the independence of the Baltic States in the course of the entire Cold War years, was not ready to take them under its umbrella. A Baltic military union, judging by the efforts of the past, would not come to fruition either.

The formation of the Council of the Baltic Sea States (CBSS) in the spring of 1992 did not envisage any security guarantees to any of its member-states. No security from Russia! The Soviet bases imposed on Estonia in 1939, which led to its annexation, and the following bitter Soviet experience had made Estonians take the idea for granted.

Thus, Estonian politicians started moving in two directions – the

European Community (to become the European Union) and NATO, which both, according to their perceptions, could help them to get out of Russia's sphere of influence.

VARIETIES OF SECURITY

For quite a long period the notion of security in Estonia was just associated with defence or military security. The ignorance of Estonians in security matters could be easily explained and even justified – for almost half a century it was the Soviets who kept the Estonian Soviet Socialist Republic 'secure' from the outside world. With the passage of time, local politicians started becoming aware of economic, political, social, environmental, psychological, informational, health and other aspects of security.

Military security, however, seemed the most important: the fear of neighbouring Russia overshadowed everything else. Estonians began to learn early on in the first years of independence at the beginning of the 1990s that the way to the EU and NATO would be a long and thorny one. However, Estonian politicians turned out to be persevering and obstinate – both 'Europeanism' and 'atlantism' would remain the pillars of their policy until those dreams came true.

HOPING AGAINST HOPE

It was very unpleasant for Estonians to acknowledge that, contrary to their expectations, the nation's clearly expressed adherence to the West would most probably not make the Westerners rush to Estonia to lay down their lives for the independence of the country, in case *force majeure* circumstances were to occur there. Overt and covert signals coming from Western friends made Estonian politicians ponder the steps Estonia should take to meet its security needs. The latter, however, were again linked to the military aspect of security, such as the acquisition of armaments from Israel, the striving for the compatibility of purchased arms with the NATO ones, the creation of the Baltic Battalion to be used as part of a UN peacekeeping force, conclusion of bilateral agreements of military cooperation with a number of European countries, inclusion in the activities of NACC and PFP programmes and so on. All those measures, in fact, made rank-and-file Estonians hope against hope for a quick settlement of their security problems. Besides, some foreign and domestic policy moves made them forget for a while that Russia was too serious a neighbour to ignore its interests even temporarily. Boris Yeltsin was practically the first head of state to recognize Estonia's independence in August 1991. In January of the same year he was regarded in Estonia as a sort of hero, who, defying the anti-Baltic Soviet policies of Mikhail Gorbachev, came on 24 hours' notice to Tallinn to support the cause of Baltic independence. The feelings for the Russian leader were, however, soon over. The strong emotions created in the regaining of independence subsided and the nation was confronted with everyday realities. It now turned out that the Soviet past had heaped up a tremendous amount of problems which blocked the restoration of the Estonian Republic of the inter-war years, officially proclaimed as a primary task of the country. Alongside this, the idealization of the previous period of independence made the emerging Estonian politicians ignore anything that did not match that model. It was somehow difficult for them to realize that in the 45 postwar years the Western European countries had undergone crucial changes, their societies were radically transformed and that the Estonians' nostalgic idea of 'rebuilding the country as it had once been' could only bring them into an impasse. Thus, the adoption of the Constitution based on its predecessor of 1938 paved the way for other legislative acts which also disregarded the postwar realities, first and foremost, the very fact that the Estonian society formed in the Soviet period was to encounter a completely new phenomenon – a huge Russian-speaking population, a result of the distorted Soviet ethnic policies. The first moves were to build a new Estonia, if not just for Estonians, then for Estonians and relatively few Russians.

It was not accidental that local Russians were equated with Soviets. The Soviets, in fact, brought about the Russification of Estonia, advocated Russians as the model nationality and practically turned Russian into the official language of Estonia. Thus, the Soviets provided a matrix for the prejudices of Estonians against Russians and for the feelings of those who suffered at their hands.

Russians, who had become overnight a national minority, started labelling themselves second-rate citizens. The Estonian Republic's doors gradually closed to those who could not get Estonian citizenship and had little or no knowledge of Estonian. Many Russians were just unable to accept the situation. They suffered shock. As members of a large proud nation it was hard for them to understand why Estonians did not prefer speaking their beloved Russian. With no prior experience in having to use the Estonian language, they were confronted with a humiliating situation – Estonia had become an independent state with one official language, Estonian. Psychological pressures hampered those who studied Estonian. The policy of the Estonian authorities to require everybody to speak Estonian created in the Russians similar feelings to those that Estonians experienced during the Soviet period when Russification was under way.

These events did not leave the Russian leadership indifferent. The relations between the two countries took a sharp turn for the worse. The claims of the Estonian politicians to Estonia's pre-Second World War territories, presently under Russia's jurisdiction, complicated the situation even more. (Estonia, it is true, dropped the claims later). The two countries found themselves in a real conflict.

INTERETHNIC RELATIONS – A DOMESTIC AFFAIR OF ESTONIA?

The interethnic policy of Estonia became quite unfriendly towards local Russians turning into the key bone of contention with Russia. Over 35 per cent of Estonia's population of 1.5 million were Russian-speakers with north-eastern Estonia having one of the largest concentrations. An inadequate language environment was formed there, where over 82 per cent of the population were non-Estonian.

The main reasons for Estonia's discontent resided in the situation in Estonia after 50 years of Soviet rule and in the dynamics of the nation-building process. It was accentuated by the Estonian authorities' attitude that there had always been interethnic problems in many other countries of the world and in some cases their solutions were harsher than in Estonia. Estonian authorities considered it unfair to judge their attitude towards the Russian-speaking population in Estonia by democratic principles only, since Estonia had been forcibly incorporated into the USSR in 1940 and the inherited 'Russian question' constituted a serious problem for the very existence of the nation.

Russia repeatedly expressed serious worries about the status of the Russian-speakers in Estonia. The Estonian authorities, in their turn, addressed different international organizations with the request to check their laws for alleged discrimination. Most of the Estonian laws which irritated Russia had, in fact, benefited from the expertise of international organizations and had been judged non-discriminatory, although with qualification. In reality, their discriminative character became evident primarily in their practical application. Since the adoption of the new Citizenship Law (19 January 1995) and the new Language Law (21 February 1995), the dissatisfaction of Russian-speaking non-citizens with the Estonian authorities has become more acute. It became quite evident that the latter aimed at making the situation uncomfortable for the Russian-speaking population, to show them that now the Estonians were the masters in Estonia. To a certain extent, it could be called a sort of revenge for the humiliations which Estonians had constantly endured in the Soviet period. Although revenge was psychologically understandable, it had to be overcome at some time, if more practical policies and practices were to prevail.

In the meantime, the situation did not change much. Russia urged the Estonian authorities to implement the recommendations of the OSCE High Commissioner for Human Rights Max van der Stoel regarding the treatment of non-citizens and, in particular, to ease naturalization requirements through amendments to the Citizenship Law. This, however, fell on deaf ears.

The Russian politicians repeatedly stress that the alleged human-rights abuses against Russian-speakers in Estonia and the slow pace of naturalization are not contributing to the future development of politico-economic relations between Tallinn and Moscow.

From 1993 political relations have been driven into a blind alley. Economic relations have deteriorated by leaps and bounds. Estonia has remained one of the few countries in Europe which does not have a most-favoured-nation regime in trade relations with Russia. The highly profitable Russian transit transportation of goods through Estonia was partly directed by Russia via other Baltic States. Despite all that, the Estonian authorities, it seemed, preferred to sacrifice the economic well-being of the nation, by not yielding to the demands of Russia and of the international community to introduce changes in their interethnic policies. They, who had always condemned Soviet policy-making, were in a way behaving as the Soviet state did. The well-known Sakharov case provides a useful analogy. In the 1980s the US administration made it clear to the Soviet leadership that if academician Sakharov were to be let out of his Gorki exile, the USSR would be granted most-favoured nation status in trade relations with the USA, which meant billions of extra dollars for the socialist economy. The then Soviet leaders preferred to sacrifice the well-being of their citizens. The Soviet policy towards the Sakharov case was discussed all over the world and it must have been rather naive, on the part of Estonian politicians, to think that nobody noticed their obstinacy and that the interethnic situation in Estonia would remain just a domestic affair.

RUSSIA VERSUS ESTONIA

Russia has officially assumed responsibility for Russian citizens in the former Soviet Union. In practice, the Russian authorities take an interest in the problems of all Russian-speaking communities. Although their situation is very alarming in most of the areas of the CIS (huge numbers of them abandon their houses in Central Asian and Caucasian states leaving for Mother Russia), the Russian authorities are still rather tolerant towards the laws adopted in these republics, as well as to their political leaderships. However the Baltic States, in particular, Estonia and Latvia, where the Russian communities feel much better than they would in Russia, have become targets of harsh Russian criticism as discriminators and violators of human rights. Lithuania seems to be Russia's pet Baltic State, due to the zero option in granting Lithuanian citizenship to local Russians.

According to the Russian military doctrine of 1993, the situation with the interethnic relations might easily qualify Estonia as a threat to Russia's security with all the possible consequences deriving from it. It may suffice to recall the rather amateurish arrest of two Russian generals in Latvia in the spring of 1994, which provided the Russians with an opportunity to inform the Latvian leadership that a Russian airborne division would take off from a neighbouring area of Russia and land in Latvia in 15 minutes. Or the deportation on political grounds of Pyotr Rozhok, representative of the Russian Liberal Democratic Party in Estonia in the spring of 1995. In both cases, the Baltic authorities damaged their reputation, showing themselves as inexperienced politicians.

With the involuntary contribution of Estonian politicians, the Russian propaganda machine is becoming rather anti-Estonian. To a certain extent, it is reinforced by other factors. For one thing, there are no special Baltic Study Centres in Russia yet and the number of those who know the Baltic languages in Russia is extremely small. Thus, information about the complexity of the state of affairs in the Baltic States reaches Russia through the Baltic local Russian language newspapers. Besides, the role of the Baltic Russians' visits to Moscow to report on the domestic situation cannot be underestimated. All this, taken together, exerts a considerable influence on Russian policy-makers, who call for sanctions (fortunately enough, not military ones) against Estonia.

At the same time, the shortsightedness of some Estonian politicians may one day lead to disastrous consequences for Estonia. Commenting on the increasing number of Russian citizens in Estonia, Tiit Vähi, the former Estonian prime minister, just did not see any reason for monitoring the situation. Eventually, the number of Russian citizens could reach a critical point from Estonia's perspective (it is currently claimed by the Russian Embassy in Tallinn to be over 125,000 people). It is becoming probable that if Estonian authorities do not change their citizenship policy, the number of Russian citizens could grow to the point that Russia might demand equal political rights or autonomy for Russian citizens residing in Estonia.

It goes without saying that no nation likes to be lectured on morals or take orders or instructions from abroad as to what it should do. Estonian politicians, representing a small nation, take particular exception to this. Thus, anything instructive coming from Moscow makes them behave the other way round, even to the detriment of their country. They are, naturally, giving a more attentive ear to Western advice, even if it turns out to be conflicting, but this can also be easily ignored by them. The majority of Estonian leading politicians are, as a rule, convinced of the correctness of their ideas and do not feel obliged to consult experts outside the country's political circles.

An international commotion about Estonia's interethnic policies has created quite a peculiar situation. Due to the abundance of anti-Baltic statements made by Moscow (in fact, there has been lots of speculation about EU and NATO enlargement with the possible integration of the Baltic States and Estonia has already been invited to start EU negotiations), Estonian politicians feel sometimes that they are at the centre of attention of international public opinion. However, they miss a very important point: neither the EU nor NATO would ever accept Estonia as a full member with its interethnic problems unsettled and its unfriendly policies towards Russia fraught with a possible conflict between Russia and these international organizations. One could just imagine the possible joy of the West in integrating Estonia with nearly one-third of its population being Russian citizens with all their problems. This, of course, would not matter if Russia were also regarded as a prospective EU or NATO member. Russia's intentions are rather unclear.

Does Russia's present attitude towards Estonia mean that it intends to absorb the country again? Or do Russia's policies merely meet the requirements of its domestic controversies? Or does Russia want to maintain the 'image of the enemy' associated with small Estonia? Or is it just interested in having a weak neighbouring state on whom to vent steam sometimes?

ESTONIA VERSUS RUSSIA

For a small nation, nationality is a special value that must be protected. A big nation, on the other hand, attributes less importance to nationality, for its basic existence is not as threatened. Russians who have settled outside the territory of the Russian Federation (as it stands today) do not worry about their national identity – it is safeguarded by the significance of the Russian language in the world and by Russia's role in international relations. In the Soviet period it was emphasized that the presence of Russian-speakers in Estonia was needed to run the country. The independent Estonian state does not have such a necessity. The Estonian authorities would not mind if the Russians who have come to Estonia upon the call of the Communist Party, left the country. Estonia is ready to accept all those who learn the Estonian language and accept the Estonian culture. Local Russians, however, consider it too tough a task. They prefer to keep apart from Estonians and maintain their unity to oppose Estonians, whenever needed. There is still a hope among many Russian-speakers that under strong inter-national pressure Estonia will give up its strict language requirements. The reinforcement of the Russian Communist Party also contributes to Estonian Russians' 'wait-and-see' attitudes. Those of them who still believe that Estonia voluntarily joined the USSR in 1940 hope that one day, after the nationalist forces lose their influence in Estonia, the Estonians will come back as prodigal sons to join the CIS. Moreover, people in most parts of the CIS seldom differentiate between a regular former Soviet republic and an ex-annexed Baltic State. Some of the more knowledgeable among the Russians in Estonia are looking forward to Russian hard-liners finding a pretext to take over Estonia.

Estonia, opening to the West, is gradually restricting access to the country from the East.

The majority of Estonians are prejudiced against Russia. Their fear of Russia originates from ancient as well as recent history. This fear, whether conscious or subconscious, is enhanced by the statements of Russian Federation leaders and by official documents adopted in Russia. Russians living in Estonia are sometimes regarded by Estonians as a 'fifth column'. Besides, Estonians, as a rule, make little distinction between Russians and Russian-speaking people originating from other republics of the ex-USSR.

The Russian language elicits negative emotions in some Estonians. While communicating with their colleagues from other Baltic countries they prefer to switch over to English, which is, however, the privilege of the younger generation. The Russian language has lost its impor-tance at Estonian schools. It is most probable that in the next few years the emerging younger generation will have to communicate with neighbouring Russia by means of the English language.

Estonians avoid travelling to Russia. Besides the crime reports that they constantly hear about, they are frustrated by Russian bureaucracy, the bad quality of services offered and the incredibly high prices there. Apart from that, they fear that other Estonians might disapprove of their Russian connections.

Most Estonians still perceive Russia as a backward country. With the exception of local businessmen they do not care much for the development of the Estonian–Russian dialogue. They would just like to get back from Russia what once had belonged to Estonia: part of the Tartu University library moved to Voronezh before the First World War, the necklace of Konstantin Päts, the last president of the Estonian Republic of the first period of independence, from the Armoury Palace in the Kremlin, Estonia's frozen accounts in Moscow's ex-Vneshtorgbank, as well as the latest files of the KGB archives taken out of the country on Moscow's orders in 1991 to end the witch-hunt still popular in Estonian society. In a word, Estonians would like to forget forever the Soviet past and start considering themselves finally as Europeans.

WHAT ABOUT LITHUANIA AND LATVIA?

Does the above also apply to Latvia and Lithuania? The interethnic aspect does not play an essential role in Lithuanian–Russian relations because of the insignificant number of Russians living there, as well as the absence of similar language and citizenship problems. As far as Latvia is concerned, irrespective of several formal similarities (large Russian-speaking community, stricter rules than in Estonia for obtaining citizenship, strict requirements on the knowledge of the Latvian language), it is difficult to draw parallels, since the entire complex of other (political, economic) relations between Latvia and Russia is built up in a different way. Much depends on the political relations between Moscow and the individual Baltic State. Up till spring 1998 Estonia was subjected to more criticism than Latvia. Now the rhetoric of the Russian authorities towards Latvia has changed radically. Bilateral relations have deteriorated to such an extent that Latvia, accused by Russia of gross violations of the human rights of Russian-speakers, can expect sanctions from its eastern neighbour. The latter has addressed various international organizations with the request to condemn Latvia's ethnic policy. At the same time, the Russian authorities have changed their tone towards Estonia which, generally speaking, can be accounted for by the start of integration negotiations between Estonia and the EU.

FAILED CONTRIBUTION TO REGIONAL SECURITY

The fear concerning Russia's possible comeback is so great that Estonian politicians, as a rule, do not believe in the efficiency of the build-up of a security system in the Baltic Sea area. They would feel secure only after having been able to join the most diverse international security structures. That is why Estonia is rather hesitant to act as a peace-promoter in the region, although Estonia's President Lennart Meri once came out with an ambitious idea for Estonia to host a conference of the small states of the world.

At the same time, Estonia could play a significant role in easing tensions in the Baltic Sea region, first and foremost, by regulating its interethnic policies. According to all logic Estonia should have done it a long time ago. Local legislators either do not realize its importance for Estonia and for the international community, or their unhappy Soviet experience would not permit them to take such steps. By proposing changes in the basic laws they are afraid of an increase in Russian-speakers' influence in Estonia as well as running the risk of losing the electorate.

THE FUTURE OF ESTONIAN–RUSSIAN RELATIONS

Take it or leave it, Russia will never drop its role of protector of Russian citizens as well as Russian-speaking minorities outside Russia. It concerns, above all, the Baltic States towards which Russia has been most particular. This idea was also confirmed in the document 'Russia and the Baltic States' approved by the State Duma of the Russian Federation in 1997. Whether Estonia likes it or not, the interethnic issue will have to find a solution acceptable to Estonia, Russia and the international community. For one thing, the interdependence principle is valid in this triangle as everywhere else in the world, for another thing, the course of events in Estonia shows that the further the Estonian–EU integration talks go, the more urgent becomes the necessity to introduce changes in Estonian–Russian relations. The first swallow appeared on 10 February 1998 when the Estonian government adopted the bases of the Estonian state integration policy from April 1998 till April 1999, which is undoubtedly a new step in the attitude of the state towards the non-indigenous population in Estonia. It was said to be guaranteeing a quick modernization of Estonian society within the context of integration with the European Union. Most probably, the implementation of the document will lead to a better understanding with Russia. Nevertheless, this step ought to be followed by others in order to remove the main stumbling-block from the way of Estonian–Russian relations. The sooner the better.

NOTE

1 For further reading, the following literature is recommended: Herd (1997), Järve (1997), Kirch and Kirch (1995), Park (1995), Ruus (1996), Smith, Aasland and Mole (1994), Vares (1993), Vares (1994), Vares and Zhuryari (1995), Vares and Zhuryari (1996), Zhuryari (1993), Zhuryari (1994).

Part III

Intergovernmental Cooperation

11

The Security Policies and Concepts of the Baltic States – Learning from their Nordic Neighbours?

CLIVE ARCHER AND CHRISTOPHER JONES
Centre for Research in International Security,
Manchester Metropolitan University

INTRODUCTION[1]

The passage to security and stability for the Baltic states is being charted as it is explored and discovered. The way ahead is undoubtedly difficult, as have been the years since the states regained their independence from the Soviet Union in 1989–91. Placed in their current situation by the legacy of history and their geostrategic location, the three Baltic states are caught between continued and often threatening Russian opposition and hesitancy on the part of the North Atlantic Alliance to extend 'hard' security guarantees to their part of the Baltic subregion.

The Baltic states have managed to move from a Hobbesian security environment – wherein their very existence was uncertain – to one where it is not seriously contested. This process has been helped by a number of factors. Not least, the general international environment has moved in their favour. Russia is somewhat neutralized and its leadership has accepted general norms that include respecting the territorial integrity of former parts of the Soviet Union. The Presidential election in Russia in 1996 created an element of improved stability for the Baltic states, as had the agreements for the drawback of Russian troops from their soil in 1993–94. This has given them time and space.

The Nordic countries have provided some of the concepts – and their operationalization – that may allow the Baltic states to move into an environment of greater stability, providing they make the necessary choices in their own internal politics. Though their actions fall short of Baltic desires for 'hard' security guarantees, the Nordic states in particular have established cooperative tuition and practical programmes to provide the Baltic states with an element of what could be termed 'coping security'. Concepts of collective defence or co-operative and comprehensive security are idealized, but practice is well short of attaining such security. In the interregnum between their Cold War legacy and moving towards these concepts of security, the Baltic states are having to cope as best they can with current demands upon their statehood and their security, with limited resources.

This chapter examines the stated aims and objectives of the security policies and concepts of the three Baltic states, since their independence in 1991. The process by which the Nordic countries have contributed to these policies and concepts is then discussed. The 'schools' in which these lessons are being learnt are examined, by focusing on several political and military cooperative programmes designed to bolster Baltic independent statehood and 'tutor' them in the ways of Western security concepts and practice.

SECURITY POLICIES AND CONCEPTS

There are several distinct themes which run through the security policies of Estonia, Latvia and Lithuania. Most appear to be common to all three, and this has undoubtedly led to limited Baltic cooperation. One overriding theme is that of history, most recently that of the Soviet occupation from 1940–91. The Baltic states are determined to escape history and not to return to any Russian/CIS 'sphere of influence'.[2] This has raised two concerns: the development of the Russian concept of the 'Near Abroad' with the policy of 'peacekeeping' in such an area;[3] and the question of the 'open door' policy proposed by NATO in regards to its planned enlargement.[4] Lack of a firm commitment on NATO's part to include the Baltics in the expansion, in their view, would have relegated them to a 'grey zone' between Russia and NATO, drawing a dividing line between the Baltics and the rest of Central and Eastern Europe, or, more bluntly, would have meant a renewal of Russian domination (Haab, 1997: 3).

The main policy priority of the three Baltic states since independence has been to move as far as possible from Russian influence. This is evidenced by the current stated aims of their foreign and security policies, which are:

- to re-establish national independence in a continuation of the inter-war state (1918–40);
- to ensure national security through integration into the trans-Atlantic community and its institutions;

- to join the North Atlantic Alliance and European Union at the earliest possible time.[5]

Baltic decision-makers have stressed their countries' return to the Western and European pole, hence the link to the inter-war period of independence. Association with and ultimately membership of the Western political and security structures is seen as the only way to achieve this, thereby being a means to the goal of Baltic security and stability, rather than as an end in itself (Miniotaite, 1997: 13). The fundamental utility of these relationships has been to bolster Baltic independence at a time of uncertainty, and to order and promote development in the fields of Baltic domestic and international politics, economics, social cohesion, and military planning and cooperation. Though the objective of joining the trans-Atlantic institutions is common to all three, the order in which they rank the institutions differs. While Estonia, with its proximity to the Nordic states, has stressed Nordic and Baltic Sea cooperation, it has also placed emphasis on its advantages in the economic field and has been prepared to go ahead of its Baltic neighbours in the move towards EU membership. Lithuania has in recent years become closer to Poland (Brazauskas, 1996b; Ministry of Foreign Affairs, 1996) and has therefore been able to tie its future to the Central European 'hopefuls' more than the other Baltic states. Latvia hopes to act as the bridge between its neighbours to the north and south, and as a result is more inclined to stress Baltic cooperation, particularly in the military field (Heurlin, 1996: 86). Despite the differences in ranking the priority of the Western institutions, the Baltic states are adamant that they seek full membership 'because of what (each institution) offers in and of itself' (Ilves, 1997b: 3). There is to be no compensation membership.

The period of their previous, although short, experience of independence in the inter-war period has impacted upon current security thinking. Lack of cooperation between the three Baltic states, and the distinct failure of any resistance or self-defence, led to their individual surrenders of independence in the face of Soviet and Nazi pressure. In the initial phase of their renewed independence (1990–92) – and even previously in the run-up period (1989–90) – security policy in the Baltic swung towards the policy of neutrality. This would have been in keeping with their inter-war record, and akin to the policies of their Nordic neighbours Sweden and Finland. Furthermore, it was seen that neutrality would provide them the 'breathing space' necessary whilst they negotiated with Russia for the withdrawal of troops from their territories (Archer, 1997; Haab, 1997: 9–10). However, the history of Baltic security policy also spoke against neutrality, to the extent that by 1996 neutrality was seen as a dangerous policy option (Haab, 1997:

11; Dalbins, 1996). Self-isolation is contrary to the Baltics' expressed need to involve themselves in European security.[6]

Paramount in their statements of defence policy has been the need to build the ability to defend themselves individually and, if possible, collectively. This again is a response to the interwar experience, and the second element is a logical extension of the exclusion of neutrality. Latvia has emerged as the chief proponent of Baltic defence co-operation, seeing its security posture as resting on the twin pillars of 'an effective and co-ordinated military capability on the part of the three Baltic States, backed up by integration into the wider Western security structures' (Dalbins, 1996). The Baltic states have had to create their defence forces anew, which in itself can be regarded as a blessing in that they are not faced with the problem of putting 'new wine into old bottles' as are the Poles. However, the tremendous task of constructing their defence forces is hampered by scarce economic resources, a growing sense of apathy to military service amongst conscription-age men,[7] and a profound lack of experience at all levels of command (Öövel, 1995: 3; Libak, 1997: 12). To a degree, these problems can be offset by increased support, training, and *matériel* transfer from Western defence forces, notably the Nordics, and by an increased commitment from the Western defence institutions. The Baltic states have thus placed much faith in the response of the West. Failure to confirm the integration of the Baltic states into the European political, economic and military framework is portrayed as jeopardizing the efforts of reformers at home, and casts doubt on their building and maintaining strong democratic independence.

At the conceptual level, Baltic security is placed in the context of European security, and vice-versa. Security in Europe, according to the thinking of most Baltic states' commentators, must be indivisible, where the security of one or more should not be gained at the expense of another. This thinking is prominent in Baltic statements regarding the expansion of NATO and means that the Baltic states would expect that their security would be the concern of all other members of the Alliance. There is some doubt whether an expanded Alliance would have the feelings of solidarity needed to maintain such a position. Furthermore, it seems unlikely that the Baltic states also wish to include Russian security in this expansive view of security which, if taken to its logical conclusion, would show equal concern for Moscow's insecurities as those in the Baltic states' capitals.[8] In essence, it appears that the Baltic states are presenting NATO with a dilemma, whereby the Alliance's already fragile relationship with Russia could be threatened, if not completely destroyed, or, alternatively, Baltic insecurity would feed European insecurity. Indivisibility, it seems, is a two-edged sword. However, the Baltics are quick to stress that their applications for NATO membership are made in the absence of any direct threat (Gylys, 1996, p. 5), and point to their 'good neighbour' policies of actively engaging Russia in bilateral negotiations and agreements. Indeed, Baltic spokesmen state that they do not wish to join the NATO of the Cold War. In this they mirror the statements made by Nordic spokesmen, especially those from Denmark, in talking about Baltic membership of NATO (Hækkerup, 1997a). In a shift towards the developing idea and practice of cooperative security, most ably illustrated by IFOR and SFOR in Bosnia, the Baltic states make it clear that their desire is to join a 'new NATO in a new Europe' (Ilves, 1997a: 5; see also Birkavs, 1997b: 1, and Gylys, 1996: 6), a NATO concerned not so much with the territorial defence of Western Europe, but with the creation of a secure and stable Europe through the promotion and maintenance of shared democratic values, transparency in all aspects of national defence, and peacekeeping. The three Baltic states have come a long way since their earlier flirtation with neutrality.

Yet despite this move towards a 'new NATO', the overriding under-standing of security is that of 'hard' military guarantees, particularly Article 5 of the Washington Treaty. As part of their view of security commitments, the Baltic states have accepted the need to rebuild national defences, and to achieve this by their own efforts, by co-operation with each other, and – more importantly in face of the need to develop interoperability – with Nordic and other Western forces. It is clear they understand that they will not get 'something for nothing' from NATO, and in this respect interoperability marks the driving force behind Baltic security policy (Öövel, 1995). By being able to work with NATO and 'supporter' forces they can claim to be 'providers' as well as 'receivers' of security in Europe. This is evidenced by the creation of the joint Baltic peacekeeping battalion – BALTBAT – and the contributions of all three states to IFOR and SFOR. Interoperability is to be attained not only with NATO forces, but also with each other, a policy priority expounded by all three, but to differing degrees (Dalbins, 1996; Öövel, 1995).

Increasingly though, Baltic leaders are beginning to appreciate other – 'softer' – security threats. These are directed to the societies of the three countries rather than against their borders, and include elements such as organized crime, pollution and ethnic divisions. Given their dramatic demographic construction, the outstanding questions of borders and the social, political, and economic weaknesses of Russia are clearly to the fore in determining security policy. In this regard, NATO and EU membership are seen to meet the needs not only of hard security, but of these softer problems (Haab, 1997: 18–19). The Baltic logic behind their applications is to firm up their own fragile circumstance in these areas, and thereafter be able to transfer security and stability over the border into Russia, given their '*fingerspitzengefühl*, or finger-tip feel for Russia' (Velliste, 1993b).

NORDIC CONTRIBUTIONS

Before the events of November 1989, the security policies of the Nordic states – despite their differences – had two important unifying factors. First, all five Nordic countries sought to maintain the superpower presence in the north of Europe at a minimum level consistent with their own security. Secondly, each of the states attempted – in a construction sometimes referred to as 'the Nordic balance' (Brundtland, 1966) – to follow a policy that at least had no adverse effect on the security positions of the other Nordic countries and might even have enhanced them. To that extent, the Nordic countries were not totally self-regarding in their security policies which, anyhow, they defined widely to include diplomatic, economic and social elements in their implementation (Andrén, 1975: 1).

The changing security situation in Europe after 1989 not only presented a challenge to the security policies of the five Nordic states – as to other Western states – but also provided an opportunity, unrecognized at first, to extend some elements of Nordic neighbourhood security to the Baltic states that re-emerged as independent entities in 1991. It soon became apparent that not only was the stability of the three Baltic states of direct importance for the Nordic countries, but the latter could make a contribution to that stability in a way that other states – especially the United States and Germany – could not. During the years since 1991, the Nordic states have undertaken a process in relation to the Baltic states that could be called socialization, tutoring or, more modestly, cooperation. The nature of this process may reflect on the missionary element in Nordic foreign policy or it can be seen in terms of economic and security self-interest. Either way, it has been displayed in a number of joint projects (see next section).

In the period from 1989 to 1991, there was a growing realization in the Nordic countries that events in the Baltic states were mirroring those in the rest of Central and East Europe and most of the people in the three states wished to break away from the Soviet Union. However, the Nordic countries were not originally united in their response to this process. According to the Danish foreign minister at that time – who may be seen to have a vested interest in the matter – his Swedish and Finnish colleagues resisted recognition of the Baltic states in 1991 while Denmark and Iceland pressed for such action (Ellemann-Jensen, 1996: 136–7; see also Hansen, 1996: 44). This difference reflected the political stance of the relevant foreign ministers but, more deeply, the 'strategic distance' of Denmark and Iceland from the Soviet Union compared with the closeness of Finland and Sweden, captured in the caution bred from the non-aligned policy of the latter two states. Norway's approach was also originally cautious, reflecting concerns about relations with Moscow as well as internal political divisions (Knudsen, 1996a: 118–19).

Nordic policies towards the Baltic states from 1991 developed certain basic elements. Faced with the new reality of three new states in the Baltic region and an unstable Russian Federation with its troops still based on the soil of those states, the Nordic states attempted to bolster the sinews of sovereignty of the three states, encouraged them to reach negotiated settlements on outstanding issues with Russia and to join with Russia and other Baltic sea states in cooperative efforts, and tried to ease their way into Western institutions. In pursuit of these objectives, the Nordic countries exported some of their own security concepts to the Baltic states – who have not always been willing recipients – and have sometimes disagreed among themselves as to which Nordic state should lead the Baltic project.

What security concepts were exported? The Nordic countries – mainly through example and practice – set out a more complicated and widely-embracing notion of security than that which seemed to be dominant in the Baltic states in the 1991–93 period. Some of the elements of these security concepts can be identified in Nordic official statements:[9]

- *comprehensive security*, implying that 'security is no longer primarily a military issue' (Hjelm-Wallén, 1996). Instead, it brings into focus such elements as environmental issues, human rights, economic elements, social questions and even crime (ibid.; Ministry for Foreign Affairs, 1995: 19). Implied in this list is the need to use a wider range of institutions in pursuit of security than those primarily concerned with defence (such as NATO). These non-military elements of security have been referred to as *soft security* though these were seen as 'much more effective when they are underpinned by a "hard security" framework' (Helveg Petersen, 1996: 1 and 7).
- *civic security* implies that security is not just about the state but also society and, according to the Danish foreign minister, encompasses the non-military, civic aspects of 'soft security', where the Council of the Baltic Sea States was seen as having a key role (Helveg Petersen, 1996: 1 and 8). Meetings at Visby and Kalmar took up this rather ill-defined concept,[10] mainly in the context of the fight against organized crime (Baltic Sea States Summit, 1996: 1; Council of the Baltic Sea States, 1996: 2–3).

- *cooperative security* which deals with the subject and object of security. No longer is there a question of *us versus them*, either with a defined *us* and *them* (collective defence) or an unstated *us* and *them* (collective security). Instead, the subject would be a European *us* and the objects are the more indeterminate forces of instability and disorder. An earlier version of this was common security when the main threat was seen to be the possibility of warfare and nuclear annihilation. Cooperative security means building security 'not by blocks (sic), not by balances of power, not by spheres of interest and grey zones, but through integration, webs of interdependence and networking' (Hækkerup, 1997a: 135). In particular this concept has been pursued through the OSCE (Helveg Petersen, 1997: 146; Lipponen, 1997: 2).

The Nordic countries by no means have the copyright on these concepts. However, in making the link between them and the Baltic states in the flow of security ideas a number of points should be borne in mind. While the above concepts have now become commonplace, that was not always the case. These ideas – especially the notions of a comprehensive approach to security and common security – were more prevalent among the official thinking of the Nordic states before the end of the 1980s than in other West European countries (Archer, 1994). Secondly, official statements since the end of the Cold War by the Nordic states have seen much wider acceptance and a development of these ideas (Archer, 1994; Archer and Jæger, 1997). Thirdly, Nordic adoption of these notions has also been seen in practice, in particular in their support for international institutions, not least regional organizations such as the Council of the Baltic Sea States, the Nordic Council and the Barents-Euro Arctic Council.

Why, since 1991, have the Nordic states shown an eagerness to spread their appreciation of international security?[11] Why could they not have left the three Baltic states with their original view of their security situation that portrayed Russia as the enemy, and saw armaments from the West as a necessity and, eventually, membership of the Atlantic Alliance as a balance to and protection from Russian power?

The answer to this question must deal with both the *opportunities* that opened up for the Nordic states to export their ideas and their *willingness* to do so.[12] The opportunity arose with the recognition in 1991 of the renewed independence of the three Baltic states and in their post-independence relations with the Soviet Union/Russian Federation. Those relations in what might be called the Nordic 'near abroad' were perceived as offering an important threat to the stability of the Baltic Sea region and thus of the Nordic states. Not only could conflict between the Baltic states and Russia possibly lead *in extremis* to those three states losing their independence, but their involvement even in low-level conflict could have adversely affected the Nordic states with refugees, and a certain amount of social and economic disruption. In a wider context, any Russian aggression could have led to a disruption in the improved East–West relations,[13] and this would certainly have had a negative effect on the Nordic states. The task was to persuade both sides – Russia and the Baltics – to change their attitude towards each other and to preclude rash action by either. To that extent, the Baltic states had become a 'litmus test' of Russian intentions (Bildt, 1994). The Baltic states needed to be persuaded not to provide the occasion for a Russian *démarche*. Furthermore, the new set of post-Cold War opportunities allowed for a regionalization of security. While the concepts mentioned above were meant to have universal application, the 'divisibility of security' increasingly seen after 1989 (Heurlin, 1996: 76–7), allowed for their trial in regional arrangements.

The willingness of the Nordic states to take up the torch lies in a number of factors. One reason could be negative: the Nordic states may have wondered 'who, but us?' and answered 'Germany and the United States', the direct involvement of both being less acceptable internationally than that of the Nordic countries. The direct security involvement of the United States on the border with Russia – and in territories of the former Soviet Union – could have been seen as provocative to Moscow, and a heavy German presence could have revived historic memories not just in Russia but also in Poland and the Baltic states themselves. More positively, the Nordic countries' concept of liberal institutionalism does require that international norms, rules and institutions are spread more widely than just the Nordic region or Western Europe (Holm, 1997). Furthermore, there have been pressures within the Nordic states to embark on this mission.[14] It does seem that domestic opinion within the Nordic countries, added to international acceptance, has allowed Nordic politicians to be consistent in their security concepts. If the ideas outlined above – comprehensive, societal and cooperative security – were to work anywhere, they had to work in the Baltic region.

If the Nordic states have been ready to export their concepts of security to the Baltic states, have those countries been willing to import them? The next section deals with the cooperative programmes that involve the Nordic and Baltic countries and a number of these – such as those involving the training of peacekeeping forces – implicitly involve the acceptance of a cooperative view of security. Likewise the Nordic schemes of assistance for 'sovereignty support' place emphasis on notions of comprehensive and civic security. The extent to which these ideas have been truly accepted by the three Baltic states is arguable. Their defence doctrines seem to nod in their direction, though greater emphasis is still placed on the collective defence needs of the states (Birkavs, 1997a, p. 5; Öövel, 1995; Brazauskas, 1996a). However, their foreign and defence ministers have had regular contact with their Nordic counterparts and their public statements have echoed some of the Nordic themes, especially in the area of peacekeeping and civic security (Saudargas, 1997; Brazauskas, 1996b; Ministry of Foreign Affairs, 1996). Perhaps it has been the case that the Baltic states have learnt from the Nordic states that a different dialogue now has to be conducted in the security field. It should also be noted that some of the Nordic participants in security cooperation with the Baltic states felt that they had learnt some lessons, for example, about the need to integrate the regular army into the home-guard structures (Libak, 1997: 12).

THE COOPERATIVE PROGRAMME

In an address in 1996, Lithuanian President, Algirdas Brazauskas spoke of the value to his country of being associated with European security institutions. Although limited in some respects, it does give the Baltic states 'access to the "kitchen" of European security policy-making', and provides them with the opportunity to 'observe and participate in the decision-making process' (Brazauskas, 1996a). Implicit in this 'observation and participation' is the idea of a 'socializing' effect upon Baltic decision-makers and, consequently, upon Baltic security policies and concepts. The presence and participation of the Baltic states in political, military and economic fora seeks not only to bring them closer to the framework of European security but, more importantly, to entrench in them the values and principles incumbent upon members of those institutions. The cooperative programme that has developed since 1992, with association, partnership and membership of a wide range of international institutions, has addressed not only the practical and logistical matters of 'interoperability', but also the more conceptual ones. In this way, security and stability in the Baltic region, and in the Baltic states in particular, will rest upon indigenous security, backed up by external affiliation – a much stronger prospect than 'importing' security guarantees.

The cooperative programme must be seen in the context of two parallel frameworks: multinational activity, such as the so-called '5+3' cooperation between the Nordics and the Baltic states (Finansministeriet, 1997: 73; Gylys and Norrback, 1996); and bilateral cooperation, which for some 'supporter' states, makes up the lion's share of their cooperative activity in the Baltic. For example, Norway's support for the Baltic peacekeeping battalion – BALTBAT – constitutes their largest single defence-related project directed towards the Central and Eastern European countries. The bulk of Denmark's cooperative activities in the Baltic is bilateral, with a budget in 1997 of 70mil. Dkr., rising from 10mil. DKr. in 1994 (Ministry of Defence, 1997b: 3). Prior to the launch of NATO's Partnership for Peace in January 1994, Denmark had concluded bilateral Cooperation Agreements with Poland and Latvia, with Estonia and Lithuania following soon after. These Agreements allow for the development of Annual Work Programmes, determined between the signatories according to need, and include such activities as high level visits between Ministries and Chiefs of Staff, and staff talks and courses on security and defence issues, as well as military training at officer and NCO levels, though it should be noted that the latter are not utilized to their fullest potential (Libak, 1997: 12). Not only are the Baltic defence forces being trained at a practical level, as a consequence of their being created anew, but the Defence Ministries themselves are being constructed, developed and trained – tutored by the Nordics in such issues as 'personnel management, civil-military interface, environmental management in the armed forces, the legal framework of defence, procurement, and information technology' (Ministry of Defence, 1997b: 8).

The Nordic countries have helped the Baltic states by giving 'sovereignty support' to assist their police forces, border controls and defence administrations 'to bring them up to the level required for safeguarding sovereignty and self-determination' (Ministry for Foreign Affairs, 1995: 23). For example in December 1994 a fast patrol boat was transferred from Norway to each of the Baltic republics; Estonia has received additional patrol ships and radar equipment from Finland and Sweden, as well as surveillance equipment and instruction for its border guards. Sweden has also opened an assistance programme – a 'Sovereignty Fund' – aimed at providing financial assistance for the development of border controls (Ministry of Foreign Affairs, 1997). Secondly, they have held meetings of Nordic and Baltic prime ministers (the fourth was held in November 1996) at which they have planned cooperation in wider fora and also established joint task forces such as that to fight against criminality in the area. Also seminars have been held between the defence ministers of the Baltic and Nordic states.

The new security agenda has placed an emphasis on institutions and on regional solutions. In the Baltic region, the Nordic Council acted as model and stimulus for the creation of a Baltic Council between the three Baltic states, and a Danish–German initiative led to the creation of a Council of the Baltic Sea States (CBSS) in 1992, on which is represented the governments of all the Baltic coastal states, as well as Norway and Iceland. The CBSS was organized to improve cooperation around the Baltic Sea, promoting democracy, the rule of law, economic cooperation and environmental development, and thereby addresses the needs of 'soft' security (Carlsen, 1997: 6; Council of the Baltic Sea States, 1997). Indeed, it was established in light of the wider understanding of security – that of a more comprehensive, and a decidedly cooperative approach. The CBSS has produced an Action Programme for Baltic Sea States Cooperation that has the aim of increasing people-to-people contacts and 'civic security', identified as the non-military elements of 'soft security', which in itself was defined as 'all aspects of security short of military combat operations including the defence of the national territory' (Helveg Petersen, 1996: 1). It has been stressed that the CBSS 'could not and should not provide security in the traditional sense of the word' (Poulsen-Hansen, 1997: 67), and this is perhaps not surprising given the negative reaction of decision-makers in the region to subregional security solutions (Knudsen, 1996b: 9). It is clearly not a substitute for integration into the European security structures, but its value is to be seen in the 'training' of 'participant countries in the peaceful resolutions of common problems and promotion of mutual trust' (Carlsen: ibid.).

The other – military – aspects of 'soft security' have been addressed in the programme of cooperation undertaken within the North Atlantic Cooperation Council and the Partnership for Peace, but also by the Nordic states in the way that they have encouraged Baltic defence cooperation as a contribution to UN peacekeeping. A peacekeeping battalion – BALTBAT – was established following a Baltic initiative in 1993 to enhance their individual and joint security (Dalbins, 1996: 10; Ministry of Defence, 1997a). After the signing of a Nordic–Baltic Memorandum of Understanding (MOU) on the formation of the battalion in June 1994, and a similar agreement with the addition of the United Kingdom, the Nordic states, together with the United Kingdom, developed a framework of cooperative activity with the Baltic states, to assist and advise in the establishment, training and operation of the battalion, and to provide for some *matériel* transfer (Ministry of Defence, 1997a). Preparations were made throughout 1994, and beginning in August 1996 the three national rifle company elements of the battalion joined Nordic units in both the IFOR and SFOR operations in Bosnia, and the Norwegian UN deployment in the Lebanon. The battalion planned for full deployment as a unit in early 1998. BALTBAT represents the Baltics' common objective of developing the interoperability of their defence forces with other Western forces. Furthermore, BALTBAT represents the Baltic states' commitment to being a 'contributor' to international security and stability.

In addition to language instruction, basic (NATO style) military skills, and UN peacekeeping training, the MOU stipulates that 'the multinational programme of practical assistance ... is designed to put in place mechanisms by which the Baltic States can take over the sustainment of BALTBAT' (Ministry of Defence, 1997a). Given that the battalion marks the chief development of Baltic defence restructuring, cooperation and interoperability, it is imperative that the Baltics learn the lessons being taught in this intensive programme, and in view of the fact that the support for the formation of the battalion is finite, that they learn these lessons quickly.

Following on from the BALTBAT project, and using its model of support and cooperation, the Baltic states are also developing a joint air-surveillance network – BALTNET – based in Lithuania, and a joint naval squadron – BALTRON – based in Estonia, tasked with mine-sweeping and minelaying, and coastal defence (*Baltic Times*, 1997a: 3; Ministry of Defence, 1997b: 12; Hækkerup, 1997b: 11–12). Plans are also in hand for a Baltic Defence College. These cooperative efforts are overseen by steering committees of a number of Nordic and NATO states and the Baltic states themselves, with the BALTBAT and BALT-NET committees being chaired by Denmark and Norway respectively, and Germany chairing the BALTRON committee.

The Nordic–Polish brigade deployed in IFOR in 1996 contained contributions from the Baltic states folded into the Danish battalion (Hækkerup, 1996: 11–13). This represented perhaps the most direct link between the Nordic and Baltic military. It was also part of the bilateral contribution made by Denmark to the Baltic states to allow them to build up their forces. Danish military assistance over three years to the three states has been estimated at about half the annual Latvian defence budget (Libak, 1997: 12). Finland has given considerable assistance to Estonia, building on the cultural and linguistic link between the two states. This bilateral aid has been placed in the context of a now regularized Nordic–Baltic defence cooperation (though excluding Iceland) seen in annual meetings of the defence ministers from the seven countries. These gatherings are underpinned by regular contacts between officials, and cover a wide range of issues from technical details to the question of the Baltic states' membership of NATO.

The Nordic states have played the dominant role in the question of the Baltic countries' search for NATO membership. The Baltic states are clearly attracted by the collective defence aspects of NATO and have rejected the alternative course taken, so far, by Finland and Sweden in their adherence to a policy of staying outside alliances. Norwegian practice has been to advise caution in relation to expectations about NATO membership (Brundtland, 1996: 15–16). Denmark, in particular, has been an advocate for the Baltic states' membership of NATO. However, its ministers have made it clear that it should be a reformed, more open NATO that takes in the Baltic states and that an agreement should be reached between NATO and Russia first. In other words they foresee NATO becoming more of a cooperative security organization in its relations with Russia, whereas Baltic leaders still see its value as a collective defence organization *against* Russia. The extension of NATO to include Poland in the Baltic region will do nothing to ease this dichotomy, and could even lead to greater pressure by Russia on the Baltic states to stay out of NATO. At the NATO Madrid summit, Denmark was among those members pressing for a positive mention of the Baltic States as potential candidates, and considered the outcome satisfactory in that respect. Furthermore, in the absence of immediate NATO membership, Danish representatives have pressed for closer Baltic links with NATO so that there is 'less difference between being a member of the Alliance and being a partner' (Hækkerup, 1997b: 15, author's translation).

The hope for the Nordic states must be that there is sufficient agreement between Russia and NATO over the question of NATO expansion and that the process does not just produce a new dividing line in Europe. Continued Finnish and Swedish absence from NATO will help to dispel such an idea, but meanwhile the Nordic countries are encouraging the Baltic states to deal with the very real threats to the fabric of their societies and to continue a political dialogue with all their Baltic neighbours in the regional organizations. In order to succeed, the Nordic states need not just a reasonable Russian–NATO relationship but also a willingness on behalf of the Baltic states to look to regional solutions while they are waiting for NATO. For many Baltic politicians, there is the fear that playing the regional game could be at the expense of their longer-term aims.

SUMMARY AND CONCLUSION

This chapter has sought to provide a brief overview of the interaction of the Baltic and Nordic states in the security field. It has portrayed the Baltic states as having one major concern in 1991 – establishing their independence and, for them, the main threat was the forces of the Soviet Union, later Russia. As time went by, and the withdrawal of Russian troops from their territory was negotiated, it became obvious to their leadership that other elements would have to be considered in the security field.

The Nordic states provided not only *matériel* assistance and training aid, they also had a number of security concepts that were in tune with those espoused by Western Europe and which came to prominence in the EU, WEU and NATO. If the Baltic states were to use the same language as that in these institutions, then it made sense to pick up, for example, Danish ideas about civic security or broader notions of cooperative security. This suggests a rather crude, instrumental use of the concepts that went along with the Nordic sovereignty assistance and training. There was another reason to listen. As it became clear that both NATO and EU membership would take some years – if achieved at all, that the threat from Russia was either overestimated or subsiding, and that other instabilities – economic, environmental and societal – were perhaps just as great threats to the three countries, the content of the concepts started to seem more relevant.

It may be that the Nordic states have little to teach the Baltic states in the area of security. On the other hand, the Nordic countries have managed to emerge from the shadows of their more powerful neighbours and have gained experience in dealing with prospective foes and with friends alike. It has been suggested in this chapter that the Nordic countries have had good cause to export to their new Baltic neighbours some of their security concepts as well as more direct assistance. This involves a particular way of looking at security that seeks as an outcome in the Baltic region cooperative and compre-hensive security, preferably in an institutionalized form that includes Russia and the Baltic states. There remains some doubt whether the Baltic decision-makers have accepted this viewpoint, though there seems to have been progress in that direction since 1992. Nevertheless, they have adopted some of the rhetoric and have matched that with action in limited areas. Perhaps one of the important lessons still to be learnt from the Nordic states is that, in the long-term, peace, prosperity and harmony will be achieved more readily when the values of social cohesion and solidarity, human rights and a functioning civil society are attained within a state.

NOTES

1 The authors would like to thank the Copenhagen Peace Research Institute, COPRI, Copenhagen, and the Norwegian Atlantic Committee, DNAK, Oslo for their assistance in the preparation of this paper.
2 This occupation would be seen by the Baltic states as extending until 1993/4, when Russian troops left their territory. Since declaring independence the Baltic states have repeatedly declared their orientation to Western cultural, economic, political and military values and structures. Though this means 'good neighbourly' relations between the Baltic states and Russia, it does not provide for acquiescence or weakness *vis-à-vis* Russia. (See Ulmanis, 1996b; Velliste, 1993b; Gylys, 1996.)
3 Developed in 1992 and adopted as a central tenet of Russian defence policy, the concept of 'Near Abroad' was essentially a way of redefining Russia's 'sphere of influence', particularly with reference to non-Russian former Soviet republics. Central to this policy was the military defence of Russian-speaking minorities in non-Russian territory, labelled 'peacekeeping'. Estonia feels

particularly threatened by this policy, given its large Russian minority and geographic proximity. (See statements by Estonian Foreign Ministers Velliste, 1993a; Luik, 1994).

4 Briefly, the 'open door' policy proposes that the first round of NATO enlargement should not be the last, that the policy of accepting new members to the Alliance be an ongoing and open-ended process. (Solana, 1997. For an Estonian perspective on NATO enlargement, see Ilves, 1997b. See Asmus and Larrabee, 1996 and Asmus and Nurick, 1996 for further discussion on the 'open door' concept).

5 See for example Ministry of Foreign Affairs, 1996, 'Action programme of the Government of the Republic of Lithuania for 1997–2000'.

6 Latvian President Guntis Ulmanis noted his country's 'responsible determination not to stay neutral as our greatest contribution to the international security policy'. Neutrality in this sense is understood to mean self-seclusion (Ulmanis, 1996a).

7 Recent studies have shown a marked lack of interest in national service amongst 'candidate' young men. The question of apathy to some extent derives from the perception of futility, given the apparent overwhelming odds facing Baltic security and their history of occupation. See report in *The Baltic Times*, 1997b: 7.

8 For a discussion of the question of (in)divisibility of security and the Baltic area see Heurlin, 1995: 63–4.

9 For a critical evaluation of a number of these security concepts, see Heurlin, 1996: 74–6.

10 For an academic appreciation of the problem, in a post-modernist evaluation, see Joenniemi, 1995: 6.

11 It should be noted that the five Nordic states embarked on the Baltic mission with different degrees of enthusiasm at different times. Here, the five are treated together as all made some contribution. However, for a treatment of their differences see Clive Archer 'Norden and the Baltic Region: Is there a security dialogue?', paper given at COPRI, Copenhagen, 22 April 1997, pp. 4–7.

12 These concepts are advanced in Bruce Russett and Harvey Starr, 1992: 20–24.

13 This had been the case in early 1991, when Soviet special troops had intervened in the Baltic states, which were still then regarded by Moscow as part of the Soviet Union.

14 Mouritzen (1997: 45–6) claims the reasons for Danish activism in the Baltic are domestic sympathy with the Baltic states with a wide political consensus on action; parallel action by the Nordic states with its aspects of rivalry and co-operation; serving the US interest (a factor he does not consider likely as an incentive); and Danish ideas about no longer being a small state. Knudsen (1996a) also deals with the domestic factors behind Norway's Baltic policy.

12

Bridging the Nordic–Baltic Gap or – the Nordic Predicament in the Baltics

GRETHE VÆRNØ

Norwegian National Defence College Alumni Association, Oslo

INTRODUCTION

Over the last few years since the beginning of the NATO enlargement process, the Nordic countries have been exposed to considerable expectations from Western partners, particularly NATO allies, to increase their contribution to the enhancement of the security of the Baltic states.

This chapter will discuss the Nordic attitudes, policies and roles in the regional security issues. It will also touch upon the question of the long-term organization of implicit or explicit security regimes in the area.[1]

The security problems of the area are fully discussed in other contributions in this volume. The particular challenge for the Baltic countries is a twofold one. It is a function of the relationship of Russia to the rest of Europe and the Euro-Atlantic community. It is also a specific one as elaborated by Olav Fagelund Knudsen in his chapter on the generic problem of security and sovereignty for small states at the great power fringe. In our case it concerns particularly Russia's relations with states and areas where she considers that vital security interests are at stake – and seen from Moscow as Russia's 'near abroad'.

The overall policy goals to which all the Nordics adhere, are on the one hand to secure stable internal conditions in Russia by economic, democratic and social development; to integrate Russia as an equal partner in European affairs; to modify Russia's foreign policy behaviour by satisfying her needs for security and identity as a big power. The different approaches are extensively discussed in this volume by Hermut Hubel.

On the other hand, the national sovereignty of the Baltic states must be strengthened – again partly by means of stabilized internal conditions; partly by the establishment of a minimum defence; and partly by integration in Western European multilateral organizations, providing a subtle kind of 'balance of power' in a comprehensive European security system.

These goals are not necessarily easy to reconcile. The relative emphasis on the two approaches will be influenced by the way the actors perceive the driving forces behind Russian foreign policy behaviour and how to influence its direction. Also it is a matter of proximity to the problems and national interests involved. Failing to find 'inclusive' solutions satisfying the Russians as well as the Balts, may force the choice of a 'Russia-first' policy, tacitly accepting Russian spheres of interest, or a 'Baltics-first' policy denying Russia this right and thus risking increased tension. These are particularly sensitive issues for the Nordics facing the problems at close range, in contrast to their Western allies and partners.

In this chapter I am first and foremost concerned with the issue from the perspective of the security of the Baltic countries. Bolstering Baltic security may be seen as a question of providing support to balance Russian influence. However, as Russia represents the security 'problem' of the area, there can be no stability in the area without Russian co-operation.

There is a tendency among policy-makers and academicians alike to think along lines of regionalization and regional responsibility for handling the most likely threats to European security: 'local' conflicts with a potential for developing into more widespread conflicts putting at risk the cooperation between the big powers – without really touching their national interests. Regionalism seems to become the centrepiece of the OSCE efforts to create a theoretical 'Model for the 21st Century'. Regionalism may also be understood as 'balancing on a lower level', without the direct involvement of NATO or the US, in this case to let the Nordics provide the 'balance' for the time being.[2] This view has probably been encouraged by the proactive policies of the Nordics themselves. They have incessantly stressed their individual and common important roles and responsibilities in the area which is now the EU/NATO 'flank' and doorway to and from Russia; and by their inclination to take initiatives and act as spokesmen for Baltic interests.

Inevitably this raises the question of which region we are talking about. In this paper I take the Baltic Sea Region as a point of departure. However, we also have to take account of a 'Nordic' region comprising only the Nordic countries, as well as a Nordic–Baltic context or axis. The Baltic Sea region is generally supposed to be centred around the Baltic Sea including the whole or part of Russia and extending to Norway and the High North with a frequent question mark. In security terms, however, it is an open question whether a Baltic Sea region concept is appropriate – in the sense that all the littoral states are somehow involved in the same security problem. The security interrelationships between these states are not at all clear, as discussed by Raimo Väyrynen. This region is not itself a 'zone of conflict'. The functional context of the Russian–Baltic security problem may perhaps more appropriately be thought to comprise states of the former Soviet Union and the Warsaw Pact in an East- and Central-European axis or triangle described elsewere in this volume.

We may also see the problem as a structural one to be handled on the European or Euro-Atlantic level, with the Nordics more or less disassociating themselves from any specific security link.

THE NORDIC COUNTRIES – BACKGROUND

The Nordic countries are integral parts of a Baltic region as defined in this case. They are not only contributors to stability, or to Baltic sovereignty. They, particularly the Fennoscandinavian ones, Finland, Sweden and Norway, are fringe states themselves, in a sensitive strategic area and close to one of the potential zones of conflict among states formerly parts of the Soviet Union.

'Norden' is the common Scandinavian name for the region comprising the five Nordic states. This term will be used even in this English text. As Iceland as a Nordic country still represents a particular case in security questions, this country will be mentioned explicitly when the text includes Icelandic positions.

The terms 'Norden' and 'Nordic' are often being used rather carelessly when referring to any constellation of Nordic states: either the two militarily non-aligned Baltic Sea states Finland and Sweden; the three NATO states Iceland, Norway and Denmark; the three EU states Denmark, Finland and Sweden; or the same three Baltic Sea states. In security matters the term 'Fennoscandinavia', indicating the three countries most influenced by the Russian neighbourhood, is increasingly being used.

In the following I shall first look at Norden as a subregion in itself, to see how they perceive their own interests and what experience and security concepts they bring to the regional questions. To analyse the prospects of any common Nordic strategy, one has to have a sober view of convergencies and divergencies. Norden is a typical example of 'now we see it, now we don't'. The reason for this is perhaps that the Nordic identity today is a product as much of a political 'project', as of a legacy of common history for good or bad; cultural similarities, a common language group except for Finnish, and the geographic proximity of a group of like-minded, small neighbours. The Nordics do not constitute any entity of states that can easily be lumped together as a component in any regional regime, despite their highly developed patterns of cooperation. This is particularly true in security questions.

There are several ways of looking at Nordic history. The prevailing theory today takes as a point of departure that Nordic interstate relations and Nordic security politics are the product of the law of gravitation within a 'Nordic Triangle' – where outside powers, notably the Atlantic powers, Russia, and the Continental powers (Germany or now the EU) exert a 'pull and push' effect on the Nordic states in three different directions, in a permanent geopolitical pattern. Gravitation is understood as the degree of influence exerted by a large power on small neighbours subject to variations in mass, distance and counterweights. The 'Triangle effect' became most evident during the pre-war and war years 1939–45 when the Nordic states were caught – each in its way – in the pinch between the contending parties.

The Second World War was a demonstration of the instincts for self-preservation of each Nordic country under strain, the lack of a perceived common security interest, and the absence of sufficient power, individually or combined, to resist the great power influence and deter or deflect pressure or aggression. Sweden, in particular, had also learned that weak neighbours are a security risk.

The 'Triangle theory' has gained substance by the way the Nordic countries – with the possible exception of Denmark which might have preferred a Nordic defence pact – had either to adjust or, if possible, to counterbalance the pressure from the Soviet Union by attachment to another pole of power. In this calculation they had to take into account what areas the big powers considered 'legitimately' within their and the other states' spheres of interest. Finland accepted her accommodation to the Soviet Union, formalized by the Pact of Friendship and Cooperation of March 1948. At the same time she fought for recognition as a 'neutral' state, politically placing her outside the Eastern Bloc. Norway had been recognized as a part of the Western sphere of interests. She used her freedom to enlist wartime allies in an overt balancing act and escaped definitely into the Western bloc as a charter member of NATO in 1949. Denmark and Iceland followed Norway with some misgivings. Denmark was traditionally perceived as being subject to Continental, particularly German forces of gravitation. Sweden might have had a choice – finding herself at the balancing point where she, at a probable cost to Finland, might have chosen a Western affiliation. She chose a continued policy of 'non-alignment in peace with the purpose of neutrality in war'.

At the same time they all tried to find a balance between a non-provocative, reassuring adjustment policy *vis-à-vis* Moscow – and a national defence of a sufficiently deterring capacity. In all the Nordic states, rational considerations as well as the effect of the shadow of the Soviet Union on their psychology, shaped policies with strong components of adjustment. The Nordic countries had, however, all definitely learned that collective security did not work, and that a declaration of neutrality was of no avail if warring parties did not respect it. They felt the need to defend their independence by demonstrating their will and ability to resist armed attack. While Finland and Sweden counted on independent national defence, Iceland became for all practical purposes a US 'client' with NATO membership, no national defence and bilateral defence agreements with the US. Norway and Denmark counted on allied deterrence and reinforcement of their own inadequate defence capabilities.

Pattern or Balance

The imposed or chosen security posture of the Nordic countries necessarily resulted in different emphasis on the respective deterrence and détente/accommodation factors in the handling of the Soviet 'challenge', as well as in different official interpretations of the nature of the East–West confrontation. However, all of them officially preferred to define the tension and the risk of war purely as a function of superpower or East–West confrontation. The Nordics may have 'chosen to itch where they could scratch'.

All the Nordic states considered their policy during the Cold War a success and a contribution to stability in the area as a whole. One trend of thought, most prominent in Norway, has seen Norden as a dynamic system of balances to offset or deter Soviet 'imperialism' or 'expansionism'. A 'Nordic balance', whereby changes in the policies of one of the power blocs *vis-à-vis* one of the Nordics would incur reactions from the other bloc in a self-adjusting equilibrium. For Sweden and Finland to discuss security in those terms during the Cold War would be to recognize a certain right of the great powers to adjust the balance at the expense of the Nordics and to admit that deterrence was necessary for their own security as well.

Sweden countered with the concept of a static 'Nordic pattern'. The combined effect of Finland with its adjustment policy, Norway and Denmark as NATO members on 'minimum conditions', and Sweden with its non-alignment policy with a large element of political 'bridge-building', created an area of stability as a buffer between East and West. The area was characterized by a high degree of predictability and relatively low levels of armaments – on the Nordic side.

Nordic Security Interactions

Thus the Nordic countries have lived with widely different security postures. However, the Nordic area has had a strong internal security dimension in several respects. Firstly, the term 'security community' is used to connote the character of Nordic relations, where disagreements are routinely played down and usually solved at a very low level. 'Peace structures' have been built up in all segments of the societies to absorb differences.

Another feature of the relationship is their shared concern as neighbours of the Soviet Union/Russia in a sensitive strategic area. The security and defence policy of each country was seen to have important potential consequences for the security of the others, and were taken into consideration in the defence planning of each country. In some ways Norden, particularly Fennoscandinavia, could be seen as a strategic unity, where it would be impossible for any country to avoid being touched by a superpower conflict taking place in the North. After the Sweden-initiated negotiations for a Nordic defence pact aborted in 1948, a secret wish lingered on for a combined defence effort of the Fennoscandinavian countries should they all become involved in the same war. Such sentiments were found among the military and were perhaps most openly expressed in Norway.

Yet another security aspect was obvious in the postwar years in the strong Finnish but also Swedish interest in using Nordic cooperation as a link to the West in order to counteract isolation and conduct the two 'neutrals' into the Western orbit. Such measures were considered to have a function as a low-level 'balance' to ward off undue pressure from the Soviet Union and to increase the self-confidence and resilience of the small countries. Most noteworthy has been the intimate Nordic–UN cooperation, with the exception of sensitive East–West and disarmament questions, where the split was absolute and sometimes quite embarrassing.

Thus the Nordic states bring to the matter of regional security a rich and varied experience of living with geopolitical realities and each other. The open questions are: Which of these elements are still relevant for the Nordics today? Which elements may be applicable to the larger region under new circumstances?

CHANGES: CHALLENGES AND POLICIES IN A REGIONAL PERSPECTIVE

With the fall of the Soviet Union the position of each country changed in ways which are as yet hardly digested. The old concepts of a Nordic pattern or balance within the old Nordic region has to be redefined.

For Sweden and Finland the most momentous change was EU membership from 1995, which entrenched them firmly in the Western sphere, providing them with the political security of belonging to a powerful entity. However, it still leaves open the question whether the 'small state' syndrome at the Russian fringe has been permanently eliminated for those countries.

Geography explains why the Nordics – though in varying degrees – are still highly sensitive to Russian policies. Finnish relations to Russia are determined by the long common border with Russia from the Barents region to St Petersburg, and the correspondingly important economic and security interests. Finland emphasizes that Finnish foreign policy is now defined by EU membership and that Russia is not so important to Finland any more. However, it remains to be seen whether Russia will consider Finland outside its reach, or only on a very long leash.

Norway also shares a short land border with the military complex in Murmansk and an extensive, partly disputed sea border with Russia in the strategically important Barents Sea, rich in oil and fish. Her primary security interest is to safeguard her sovereignty in the North and secure her relationship with Russia with the support of the allies.

Sweden for her part has no common border with Russia. She is protected militarily by the Finnish buffer, and reaps a security dividend from the independence of the Baltic states. Traditionally, however, Russia has been seen as the main threat. Still today a majority of the population sees Russia as the main security problem.

Denmark's situation and policies are clearly different. She is by geography not a 'fringe state', and the strategic changes in the Baltic area have further removed her from the potential 'front line'.

In response to this situation, one of the characteristics of all the Nordic states at the moment, is their parallel courses towards the Western centres of power. The logic of the situation drives Finland and Sweden towards as full and comprehensive an integration as possible in the West European based 'security community' – though not to the price of reciprocal defence obligations in an alliance. Finland and Sweden will be extremely wary of any developments that may put in jeopardy the security bonus they have won by EU membership, particularly as they have once and for all relinquished the idea of uni-lateral neutrality as a security shield.

Changing Security Structure

The general development is, however, constantly introducing new elements of uncertainty into the security equation of the Nordics. There are diverging views among the Nordics on the different models of

European security architecture. The differences are due to reliance on different security concepts, membership in different organizations, and different military alignment policies. Each Nordic country wants to strengthen the security impact of the organization where it itself seeks security. It is important to each of them that cooperative efforts are initiated in fora where they themselves can participate in the decision-making process.

The two militarily non-aligned have expressed a certain concern that the Russian–NATO agreements might weaken the position of third countries by giving Russia too much influence in new structures that are instrumental for the security of the small countries. NATO enlargement and the development of a European security and defence identity (ESDI) within NATO might work in the same direction. Norway for her part is satisfied with continued emphasis on NATO even though she has reason for concern that enlargement, Russia–NATO deals, and a shift to 'new NATO' tasks might weaken the military guarantee element in Article 5. Denmark appears to see her interests fully served by NATO developments and conducts a proactive policy in support of them.

One important element of change is the development of 'co-operative defence' – an all-European cooperation in crisis management and peace operations – invariably greeted with enthusiasm by the Nordic governments, including the Icelandic one. It has opened a road for Sweden and Finland to integration without alliance obligations, whether in the EU, WEU or in the 'new NATO'. For them this is a security bonus to the extent that participation serves to increase their influence and relevance and, perhaps, offers them some support in times of need. However, by participating actively in shaping a system for crisis management, they will themselves be entangled in it. In regard to peace operations in their 'near abroad', the Nordics have to varying degrees been careful. They are hedging against conflict with Russia by insisting that such operations should only be undertaken under mandate from OSCE or UN.

Finally the 'neutrals' in the Baltic region risk being seen as part of a 'grey zone' to be covered by peacekeeping or NATO out-of-area operations. A critical point for these two countries is that they do not have full and equal access to the decision-making fora either in NATO or in the WEU, even if the establishment of the Euro-Atlantic Partnership Council (EAPC) and other developments may point to a more influential role for the non-NATO partners.

For Norway there is a major difference. While a shift of emphasis from NATO's Article 5 to the 'new NATO' tasks makes it easier for Sweden and Finland to approach NATO, it may lessen the security guarantee to Norway instead of increasing it.

Nordic Convergence?

Developments have led to a convergence in the security situation of the Nordic countries, in particular the Fennoscandinavian ones. First of all Sweden and Finland as EU members are today closely associated with Western interests, and have a stake in West European and Atlantic security – to the point of now openly admitting the necessity of a US presence in Europe and in the Baltic Sea.[3]

They are tied up with the formulation of European security policies through overlapping NATO and EU procedures. Still the historic experience continues to be reflected in their policies. Limits to convergence and military cooperation are set by continued though increasingly conditioned unwillingness on the part of Finland and Sweden to enter into binding alliances. Norway and Denmark are tied up with NATO obligations. They have to risk involvement when NATO as a whole involves itself – self-evidently in Article 5 operations, but probably also in out-of-area operations. Sweden and Finland on their side both maintain that their countries are able and prepared to defend themselves – and themselves only. They do not need – or wish for – any defence commitments. Sweden has reformulated its neutrality policy to a policy of non-adherence to military alliances with the purpose of 'being able to stay neutral' in a conflict in its close neighbourhood.[4]

Secondly the threat perceptions of the Nordics are remarkably similar. The official line of all the Nordics is that there is no military threat foreseeable against their countries. The East–West confrontation is over, and there are no bilateral problems apart perhaps from the still unsolved border problems in the High North. However, they all concede that the uncertainty about developments in Russia persists, and that the vast military concentrations and nuclear weapons in North-West Russia are facts of life. The Fennoscandinavians structure their reduced forces with a view to a possible confrontation with the only potential military threat.

They are worried by the irreconcilable attitude of Russia *vis-à-vis* the Baltic countries and by Russian perceptions of their 'legitimate' spheres of interest and views of Russian security problems in the region as explained in the contribution of Arkady Moshes. In Nordic politics we can distinguish two different views of Russia – as a state with a legitimate fear of encirclement and US/NATO 'threat', or as a state lingering on the brink of imperialism or expansionism. Today, when the Western allies strive to portray Russia as a security partner, it is not politically opportune to portray Russia as an imperial threat to its neighbours. Logically this leaves the Nordics with the not altogether popular notion of accepting legitimate Russian security interest in its 'near abroad'.

Thirdly defence and security cooperation has been a growth sector since the fall of the Berlin Wall. The political dialogue expanded rapidly on regional and European security issues. So did practical military co-operation particularly in relation to UN operations, Nordic defence equipment cooperation, and cooperation in relation to the Baltic states. The North Atlantic Cooperation Council (NACC), the Western European Union (WEU) and the Partnership for Peace (PFP) provided common meeting grounds for politicians and military alike. The integration of Sweden and Finland into European cooperative defence (in a NATO context), was helped along by the Nordic connection as well in IFOR, where the 'Nordic brigade' provided the initial 'fig leaf', as in PFP. Once the mental and political road blocks were removed, the concept of cooperative defence itself paved the way for extended Nordic military cooperation, not least in the military assistance to the Baltic states – soon to become one of the official reasons for Nordic military cooperation.

Policy practitioners seem in general to have sensed a marked reduction in enthusiasm for a purely Nordic military cooperation since the 'EU rift' in 1995. However, we should not disregard continued military interest in a kind of cooperation that might reinforce the defence of the whole Fennoscandinavian area, particularly as the small Nordic countries all have problems with keeping up a credible, balanced defence. There seems anyway to be considerable interest in bilateral military cooperation, not least between the 'neutrals' Finland and Sweden, while any Nordic cooperation in national defence is limited by the non-NATO membership of the 'neutrals'. The theory of increasing convergence of the Nordic countries also opens up the highly contentious question of whether technological, military and political development has made the Nordics even less able than before to distance themselves from an armed conflict involving one of the others.

Despite the convergence of security positions in Norden, a new and negative factor, particularly for Norway and Iceland, is the relative deterioration of the five-state *Norden* as an exclusive framework for general cooperation implying a further marginalization of the Nordic non-EU members. True enough the parliamentary assembly Nordic Council may have a residual value as a framework for neighbourhood cooperation; as a disguised Nordic caucus for the Nordic EU members; and as a forum for the co-ordination of their regional policies. It has been a useful avenue for a concerted effort directed at the small Baltic states exclusively, without raising Russian hackles, or exposing any of the Nordic governments individually.

There are however three main reasons for the weakening of the inner Nordic cohesion. One is obviously that EU membership leaves little room for 'sideshows'. 'Nordic cooperation' is a term increasingly synonymous with intra-EU cooperation between the Nordic EU members.

Secondly, the increasingly intimate cooperation of Sweden and Finland with the 'new NATO' creates direct links of communication to the centre, gradually reducing the need for Norway and Denmark as intermediaries.

The last but not least important reason is the emergence of the Baltic Sea area as a dynamic, challenging area for the Nordic Baltic Sea states. The term 'Nordic' is often seen as inclusive of the small Baltic states. Conceptually the 'Nordic region' is being absorbed in a Baltic or North-East European region, and seen as a subregion in a EU or NATO/PFP context.

The Regional Factor

Thus we are brought to the introduction of the extended regional aspects of security. With the independence of the three Baltic states the Nordics had to see their own vital and common interests linked up with stability and security in the Baltic Sea or in a 'Nordic–Baltic zone of conflict'.[5]

Low-level risks threaten to spill over into the Nordics' territories. Any conflict might confront them with severe political dilemmas, cause 'East–West' tension which they could hardly escape as EU or NATO members respectively, and influence their own neighbourly relations with Russia.

The national interests of the Nordics are definitely also brought into focus by Russia's continued interest in and proposals for regional arrangements to meet Russian security problems. We may even add the important proposition by Olav Fagelund Knudsen that the Nordic countries have identical interests in modifying the hegemonistic leanings of great power neighbours. It can also be argued that the strategic gains brought by Baltic independence, particularly for Sweden and Denmark, are worth fighting for.[6]

The Nordic countries are, however, divided internally as well as among themselves in their views as to the limits to their responsibility and to the degree of challenge to their own national interests inherent in the issues. They find themselves to varying degrees caught between Russia and the Baltics.

In the case of Finland potential conflicts between Russia and Estonia would leave her extremely exposed politically and militarily. Despite its close relations, especially to Estonia, Finnish policy could probably be labelled a very careful 'Russia-first' policy, with a reservation about the impact of EU policies. Norway, while sharing Finland's preoccupation with Russia, is not a Baltic Sea state. Norway is devoting her main energy to the Barents cooperation and stresses the value of a multi-lateral framework that highlights inclusive Russia–West cooperation as a contribution to the stability of the whole 'Nordic–Baltic flank'. Norway also has a leaning towards a non-confrontational adjustment policy despite its own policy of deterrence *vis-à-vis* the Soviet Union/Russia. Not until the NATO Madrid meeting in July 1997 did Norway take a firm official stand on Baltic NATO membership.

Sweden on the other hand is not squeezed between Russia and the Baltic countries in the same way as Finland. She can afford a more pronounced 'Baltics-first' policy, stressing a Nordic–Baltic axis of co-operation. At the same time Sweden is perhaps the most insistent advocate of stabilizing regional cooperation, with a heavy emphasis on Baltic sovereignty, combined with an accommodating attitude towards Russia for Sweden as well as for the Baltic states.

Denmark's interests in the area – and the remarkable level of activity on behalf of the Baltic states and Poland in a clear 'Baltics-first' policy – have been explained mainly as a strategy for increased national relevance in the fora determining policies of vital importance to Denmark. The Danish government seems to be thinking along the lines of a EU–NATO region with an axis through Denmark, Germany and Poland up to the Baltic countries, with the purpose of providing security support and NATO connections to the exposed countries.[7]

The involvement of the three Nordic EU members in the Baltic states may also be explained by the fact that the Baltics are candidates for membership in the EU, and as such participate in EU activities on a large scale together with the EU Nordics.

In addition to the evident self-interests, the Nordics are exposed to external pressures from several quarters. Firstly the Nordics had the problems put on their doorstep by hard-to-resist pressure for support from all three of the Baltic nations from long before the acknowledged independence.

Secondly the Nordic NATO members have to share NATO responsibilities for the situation NATO has itself created for the Balts by the enlargement process. The Nordic EU members for their part have done their utmost to have the Baltic states accepted as EU candidates. They have to face the possibility of extending to new EU members the same solidarity and political security that they themselves expect from their membership. The same applies of course to Denmark and Norway in relation to NATO.

In a more recent development the main pressure stems from EU as well as NATO partners. The issue of NATO enlargement forced the question of how to counteract the impression of Western abdication of power by providing compensatory security to countries not likely to become NATO members. Western powers were caught in the dilemma of not being willing or able either to accept Russian views of the Baltic states as 'near abroad', or to extend any military guarantees. The Nordics suddenly figured as important actors in the region, and references to Nordic responsibilities could be heard at high official levels. These vague ideas were gradually tuned down, and substituted with a more subtle approach. The Americans appealed to the Nordics in turn, in order to maximize their contribution to whatever could be done to accommodate the Balts – barring NATO membership.

All the Nordics categorically stated that it was out of the question for them to undertake any obligations for the defence of the Baltics, or to enter into any special arrangement of non-alignment. They were left with two options – in reality if not in words. They could tacitly accept the Baltic states as a 'grey zone' in the name of stability, as they had done before in the case of Finland. Or, they could work to lift the security of the small fringe states out of a 'grey zone' and into a common European responsibility involving the big powers – also by indicating willingness to do their share.

The idea of organizing PFP activities on a regional basis that could weave the Balts into the NATO-based cooperative defence system took hold. The Swedish Moderate leader Carl Bildt was inspired during the fall of 1996 to introduce a proposal for a Nordic–Baltic Partnership, with or without the Nordic NATO countries included. Half a year later the Swedish defence minister flatly declared himself against any thought that Sweden or any other small country should take the lead in regional security initiatives.[8] Also, the Swedes constantly pronounce themselves against any regional PFP not firmly linked with NATO at a central level.

The bottom line would be that increased Nordic contributions to Baltic security would only be acceptable if combined in package deals of structures that would also reinforce the security of the Nordics. How to do this has obviously been a contentious issue among the Nordics, particularly as it involves the question of internal organization within NATO. While Norway has advocated 'regional tables' within the new Euro-Atlantic Partnership Council, EAPC, Denmark has promoted her own role as centre for a regional NATO structure with responsibility for NATO-based cooperative defence activities in the Baltic region.

BRIDGING 'THE NORDIC–BALTIC GAP'?

Overall policy

The NATO enlargement issue put a spanner in the works of the 'soft security' – or 'stability' cooperation – by its unwelcome focus on national defence for the states that are not members-to-be of the Alliance. The 'hard' security dimensions brought out the differences in security concepts among the Nordic countries and made the already quite difficult balancing acts even more delicate. The Nordics still prefer to keep up the good works in what has been termed 'fair weather policies'. As a first line of explanation of policies they tend to say that 'soft is the answer' because there is no threat of a military kind. Conflicts should be handled by peaceful means within a collective security framework.

The Finnish and Swedish governments initially maintained that NATO membership would be an unnecessary and undesirable militarization and a threat against stability in the area.[9] This official stance was an implicit message to the Balts to learn from their example. Besides, in the opinion of Nordic governments, military action is no solution to problems. It is difficult to determine whether this policy represents a real belief in pan-European collective security or whether it is an attempt to bridge inconsistencies by offering a 'grand design'. The message is, however, hardly credible in light of their own defence policies.

The second line of explanation is quite simply that 'soft is the answer' because nobody has any other answer for the moment. If and when the Baltic countries become members of either the EU or NATO, the Nordics will have to take on full responsibilities in line with their partners and allies – a fact that does not go unnoticed. Meanwhile other mechanisms to handle potential conflicts are called for, among others to exploit to the full the new openings offered by cooperative defence. This position does not, however, answer the question of whether intensified military cooperation among the littoral states (including Russia and Norway) in reality constitutes a barrier to any thought of the use of violence among neighbours in the area.

Obviously, despite the 'no-threat theory', the Nordics admit the need for some deterrence factors as seen in the discussions on 'military vacuum', cooperation on sovereignty support, and in the advocacy of EU membership for the Baltic states. They have different views on whether anything more is called for, as was evident in the solitary Danish and Icelandic campaign for Baltic NATO membership until the Madrid meeting, when Norway openly followed suit. However, today they all refer to the agreed OSCE principles on interstate relations, including the right of all states to choose their own security arrangement – without the reservation that their choice must be accepted by their would-be partners!

At the same time they advocate a modicum of adjustment to a large neighbouring power whose constructive cooperation is fundamental to stability. At the bottom of this policy lies the wish to avoid any conflict with Russia and to prevent challenges to Russia's psychology which might turn Russia into a more troublesome neighbour. Also, by this 'soft' and as far as possible impartial policy, the Nordics escape the Russia- or Baltics-first dilemma.

Cooperation and Challenges

From the first possible moment, bridges were built across the Baltic Sea. Activity at the bilateral level has been considerable. The level of activity is so high that the Nordics time and again are stumbling into each other.

Joint Nordic initiatives have taken place first and foremost through the Nordic Council (NC), the Nordic Council of Ministers (NCM) and several Nordic loan and investment institutions. Nordic information offices were set up in the Baltic capitals and St Petersburg. Several joint Nordic projects were initiated at the governmental level. In the NCM and the regular meetings of foreign and defence ministries, the Nordics have consulted on Nordic positions on overall policies in the region, for example, on Baltic independence, Russian troops, Russian minorities and lastly on a common position on Baltic EU membership.

Baltic independence was followed by an interlude of Nordic euphoria. The question was raised whether to enlarge the NC with the three Baltic states – and throughout the years a tug-of-war has been waged as to the extent of integration of the Baltic parliamentarians in the NC. Baltic 'guests' participate regularly and Nordic–Baltic sessions or conferences are held on an almost regular basis. The NC stimulated Baltic parliamentary cooperation, and took the initiative to arrange the Baltic Sea Parliamentary Conferences. When the NC reorganized its work as a reaction to the Nordic EU split, a Nordic 'near abroad' programme constituted one of three pillars of the restructured NC, the other pillars being intra-Nordic cooperation, and common European issues, mostly concentrated around EU matters.

Sovereignty Support

Outside this formal Nordic framework initiatives were taken to enlist the Nordics in an effort to bolster Baltic independence and sovereignty by means of military assistance, for example, air and border control. This was followed by initiatives to encourage inter-Baltic military cooperation and to help the Balts prepare for and participate in international peace operations and PFP-exercises. These initiatives quickly turned into an extensive international endeavour where countries other than the Nordics increasingly played an active and initiating part. For all practical purposes none of the projects are purely Nordic in character. This development was highly welcome from the Nordic point of view.

However, the role of other states – and of the other Nordics – more often than not disappears in the official presentations of national achievements. The importance of national flagwaving apparently is so great that it has even been difficult to agree on a common approach to the co-ordination of activities.

Multilateral Structures and Networks

This brings us to the level of multilateral structures. Multilateralism may take many forms, in the choice of which we meet again the classical dilemma: 'Inclusive' institutions and regimes with the Russians as equal partners may fall into the category of 'adjustment' to Russian needs and demands, while organizations without the Russians will be perceived as support for the Balts (and part of a 'soft deterrence' or balance strategy.)

One kind of multilateralism is the integration of Russia and the Baltic states in 'inclusive', overall European organizations, whether extended Western organizations or pan-European ones like OSCE. Here we may include the NACC, now turned into the EAPC, and PFP programmes. However, even if the PFP has been defined as an *inclusive* programme, the Russians are clearly keeping their distance from this NATO-based programme, thus giving it a more Baltic-oriented profile.

Another kind of multilateralism is evident in the attempts to integrate specifically the Baltic countries into Western institutions where Russian membership is still out of the question, like the EU and NATO.

A third model of organization, and more easily attainable, is to work horizontally among the fringe states – setting up different kinds of 'Nordic–Baltic' cooperation. The scope of Nordic–Baltic cooperation has widened to a point where it might have been natural to ask whether institutionalizing this informal cooperation, for example, within the framework of the Nordic Council, would yield additional security benefits. Could it be a repetition of the Finnish strategy – to construct a 'Nordic' identity or link that would take the country a few steps out of Russian reach?

In their chapter in this volume, Heisler and Quester ask of existing organizations how much might be sacrificed existing purposes in order to support newer purposes. For the EU Nordics this could be seen as simply extending their EU obligations *vis-à-vis* third countries as part of the EU endeavours to stabilize its periphery by trans-EU-border regional cooperation. The possible reluctance of the non-EU members Norway and Iceland could be solved by establishing a Joint Council of the Nordic and the Baltic Council respectively, instead of enlarging the NC.

A more serious objection might be the doubt felt today among Nordics and Balts alike about the usefulness of reinforcing an impression of a Nordic–Baltic axis as a subsystem of fringe states or contributing to perceptions about an extended 'Nordic balance' or 'Nordic pattern'. There might also be a discussion about how much more can be obtained by an association with the Nordic states only, than that which is already obtained by the CBSS or the BS Council of Parliamentarians. These options also reflect preferences along the lines of regional, inclusive stability, or specific support to the Baltics.

Regional Inclusive Structures

A fourth kind of multilateralism can be found in regional structures including Russia, the Barents Euro-Arctic Council (BEAC) and the Council of the Baltic Sea States (CBSS). There is full political support in all the Nordic countries for the BEAC taking in hand practical cooperative measures between Western states and Russia in the North, and the CBSS. There have been, however, two main preconditions on the part of the Nordics. One was the participation of heavy external Western actors to provide the balance in otherwise lopsided frameworks, as well as a link to more substantial sources of funding. In both councils the EU became a full-fledged member.

The other precondition was the exclusion of issues that concerned the national security of the partners – out of three main considerations.

Firstly it did not make sense to allow conflicts between two countries or more to overshadow the effort to upgrade a common interest.

Secondly it is desirable to avoid issues that might imply – or raise expectations about – involvement in or obligations to the defence of the Baltic states in the case of a conflict with Russia.

Thirdly multilateral regional cooperation should not provide the point of departure for establishing any regional security regime. The Nordics have, for instance, had to face considerable interest from the Russian side to use the CBSS as the basis for a regional security forum introducing questions of regional arms control, discussion of 'models for the 21st century' and re-emerging thoughts about the 'Sea of Peace' and nuclear weapons-free zone as regional issues. The Nordics have insisted that regional fora should not discuss issues that should be left to treatment at a balanced European level as they are not 'regional' in character, whether they are Russian–Baltic ones or related to wider Russian military and strategic interests. The concerted Russian diplomatic initiatives in the Baltic area from the autumn of 1997 have caused headaches in all the Nordic capitals.

One major problem has been and still is the need to define and

defend a distinct line between those 'soft' issues that lend themselves
to regional cooperation and confidence building and the 'hard' issues
that in the opinion of the Nordic governments do not. They are finding
themselves on a slippery slope. Developments have diffused the border
line between soft and hard security, with the introduction of 'civil
security issues', CBMs at a Polish initiative, WEU parliamentary
resolutions about an emergency 'Hansa' naval corps for the Baltic Sea,
sovereignty support and projects for joint air surveillance, among
others, and 'cooperative defence' whether preparations for peace
operations or Partnership for Peace. PFP cooperation might be seen
to cover a broad spectrum of security, from low-level risk management
all the way to a substitute NATO membership.

There have been several reasons behind the Nordic reticence to any
regional security concept touching on military and defence matters.
First of all the Nordics' aim is to promote their own security within an
indivisible European security (whether it be the pan-European collective security one or the NATO-based military and EU-based political
one) and maintain a US balance of power/engagement in Europe, the
Baltic Sea included. In the context of a regional zone of conflict they
might be marginalized in overall European security because of the
lesser importance assigned to the region by their Western allies and
partners.

Secondly they do not want regional arrangements that might draw
them into Russian–Baltic conflicts by somehow inferring that they are
part of the same conflict. The Nordics might rather want to distance
themselves from Baltic–Russian controversies. The mere possibility of
being themselves drawn into such a conflict is one more reason for
insisting on big power responsibility in the region.

Neither do they want to be placed in the same category of states.
Even if the security problem as defined by Fagelund Knudsen concerns
all fringe states, any identification might be felt to be harmful, as it
could imply that their own positions were in question.

Thirdly the Nordics do not want to be locked into a separate
arrangement or into a concept of a security region in an area where
Russia was striving to be a hegemonic power. Trying to satisfy Russia's
security needs in a regional context would necessarily happen at the
expense of the small neighbours.

Most unwelcome would be the idea of establishing a formal, static
security regime, within the region, a pattern of national defence and
security postures designed to project stability by freezing the positions
of the littoral states.

We may suppose that this was not what Finland and Sweden opted
for when they exchanged their unilateral neutrality policy for EU
membership.

CONCLUSION

Parallel to the question of formal organization of security runs the question of whether there is already in place informal regional inter-relations, mechanisms of checks and balances, or a pattern of security structures. In that case, to what degree do the Nordic states play a part in the process and what kind of impact do the policies of the respective Nordic countries have today or might they have in the future on the Russian perceptions of their main security concerns?

The interactions in the area are exceedingly complex and a full analysis of this issue would fall outside the scope of this chapter. However, by way of conclusion, we may consider a few elements brought out by the fact that the Nordic Cold War theories of a 'Nordic pattern' or a 'Nordic balance' have been introduced in the debate on long-term solutions to the Baltic problem.

We may take as a point of departure that today there is no fixed or stable pattern in the area – quite to the contrary – even if all the Nordics have reconfirmed their alliance or non-alliance policies. A pattern may emerge in a painful process over several years. Meanwhile it is more appropriate to ask which 'balances' – including incentives – are at work and whether they are strong enough to restrain or modify Russian behaviour.

In this process one might consider ways of offsetting Russian power *vis-à-vis* the Baltic countries by having available a flexible set of responses from neighbouring states. Keeping options open for NATO membership for Sweden and Finland as well as for the Baltic states is possibly an element in a balancing policy.

However, there is probably a tendency in Norden to overestimate the importance of the Nordic countries. The 'Nordic balance' concept has mostly been used lately in relation to another axis of balances, namely the one linking Germany, Poland, Kaliningrad and the Baltic states. Here we may refer to other contributors in the present volume.

Secondly the Nordics probably do not have at their disposal any large arsenal of instruments. Any changes in policy in whatever direction would be subject to severe internal and external constraints.

Thirdly, it may be difficult to upgrade the – not necessarily compatible – Nordic views and interests into a coherent Nordic strategy. There are clearly common denominators in the policies of the Nordic countries thus far. However, the moment we start talking about Nordic contributions to the balancing of Russian behaviour, we should not expect too much by way of Nordic cohesion, except within the framework of a larger European and Atlantic strategy. A common platform seemingly depends upon continued fair weather where the 'soft' approach is possible and yields results.

Lastly we should not, however, preclude a very different development. The Nordic positions have moved very quickly along with the
overall developments, pushed forward by multiple pressures. As small
and vulnerable countries their freedom of action is limited by their
need to adjust to their big partners with whom they have linked their
destinies.

NOTES

1 Sources, documentation and literature: this paper leans extensively on docu-
mentation in connection with the following studies. In the list of references, see
Barth and Brodshaug (1997), Brundtland (1996), Dörfer (1997), Huitfeldt and
Gjeseth (1996), Neumann and Ulriksen (1996), Værnø (1990), Værnø (1993),
'Totalförsvar i förnyelse' (1996). See also the following documentation, not
included in the volume's common list of references: Værnø, Grethe (1996a)
'Norge og det nye NATO' (Norway and the New NATO), *Norsk Militært Tidsskrift*
(12); *idem* 1996b). 'Svensk og finsk hinderløp mot NATO' (Swedish and Finnish
Obstacle Course to NATO), *Norges Forsvar* (10); *idem* (1996c) 'Østersjøen, Norges
nye interessesfære' (The Baltic Sea, the New Norwegian Sphere of Interest),
Norsk Militært Tidsskrift. Also: Reports from the Norwegian Defence College
Alumni Association Study Committee (FHSFS): Værnø, Grethe/Project Group
'Norden': 'Felles sikkerhetsinteresser i Norden?', Oslo, 1996. 'Sikkerheten i
Norden i nytt lys', Nordic Seminar, 21–23.4.1995, Publication no. 3, 1995. –
'Hva skjer med Europa', Seminar 24–25.4.1996, Publication no. 1, 1996. – 'De
nordiske land mellom EU og NATO', Conference 20.2.1997, Publication no. 1,
1997, – 'Felles sikkerhet fra Barents til Østersjøen?' Conference 25–26.11.1996
arranged by Voksenåsen Foundation, The Embassy of Sweden and the Defence
College Alumni Association. See also speeches and addresses by leading decision-
makers: Gustafsson, Bengt: Statement by the Chief of Defence in Kungl.
Krigsvetenskapsakademien, Stockholm, 13 Nov. 1996. – Persson, Göran:
Address by the Prime Minister of Sweden at the Foreign Policy Association, New
York, 25 Sept. 1996. – Taina, Anneli, 'Säkerhetsutvecklingen i Europa och
Finlands försvar'. Statement of the Minister of Defence to Parliament, 17.3.1997.
SRR 1/1997, Helsinki. Official documents: 'Dansk sikkerhedspolitikk'. Publication from Ministry of Foreign Affairs, Copenhagen, Nov. 1996. – Papers from
'International Seminar on Regional Cooperation in the Barents, the Baltic Sea
and the Black Sea Regions'. Norwegian Ministry of Foreign Affairs 13–14 March
1997. – *Politik i NORDEN*. News bulletin published by the Nordic Council and
the Nordic Council of Ministers, Copenhagen. – Current communiqués from
OSCE, NATO and the EU.
2 See Olav Fagelund Knudsen's chapter in the present volume.
3 The Swedish Minister of Defence Bjørn von Sydow in a speech made on 29.4.97
in the Oslo Nobel Institute, arranged by the Norwegian Atlantic Committee.
4 This gives Sweden a bit of leeway – and keeps an option open as a signal to
Russia 'that Sweden cannot stay indifferent to any aggression towards the Baltic
states'.
5 This term was used by Norwegian Minister of Defence Jørgen Kosmo in his
message to the Storting in the autumn of 1995, inferring that none of the Nordics
would be able to escape a political or military conflict.
6 The early and spontaneous statement from the Swedish prime minister Göran

Persson when newly elected, to the effect that 'The Baltic case is ours', however, found no echo in the other Nordic countries.

7 Bertel Heurlin, FHS Conference Report no. 1, 1997.
8 Defence Minister Björn von Sydow.
9 See in particular simultaneous statements by Finnish president Ahtisaari and Swedish Foreign Minister Hjelm-Wallén and Defence Minister Thage Peterson, June 1996.

13

The Security of the Baltic Countries: Cooperation and Defection

RAIMO VÄYRYNEN

Joan B. Kroc Institute for International Peace Studies, University of Notre Dame

1. THE BALTIC CHOICES

Independence often brings with it a sense of almost unlimited opportunities. When the old imperial constraints have been removed, the new state starts a crash programme to integrate itself with the international institutions expecting them to recognize its sovereignty and confer on it protection and assistance. Soon it turns out, however, that sovereignty is almost a quasi-concept; while its legal and political meanings are quite specific, its practical implementation depends on the nature and capacity of the states involved and the situations in which they have to arrange their mutual relations. Therefore, the capabilities of states to meet the obligations of sovereignty and the commitments of other states to assure them always fall short of the ideal model.

1.1 Relations with great powers

This caveat also applies to the newly independent Baltic states whose options to find their place in the emerging post-Cold War structure of Europe are more limited than perhaps they originally expected. Moreover, they have themselves excluded some options; after having been occupied by the Soviet Union from 1940–91, they are now in no mood to ally with its successor state, Russia. In terms of alignments, Estonia, Latvia, and Lithuania have essentially only two options: non-alignment or an alliance with the West.

Neither of these options excludes a *rapprochement* with Russia and it is, in fact, a certain precondition for the admission of the Baltic countries to the European Union and NATO. However, until recently, neither these three countries nor Russia have shown any genuine interest in a mutual *rapprochement* to mitigate the security dilemma (unless the other party significantly alters its policies). The three most important elements in Baltic–Russian relations are the historical legacies, the security issues, and the Russian minorities, especially in Estonia and Latvia.

The position of the Russian minorities is not only a political problem, but it also has direct implications for the sovereignty of Baltic countries. Interethnic conflict tends to manifest the inherent tension between self-determination and sovereignty; its logic demands the former and challenges the latter. The intensity of this tension varies, of course, from one situation to another depending on the strategic importance of the country and the escalation potential of the dispute. Ethnic conflicts are also risks to security not only because of their potential for escalation, but also because of the conflicting and unpredictable responses of third parties to them (Shedadi, 1997).

The challenge of Russian minorities to the sovereignty and security of Baltic countries is not one of their secession, as these minorities are rather content with the economic and even political situation in their host countries. Tensions in Latvia escalated, however, in the spring of 1998 after 500 former SS troops organized a demonstration which faced a counterdemonstration by the Latvian Russians. Tensions have also been heightened by extremist bombings in Riga and calls by Russian politicians for the imposition of economic sanctions on Latvia.

Even these problems reflect more the primacy of the political and cultural minority rights of the Russian populations – which Estonia and Latvia have been somewhat slow to accept – than external Russian threat. Moscow has made it very clear that it intends to obtain these rights for Baltic Russians, by external measures short of military force if needed. Thus, Russia does not seem to seriously threaten the sovereignty of Baltic states, but poses a certain threat to their security.

Stalemate is perhaps the best way to describe the current Baltic–Russian relationship; both parties consider major concessions impossible, while Russia as the bigger power is unwilling, and possibly unable, to use force to break the political logjam. This stalemate is, however, dynamic in the sense that political and legal talks between the states continue and thus their relationship may be gradually redefined. In this dialogue, the Baltic countries also define the territorial, political, and cultural boundaries of their sovereignty, which is also reconstructed by their evolving relationship with the West (for a general analysis on the construction of sovereignty, see Biersteker and Weber, 1996).

All three Baltic countries have made a firm choice to seek an early membership in both NATO and the European Union as the best assurance for their political independence, national security, and economic development. This decision amounts to admitting that they are too weak, even together, to defend themselves and acquire a strong international position. Therefore, the Baltic states try to borrow support from the West to stabilize their independent existence. It seems that the Baltic countries do not have any specific Russia policy nor does Russia have any Baltic policy. Instead, they both try to manage mutual problems in larger contexts, and especially through the United States and NATO (Stranga, 1997: 193).

An intriguing question is whether the Baltic countries, in seeking Western support, are balancing the Russian threat or bandwagoning with the West. The most common view seems to be that the Soviet successor states have not, with the exception of the Baltic countries, balanced Russia and many have, in fact, bandwagoned with it. The reasons for this include Russia's military and economic support to the successor governments and the political coalitions running them and its disregard for the ideological orientations of these governments (Roder, 1997: 232–9).

If there is more than one great power in an international system, it may be difficult to distinguish empirically between balancing and bandwagoning, and motives for a choice between them. That is to say, bandwagoning with the West and the balancing against Russia are easily equated with each other, even though they may contain two different processes. The standard argument is that the Baltic countries have oriented themselves to the West to obtain security guarantees against the Russian threat to their independence and security. However, I would like to suggest that the Baltic policy of aligning with the West is informed as much by the effort of bandwagoning with it as balance against the Russian threat.[1]

The Baltic countries are not, of course, bandwagoning with the West because it threatens them, but because of its superior material capabilities and cultural attractiveness. The Baltics want to be a part of the West as such an association is in all respects more rewarding than a place in the Russian orbit. This suggestion is based on a somewhat controversial premise that the Russian threat to the security of Baltic countries is either small or at least exaggerated. Obviously, there is evidence about the Russian intentions to apply political and economic pressure on the Baltic countries and even intimidate them. To the extent Russia has resorted to pressure tactics, it may reflect confusion in its foreign policy-making and inability to decide how to deal with the strategically important region.[2]

While recognizing the reality of the Russian presence in and pressure on the Baltic countries, one cannot completely exclude the possibility that they are also making up these factors to draw Western attention. Their real motivations may be more linked with the realities of the unipolar world in which the dominant power and the politico-cultural system of the United States appeals to small states. Such states also have more freedom of action and regional opportunities in a uni-polar than a bipolar international system (Hansen 1998). Thus, the dominance of the West and its international institutions rather than the Russian threat may be the primary reason for the course of the foreign policies by the independent Baltic countries in the post-Cold War world.

The economic and cultural pull of the West and the perceived military push of the East as grounds for the Baltic external alignments are complemented by their historical learning experiences. This theory argues that 'formative historical experiences' provide lessons which inform the subsequent choice of alliance partners by small states (Reiter, 1994). It is quite clear that, in addition to the perceived threat from Russia, the policies of Baltic countries are even today influenced by the Soviet occupation, which beyond any doubt has been the most traumatic historical experience for them.

The West has adopted a cautious attitude towards the Baltic countries in considering their admission to NATO and the EU. There-fore, the Balts have to adopt, out of political necessity, a gradual, long-term perspective towards Western institutions. They would like to become card-carrying members of NATO and of the European Union as quickly as possible, but now they have to be content with the schedule prepared by others for them.

No doubt, this has frustrated the Baltic states; none of them is to be included in the first round of NATO enlargement in 1999 and the European Commission included only Estonia among the six countries with which it will start negotiations on membership. Even for Estonia, membership is unlikely before 2005. Thus, for the Baltics, life on the fault-line of Western and Eastern Europe continues to be a fact of life in the foreseeable future.

1.2 Intra-Baltic relations

After having attained independence by both separate and common efforts, the Baltic countries were clearly committed to a higher level of mutual cooperation than had been the case in the interwar era. Their collaboration then was plagued by mutual suspicion and unilateral solutions. In the 1990s, on the contrary, they have made serious efforts to cooperate. By establishing the Baltic Assembly, the Baltic Council of Ministers, and their joint session, the Baltic Council, intra-Baltic co-operation has gained an institutional dimension. Various environ-mental and economic projects have also been launched to strengthen the infrastructure of Baltic unity (Lejinš, 1997: 162–9).

However, there are still major gaps in the collaboration between the Baltic countries. In particular, their political cooperation seems to have become increasingly difficult after NATO and the European Union have started making real decisions on their enlargement, and the Baltic states have realized that they will neither sit in the front row nor be treated as a homogenous group. This has, of course, been the basic tenet of Western policy; all applicants to NATO and the EU have been scrutinized separately and strictly on their own merits.

In this competitive situation, commitments to mutual support have been evaporating among the Baltic countries and they have started pursuing their own strategies to gain access to NATO and the European Union. Mutual cooperation has had to yield to safeguarding one's own position. Realizing that they have been dealt weaker cards, Latvia and Lithuania have, since the summer of 1997, demanded that the European Union start membership negotiations with all three Baltic countries instead of only one.

Estonia has not refused to support this position, but it has not made its own position *vis-à-vis* the European Union dependent on what happens to the other two Baltic countries. Estonia justifies its separate treatment by its strong and consistent commitment to liberal market reforms. On the other hand, Latvia and Lithuania are thought to lag behind in aspiring towards membership conditions, an argument vehemently denied in Riga and Vilnius, which have repeatedly stated that the European Commission has been using outdated economic statistics which underestimate their progress (for background, see Lofgren, 1997).

The present situation in intra-Baltic relations can be illustrated by the distinction between 'dilemmas of common interests' and 'dilemmas of common aversions' (Stein, 1990: 32–8). Although some national differences exist, the Baltic countries have a common aversion to being subjugated again by Russia. Such a fear is probably exaggerated, but existential, shared by the Baltics for whom the preservation of national sovereignty is a key objective. On the other hand, their position towards the European Union has features of a prisoner's dilemma in which an equilibrium can be achieved only if Estonia eschews its chance to become an EU member and joins the ranks of Latvia and Lithuania outside the Union.

To guarantee a Pareto-optimal outcome in such a situation, 'the parties must collaborate, and all regimes intended to deal with dilemmas of common interest must specify strict patterns of behaviour and ensure that no one cheats' (Stein, 1990: 39–40).[3] Because of the great value attached by the Baltic countries to a membership in the European Union, this is an unlikely outcome. Thus, the determination of the Union to treat all countries only on their own merits has complicated intra-Baltic cooperation. On the other hand, the Baltics bear in mind the lessons of history and avoid an explicit break in their mutual relations as this would only give new means to Moscow to divide them.

2. THE NORDIC DIMENSION

The differential access of the Baltic countries to the European Union has also divided the Nordic countries. Sweden, but also Denmark and even Norway, have argued that all the Baltic countries should have an equal chance to test in negotiations their ability to meet the EU membership criteria. On the other hand, Finland favours the stance taken by the European Commission according to which only Estonia should be a candidate for membership this time. Nordic countries have been criticized for squabbling and failing to develop a coherent strategy to bring the Baltics into the wider European framework (e.g. Udgaard, 1997).

The Finnish position has been defended by saying that in several respects, including the viability of its economic and financial structures, Estonia is more ready than the others for membership. A reference has also been made to the spill-over effect which would help to bring Latvia and Lithuania to the European Union in the wake of Estonian membership.

To see the larger picture, one should go beyond these arguments and note that, as Cyprus is not a serious candidate, the European Union can probably take only five new members without changing its own institutional arrangements. The Amsterdam summit in June 1997 showed how difficult any major changes in the composition of the Commission, voting in the Council, and the power of the Parliament are for the Union. From this it follows that if the Union's internal politics exclude Latvia and Lithuania, then they should understand that even the admission of one Baltic state, that is, Estonia, also serves their real interests.

The Estonian candidacy sends a message to Russia that Western institutions are not afraid to admit Baltic countries. It has been argued in Finland that the demands of the Nordic–Baltic coalition to start membership negotiations also with Latvia and Lithuania may lead to Estonia's exclusion, which the Mediterranean members of the Union are all too willing to accept. This would dilute the message sent to Moscow and undermine future opportunities for the Baltic countries to become members of NATO (Kivinen, 1997). The weight of this argument is somewhat diluted by the fact that Russia seems to be accepting Estonia's talks with the European Union without protest, although the mutual relations between the countries are strained.

Thus, the discussion on Baltic membership in the EU cannot be seen in isolation from the decision by NATO in the Madrid summit in July 1997 to leave all Baltic countries on the waiting list. The Clinton Administration has publicly ridiculed the European Union for the timidity of its eastward expansion (Albright, 1997). Now the European Commission has sent a signal, albeit a cautious one, that it is ready for a bolder move than NATO, and may admit at least one Baltic country.

It is interesting to note that the Finnish and Swedish governments have been divided over the enlargement of the EU, while they have been largely united on their strategy towards NATO. On the other hand, one should not exaggerate the seriousness of this disagreement; it may only reflect the traditional tension between Finnish pragmatism and Swedish high-mindedness. Moreover, Finns work more closely with the European Commission, while Swedes, partly due to stronger domestic opposition to EU membership, have opted for a looser connection.

However, neither Finland nor Sweden plans, at least for the time being, to join NATO. They understand fully that Russia is opposed to their membership and, what may matter even more, that the United States is reluctant to engage with Russia in a new row over the Finnish and/or Swedish membership. On the other hand, if these two countries decide to apply, NATO cannot easily say no.

The cautious Finnish and Swedish attitudes towards NATO membership and satisfaction with their non-aligned status is not only due to their effort to satisfy the major powers, but also to their responsiveness to Baltic interests. The potential Finnish and Swedish membership in NATO would single out the Baltic countries as the ultimate outsiders and give Russia yet another reason for opposing their efforts at joining the alliance.

In this issue, Finland and Sweden face a (pro-Baltic) dilemma of common aversion which restrains their policies; by joining NATO they would, in reality, undermine the Baltic position. Some analysts have reversed the direction of causality by assuming that if the Baltic countries are 'left in a vulnerable position, the Russians will react harshly, and that their [Finland and Sweden] own security will be eroded as a result' (Asmus and Nurick, 1996: 126–7). This observation is based on the premise that Russians harbour aggressive designs towards the Baltic countries; however, in spite of all the rhetoric and violations of the CFE quotas, the chances of such a policy are limited.

The Finnish and Swedish policies *vis-à-vis* NATO reflect not only their prudent judgement of the international political realities, but also signal their responsiveness to Baltic countries, a criterion by which Karl W. Deutsch used to judge the existence of a pluralistic security community. Responsiveness is a more demanding criterion than the mere absence of military threats between the countries (Deutsch *et al.*, 1957). Recently, the theory of a pluralistic security community has been advanced by social constructivist scholars who argue that such communities share common identity. As a result, their members uphold the same norms and institutions and feel cultural affinity with each other (Adler and Barnett, 1996).

Karl W. Deutsch concluded that the Scandinavian countries formed one of the 13 pluralistic security communities that had existed in the nineteenth and twentieth centuries. In the present context the question is whether it is possible to speak of a pluralistic Nordic–Baltic security community. My answer is a tentative yes; although the common institutional ties are not very strong, all the eight Nordic and Baltic countries ('5+3') identifying with similar values and expecting any change in their mutual relations to be peaceful. They may even be ready to respond to selective, limited threats faced by other countries. The Baltic–Nordic security community is not, however, autonomous, but it is strongly influenced by the larger European and Euro–Atlantic security complex which includes Russia (Väyrynen, 1998: 167–70).

3. ARE LITHUANIA AND ESTONIA DEFECTING?

3.1 Lithuania

To a degree, disagreements among the Baltic and Nordic countries can be accounted for by real geopolitical, economic, and political differences. Because of the small share of the Russian population in Lithuania (9 per cent) compared with Estonia and Latvia, and its early decision to confer on them all citizenship rights, relations between Vilnius and Moscow are, with the exception of the Kaliningrad exclave, reasonably good.

Relieved of the burden of poor relations with Russia, Lithuania also has the possibility of developing new relations with its old nemesis, Poland, which brings in a new element to the relations of the Baltic countries with their immediate environment. In the interwar period, the disputes between Lithuania and Poland over the status of Vilnius, a historically multi-ethnic city occupied by the latter in 1920, and other issues made Polish involvement in Baltic defence impossible. Estonia and Latvia were unwilling to ally with Lithuania as it might have led to a war with Poland. Today Vilnius does not pose any problems and economic and political cooperation between Lithuania and Poland is making progress. This has permitted Lithuania to pursue a policy which has deviated from a common Baltic line (Lieven, 1993: 76–8; Miloz, 1993).

The Lithuanians have not exactly defected from Baltic cooperation, but they have rather pursued a double strategy. In the hope of being admitted to NATO and the European Union earlier than Estonia and Latvia, which has turned out to be a chimera, Lithuania has relied increasingly on Poland and Denmark to speak on its behalf in Brussels. Consistent with its traditional support to the Baltics and as an informal US liaison in the region, Denmark has adopted an active, positive policy towards the Baltic countries reflecting the US preference for an integrated 'minilateral' approach to the Baltic Sea region. This approach is intended to reduce the US need to deal bilaterally with individual countries (Hansen, 1996). The 'minilateral' strategy culminated in the conclusion of the non-binding Charter of Partnership in January 1998 between the United States and the three Baltic countries.

Another example of 'minilateralism' was the meeting held in Denmark in May 1997 between the Danish, German, and Polish defence ministers who were, in its second part, joined by their three Baltic colleagues. In August 1997, Denmark, Germany, and Poland decided to set up in Szczecin the headquarters of the multinational army corps of 30,000 troops which will become operative in 1999. By September 1998, the three countries had enlarged their joint military corps to 60,000 troops comprising one mechanical division in each of them (Helsingin Sanomat, 2 September 1997: C3 and *RFE/RL News-line*, 7 September 1998).

A broader endeavour was the ten-nation summit organized in Vilnius in September 1997 to bridge the Baltic and Black Sea nations. This summit was clearly an effort to establish a new, loose coalition of states to reduce the impression that the enlargement of NATO is creating new dividing lines in Europe (Goble, 1997).

Germany is in a position to forge new constellations in the Baltic Sea region. The new multinational army corps, inspired by the forth-coming Polish membership in NATO, will create new links also with the Baltic countries, especially with Lithuania. The Speaker of the *Seimas*, Vytautas Landsbergis, has in fact stated that 'the triangle of Poland–Germany–Denmark could transform into a quadrangle to include Lithuania' (Dispatch of the Lithuanian news agency, *ELTA* on 25 June 1997).

Today, Polish–Lithuanian economic cooperation is limited. In 1994, Lithuania's exports to Poland were $102 million and its imports from there $104 million, representing 5 and 4 per cent, respectively, of its total exports and imports. It is, however, more than its trade with either Estonia and Latvia. In 1994, Lithuania's main trading partner was still Russia, which received 39 per cent of its exports and sent 28 per cent of its imports.[4] The corresponding shares for Germany, its second most important partner, were 14 and 11 per cent, respectively.

Polish–Lithuanian cooperation relies on historical and cultural links between the countries. These links can play a positive role now that the disputes over territories and minorities have been settled to mutual satisfaction. A concrete example of their mutual ties is the establishment in September 1997 of the inter-governmental Polish–Lithuanian Cooperation Council which promotes cooperation in security, economy and culture. The Council will also form a bilateral peacekeeping battalion, to be stationed in Poland. It remains to be seen whether the Polish–Lithuanian battalion will compete with the joint Baltic peace-keeping battalion (BALTBAT) established in 1995 by an Agreement on Cooperation in the Fields of Defence and Military Relations.

Lithuanians seem increasingly to think in north–south terms in which Poland becomes an intermediary and access route for co-operation with the Central European countries. Polish–Lithuanian ties are also buttressed by the common risks posed by the heavily militarized Kaliningrad exclave wedged between the two countries (Jurgaitiene and Wæver, 1996: 204, 209–12; on Kaliningrad, see Wellmann, 1996). In the early 1990s relations between Lithuania and Poland were near crisis point, but in 1994 a change took place when Vilnius realized that 'Poland was becoming a bridge linking Lithuania with the EU and NATO' (Miniotaite, 1997: 7).

In 1997, Lithuania's relations with Estonia and Latvia were defined by its then President, Algirdas Brazauskas, as 'one of the priorities in our policy', but he also noted that 'they have become a subject of debate lately'. On the other hand, he stated that relations with Poland 'have never been better throughout our history than they are today' and our southern neighbour had become our 'strategic partner in the integration into the EU and NATO'.

Brazauskas stressed Lithuania's position at a crossroads of several regions – the Baltic Sea area, the Baltic states, and Central Europe. Among them, Central Europe has a priority as cooperation with it 'secures the Lithuanian position as an integral part of Western civili-zation' and 'brings us closer to the CEFTA membership'. Except for Denmark, Nordic countries are not mentioned by name: 'I would like to single out bilateral relations between Lithuania and Denmark, especially our practical cooperation in the military sphere and peace-keeping.'[5]

The relative neglect of intra-Baltic cooperation in Lithuania's policy is no accident. Its preferences have been clearly stated by the Foreign Minister, Algirdas Saudargas. In his view, major powers should not treat the Baltic states as a single category simply because they have a common Soviet past. In this context, he has even pointed out that 'Lithuania wants to be a Central European country, not a Baltic republic.'[6] On the other hand, there are some differences between the political parties on the relative emphases that various regions should receive in Lithuania's foreign policy.

Lithuania's bandwagoning with Poland makes political sense as Warsaw is clearly emerging as the linchpin of NATO strategy in Eastern Central Europe. Its role in the eastward enlargement of the European Union is less clear. Poland, with 37 million people, is surely an important actor also for the Union, but the demographic size of the country has a different meaning for it than for NATO. Due to its size Poland, with its unproductive agriculture and regional differences, poses a major problem for the general budget and the structural funds of the Union. For NATO, the size of the country's territory matters more than its population. Moreover, the NATO enlargement costs are, at most, one-tenth of the Union's admission of the same new members.

3.2 Estonia

If Lithuania has been seeking its own way to Western institutions, so also has Estonia. It has realized that because of the progress of its privatization programme, stable currency, and strong free-trade orientation, it has gained a warm spot especially in the hearts of Germany and the United States. This has, in turn, increased the Estonian tendency to formally stress the importance of the common Baltic orientation, but, in reality, to pursue unilaterally its membership in the European Union.

While Poland has been Vilnius' conduit to Europe, Tallinn has stressed its Scandinavian credentials: 'Estonia, fearful of being held back from its neighbors, Latvia and Lithuania, had started to advertise itself less as a Baltic state than as a bit of Scandinavia stranded across the Gulf of Finland ... The ploy seems to be working' (*The Baltic Front-Runner*, 1997). The relationship with the Nordic countries is not only cultural and political, but also economic in nature.

In 1996, 18 per cent of Estonia's exports went to Finland, 17 per cent to Russia, 12 per cent to Sweden, and 7 per cent to Germany, while the corresponding percentages for imports were 36, 13, 9, and 8 per cent, respectively. On the other hand, Estonian foreign trade is more oriented to the other Baltic countries than Lithuania's; in 1996 their share of Estonian exports was 14 per cent, but only 6 per cent of imports.[7] Since 1987 more than $850 million have been invested by foreign companies in Estonia, roughly one half of this money going to industry. In 1996, 37 per cent of the FDI came from Finland, 23 per cent from Sweden, and 7 per cent from Russia. The share of the Nordic countries has been declining somewhat, however.[8]

Without being excessively materialistic, one can argue that the different economic links of Estonia and Lithuania have shaped their strategies to gain membership in the European Union. Lithuania has oriented itself to Central Europe and Estonia to the Nordic countries.

While the Baltic countries have wanted to preserve the veneer of mutual cooperation, they have refused to commit themselves to a 'pact of mutual assistance' in relations with NATO and the European Union. This became clear, for instance, in the summer of 1997 when they became involved in verbal jousting over membership candidacy in the EU. Estonians also allowed the other two to understand that they are, because of their economic achievements, closer to membership in the World Trade Organization (WTO) than the other Baltics.

3.3 Latvia

Latvia has been a silent partner in the Baltic squabbles on EU membership. In the absence of strong bilateral ties either with Central Europe or the Nordic countries and under stronger Russian influence, it has stressed the importance of inter-Baltic cooperation (on the Latvian case, see Dreifelds, 1996). This is reflected in the opinions of the Latvian elites that cooperation with other Baltic countries is more important than with any other countries (see Table 13.2 below).

In foreign trade Latvia continues to be oriented to Russia, which in 1996 absorbed 6 per cent of its exports and originated 23 per cent of its imports, but also to Germany (14 and 14 per cent, respectively). The next trading partners were Sweden (7 and 8 per cent), United Kingdom (11 and 3 per cent), and Finland (2 and 9 per cent). Trade with other Baltic countries accounted for roughly 12 per cent of Latvia's total trade.

Both in absolute and per capita terms Latvia has attracted less foreign direct investment than Estonia, but more than Lithuania. Of the total FDI stock of $369 million in 1996 about 15 per cent came from the United States, 13 per cent each from Russia and the United Kingdom, 7 per cent from Germany, and 5 per cent from Sweden (*Economic Development of Latvia*, 1997). Because of the high share of Russian population, Latvia is often considered politically more vulnerable than the other two Baltic countries.

The Latvian dependence on Russia and its oil exports through the main harbour in Ventspils is obvious; in 1997, the transit trade accounted for 18 per cent of its budget. This dependence has given rise to some bitter comments on the neighbouring countries. The new Lithuanian oil terminal in Butinge, close to the Latvian border, has been criticized as an environmental risk. Neither do the Latvians like the Russian plans to build three new harbours at the Gulf of Finland, the biggest one being planned for Primorsk (Koivisto). The Finnish initiative on the Northern Dimension of the European Union is considered a ploy to capture the lucrative Russian oil trade (Helsingin Sanomat, 2 September 1998: C1).

4. BALTIC RELATIONS WITH RUSSIA

Obviously the perceived Russian threat, the economic attractions of the European Union, and the expectation of security assurances from the United States dominate in the decision-making of the Baltic countries. From that point of view a key issue concerns future Russian policy towards the Baltic countries. Through most of the 1990s, this policy was rather simple in its dual effort to reduce Western influence in the Baltics and protect and endorse the position of the Russian minorities in the three countries.

The role of the Russian minorities especially in Estonia and Latvia is a complex issue. On the one hand, these countries have introduced and implemented quite restrictive legislation on citizenship and associated political and social rights. A guiding idea behind this legislation seems to be that those Russians and other non-Russian former Soviet citizens who had immigrated to Estonia and Latvia during the occupation period should face a particularly high barrier of entry to citizenship.

The restrictive, nationalist nature of the citizenship legislation has received a lot of international criticism, not only from Russia, but also from Western countries and international governmental and non-governmental organizations. This criticism has influenced Estonian and Latvian policies, mostly because the Council of Europe, NATO and the European Union expect the members to meet some basic human-rights standards: equitable treatment of minorities, acceptable human rights legislation, and the resolution of territorial and other conflicts with neighbouring countries.

These external demands have, in fact, shaped the Estonian and Latvian minority policies, even though the changes have been slow. Obviously, the treatment of Russian minorities in Estonia and Latvia is going to be a thorn in the side of their relations with Moscow for a long time to come (Saffrais, 1998). This is reflected in Moscow's new emerging approach in which it differentiates more strongly between Lithuania on the one hand and Estonia and Latvia on the other. Where Vilnius is praised and rewarded by Moscow, the policies of Riga and Tallinn are condemned and punished.

One aspect of Moscow's economic leverage is the transit fees it has to pay for the shipment of Russian goods from Baltic ports. There seems to a growing tendency to pay the fees to the Lithuanians. As a result, Estonia has been estimated to lose some $500 million annually (Goble, 1997a; Goble, 1997b). There is some evidence that during the Russo-Latvian conflict in the spring of 1998, Russia diverted some of its traffic from Latvian to Lithuanian ports.

This economic differentiation is accompanied by Moscow's collective treatment of the Baltics at least in the area of security. On 24 October 1997 President Yeltsin formally proposed to his then Lithuanian counterpart, Algirdas Brazauskas, on signing the border treaty between the countries, that Russia is ready to guarantee unilaterally the security of the three Baltic countries. This is another prong of Moscow's strategy in the region: to reduce the threat perceived by the Baltics to emanate from Russia and thus reduce their determination to join NATO. The other prong is to criticize the inadequate protection of the Russian minorities by Estonia and Latvia and to make them in that way less attractive to the West.

The presidents of the three Baltic countries rejected the Russian offer of security guarantees in their summit meeting in November 1997 held in Lithuania. They stressed that the security of the region would be best enhanced by the integration of Estonia, Latvia, and Lithuania into NATO and the European Union. The Baltics did not want to reduce their freedom of action in the West in return for the verbal commitments by Moscow (Möttölä, 1998: 12). After the rejection, the Defence Minister, Igor Sergeev, continued the new policy to reassure the Baltics that 'Russia will never resort to force in solving problems with the Baltic States' (*RFE/RL Newsline*, 27 November 1997).

5. IDENTITY AND CULTURE

Security is the most central concept in the external, and even internal relations of the Baltic countries. Due to historical reasons, the Baltics cannot but 'securitize' their relations with Russia, from which it follows that the intra-ethnic conditions within the countries and their relations with the West are also understood in security terms. The foreign relations of the Baltic countries render them readily describable by various balance-of-power and balance-of-threat theories.

However, cultural and institutional factors cannot be discarded in the analysis of the choices made by the Baltic elites. These factors seem to be more pertinent to the elites than the ordinary people. This is reflected in the fact that despite the penchant of the elites for joining NATO and the European Union, only about 30 per cent of Estonians, Latvians, and Lithuanians are unequivocally in favour of membership in these organizations; the rest are either uncertain or opposed.[9]

Social constructivists tend to argue that cultural predispositions, institutional affiliations, and historical learning experiences tend to define the identity of states and shape their incentives for action. The constructivists thus stress that both the formal security institutions, international political environment, and the patterns of interstate amity and enmity have important cultural aspects. This means that the material perspective on international security is inadequate to grasp its meaning fully.[10]

Obviously, the constructivist shift brings new perspectives to the study of security. It has at least one major defect, though; 'the question of military power and instruments of violence is crucially under-theorized in interpretive ... approaches' (Krause and Williams, 1997: 51–2). This point has direct implications for the study of Baltic security. As will be documented below, the Baltics have well-formed cultural identities which correlate with their stated policies to join Western economic and security institutions and build their societies on Northern and Western European models.

The orientation of the Baltic identities are reflected in Table 13.1 that summarizes the results of an opinion survey in which various Baltic elites were asked about their preferences concerning the socio-economic and political model offered by various countries (for data, see Steen, 1997):

Table 13.1. The attitudes of Baltic elites towards other nations as a model, per cent

	USA	Russia	Germany	Scandinavia	Others	Total
Estonia	7	–	35	34	24	100
Latvia	4	1	30	58	7	100
Lithuania	3	1	20	57	19	100

It is clear that all the Baltic elites have a strong German–Scandinavian orientation in their approach to the external world. Obviously, this is partly as a result of geographical location, but is also due to the recognition that Germany and the Nordic countries, as members of NATO and/or the EU, are the key bridges of the Baltic countries to these institutions. Moreover, the stability of the liberal-corporatist model of society may attract the elites which are experiencing the vicissitudes of transition. The Nordic model attracted especially the Baltic political and legal elites, while Germany was, in relative terms, more popular among the business elites. It is interesting that the United States did not turn out to be more popular as a model for the Baltic countries.[11]

The practical interests in functional cooperation may be dictated, however, by factors other than the social model offered by a particular country. Therefore, it is relevant to check which countries are regarded by the Baltic states as the most important partners in cooperation (the percentages indicate the share of those respondents who rank a particular country as the most important partner on a 1–5 scale) (Steen, 1997: 85):

Table 13.2. The centrality of cooperation with various countries, per cent

	Estonia	Latvia	Lithuania
Estonia	–	65	55
Latvia	42	–	53
Lithuania	42	66	–
Russia	55	58	37
USA	53	45	52
Germany	70	60	65
Sweden	63	57	36
Denmark	29	51	34
Finland	54	28	23
Norway	18	24	23

Germany and Sweden are considered to be of primary importance by all Baltic countries as partners in cooperation (though Sweden is less relevant for Lithuania). In fact, the other Baltic countries are in most cases less relevant than Germany and Sweden. Finland and Norway, except for Finland for Estonia, are clearly only of secondary importance for the Baltic countries, probably because they are outside the Central and West European core.

The main difference between these two tables is that, while the US and especially Russian social models are detested, these two countries are regarded by the Baltic countries as important partners of co-operation. This is not difficult to understand; the United States is the leading country in NATO whose membership they are aspiring to, while Russia is the big eastern neighbour with whom they have open disputes concerning borders and national minorities and from which a potential military threat emanates. The main exception is Lithuania whose elites do not consider cooperation with Russia to be of prime significance. This is not due to the anti-Russian opinions of the Lithuanian elites; in fact, they are more positive than the Estonian and Latvian attitudes towards Russia and the Russian minority in their own country (Rose and Maley, 1994).

These findings are somewhat puzzling for constructivist perspectives. The attitudes of the Baltic elites seem to reflect, on the one hand, their cultural affinity and historical ties with Germany and the Nordic countries, and keep their distance from Russia. On the other hand, they reflect a *Realpolitik* approach by recognizing the need to cooperate with Russia and the United States, even though their societal and cultural models are not considered attractive. In the end, both cultural-institutional and realist interpretations capture different aspects of the social reality.

The tension between constructivist and realistic interpretations can be, at least in part, solved by emphasizing more the role of institutions.

In this context the term can be used in two different senses: institutions of cooperation and the structures of knowledge, power, and trust. Today, the Baltic countries are involved in several subregional and regional organizations, and also in the global United Nations. These institutions link the Baltic countries with each other, with the neighbouring states in the Baltic Sea basin, and with the member-states in the OSCE space.

Institutions help the Baltics both to organize their cultural identities in a pattern of lasting relations with each other, but also to set up mechanisms for conflict-resolution and confidence-building. The more dense the institutional networks are and the more the Baltic countries are embedded in them, the more secure they are (Möttölä, 1998). Institutions mean, however, more than organizations; they also contain particular patterns of knowledge, power, and trust (Williams, 1997: 290–6). In the present context it is of considerable importance how the Balts describe, narrate, and argue about their friends and adversaries and how these symbolic representations affect the relations of trust and power with the main powers.

6. CONCLUSIONS

Since their independence the Baltic countries have developed common institutions and practices of cooperation. They share the dilemma of common aversion towards Russia and may even exaggerate it. While Russia certainly has material capabilities to threaten and punish the Baltic countries, military threat and insecurity are only one part of their tension-ridden relations with Russia. Relations of insecurity are also underpinned by politically coloured symbolic representations of the other party which undermine, in turn, the mutual relations of trust.

The sharing of the aversion dilemma has not solved, however, the dilemma of common interests among the Baltics on how to forge a common front in relations with NATO and the EU. The patterns of economic cooperation by the Baltic countries do not differ appreciably as for all of them Germany and the Nordic countries are the most important partners. There are, however, differences between the Baltics on the extent to which they continue to depend economically on Russia and how important Poland and the individual Nordic countries are for them.

Both Estonia and Lithuania have concluded that orientation to non-Baltic countries – Estonia to Finland and Sweden, and Lithuania to Poland and Denmark – promises a more direct path to NATO and especially the European Union than the establishment of a united Baltic front. There is an interesting difference between Russia and the United

States concerning the advisability of such a front. Russia is inclined to drive a wedge between Lithuania and the other two countries, while the United States prefers to deal with all three collectively.

The defection of Estonia and Lithuania from the united Baltic front has been only partial, but nonetheless clearly discernible. The Nordic countries have not even tried to forge a Baltic front from outside. They even have a mutual disagreement on whether the Union should start negotiations with all the Baltic countries or only with Estonia. The membership negotiations are now restricted to Estonia, but the Union has started preparatory talks on accession also with Latvia and Lithuania.

Disagreements between the Baltics and the impotence of the Nordic countries have opened the door for the larger powers to become involved. Russia has continued to express its opposition to NATO membership for the Baltic states, but otherwise it has been rather passive in relation to them. It has been surmised, however, that Russia's tactics to delay border agreements with Estonia and Latvia may have been informed by its effort to complicate their accession to the European Union, which expects member-states not to have disputes with neighbouring states (Stranga, 1997: 199–202; Nielsen-Stokkebye, 1997: 14).

The divisions among the Nordic countries mean that they are unable to help the Baltic countries to overcome their 'dilemma of common interests'. As befits the biggest country in the region, Germany has assumed the role of conciliator and mediator. The Kohl government is working to reduce the political gap between Estonia on the one hand and Latvia and Lithuania on the other. This may be an omen for the future; Germany provides a measure of regional order which alleviates the divisive tendencies among the Baltic countries and makes sure that their relations with Russia remain stable.

NOTES

1 For a general discussion on the motives and conditions for balancing and bandwagoning, see Walt (1987: 17–33). Obviously, bandwagoning with the West can have balancing effects in relation to Russia: 'Integration with western markets and political mechanisms will help to diminish the inevitable economic asymmetry that exists between the small Baltic states ... and big Russia, thus creating a more solid basis for the development of Baltic sovereignty'; see Bleiere (1997: 63).
2 For a nuanced interpretation of Russian interests and policies in the Baltic region, see Sergounin (1997).
3 After sociologist Vilfredo Pareto. Pareto-Optimal solutions are commonly known in the social sciences as solutions such that none better can be found for any of the participants.

 4 On Russia's economic relations with the Baltic countries in general, see Stranga, op. cit., 1997, pp. 207–17.
 5 These quotations originate from the 1997 report of the Lithuanian President to the Lithuanian parliament, the Seimas; see *Http://rc.lrs.lt/prezident/mp97at.hm*. I am very grateful to Ricardas Kasperavicius, who helped me to unearth this material on Lithuania and also collected other material on Baltic countries.
 6 Karpinski, 1997: 15–17, 56 and interview of Algirdas Saudargas in *Helsingin Sanomat*, 20 March p. C2.
 7 See, Estonian Foreign Trade in 1996. *Eesti Pank Bulletin*, no. 2, 1997.
 8 The source of information: The Estonian Investment Agency. *http://www.eia.ee/factshee/fact8.htm*.
 9 This a result of the Eurobarometer public opinion poll, reported in *Christian Science Monitor*, 9 June 1997, pp. 1, 8.
10 For a detailed account of the cultural approach, see Jepperson, Wendt and Katzenstein, 1996. For a slightly different interpretation, see Finnemore, 1996.
11 It is even more interesting that 6 per cent of Estonian and Latvian elites, as much as 15 and 43 per cent of the private business elites, considered Taiwan as the appropriate model. This may reflect the Taiwanese campaign among small and newly independent countries to gain support for its sovereignty.

14

The Baltic States and Europe: Identity and Institutions

PETER VAN HAM[1]

George C. Marshall European Center for Security Studies,
Garmisch-Partenkirchen

INTRODUCTION

The concept of 'Europe' is a fluid one. Even in institutional terms, 'Europe' has not found one common denominator. More often than not, analysts refer to 'Europe' as the European Union (EU), but since this would exclude such quintessentially European countries as Norway, Poland and Switzerland, this obviously lacks geographical as well as cultural and geopolitical precision. This can hardly be considered as something worth worrying about, since this volatility reflects the fuzziness of political and cultural borders setting 'Europe' apart from the rest of the world. For the majority of former communist countries, the wish to 'join Europe' is not limited to entering Europe's main economic and security organizations, but also to join the European security community that has come into being during the decades of the Cold War. As the British historian Tony Judt recently argued: 'Europe today is not so much a place as an idea, a peaceful, prosperous, international community of shared interests and collaborating parts; a "Europe of the minds", of human rights, of the free movement of goods, ideas, persons, of ever-greater cooperation and unity.' Judt (1996: 3).

In this respect, the position of the Baltic states (that is, Estonia, Latvia and Lithuania) is a special one, since they have been an integral part of the Soviet Union for more than five decades. This has not only affected their own national identity, but it has also made it more difficult for these countries to again show up on the geopolitical radar screen of Western policy-makers after an involuntary absence of more than half a century.

During the Cold War, Western European countries have predominantly used the Atlantic framework to manage their security and defence efforts. For decades, Europeans could continue with the process of economic and – to a certain extent – political cooperation and integration within the European Community (EC), meanwhile conveniently leaving security and defence to NATO. The historical reasons for this institutional division of labour are well known: most European countries preferred to counter the Soviet threat jointly with the United States within NATO. With these strategic certainties now gone, the Western part of Europe is engaging in the development of a so-called 'European Security and Defence Identity' (usually abbreviated as ESDI), which is institutionally embedded in the EU and Western European Union (WEU). Large parts of this paper will examine the place and role of the Baltic states in this process. It will focus on the institutional relationship between the EU and WEU with the Baltic states, and ask whether full or partial membership of these organizations can serve as a (perhaps sub-optimal and certainly temporary) solution to fill a perceived Baltic 'security vacuum' now that NATO membership for these countries has become a prospect for the next millennium. The Baltic states are already involved in the EU's 'structured dialogue' with candidate countries and have participated as Associate Partners within WEU's debate on the development of the ESDI; they can also expect to be offered an upgraded PFP (programme) – Partnership for Peace with NATO.

Although important, these institutional links are still rather loose and fail to provide the strategic moorings that bind the Baltic states to political 'Europe'. This paper will conclude that this ambiguousness is likely to linger for some years, and that the place and role of the Baltic states in Europe will depend as much on the development of Europe's security and defence identity as the Russian reaction to it. It will conclude that although the Baltic states have, all in all, been successful in both redefining and reinforcing their national identity and getting the political attention of the West, they still have a long way to go in becoming an integral component of Europe's security community.

THE BALTIC STATES, CENTRAL EUROPE, EUROPE ...

One of the most challenging tasks on the foreign policy agenda of Central European countries has been to carve out a place on the mental map of European and American policy-makers and analysts. The difficult process of nation-building does not only have a domestic component, but also depends upon whether or not these 'new' nations are readily and fully accepted as new members of the European family. Central European countries not only had to overcome economic and political hurdles in 'joining Europe', but they also had to convince the

Western European audience (which includes the political élite as well as the regular populace), that Budapest and Sofia as well as Tallinn and Riga are capitals of 'European' countries, with a 'European' history, culture and mentality. Since the Cold War has for so long limited the definition of 'Europe' to the western half of the continent, Central European countries – and the Baltic states in particular – have had to put much energy in regaining their proper place as sovereign, 'normal' actors on Europe's post-Cold War stage. All this was meant to overcome the psychological divide that had grown over time during the forced separation of Europe by the Iron Curtain.

It is important to note that West European ignorance concerning Central Europe stretches back to the pre-Cold War era. The British historian Hugh Seton-Watson observed in 1945 that for many of his countrymen the countries of Central Europe '… have unpronounce-able names and live in plains and forests, on mountains and by rivers which might be in another world. When Mr. Chamberlain spoke of the Czechoslovaks as a "people of whom we know little", he was telling the truth and he was speaking for the British people.'[2] Although modern media have made it easier to know much more about this part of Europe, it is probably fair to say that the level of public knowledge as well as understanding of the developments in many countries of this region remains rather limited. This especially applies to the Baltic countries, who have been subjected to forced Russification by Moscow and have dwelled for decades within the 'Black Box' of the USSR. The Baltic quest to 'join Europe' is therefore more than a contest to enter European economic and politico-military organizations as soon as possible; it is also an effort to raise the level of awareness and sensitivity of their national and regional problems in the rest of Europe (as well as the United States). A major task of the Baltic states has been to convince their European and American audiences that they belong to 'Europe', culturally, politically as well as strategically. Only if the Baltic states are accepted as an integral part of 'cultural Europe' can they expect to be accepted as full members of the politico-security organi-zations of the 'institutional Europe'.

Given the controversial thesis put forward by the American scholar Samuel Huntington that future conflict will increasingly be between different 'civilizations';[3] it is interesting to note that the three Baltic states clearly fall inside the category of 'the West'. Huntington's rough line dividing the Christian western part of Europe from the Orthodox eastern part, splits Belarus, Ukraine and Romania in half, but clearly places the Baltic states – with their Lutheran and Roman Catholic traditions – in the area of the 'Western Christendom'. One could easily dismiss this as irrelevant to the discussion of the Baltic states' place and role in Europe, and this paper certainly does not propose to follow

Huntington's argument and make it a central element of analysis. Huntington's thesis has many flaws. But although the strategic and analytical relevance of this thesis might be doubtful, one could ask whether it is mere coincidence that the majority of prospective EU members fall into Huntington's category of 'European civilization'? Clearly, countries like Belarus, Ukraine, Moldova, Yugoslavia, Albania and Macedonia, have little chance of joining the EU even in the remote future; the prospects of Bulgaria are certainly better, but its democratic (let alone economic) development is far from assured. The main point to make here is that for those who think of 'Europe' in 'civilizational terms' (and the repeated off-hand rejection of Turkey as a possible EU member for exactly that reason illustrates that many keep these arguments in mind), the Baltic states are certainly an integral part of 'cultural Europe' and the even wider catch-all category of 'the West'. Europe's cultural, political and security identity are therefore organically linked, and one can see a clear reflection of this identity in the institutional arrangement of European integration. For the Baltic states this acceptance as part of the 'European family' has therefore been the basis on which to build a strategy of 'joining Europe' in institutional terms.

Joining the EU is one of the top priorities on the foreign policy agenda of the Baltic states. It needs hardly to be said that all Central European countries are already part of geographic Europe and that they have been excluded from the European integration process involuntarily. Most West European policy-makers therefore depict the enlargement of the EU towards Central Europe as an historical opportunity as well as a duty to undo the injustice done to these countries during the Cold War. For the Baltic states being recognized as a candidate country for EU membership has been a first, but very important, symbolical phase in their closer association and future integration into the European project. For Estonia, Latvia and Lithuania, the first challenge has been to become recognized as 'Central European' countries, that is, those countries that both geographically and strategically belong to the 'natural' area to which Europe's institutions would want to enlarge. The Baltic states have therefore made it clear from the beginning that although they have been part of the USSR for decades, they are not among the so-called 'Soviet successor states', that is, those countries that take on the responsibilities of the Soviet heritage. Obviously, for similar reasons the Baltic states have refused from the outset to join the Russian-dominated Commonwealth of Independent States (CIS); Baltic diplomats have also aired regular complaints that Moscow continues to include the Baltic states in their concept of the 'Near Abroad'. The result of these efforts has been that both Russia and the West now seem to consider the Baltic states as an area of 'special interest'. It should be appreciated that this has never been a foregone development; it has taken both active lobbying on the part of the Baltic states themselves, as well as a shift in the political mind-set of Western policy-makers, to accept these countries as candidates for joining the core of European integration.

It is well understood that joining the EU provides the Baltic states *de facto* participation within the security community that underpins Europe's integration process. The Baltic states realize that although the Union cannot provide an Article 5 military security guarantee à la NATO and WEU, full EU membership will make them an integral element in the process towards European unity. Finnish President Martti Ahtisaari stated in December 1996, that 'as a member of the European Union, Finland is part of a community of political solidarity. A threat to one member-state is directed against the whole community.'[4] The rationale behind this argument is that it is practically inconceivable that a EU member-state which participates fully in the three pillars of the Union would, in the case of external military aggression, even in the absence of official security guarantees, not be assisted by its European partners. In this respect, joining the Union would not only crown more than a decade of economic and political transformation, but it would also be testimony to the fact that the Baltic states are no longer to be considered peripheral to the construction of 'Europe', but have become part of the mainstream.

The United States in particular has pushed the idea of giving the Baltic states (among others) closer ties with the EU, or even full EU membership, as a sort of 'consolation prize' for being left out of NATO's first enlargement wave. After the NATO Madrid summit of July 1997, it has become clear that the Baltic states will not see their wish fulfilled for speedy acceptance into the Alliance. Anticipating the decision to have only a limited first wave of NATO enlargement, Washington has informally proposed to limit the shock of being rejected by calling upon the EU to include Estonia, Latvia and Lithuania in its own first 'wave' of enlargement, and speeding this process up so that EU and NATO enlargement will roughly coincide.[5] Washington's proposals seem to have been prepared by a RAND publication (in the summer of 1996), that has made a strong case for NATO and the EU to develop an enlargement strategy specifically aimed at sustaining Baltic independence and security (Asmus and Nurick, 1996). One of the key elements in the advice of the RAND analysts (apart from encouraging political and economic reform, as well as Baltic defence cooperation and Nordic–Baltic cooperation), is that the EU should seriously consider including Estonia (but not Latvia and Lithuania) in the first wave of enlargement. The RAND paper suggests that it should be made clear beforehand to Tallinn that this would – exceptionally – not result in an invitation to also join WEU as a full member, since this would mean a backdoor NATO security guarantee. At the same time they call for an expanded PFP-programme in the Baltic region. The principal benefit from such a strategy would be that it would provide an 'institutional manifestation of the West's commitments to and engagement in the Baltic region'. The RAND analysis and recommendations have certainly boosted the debate on the Baltic states and their place in Europe's evolving security framework. Especially (temporarily) decoupling the semi-automatic link between EU and WEU membership might be a useful, pragmatic solution to the challenge of finding a way out of the Baltic's security predicament.

The European Commission's 'Agenda 2000' (which makes proposals for the EU's enlargement strategy), published in July 1997, has followed much of the course suggested in the RAND analysis: only Estonia was deemed economically, socially and politically ready to take up accession negotiations with the EU; it was suggested that Latvia and Lithuania wait and introduce more market-oriented democratic reform measures. The Commission has suggested starting accession negotiations with a limited group of Central European candidate countries whose economies and societies could be integrated into the Union without too many complications: the Czech Republic, Estonia, Hungary, Poland and Slovenia (as well as Cyprus). It comes as little surprise that the European Commission's proposals have met with a mixed reaction from the EU's 15 Member-states and have been a tremendous disappointment for policy-makers in Riga and Vilnius. At the time of writing it is still not clear whether the Commission's evaluation of the accession chances of the Baltic will be accepted by the Fifteen; the 'Agenda 2000' still has to be officially endorsed by the EU's Council of Ministers.

The Scandinavian countries, in particular, can be expected to make a case for including Latvia and Lithuania in the first round of accession negotiations (although their chances of being successful seem rather bleak). For all three Baltic states it has been of tremendous importance that the European Union initially (at its Madrid Summit of December 1995) promised to start accession negotiations with all Central European (and Mediterranean) candidate countries simultaneously (that is, in January 1998, six months after the IGC's close). Initially, Germany put pressure on its partners to give priority to Poland, the Czech Republic and Hungary, arguing (quite correctly) that these countries are in the forefront of economic and political reform. After much criticism from other Central European countries, this proposal was quickly dropped. For the Baltic states, in particular (but also for countries like Bulgaria and Romania) it would have been of great importance to start negotiations at the same time as the three Visegrad countries, underlining their shared commitment to join the European integration process. As in many other cases, the process and clear prospect of joining the EU is probably as important for the economic and political development and security of the Baltic states, as the final signatures under the accession treaties. With this change in EU policy, Latvia and Lithuania will probably have to get used to the idea of waiting for another decade or so before they will be able to share the benefits of full EU membership.

Even though there are certainly arguments for co-ordinating NATO and EU enlargement, Brussels (as well as most EU member-states) has rejected the American idea that EU membership is some sort of compensation, merely an instrument for sending political signals. The European Commission has made it clear that EU membership is no political consolation prize to be given to disappointed Central European countries who have missed the boat in NATO's first enlargement wave. Günther Burghardt, the German European Commission general director responsible for EU foreign relations argued in February 1997, that there are many differences between EU and NATO enlargement: 'EU expansion involves between 70,000 and 80,000 pages of legislation whereas NATO involves Article 5.'[6] The Union is also disinclined to do something that NATO itself does not seem to be capable of – incorporating three former Soviet republics whose security remains feeble and whose relationship with Russia is still far from good. All in all, the political argument that EU membership for at least one Baltic country will have a positive effect on the stability of the Baltic region as a whole is a convincing one, but of course does not find much political support in Latvia and Lithuania.

It should also be well understood that European integration is not a static but a dynamic process, and that Baltic (and Central European) membership of the EU will seriously affect the nature as well as the institutional set-up of the Union. A wider Union will not simply incorporate *more* member-states, it will also be a substantially different, more diverse grouping of countries.[7] Whereas the West confronted a clear and overwhelming but remote security threat during the Cold War, Western Europe now faces diffuse and minor but direct challenges to its stability and safety. One of the key problems is that consensus on the nature and importance of these crises is lacking among West European governments. The new security environment has exposed differences which have been papered over in the past, accentuating the diverging security perceptions and interests between EU member-states as well as the long list of candidate countries that are now lining up to join the Union. Accepting countries with different economic and political backgrounds as full EU member-states is one thing, but coming to terms with the consequences of including three, be it rather small, former Soviet republics in quite another. Admitting one or more Baltic states as a full member of the EU therefore inevitably increases the risk of a further 'regionalization' of European security.

It almost goes without saying that for the EU's northern members crises and instability in the former Soviet region are of vital importance,[8] whereas developments in Northern Africa are of more immediate relevance to the EU's Mediterranean members. Although it is equally obvious that serious political turbulence anywhere in the periphery will eventually affect all West European countries, different priorities and foreign policy agendas make a common threat assessment and a common European response difficult. There is already a clear tendency in the EU for 'Baltic initiatives' to come mainly from the Nordic countries, even though financial resources to back these initiatives may come from the EU as a whole. The incorporation of Austria, Finland and Sweden has further provoked some alarm about the possible strategic consequences of a shift in Europe's centre of gravity towards the North, and has stimulated France, Spain and Italy to emphasize the so-called 'Mediterranean Dimension' of the EU. Such tensions are now certainly manageable, but they are likely to increase when the Union (as well as WEU) enlarges towards Central Europe, which is bound to again stimulate suspicions about the creation of a pan-Germanic *Mitteleuropa*.

These centrifugal tendencies, in combination with the soul-searching that is going on in Brussels as well as in West European capitals concerning the ultimate future of the European integration process, have raised the basic question of what 'Europe', and the ESDI in particular, is all about? Although countries such as Ukraine, Belarus and Moldova have not officially applied to join the Union, the question of how wide 'Europe' can stretch itself without snapping is an important one that will definitely become politically relevant before too long. EU member-states are unlikely to take the Huntingtonian civilization-map as their strategic guideline to make these portentous decisions, but one should nevertheless ask how 'flexible' the EU can and should be before it loses the quality of a cohesive group of more or less like-minded countries that basically share a similar (or at least compatible) vision of what 'Europe' should be and do?

EUROPE'S ESDI: WHAT PLACE AND ROLE FOR THE
BALTIC STATES?

In 1951, one of the founding fathers of European integration, Robert Schuman, argued that 'before Europe develops into a military alliance or an economic community it has to be a *cultural community*'.[9] (Emphasis added). Underlying this statement is the idea that integration in the political, and especially security and military sphere, cannot be pushed too far unless states, and their peoples in particular, feel sufficiently 'European', that is, think in terms of *European* security and *European* policy responses to risks and challenges to *Europe*. Schuman's statement was certainly relevant to the political situation in the early 1950s, and has now again become central in a period where European governments are planning to pool their foreign, security and defence resources and co-ordinate their policies within the EU (and WEU).

It is clear that the development of a European security and defence identity does not only depend on feelings of common roots and a common destiny, but also requires an institutional framework with clear, efficient and effective rules of decision-making and similar norms for burden-sharing. Just as the construction of an economic and monetary union in the EU needs the cement of complex interdependence combined with a necessary minimum of solidarity, a European foreign and security policy must have a foundation of common interests and values, a shared assessment of the principal risks, challenges and threats to the security of Europe, as well as the priority with which they should be addressed. Obviously, these challenges are not reduced by the prospect of a Union with up to 25 member-states stretching from Ireland to Estonia, and from Portugal to Romania.

This has put tremendous pressure on current EU member-states to make more than cosmetic changes to the Union's institutional make-up. The EU now has reached the limits of its institutional flexibility and taking in additional members will require serious reform of the Union's institutional set-up. Without institutional reform of the EU – streamlining its decision-making process and making room for new members in all its three pillars – enlargement will be seriously delayed. Enlarging the EU also implies that the management of the Union's Common Foreign and Security Policy (CFSP, or 'second pillar' of the EU) will become even more difficult. Apart from the different national interest that enlargement will bring to the EU's foreign policy agenda (*supra*), an organization of 20 to 25 member-states may well be a qualitatively different one from the EU/EC of the past with a mere ten to 15 members. Just a regular *tour de table* of the future EU of 25, if each government representative is allowed to speak for five minutes, will already take more than two hours. Integrating Central European countries in an effective and dynamic EU, while maintaining (or preferably reinforcing) the cohesion among member-states, has been among the main challenges for the EU's Intergovernmental Conference (IGC) to revise the 1992 Maastricht Treaty.

The new Union Treaty agreed upon at the Amsterdam Summit in June 1997, takes only modest steps in the right direction, but has postponed many of the tough decisions on institutional reform. The key question facing the future of the European integration process is therefore still undecided: whether such a 'wider Europe' will have the same level of coherence and solidarity as a Union of Fifteen? In other words, will a 'wider Europe' undermine the European security community, or may it, on the other hand, reinforce it? Another key question will also remain unanswered for quite a long time to come, namely: how will enlargement affect the Union's ability to act as a cohesive and powerful actor in foreign and security policy?

Even before enlargement, the CFSP is experiencing a 'low' (and one could certainly argue that the EU has never experienced anything other than that). The Yugoslav war has from the very beginning exemplified the impotence of Europe as an entity; during the war itself, the EU was an actor working in the margins. For those who had not yet realized this, it became painfully clear when the so-called 'Contact Group' for former-Yugoslavia was set up in 1994, which included the US, Russia, France, Germany and the United Kingdom, but not the EU. Only after a peace settlement was found in Dayton in December 1995, was the EU given the important and difficult (and also somewhat thankless) task of overseeing and co-ordinating the economic recovery of Bosnia. This again made it clear how the EU was seen from the outside: as basically an economic actor, not as an actor in its own right on foreign and security matters.

The EU (as well as to a lesser extent WEU) can be blamed for raising expectations, in Europe as well as in the United States, that with the signing of the Maastricht Treaty (which also established a closer link between the Union and WEU), 'Europe' was now capable of acting decisively in foreign affairs. The Bosnian *débâcle* has disproved this once and for all, thereby clearing the European air of any illusions that 'Europe' could in the foreseeable future count on forging a credible ESDI. One of the principal problems in the European effort to build a credible ESDI has been that there is little agreement among EU/WEU member-states concerning the key question of what sort of role 'Europe' should play in the foreign and security policy field. Should the EU develop into a full-fledged superpower, a regional power, a civil power or a rather complex entity with a mixed character?

If Europe strives to become a superpower which adopts a global range of interests and which has the capabilities to pursue these interests worldwide, this would require a comprehensive common defence policy with common military structures, as well as efficient decision-making procedures where majority voting would be the rule rather than the exception. Europe as a regional power would predominantly be engaged on its periphery, requiring limited instruments for crisis management and peacekeeping in neighbouring regions. As a *civil power*, Europe would promote democracy, human rights and economic cooperation, without developing European military capabilities beyond the potential which at the moment exists on the national level within the framework of NATO and WEU. One could argue that the absence of visionary goals is prudent, since the ESDI will probably only come about in an incremental way. But it should at the same time also be acknowledged that any choice will have a significant impact on the development of Europe's operational military capabilities, and that West European governments, as well as the political establishments of the Union's prospective members, should take collective steps to assure that these military capabilities will also be actually available in the future. There are few indications that the Baltic strategic elite is overly concerned with such metaphysical questions concerning 'Europe's' future role. As long as the Baltic states are not 'in', they seem to be prepared to join any 'Europe' that may finally emerge.

One could argue that WEU – the EU's defence counterpart – has gone furthest in opening its institutional doors to the Baltic states and incorporating them in the debate on the development of European security and defence cooperation. Following the logic of the Union's enlargement strategy, WEU invited all EU member-states to join WEU, which led to the accession of Greece in March 1995; Norway, Iceland and Turkey (as European NATO members) have become WEU Associate Members; and Austria, Denmark, Ireland, Finland and Sweden (as EU members) are now Observers. In May 1994, the WEU Council offered the status of Associate Partnership to the Central European countries, including the three Baltic states. This permits these (now ten) countries, who have signed so-called Europe Agreements with the EU, to regularly participate in meetings of the permanent WEU Council (on the ambassadorial level), and to be present at all WEU Ministerial Councils. Associate partners regularly participate in the Council's discussions, receive information about WEU activities, have established contacts with the WEU Planning Cell, and, perhaps most importantly, can participate in future peacekeeping, humanitarian and rescue missions of WEU.

It should be emphasized that WEU has little in the way of a PFP-scheme à la NATO, where partnership and cooperation can be developed through joint exercises and training. Associate Partnership in WEU therefore still has only a few positive concrete consequences for Baltic security. Nevertheless, despite WEU's still rather marginal and unclear role in Europe's evolving security and defence framework, it goes almost without saying that the Baltic states highly value their presence at the WEU Council table, which allows them to air their security concerns and express their views on how the ESDI should be shaped. Like most other Central European countries, the Baltic states consider WEU still too rudimentary and feeble to be any kind of alternative to NATO. This option has been informally floated by analysts in Moscow,[10] but has found little support in Western and Central Europe.[11] Not only would it undermine the current objective of making EU, WEU and NATO enlargement broadly congruent, but the functional relationship between WEU and NATO would also be impeded were membership of those two organizations to diverge (currently all full members of WEU are also NATO Allies). Probably for this reason, NATO has clearly stated that it favours the 'eventual broad congruence of European membership in NATO, EU and WEU', and that it would 'give particular consideration to countries with a perspective of EU membership' when the time comes to decide on the 'who' question of NATO enlargement.[12]

The Amsterdam Treaty has taken a small step towards linking the EU and WEU closer together. WEU has already prepared a detailed analysis of the possible options (in November 1995).[13] One of these options called for an arrangement to provide for participation by all EU member-states in joint peacekeeping and crisis-management operations which would then be conducted by WEU. This alternative (which formed the main element of a joint memorandum issued by Finland and Sweden on 25 April 1996),[14] has found the support of most EU member-states. It has been a modest success that at Amsterdam the so-called Petersburg Tasks of WEU (humanitarian, rescue and peacekeeping missions) have now been incorporated in the new Union Treaty. The prospect of a full-fledged merger of the EU and WEU still has only limited support among the Fifteen – Great Britain, Denmark and Sweden, in particular, have been opposed to such a development. Sweden's Defence Minister Björn von Sydow argued in June 1997 that an EU–WEU merger would 'represent a stumbling block for the Baltic countries in their striving for EU membership, if EU membership then becomes for NATO members only'.[15] WEU's collective defence commitments therefore remain firmly placed outside the new EU framework, but the important Petersburg missions will now be an integral part of the Union's foreign policy agenda. Partly for this reason, the results of the Amsterdam Summit have been greeted positively by most Baltic politicians.

This aspect of the new Amsterdam Treaty is of interest to the Baltic states, since they will in the future then join Sweden, Finland and Austria as full EU member-states, feeling themselves secure without necessarily having an official military security guarantee. For Western Europe and the United States, such an option would be preferred over immediate full Baltic WEU and/or NATO membership; it would also have the considerable added benefit of not antagonizing Russia. The United Kingdom has pointed out that the development of a common

European defence and the merger of EU and WEU could have the undesired side-effect of hampering the overall EU/WEU enlargement process: Russia has never raised objections to the enlargement of EU and WEU, but Moscow might reconsider its stance if the EU could be seen as turning into a 'military', as well as a politico-economic organization.

The impact of the Union's enlargement towards Central Europe, and the Baltic states in particular, is difficult to grasp. Since NATO will enlarge first, this will certainly affect Europe's strategic equation. For those Central European countries that will join NATO in the first 'wave' of enlargement (that is, the Czech Republic, Hungary and Poland), joining the EU may become somewhat less urgent since they will then rest assured that their Alliance membership will shelter them from external aggression and subordination. But for those candidate countries that are likely to face a longer wait, strengthening ties with the EU will become increasingly important. Western countries will also want to avoid a possible double disappointment in Central European countries that will feel rejected by both NATO and the EU; the proposed PFP-plus and an intensification of the Union's involvement may help to overcome the sense of isolation in this region, meanwhile preparing the ground for future membership of these countries. Moscow's reaction to the first round of NATO enlargement will also impact upon how the EU will evaluate the possible strategic risks involved in inviting (one or all of) the Baltic states to join as full members.

CONCLUDING REMARKS

Over many centuries, Europe has always had problems in determining its most eastern borders. Originally, the term 'Europe' was used for areas such as Macedonia, Albania and Serbia, but these areas have now become rather peripheral and most 'Europeans' tend to think that the wars and political turmoil in these countries reflect an absence of 'Europeanness', of civilization, rather than a reflection of deep European cultural roots. The fact that there is no maritime or terrestrial frontier that clearly separates 'Europe' from 'Asia', has stimulated definitions of 'Europe' as first a cohesive religious (that is, Roman Catholic), and later as a civilizational entity; the Huntingtonian definition of Europe (*supra*) is just the latest reflection on this disposition. It is clear that while thinking about the further development of European integration and the structure of a European security framework, these old, lingering questions about Europe's cultural and political identity again emerge. These questions are both difficult to avoid and to answer.

For the Baltic states these questions are politically pertinent since they may in the end be as important as the 'objective' evaluation of their economic and political readiness to join the European and Euro-Atlantic institutions. There is a clear tendency for Baltic politicians to identify their national and regional political and security problems as problems affecting Europe as a whole, mainly because they are considered a litmus test for Russia's international behaviour and role *vis-à-vis* its neighbours and the West in general. As Lithuania's parliamentary chairman Vytautas Landsbergis argued in April 1997: 'We are not a lone island between two thunderous oceans but, rather, a part of a continent that wishes to be stable and safe; our problems are therefore Europe's problems.'[16] It is for that reason that it is so crucial for the Scandinavian countries to continue making the 'Baltic case' in Brussels (in the EU and WEU as well as NATO). Since they cannot count on the strong and active support of a key European actor (German backing remains lukewarm), the Baltic states need all the support they can muster to make their voice heard in Brussels and other European capitals. Sweden's Moderate Party leader Carl Bildt recently stressed that his country's 'most important foreign policy task' (working closely together with Finland and Denmark) is to 'secure a place for the three Baltic states in the coming expansion of the EU'.[17]

Although this certainly sounds encouraging, given the divergent European Commission opinions on the three individual Baltic states, it is unlikely that this scenario will become reality. Recent opinion polls among EU citizens showed that only 37–38 per cent of the EU populations supports Estonian, Latvian and/or Lithuanian EU membership (just 4 per cent more than Russia),[18] which again illustrates that the Baltic states do not yet figure prominently on the 'European map' of ordinary Europeans. The risk of disappointment in Latvia and Lithuania at how they are treated by the EU and NATO is real: they will not continue accepting the EU's promise of 'jam tomorrow', and the time they want to have 'jam today' may well be sooner than later. As one prominent Latvian politician argued in May 1997: 'We cannot wait too long. People will tire of working towards integration with the West. They risk losing hope and beginning to believe they will never be accepted [by the EU and NATO]'.[19] It would therefore be appropriate for the EU to develop a clear timetable for admission, making sure that the psychological setback of the 'double rejection' is accommodated.

The relationship between Europe's slowly developing security and defence identity and the Baltic states will remain unclear for a considerable time to come. This should not come as a surprise, nor should it be a ground for serious concern. The Baltic states' ties with the EU/WEU and NATO are progressing slowly but steadily, but as long as Moscow continues to consider this area a part of their 'Near Abroad', claiming specific security interests, it remains difficult to foresee how a rather weak ESDI can gather the political will and courage to fully incorporate Estonia, Latvia and/or Lithuania. In this context it is perhaps worth recalling that 'Europe' historically does not only stand for Christianity, 'civilization' and 'progress', but, since Machiavelli's *Il Principe* (posthumously published in 1532), also for *Realpolitik* and a concern of states to carefully maintain a classical 'balance of power'. Neither the EU/WEU, nor NATO, is willing to 'unbalance' the already rather volatile post-Cold War European security framework by unduly provoking an already dissatisfied and insecure Russian Federation. Even if the Baltic states were therefore to become a full-fledged and integral element of 'Europe' in all its cultural, religious and political facets, the 'Russia-factor' will continue to cast a shadow on the full integration of the Baltic states in 'institutional Europe'. The Baltic states' full participation in the development of the ESDI is therefore a necessary, but in itself not a sufficient element on the road towards full integration in Europe's security framework. This may be a rather unsatisfactory, and certainly unpleasant, conclusion, but also one that takes into account existing geostrategic realities.

NOTES

1 Dr Peter van Ham is a Professor in the College of International and Security Studies of the George C. Marshall European Center for Security Studies in Garmisch-Partenkirchen, Germany. He was a Senior Research Fellow at the WEU Institute for Security Studies in Paris from 1993–96. This article does not necessarily reflect the views of the Marshall Center, the US or German Government.
2 Quoted in Zamfirescu (1996: 22).
3 Samuel Huntington first put forward his thesis in 'The Clash of Civilizations?', *Foreign Affairs*, vol. 72, no. 3 (Summer, 1993).
4 *FBIS-WEU-96-246*, 19 Dec. 1996.
5 *The Guardian*, 25 Nov. 1996.
6 *Handelsblatt*, 4 Feb. 1997.
7 Lee Miles and John Redmond have argued: 'Most of the new and probable future members actually or potentially favour intergovernmental cooperation and have a more constrained and limiting perception of the future shape of the EU than its founding fathers.' (Miles and Redmond, 1996: 303).
8 Sweden's former prime minister Carl Bildt argued in November 1994: 'In coming decades the Nordic countries will be forced to concentrate a large part of their foreign and security policy on present and potential problems in the area stretching from Kaliningrad in the south to the Kola peninsula in the north.' *Financial Times*, 22 Nov. 1994.
9 Quoted in Wæver and Kelstrup (1993).
10 *Russia and NATO. Theses of the Council on Foreign and Defense Policy*, (1995), point 2.3.6 which refers to the 'Enlargement of WEU in the first turn' (i.e. the autonomous enlargement of WEU towards Central Europe).

11 Although there is some support for this idea in the US. See Dean (1995: 7) and Davies (1995).
12 *Study on NATO Enlargement* (1995) and Rühle and Williams (1995).
13 *WEU Contribution to the European Union Intergovernmental Conference of 1996*, adopted at the WEU Council of Ministers in Madrid, on 14 Nov. 1995.
14 *The IGC and the Security and Defence Dimension – Towards an Enhanced EU Role in Crisis Management*, joint Finnish–Swedish memorandum (25 April 1996).
15 *Dagens Nyheter* (Stockholm), 7 June 1997, translated in *FBIS-WEU-97-160*.
16 Interview with Landsbergis in *Transition* (vol. 3, no. 6), 4 April 1997, p. 18.
17 'Bildt sees Baltics as Country's Task in Europe', in *Svenska Dagbladet*, 21 March 1997, translated in *FBIS-WEU-97-070*.
18 *Eurobarometer*, Report no. 45, Dec. 1996 (fieldwork done in January–March 1996).
19 Karlis Druva, chairman of the Latvian parliament's Defence and Foreign Policy Committee in *Dagens Nyheter* (Stockholm), 10 May 1997, translated in *FBIS-WEU-97-102*.

Part IV

Concluding Section

15

The European Union, the Baltic States and Post-Soviet Russia: Theoretical Problems and Possibilities for Developing Partnership Relations in the North-eastern Baltic Sea Region

HELMUT HUBEL
Friedrich Schiller University of Jena

INTRODUCING THE 'BALTIC TRIANGLE' AND ITS ACTORS

When the Soviet Union was dissolved in December 1991, many observers spoke of a unique chance for Europe to grow together. After the ideological division and military confrontation had ended, democracy and the market economy were to provide the model for Europe's unification. In those days Russian President Boris Yeltsin supported the Baltic states seceding from the Soviet Union, since it helped to pave the way for Russian sovereignty (in the political battle against Soviet President Gorbachev) and to stabilize his rule as democratically elected President of Russia. Also, his support for the independence of the Baltic states served to please the US and West Europe, which Yeltsin needed for achieving his goals. Later, in August 1994, Russian troops withdrew from the Baltic states, at the same time as they left East Germany.

In the early days of 'democratic Russia', politicians in Moscow advocated that their country should join Western institutions like NATO and the European Union.[1] In those early days of national independence Russia was said to be an integral part of democratic Europe and its institutions. Several years later, these dreams had vanished. Political and economic developments within Russia have demonstrated the impossibility of quickly overcoming 70 years of socialist order. While the East-Central European states have undertaken more or less fundamental changes in their political and economic systems, the post-Soviet area is still marked by grave uncertainties – ranging from neo-authoritarian rule and Soviet-type economic structures, as in Belarus, to bold reform efforts in certain regions of Russia and often inconclusive reforms in the centre of the Russian Federation (Lambsdorff, 1997).

Compared with other parts of the post-Soviet sphere and many East-Central European states, the three Baltic states have already made impressive steps towards the 'Western model'. These achievements have been supported by the fact that Estonia, Latvia, and Lithuania had been independent states in the inter-war period, that they were (in many respects the most advanced) republics of the Soviet Union for forty years 'only', that it was easier to introduce and sustain changes in their relatively small societies and economies, and that they have a favourable geographic location with supportive neighbours in Northern and Western Europe across the Baltic Sea.

This author has argued that with the ending of the East–West conflict the Baltic Sea region can be regarded as a 'laboratory' for studying in detail Europe's problems of growing together (Hubel, 1994):

– The Baltic Sea region links Eastern, Northern, and Western Europe – three 'subregions' which used to have different political, economic, and military orientations during the East–West conflict.

– With the ending of the East–West conflict the European Community/Union was the first Western institution to expand to the East and North of Europe: the GDR joined the EC on 3 October 1990 and Finland and Sweden became members of the EU in 1995.

– Moreover, since 1993 the EU has concluded 'Europe agreements' with Poland, the three Baltic states and others, thus promising them full membership. In 1997 the European Commission and the EU governments invited, among others, Poland and Estonia to start negotiations on EU membership in 1998.

– Significantly, the EU also concluded a 'partnership agreement' with Russia. This agreement does not include any provision for future membership; yet, if conditions were to become 'ripe' one day, this agreement could facilitate the establishment of an economic free-trade area. Such provisions could be of particular interest for the EU, its associated members Poland and Lithuania, and Russia in dealing with problems concerning the enclave of Kaliningrad (the former Königsberg).

When assessing the developments during the 1990s, one can state that a 'triangular relationship pattern' is evolving in the Baltic Sea Region, consisting of

- the *members* of the European Union,
- the *associated members* of EU, including Poland (POL) and the Baltic states (BS), and
- Russia (RUS) as a *partner* of EU.

Figure 15.1

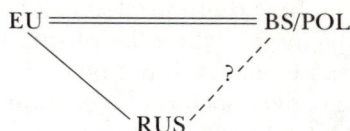

The European Union consists of states among which war has ceased to provide an instrument for managing interstate relations. The reasons are that all member-states are governed by the rule of law and democratic political systems and that they are linked together by joint economic resources and common political and legal institutions. Although still sovereign states, EU members have voluntarily given up certain elements of state sovereignty. Thus, Immanuel Kant's model of the 'democratic peace' is applicable to the European Union (Doyle, 1983).

Poland and the Baltic states, as candidates for EU membership, are in the process of joining this 'zone of European peace'. When conditions are 'ripe', their membership will be a logical extension of the 'European zone of peace'. Yet, up to this day the conditions for membership have not yet been defined. The EU 15 have decided to focus first on consolidating the previous round of enlargement and streamlining its decision-making, before starting to tackle the challenge of Eastern enlargement. Although the criteria and timetable for this process have not yet been defined, one can state that a special relationship between the EU and the candidates of the Eastern enlargement is evolving.

The other two relationships of the 'Baltic triangle' are more difficult to determine. From the EU's point of view, Russia is not, in the foreseeable future, likely to be a candidate for membership, but only – under the best conditions – for association. Seeking a stable, cooperative relationship with Russia, the EU regards it as a partner (Hubel, 1996). Given the uncertain political and economic status of Russia and most of the other post-Soviet states, the Kantian model for shaping relations obviously cannot be applied.

This theoretical conclusion creates major problems. The most important is that – for the time being – the construction of a European peace order including Russia cannot be based on the 'EU model of integration', the most advanced model for safeguarding peace among nations. This leaves only the two other major theoretical options: One is the Hobbesian paradigm of managing interstate relations through a balance of power; the other is the Grotian model of establishing common rules and institutions.[2]

In the following, these three theoretical models will be explained. A discussion will follow on how these models can be used for describing the late 1990s 'Baltic triangle' – the relationship between the EU, the Baltic states, and Russia. Poland will not be included in this 'triangle', because of the size of the Polish society and economy, its probable future membership in NATO, and the evolution of another special political relationship – the French–German–Polish 'Weimar triangle'. All these factors point to an analytical treatment different from that of the 'Baltic triangle'.

Also, this paper does not deal with the implications of NATO's Eastern enlargement. The membership of Poland, the Czech Republic and Hungary in the Western alliance will probably not alleviate the Baltic states' security problems with Russia. Rather, it will aggravate them. Even if, one day, the Baltic states were to enjoy NATO's military security guarantees – and this means primarily US protection, which they will not receive for the time being – the question would still remain how to manage relations with Russia.

This problem might become more acute, since Russia could answer NATO's East-Central European enlargement of 1999 by putting additional pressure on neighbouring states, particularly Estonia and Latvia. Under such circumstances the Union between the Russian Federation and Belarus, concluded in 1997, might gain an additional – military – importance. These are the major reasons why this author has decided to leave NATO-related aspects aside and, instead, focus on the EU.

In this paper alternative non-military options will be discussed for managing future developments within the 'Baltic triangle'. While avoiding political forecasts, policy options will be analyzed from a theoretical point of view. At the end, policy suggestions will no longer be avoided and some ideas will be presented that follow from the theoretical deliberations.

THE THREE PARADIGMS FOR ANALYSING INTERNATIONAL POLITICS

As Martin Wight and Hedley Bull have argued (Wight, 1991; Bull, 1977), there are three traditions of political thought for analyzing international relations. The first and oldest paradigm is the tradition of political realism, which thinkers like Thucydides, Machiavelli, and Hobbes first presented, and political scientists like Edward H. Carr, Hans Morgenthau and Kenneth Waltz applied in this century.

For the realist school of thought international politics is ruled by the ineluctable 'security dilemma' (Herz, 1959), forcing political units – the states – to arm themselves and seek security through military protection and alliances. For realists, shifts in the 'balance of power' – be it in the military, economic or societal spheres – are unavoidable. Consequently, there can be no permanent stability in politics among nations. In the realists' assessment the only possible safeguard against war remains military power, serving to keep potential aggressors in check. After the East–West conflict neo-realists such as Waltz (1993) and John Mearsheimer (1990) continued to argue that nuclear weapons remain the only 'guarantee' against war, be it in Europe or elsewhere.

The second paradigm has been developed by international lawyers in the tradition of Hugo Grotius. As Grotius has stressed, not conflict and war but interaction and cooperation are the dominating features of international politics. Although not all wars can be avoided, peace founded on international rules and institutions is the norm. In the twentieth century, with the formation of the United Nations and a growing web of international institutions, this school of thought has gained prominence, for example, in the writings of the 'liberal institutionalists', such as Joseph S. Nye and Robert O. Keohane. These authors argue that international institutions, by creating interdependence, can diminish or even abolish the 'security dilemma' (Keohane/Nye/Hoffmann, 1993; Keohane, 1993).

Whereas both the realists and the institutionalists regard states as the predominant and indispensable actors of international politics, the third paradigm shifts the attention to the societal and transnational factors. As the philosopher Immanuel Kant has argued, the organization of societies – democracy – and global economic activity (safeguarded by international law) is the key to organizing international peace. Woodrow Wilson's League of Nations can be understood as the first effort to apply these principles in reality. The European Community/Union, to mention just one modern institution, has managed to realize both the Kantian idea of organizing peace between democratic nations and the institutionalist principle of creating economic interdependence and close political cooperation.

As the ongoing debate on the question whether 'democracies do not fight each other' demonstrates (Doyle, 1983; Russett, 1993), the disputes between the three 'schools of thought' are still going on. This is not the place to dwell on these controversies. Suffice it to say that the recent debates demonstrate that there continue to be different paradigms of international thought. Following Martin Wight (1991) and Hedley Bull (1977), this writer believes that all three 'schools of thought' have something to say, that 'the truth' does not lie in one of them exclusively, but that it has to be found – depending on changing conditions and circumstances – in the debate between the three paradigms.[3]

THE THREE PARADIGMS AND THE ACTORS OF THE 'BALTIC TRIANGLE'

For the first time in history a group of European states have managed to organize peace among themselves without relying on a military balance of power. To be sure, both the United States and the Soviet Union heavily contributed to the formation of the European Community: the US by supporting (and partly financing) European integration after 1945 and by including most of the members of the EC in NATO, the Soviet Union by threatening Western Europe and forcing them to overcome old rivalries and act together.

Also, up to this day there is a certain 'internal balance' within the European Union, since the strongest state by population, economic and financial potentials, holding a negative historical record (Germany), has committed itself to a non-nuclear status and to the integration of its military in NATO. Also, the European Monetary Union will mean the 'Europeanization' of the Deutsche Mark – largely on German terms. The other two key member-states of the Union (France and Great Britain) are nuclear powers and hold permanent seats in the UN Security Council.

Yet, despite these asymmetries in power and status, peace within the European Union does not depend on military potentials, but rests on the democratic character of the member-states and their societies, their economic integration and joint institutions. European integration has been a remarkable success, otherwise Great Britain and the other eight 'newcomers' since 1972 would not have joined what is today the EU 15. Yet, after the end of the East–West conflict, with German unification and the democratization of East-Central Europe, the ideas and principles of European integration are confronted with two major questions:

1. How can the principles of political integration, that have been devised for a group of 6 and later 12 states, be sustained and developed further to serve an 'ever growing Union' that, one day, could encompass up to 30 members? This is the key question of 'deepening'. Its key test will be the EMU, and everybody is aware

of the recent debates in various member-states. Yet, despite all difficulties, it seems that some 10 or 11 EU members will join the EMU in 1999.

2. How far can the European Union grow to the East? In 1997, the EU members have reached a general political consensus that 'Eastern enlargement' will be on the agenda. Five East-Central European states, including Poland and Estonia, have been invited to start official negotiations on EU membership. The others will take part in preparatory talks about future membership. Yet, the criteria and timetables for the enlargement process have not yet been agreed upon. In concluding 'Europe agreements' with various East-Central European states – particularly Poland, and the three Baltic states – and following the decisions of the EU Commission and the European governments in 1997, the EU is now on record as wanting to accept these countries as full members one day. Thus, the EU–Baltic states relationship has to be characterized as an associate relationship.

The EU has also concluded a 'partnership treaty' with Russia, indicating that its future Eastern border would not include the post-Soviet states, except the three Baltic countries. From a theoretical point of view, there is already an implicit consensus within the EU that, in the foreseeable future, the 'democratic zone of peace' will not encompass the whole of Europe. As long as Russia and several other post-Soviet states have not fully managed the transition to market economies and democratic systems and have not overcome conflicts within their societies and with neighbours, they will have to stay outside the 'core' of European integration. Consequently, in dealing with Russia, the most advanced model for preserving peace – democratic peace/-homogeneity of societies – is not available, at least for the time being.

In concluding a partnership agreement with Russia, the EU has already embarked on developing a relationship according to the second paradigm: Partnership means seeking as many and as close links as possible. If Russia were to resort (again) to a conflictual relationship with the EU, it would have to sacrifice gains, such as contacts, credits, and membership in Western institutions (for example, the Council of Europe and the G-8 group, that started to emerge from the Denver G-7 meeting in June 1997).

Yet, from a realist point of view, neither the Kantian nor the Grotian approaches promise credible security. The Hobbesian school of thought, particularly in the US (Mearsheimer, 1990; Waltz, 1993), regards present Russian policies as transitory. In a Hobbesian assessment, the conciliatory policies of Presidents Gorbachev and Yeltsin were and are just expressions of Soviet/Russian weakness. As soon as a stronger leader in Moscow should manage to consolidate the economy and to overcome present military weaknesses, Russia would reassert itself. In describing such a scenario, historical analogies range from Weimar–Hitler to Chile–Pinochet.

According to the Weimar–Hitler analogy, a Zhirinovsky-type leader would turn 'Russia's humiliation' into totalitarian internal rule and external aggressiveness (Zhirinovsky, 1993). Since January 1994 we also know that Zhirinovsky's preference for 'European peace' would be based on a kind of renewal of the Hitler–Stalin pact of 1939. According to his 'plan', the Baltic states would 'come back to mother Russia'; only the Tallinn area would be left outside, similar to Danzig before the Second World War.[4]

The second scenario of a strong military leadership, one could call it the Pinochet–Lebed-type, might not be so threatening to the EU and the Baltic states. Yet, if the logic of military security and spheres of influence should dominate Russian politics again, it would be difficult for the Baltic states to become full members of the EU and, one day, of WEU as well (not to speak of NATO).

THEORETICAL OPTIONS FOR MANAGING THE 'TRILATERAL RELATIONSHIP'

Applying the Realist (Hobbesian) Paradigm

When looking at recent Russian debates about relations with the West, one has to state that the integrationist dreams of the early 1990s have largely vanished and given way to a rather traditional geopolitical way of thinking. The debates on the *'blizhee zarubezhe'* (near abroad) and the 25 million Russians living abroad are clear proofs of this.[5] Geopolitical thinking, though not necessarily in all aspects, belongs to the realist school of thought. Also, spheres of influence, broad definitions of military threats, the lack of willingness to distinguish between real and hypothetical 'threats', and the search for military counter-weights are well-known elements of Soviet Russian military thinking (Vigor, 1975).

If such features were to dominate Russian politics completely, the obvious consequences would be that relations with Western Europe and the United States would be understood again in terms of military balance; arms reductions would end, the nuclear and conventional arms race would resume. The consequence would be that the Baltic states would not be able to establish any security association with Western institutions (NATO, WEU) and probably no full (political-economic) membership in the EU. Under such circumstances, the only option for securing the Baltic states *vis-à-vis* Russia could be comparable to the Finnish–Soviet relationship, based on the 1948 treaty.

Interestingly, the Finnish–Soviet type of relationship has already been 'offered' to the Baltic states by Sergei Karaganov, one of the younger prominent Russian security experts (Stranga, 1996).

When we look at recent attitudes in the Baltic states, one has to say that the realist perspective is prevailing too: The Baltic states' politicians have been seeking NATO membership because many of them expect Russia to become an aggressive, expansive neighbour again. In this perspective, a US security umbrella is needed to thwart such possibilities.[6] Yet, the Baltic states' dilemma is that the present US government is not willing to grant such security guarantees to them. This statement remains valid also after the conclusion of the US–Baltic charter in January 1998.

While the EU provides the perspective of economic integration, which could help to stabilize the political transition process, it would not be able to grant security guarantees in the same way as the US. Also, as long as the West European Union (WEU) has not become an effective part of the EU and its political decision-making, it ultimately depends on US military capabilities and decisions.

Therefore, if we look at the Baltic–Russian relationship from a realist point of view, the very best option for the Baltic states' survival would indeed be in accordance with the 'Finnish–Soviet example'. Without investigating this scenario extensively, it seems to this author, however, that there are several factors that might make it difficult, if not impossible, to apply it to the Baltic states today or in the future:

- The first aspect concerns geopolitical conditions: To fit the Cold War Nordic pattern, Poland, as the immediate neighbour of Lithuania, would have to pursue a 'Swedish-type' policy of non-alignment. Yet, the present US, German, and NATO policies – supporting Polish NATO membership similar to the 'Danish–Norwegian example' – are in obvious contradiction to such an option.

- The second argument concerns the military capabilities of the Baltic states. The three states would have to join forces and create an independent military that would be able to let Russia 'pay a heavy price', if it should try to repeat the Soviet annexation of 1940. The questions remain whether the Baltic states would ever be able to agree to, finance, and sustain a meaningful military 'tripwire' against Russia.

- The third aspect concerns internal political conditions in the three Baltic states: They would all need political leaderships which Russia could regard as 'steady and trustworthy'. This means that these leaders would have to conduct a political orientation, demonstrating constant 'friendliness' towards Russia and caution in relations with Western countries, similar to the 'line' which the Finnish presidents Paasikivi, Kekkonen, and Koivisto have pursued. Yet, when assessing present Baltic leaders, they rather remind one of the Finnish politician Vainö Tanner, whom the Soviet (and Finnish) communists regarded as an arch enemy and helped to defeat politically.

These arguments summarize the experience of the Cold War and the specific conditions of the Nordic states. The question remains whether these lessons still have validity in the post-Cold War situation of the late 1990s and it seems that it can only be answered in Moscow. As long as traditional Soviet-Russian security perspectives and attitudes prevail and Baltic security concerns just reflect these attitudes, the outlook for safeguarding the Baltic states' independence is bleak. Policies according to the Hobbesian paradigm would leave the EU hardly any option for alleviating the Baltic states' problems.

Applying the Kantian Paradigm

Applying the Kantian paradigm would be the ideal solution for the Baltic–Russian problems. Democracy, market economy, the rule of law, and economic interdependence would create 'structural safeguards' against the domination of a big power over neighbouring small countries. Joint institutions and the creation of common wealth would necessitate and facilitate solving controversies over borders and 'ethnic minorities' and could provide long-term stability.

In such a scenario the Baltic–Russian neighbourhood would resemble the relationship which, for example, the Benelux countries (Belgium, Luxemburg, and the Netherlands) have managed to establish since 1951 (when the European Community of Coal and Steel was created upon French initiative). Another useful reminder of the achievements of European/North Atlantic integration would be the agreement between Denmark and the Federal Republic of Germany on the preferential treatment of the Danish minority in Schleswig-Holstein of March 1955 (just before West Germany joined NATO).

Yet, as has already been argued, for the foreseeable future there are no chances that Russia will be able to fully 'join Europe' and that the Baltic–Russian relationship could be based on the principles of 'democratic peace'. This means that, for the time being, the experience of European integration can serve only as a vision and point of orientation but not as a guiding principle for the practical policies of today.

Applying the Grotian Paradigm

Hedley Bull, while acknowledging the relevance of all three major paradigms, has demonstrated that the Grotian school of thought offers the best option for managing international politics and working towards international peace, as long as national societies and political systems are governed by different principles. This statement still appears valid. Only if democracy were to become the universal guiding principle and if the 'world of society' (*Gesellschaftswelt*, Czempiel, 1993) became truly universal, might the Kantian paradigm be able to supplant the other two. From both a Hobbesian and Grotian perspective there is little chance that such a universal world order will ever be possible.

Today the realist paradigm can be regarded as still valid in certain parts of the world, including the 'zones of turmoil' in Eastern and South-eastern parts of Europe (Singer/Wildavsky, 1993; Hubel, 1997). Yet, within the North Atlantic security community the realist paradigm is no longer the governing principle. Also, since the early 1970s 'Europeans from Vancouver to Vladivostok' have managed to establish security relations that are no longer based exclusively on the realist paradigm. Common norms and institutions were created, particularly within the framework of the CSCE and bilateral East–West agreements, thus adding important elements of cooperation and interdependence to the logic of East–West deterrence. These cooperative East–West elements and the persistence of Western institutions (NATO und EC/EU) provided the framework for ending the East–West conflict in 1990/91 peacefully and quickly (Keohane/Nye/Hoffmann, 1993).

Bull's analysis was based on the experience of the East–West conflict. Yet, when reading his *Anarchical Society* (first issued in 1977) again today, one is surprised at how valid his observations have remained – despite the changes we have been through since 1989.[7] As has been argued, the key reason is that – for the foreseeable future – all-European politics will not be based on a homogeneity of societies and political systems. Probably, the future borderline between the European 'zone of peace' and the Eastern parts of the continent will be Norway's north-eastern, and Finland's and the Baltic states' eastern borders. Managing relations between the European 'zone of peace' and Russia will remain the key problem for all-European stability.

The Grotian paradigm, stressing cooperation, common rules and institutions, does offer some options for dealing with this problem.

From an enlightened Russian point of view, the partnership agreement with the EU 'is one of the most important foreign policy achievements of the last years' (Zagorski, 1997, p. 52). The reason is that in 1994 the EU formally recognized that the Russian economy is a 'transition economy', that EU–Russian trade should be gradually liberalized, and that an option should be kept open to later develop the partnership to a free trade agreement. (Schneider, 1995). In particular, Zagorski (1997, p. 51) recognizes that Germany, within the EU, has strongly supported the principle of a general preferential treatment of Russia.

To be sure, for the time being these principles are more of a declaratory character. They have to be implemented and existing trade barriers on both sides have to be abolished. Yet, one can already detect a certain pattern evolving in the EU–Russian partnership. It seems to be no coincidence that the EU–Russian partnership agreement was signed in 1994, the same year when Russian troops completed their withdrawal both from East Germany and the East-Central European states, including the three Baltic states. In addition, US and European – particularly German – credits granted to Russia have demonstrated Western willingness to sustain a cooperative relationship, despite severe setbacks in Russia (such as Chechnya and other military campaigns of Russian troops in the 'near abroad', Russian–Ukrainian controversies, and the re-emergence of influential groups, opposing democracy and market economy).

In continuing cooperation with Russia, the EU and several EU member-states have also contributed to keeping Baltic–Russian controversies contained. Present Russian political leaders clearly understand that economic-financial cooperation with the EU, and the West in general, demands a certain 'code of conduct', particularly in relations with the Baltic states. Thus, one can argue that important elements of a cooperative relationship between the EU and Russia have already been developed and that they contribute towards stabilizing the Baltic–Russian relationship.

For future EU policies towards Russia and the Baltic states there is one logical conclusion. The EU should shape its measures and steps towards Russia and towards the Baltic states in a co-ordinated way, taking into account the 'logic of the Baltic triangle'. Meaningful steps towards integration of the Baltic states in the EU should always be accompanied by measures facilitating the liberalization of trade and other elements of cooperation with Russia, thus 'keeping Russia engaged' in a productive relationship. While promoting relations with the Baltic states and with Russia simultaneously, yet on different levels, the EU should also continue working on the improvement of Baltic–Russian relations.

For the time being many Russian politicians still tend to regard official trade relations with the Baltic states as a 'political weapon'. Border tariffs and other discriminatory actions are being used for putting pressure on Estonian and Latvia, particularly in order to influence their policy towards their Russian-speaking population group.[8] The EU's task would be to use its influence on both sides, particularly Russia, to remove existing obstacles and help create normal interstate relations. Also, Baltic–Russian cooperation on issues such as trade, traffic, and communication should be actively promoted. If such links were permanently established, they would help create a structural Russian interest in the existence of sovereign, prosperous Baltic states affiliated with the EU and other European institutions.

Certainly, there are major difficulties standing in the way of achieving such an institutionalist programme:

- Firstly, without political leadership in Moscow, St Petersburg, and Pskov (just to name two capitals of neighbouring Russian regions) aiming at democratic and market-economic structures and interested in a cooperative relationship with the EU, this approach will not work. For the time being the picture seems mixed – with reform-minded leaders in Moscow and St Petersburg, and pretty reactionary, Soviet-style politicians in Pskov.[9]

- Secondly, time will be needed to allow a change in Russian and Baltic political mentalities. Presently the parties concerned tend to see the other either as 'part of Great Russia' or as 'the eternal enemy of Baltic independence'. Positive experience with normal neighbourly relationships will be needed to change such stereotypes.

- Thirdly, the EU will not be able to change economic realities in the countries concerned. Rather, the results of indigenous economic and political reforms will be a major factor in EU decision-making on questions related to Eastern enlargement.

- Fourthly, any future action of the EU will depend on the results of recent deepening efforts of the Union. Without more effective decision-making procedures, questions like Eastern enlargement might be blocked by one or several member-states holding different views on the EU's priorities. For example, for several southern members of the EU the issue of relations with the Baltic states is certainly not a priority. Spain and others, for understandable reasons, are looking to the South instead of the East of the Union. Consequently, EU decisions concerning the 'Baltic triangle' will probably have to be balanced by measures concerning Mediterranean policies. As a result, available resources will be stretched and time-tables may have to be extended.

In sum, a successful application of the Grotian approach will depend on several factors within and between the actors of the 'Baltic triangle'.

CONCLUSIONS AND POLICY OPTIONS

After having investigated the three paradigms of international theory and having discussed their application to the 'Baltic triangle', the following summary emerges. The realist or Hobbesian paradigm, which presently seems to have strong supporters both in Russia and the Baltic states – if only with opposite intentions – does not provide much hope for preserving Baltic independence and security. If the logic of spheres of influence and military balance were to dominate policies again, probably the best option for the Baltic states would be a relationship with Russia similar to the Finnish–Soviet one (1944–91). For the Baltic states this would necessitate a certain accommodation with Russia, a clear distance from Western security institutions (NATO in particular), and not full membership in the EU. Several reasons have been given why this 'model' probably would not work under post-Cold War conditions.

The Kantian paradigm, stressing the homogeneity of societal-political order and transnational links, would be the ideal solution to Baltic–Russian problems. The controversial issues – such as border disputes and minorities – could be solved in a way similar to that of Western European practice since the 1950s. Yet, for the foreseeable future, Russia does not seem able to achieve a complete transition to democracy and a market economy. Therefore, for the time being, the Kantian paradigm does not provide a concrete perspective for organizing peace in the 'Baltic triangle'.

The third option, the Grotian paradigm – stressing cooperation and institution-building between states of different social-political order – does offer a theoretical perspective for managing relations in today's 'Baltic triangle'. It has been argued that the European Union has already started developing a long-term relationship with both the Baltic states and Russia. Whereas the Baltic states have already been promised future membership in the Union, Russia has gained a partnership treaty, leaving open the option for future free trade and association with the EU.

The missing link in the 'triangular relationship' remains the Baltic–Russian neighbourhood. This author is proposing that the EU should use its relationships with both the Baltic states and Russia to promote a political normalization of the Baltic–Russian neighbourhood and actively support economic interaction across Russia's borders with Estonia, Latvia, and Lithuania. As for concrete policy options, this author suggests that the EU, when talking/negotiating with any other partner of the 'Baltic triangle', should always demand that measures be taken to improve Baltic–Russian relations. In its previous talks with the Baltic states, the EU has already made clear that they could not become members of the EU as long as they continue to have border disputes with neighbours. Also, the EU and several of its member-states have demanded that the treatment of minorities should meet the standards held by the Council of Europe and the OSCE. Consequently, both Estonia and Latvia have followed the EU's suggestions and have declared themselves ready to accept the existing borders with Russia. Also, both Estonia and Latvia have made changes in their laws on aliens, taking into account suggestions from European institutions, such as the Council of Europe and the OSCE.

Now the EU and individual European member-states should start convincing Russian leaders that, first of all, Russia should sign the border treaties with its neighbours Estonia and Latvia. Otherwise, the EU should hesitate to further develop its partnership with Russia.

Secondly, when talking about commercial issues, the EU should always make clear that it expects a normalization of trade, traffic, and communication across the borders of the Baltic states and Russia. Arbitrary customs regulations, trade barriers for political reasons, threats to apply economic sanctions, and other impediments should be declared incompatible with the 'spirit and practice of European integration'. Simultaneously, the EU should be prepared to reward agreements on practical issues between the Baltic states and Russia. Also, the EU should focus some of its programmes (like TACIS) on the improvement of Baltic–Russian relations and support concrete measures, such as the development of roads, ports, and communications (Christiansen, 1996).

Such practical measures could be of major importance when dealing with the issue of Kaliningrad. After Poland and Lithuania join the EU one day, the Russian *Kaliningradskaya oblast'* (the region of Kaliningrad) will be surrounded by 'EU territory'. In order to protect its future borders and safeguard the stability of its new members, the EU will certainly be interested in a positive economic development of this enclave. Thus, creating employment and raising living standards would serve both Russia's and the EU's interests. It could also help to demilitarize this enclave. Polish and Lithuanian participation in such projects would serve to 'Europeanize' this potentially thorny issue. After the Russian–Estonian and the Russian–Latvian controversies have been – hopefully – solved one day, *Kaliningradskaya oblast'* might become the true test for an effective 'triangular Baltic cooperation', EU association and, ultimately, perhaps even integration.

Today this is more a vision than a concrete perspective. The coming years will show whether the partners of the 'Baltic triangle' are able to pursue policies according to the Grotian paradigm. Theoretically speaking, the challenge for managing the Baltic triangular relationship is to avoid falling back to the realist paradigm and to keep options open for a future application of the Kantian principles. Today the principles of the Grotian paradigm offer the better proposition: to promote a partnership while acknowledging differences in the organization of societies and political systems.

NOTES

1 This author remembers well attending a speech of then Russian Vice-President Aleksandr Rutskoi during a German-*Soviet* conference in Moscow (September 1991), calling for Russian membership in NATO.

2 In reality these models do not appear in a pure form. Rather, one has to identify combinations and links between them. For example, during the East–West conflict European peace rested on a combination of all three:

– NATO and the US 'nuclear umbrella' provided a military balance against Soviet military power and the Warsaw Pact. The Baltic Sea Region could be understood as a special area in which Finnish/Swedish neutrality policies and Danish/Norwegian 'non-base/non-nuclear' NATO membership provided a certain 'softening' (but not abolition) of the power balance logic.
– The Kantian model of democratic peace was applied only in the North Atlantic 'security community' (Deutsch, 1957).
– Since the early 1970s, with the Western and West German 'Ostpolitik', efforts were undertaken to establish a cooperative East–West relationship in Europe. East–West treaties and the CSCE can be understood as efforts towards applying elements of the Grotian model.

3 '(The theory of international politics) will remain indefinitely in the philosophical stage of constant debate about fundamentals … . The works of the new scientific theorists will … take their place alongside earlier works as partial and uncertain guides to an essentially intractable subject.' (Bull, 1969: 30)

4 See the 'future map of Europe', as drawn by Zhirinòvsky in 'Le continent vu par Vladimir Jirinovski', in *Le Monde*, 29 Jan. 1994.

5 If we used the Hitler analogy again, the case of the Sudeten Germans in the Czechoslovak Republic of 1938 would be a frightening analogy for Great Russian aspirations towards the Baltic states, Estonia and Latvia in particular.

6 This observation is based on interviews which this author has conducted in Estonia and Latvia in March 1997. For a self-criticism of recent Estonian attitudes towards Russia, see also Haab and Vares, 1996.

7 In particular, Bull's observations on 'alternative paths to world order' (Bull, 1977: 233–322) provide good arguments against the 'obsolescence of the states system', as presented by contemporary 'Kantians' like Czempiel, 1993 and Rosenau and Durfee, 1995, defending Rosenau, 1990.

8 Russian Foreign Minster Yevgeni Primakov, presently withholding the signing of border treaties, is a prominent advocate of this approach. Primakov, having served Soviet Secretary-Generals Brezhnev and Gorbachev, and now serving President Yeltsin, is obviously an embodiment of Soviet–Russian continuity!

9 Author's interviews in Riga and Tallinn, March 1997.

References

Achen, Christopher H. and Duncan Snidal (1989). 'Rational Deterrence Theory and Comparative Case Studies', *World Politics*, 41: 143–69.

Adler, Emanuel and Michael N. Barnett (1996). 'Governing Anarchy: A Research Agenda for the Study of Security Communities', *Ethics and International Affairs*, 10: 63–98.

Adomeit, Hannes (1995). 'Russia as a "Great Power" in World Affairs: Images and Reality', *International Affairs* (1).

Albright, Madeleine (1997). 'Why Bigger is Better', *The Economist* (15 February), 21–3.

Alten, Jürgen von (1996). *Weltgeschichte der Ostsee*, Berlin: Siedler.

Amstrup, Niels (1976). 'The Perennial Problem of Small States: A Survey of Research Efforts', *Cooperation and Conflict*, 11: 163–82.

Ananicz, Andrzej, Przemyslaw Grudziński, Andrzej Olechowski, Janusz Onyszkiewicz, Krzysztof Skubiszewski and Henryk Szlajfer (1995). *Report Poland–NATO*, Warsaw: Euroatlantic Association.

Andrén, Nils (1972). *Den totala säkerhetspolitiken*, Stockholm: Rabén och Sjögren.

Andrén, Nils (1975). *Problems of Swedish Security*, Stockholm: National Defence Research Institute.

Anisimov, V. (1994). 'Kaliningradskiy faktor. O pravakh nemtsev na Kaliningradskuyu oblast', *Kaliningradskaya pravda* (11 March).

Arbatov, Alexei (1994). 'The Foreign Policy Priorities of Russia', in Armand Clesse, Richard Cooper and Yoshikazu Sakamoto (eds), *The International System after the Collapse of the East–West Order*, Dordrecht: Kluwer Academic.

Archer, Clive (1994). 'New Threat Perceptions: Danish and Norwegian Official Views', *European Security*, 3 (4): 593–616.

Archer, Clive (1997). 'Security Considerations between the Nordic and Baltic Countries', *Danish Foreign Policy Yearbook 1997*.

Archer, Clive, and Øyvind Jæger (1997). 'The Security Policy Doctrines in the Nordic and Baltic Countries: Stability and Change', *NEBI Yearbook 1997*, Copenhagen: COPRI.

Argyle, Michael (1982). 'Inter-cultural Communication', in Stephen Bochner (ed.), *Cultures in Contact*, Oxford: Pergamon Press, 61–80.

Asmus, Ronald D. (1997). 'The New Hanseatic League. Remarks in Helsinki, 8 October 1997', Washington, DC: United States Information Service.

Asmus, Ronald D. and Larrabee, Stephen (1996). 'NATO and the Have-Nots: Reassurance after Enlargement', *Foreign Affairs*, 75 (6): 13–20.

Asmus, Ronald D. and Robert C. Nurick (1996). 'NATO Enlargement and the Baltic States', *Survival*, 38 (2): 121–42.

Avruch, Kevin and Peter W. Black (1993). 'Conflict Resolution in Intercultural Settings: Problems and Prospects', in Dennis J.D. Sandole and Hugo van der Merve (eds), *Conflict Resolution Theory and Practice*, Manchester: Manchester University Press, 131–45.

Axelrod, Robert (1984). *The Evolution of Cooperation*, New York: Basic Books.

Baehr, Peter R. (1975). 'Small States: A Tool for Analysis?', *World Politics*, 27 (3): 456–66.

Baev, Pavel (1996a). *The Russian Army in a Time of Troubles*, London: Sage.

Baev, Pavel (1996b). 'The Russian Debate about the Near Abroad', in Jakub M. Godzimirski, (ed.), *Russia and Europe,*. NUPI Report 210, Oslo: Norwegian Institute of International Affairs.

Baev, Pavel (1997). 'Russia's Departure from Empire: Self-Assertiveness and a New Retreat', in Ola Tunander, Pavel Baev and Victoria Ingrid Einagel (eds), *Geopolitics in Post-Wall Europe*, London: Sage.

Baltic Sea States Summit (1996). *Presidents Declaration, Visby, 3–4 May 1996*, retrieved from http://www.baltinfo.org/document.htm

Balutskiy, Sergey (1995). 'Zachem amerikanskomu kongressmenu razygryvat' kaliningradskuyu kartu, Proyekt rezolutsii o Kaliningradskoy oblasti v palate predstaviteley SShA', *Rossiyskiye vesti* (19 April).

Barth, Magne and Else M. Brodshaug (1997). 'Nordisk sikkerhetspolitikk', *PRIO-notat* 1/97.

Barynkin, Viktor (1996). 'Russia's Stand on Plans for Enlargement of NATO. A View from the General Staff of the Russian Armed Forces', *RIA Novosti – Military Review* (May).

Bazhanov, Yevgeni (1996). 'Russia's Changing Foreign Policy', *Berichte des Bundesinstituts für ostwissenschaftliche und internationale Studien*, no. 30.

Bekker, Aleksandr (1994). 'Kaliningradskaya oblast khochet ostat'sya rossiyskoy', *Segodnya* (28 May).

Bem, Sandra L. (1974). 'The Measurement of Psychological Androgyny', *Journal of Consulting and Clinical Psychology*, 42: 155–62.

Bernatowicz, Grazyna (1995). 'Regional Cooperation in Europe – Baltic Case', in Pertti Joenniemi and Carl-Einar Stålvant (eds), *Baltic Sea Politics: Achievement and Challenges*, Stockholm: Nordic Council.

Biersteker, Thomas J. and Cynthia Weber (1996). 'The Social Construction of State Sovereignty', in Thomas J. Biersteker and Cynthia Weber (eds), *State Sovereignty as Social Construct*, Cambridge University Press: Cambridge, 1–21.

Bildt, Carl (1993). 'Sweden and the Baltic countries', Address by the Prime Minister, Stockholm: Swedish Institute of International Affairs.

Bildt, Carl (1994). 'The Baltic Litmus Test', *Foreign Affairs*, 73 (5): 72–85.

Birkavs, Valdis (1997a). 'The Priorities of Latvia's Foreign Policy', Address given at University of London, School of Slavonic and East European Studies, 10 March, retrieved from http:/www.mfa.gov.lv/mfa/pub/runas/vb/vb970310.htm

Birkavs, Valdis (1997b). 'Statement by H.E. Dr Valdis Birkavs, Minister of Foreign Affairs of Latvia', at the Meeting with the North Atlantic Council, Brussels, 30 April 1997, Brussels, retrieved from http:/www.mfa.gov.lv/mfa/pub/runas/vb/vb970430.htm

Bitzinger, Richard A. (1996). 'The Nordic/Baltic Region: A New Strategic Significance?', *Defence Analysis*, 12 (3).

Bjøl, Erling (1968). 'The Power of the Weak', *Cooperation and Conflict*, 3: 157–68.

Black, Peter W. and Kevin Avruch (1993). 'Culture, Power and International Negotiations: Understanding Palau–US Status Negotiations', *Millennium*, 22: 379–400.

Blackwill, Robert D., Rodric Braithwaite and Akihiko Tanaka (1995). *Engaging Russia. A Report to the Trilateral Commission no.46*, New York/Paris/Tokyo: Trilateral Commission.

Blank, Stephen J. (1995). 'Energy, Economics, and Security in Central Asia: Russia and Its Rivals', Strategic Studies Institute, US Army War College, Carlisle, PA (10 May).

Blasier, Cole (1976). *The Hovering Giant. US Responses to Revolutionary Change in Latin America*, Pittsburgh, PA: University of Pittsburgh Press.

Bleiere, Daina (1997). 'The Integration of the Baltic States and the European Union: The Latvian Perspective', in Atis Lejinš and Zaneta Ozolina (eds), *Small States in a Turbulent Environment. The Baltic Perspective*, Riga: Latvian Institute of International Affairs, 60–112.

Boyes, Robert (1992). 'Resurgence of Kaliningrad Troubles Poles', *The London Times* (15 May).

Bozeman, Adda (1960). *Politics and Culture in International History*, Princeton, NJ: Princeton University Press.

Braudel, Fernand (1975). *The Mediterranean and the Mediterranean World in the Age of Philip II*, London: Fontana/Collins.

Brazauskas, Algirdas (1996a). Address by the President of the Republic of Lithuania at the Western European Union, Brussels, 15 October, retrieved from gopher://marvin.nc3a.nato.int:70/00/partners/lithuania/mfa/statements/1996/weu.doc

Brazauskas, Algirdas (1996b). Address by the President of the Republic of Lithuania at the meeting with European Parliament committees, Brussels, 17 October, retrieved from gopher://marvin.nc3a.nato.int:70/00/partners/lithuania/mfa/statements/1996/ep.doc

Breckinridge, R.E. (1991). 'The Interaction of Regimes', Ph.D. dissertation; Department of Government and Politics, University of Maryland.

Brown, M.E., S.M. Lynn-Jones and S.E. Miller (eds) (1996). *Debating the Democratic Peace*, Cambridge, MA: The MIT Press.

Brundtland, Arne Olav (1966). 'The Nordic Balance Then and Now', *Co-operation and Conflict* (2): 30–63.

Brundtland, Arne Olav (1971). 'The Nordic Countries as an Area of Peace', in A. Schou and A. O. Brundtland (eds), *Small States in International Relations*, Stockholm: Almqvist & Wiksell.

Brundtland, Arne Olav (ed.) (1996). 'Finsk og norsk forsvar – alltid for samme formål – alltid med ulik kurs?' Proceedings from the Conference 'Nordens stemme på Akershus', Oslo: NUPI.

Brundtland, Gro Harlem (1996). 'Prime Minister Gro Harlem Brundtland. Address at the University of Vilnius, 19 March, *UD Informasjon, no. 8*, Oslo, Utenriksdepartmentet.

Brusstar, James H. (1994). 'Russian Vital Interests and Western Security', *Orbis* (Fall).

Brzezinski, Zbigniew (1994). 'The Premature Partnership', *Foreign Affairs*, 73 (2).

Bull, Hedley (1969). 'International Theory: The Case for a Classical Approach', in Klaus Knorr and James N. Rosenau (eds), *Contending Approaches to International Politics*, Princeton, NJ: Princeton University Press: 20–38.

Bull, Hedley (1977). *The Anarchical Society. A Study of Order in World Politics*, London: Macmillan.

Buzan, Barry (1983). *People, States and Fear. The National Security Problem in International Relations*, Brighton: Harvester Wheatsheaf.

Buzan, Barry (1991). *People, States and Fear. Second Edition. An Agenda for International Security Studies in the Post-Cold War Era*,. London: Harvester Wheatsheaf.

Buzan, Barry (1997). 'Rethinking Security After the Cold War', *Cooperation and Conflict*, 32 (1): 5–28.

Cantori, Louis J. and Steven L. Spiegel (1970). *The International Politics of Regions. A Comparative Framework*, Englewood Cliffs, NJ: Prentice-Hall.

Capra, Fritjof (1992). *The Tao of Physics*, 3rd edition, London: Flamingo.

Carbaugh, Donal (1994). 'Cultures in Conversation: Prospects for New World Communities', in David March and Liise Salo-Lee (eds), *Europe on the Move: Fusion or Fission?*, Proceedings, 1994 Sietar Europe Symposium, Sietar Europe/University of Jyväskylä, Finland, 24–34.

Carlsen, Per (1997). 'Political, Economic, and Military Security of the Baltic into the 21st Century: the Long View from the Region. Confidence and Security Building Measures', Copenhagen: Ministry of Defence, May 1997 – presentation made at Sandhurst, UK, 28–30 May.

Carr, F. and K. Ifantis (1996). *NATO in the New European Order*, New York: St Martin's Press.

Casse, Pierre and Surinder Deol (1985). *Managing Intercultural Negotiations*, Washington, DC: Sietar International.

Castel, Viviane du (1996). 'Entre Kaliningrad et la Russie: les Dangers d'un Corridor Stratégique', *Défense National* (11): 69–82.

Chay, John and Thomas E. Ross (eds) (1986). *Buffer States in World Politics*, Boulder, CO: Westview Press.

Cherkasov, Gleb (1996). 'Shestogo oktyabrya Kalinigradskaya oblast izberet sebe vsu mestnuyu vlast', *Segodnya* (19 Sept.).

Cherkasov, Gleb (1996). 'Yuriy Matochkin: tsentr dolzhen podelitsya polnomochyami s regionami', *Segodnya* (19 Sept.).

Chinn, J. and R. Kaiser (1996). *Russians as the New Minority: Ethnicity and Nationalism in the Soviet Successor States*, Boulder, CO: Westview Press.

Choucri, Nazli and Robert C. North (1975). *Nations in Conflict. National Growth and International Violence*, San Francisco: W.H. Freeman.

Christiansen, Thomas (1996). 'European Integration and Nordic Security: The Role of the European Union in the Baltic Sea Region', in Anders Orrenius and Lars Truedson (eds), *Visions of European Security – Focal Point Sweden and Northern Europe*, Stockholm: The Olof Palme International Centre: 278–94.

Clement, Rolf (1997). 'Doppelten Zurückweisungsschock abfedern. Mitglied oder nicht – die relativierte Frage', *Das Parlament*, 21 (16 May).

Cohen, Raymond (1987). 'Problems of Intercultural Communication in

Egyptian–American Diplomatic Relations', *International Journal of Inter-cultural Relations*, 11: 29–47.

Cohen, Raymond (1991). *Negotiating across Cultures – Communication Obstacles in International Relations*, Washington, DC: United States Institute of Peace Press.

Council of the Baltic Sea States (1996). 'Action Programme for the Baltic Sea States Cooperation', retrieved from http://www.baltinfo.org/document.htm

Council of the Baltic Sea States (1997). 'About the Council of the Baltic Sea States: Basic Information', retrieved from http://www.baltinfo.org/CBSS.htm

Cox, Robert W. (1997). 'Introduction', in Robert W. Cox (ed.), *The New Realism – Perspectives on Multilateralism and World Order*, Basingstoke: Macmillan.

Crow, Suzanne (1993). *The Making of Foreign Policy in Russia under Yeltsin*, Munich and Washington: RFE/RL Research Institute.

Czempiel, Ernst Otto (1993). *Weltpolitik im Umbruch*, Munich: Beck.

Dahl (Nilsson), Ann-Sofie (1997a). 'To Be Or Not To Be Neutral: Swedish Security Strategy in the Post-Cold War Era', in Efraim Inbar and Gabriel Scheffer (eds), *The National Security of Small States in a Changing World*, London: Frank Cass.

Dahl (Nilsson), Ann-Sofie (1997b). 'Not if but How: Sweden's Future Relations with NATO', *NATO Review* (3).

Dalbins, Juris (1996). 'Baltic Cooperation – The Key to Wider Security', *NATO Review*, 44 (1 – January): 7–10.

Darski, Jozef (1992). *Bialorus*, Warszawa: Instytut Polityczny.

Davies, Norman (1981). *God's Playground. A History of Poland*, Oxford: Oxford University Press.

Davies, R.T. (1995). 'Should NATO Grow? – A Dissent', *The New York Review of Books*, 42 (14) (21 Sept.): 74–5.

Davydov, Yuriy (1997). 'Russian Security and East-Central Europe', in Vladimir Baranovsky (ed.), *Russia and Europe. The Emerging Security Agenda*, Oxford: Oxford University Press for SIPRI.

Dean, Jonathan (1995). 'Losing Russia or Keeping NATO – Must We Choose?', *Arms Control Today* (June).

Defence Bill 1991/1992, Prop 1991/1992: 102. Stockholm: Ministry of Defence.

Deutsch, Karl W. *et al.* (1957). *Political Community and the North Atlantic Area. International Organization in the Light of Historical Experience*, Princeton, NJ: Princeton University Press.

Deutscher, Isaak (1949). *Stalin*, New York: Oxford University Press.

Dörfer, Ingemar (1997). *The Nordic Nations in the New Western Security Regime*, Washington, DC: The Woodrow Wilson Center Press.

Doyle, Michael (1983). 'Kant, Liberal Legacies, and Foreign Affairs', in *Philosophy and Public Affairs*, 12 (3–4).

Dreifelds, Juris (1996). *Latvia in Transition*, Cambridge: Cambridge University Press.

Dubnov, Vadim, (1995). 'Prusskiye russkiye. Kaliningradskaja oblast: budushchaya Baltijskaya respublika', *Novoye Vremya* (35).

Eberhardt, Piotr (1993). *Polska granica wschodnia 1939–45*, Warszawa: Editions Spotkania.

Eberhardt, Piotr (1996). *Miedzy Rosja a Niemcami, Przemiany narodowosciowe w Europie Srodkowo-Wschodniej w XX wieku*, Warszawa: Wydawnictwo Naukowe PWN.

Economic Development of Latvia. Report (1997). Riga: Ministry of Economy, Republic of Latvia, June.

Ellemann-Jensen, Uffe (1996). *Din egen dag er kort*, Copenhagen: Aschehoug.

'Estonian Foreign Trade in 1996' (1997). *Eesti Pank Bulletin* (2).

Fairlie, Lyndelle (1996). 'Kaliningrad: NATO and EU enlargement issues focus new attention on Russia's border with Central Europe', *IBRU Boundary and Security Bulletin* (Autumn).

Fant, Lars (1992). 'Scandinavians and Spaniards in Negotiations', in Annick Sjögren and Lena Janson (eds), *Culture and Management*, Stockholm: Stockholm School of Business, 125–53.

Feghali, Ellen (1997). 'Arab Cultural Communication Patterns', *International Journal of Intercultural Relations*, 21: 345–78.

Finansministeriet (1997). *Danmark som Foregangsland. Den Udenrigspolitiske Insats for Central-og Østeuropa herunder de Baltiske Lande*, Copenhagen: Finansministeriet.

Finnemore, Martha (1996). *National Interests in International Society*, Ithaca, NY: Cornell University Press.

Fisher, Glen (1988). *Mindsets – The Role of Culture and Perception in International Relations*, Yarmouth, ME: Intercultural Press.

Foreign Policy Concept of the Russian Federation (1993). *FBIS Report*, FBIS-USR-93-037 (25 March).

Forsberg, Tuomas (ed.) (1994). *Contested Territory. Border Disputes at the Edge of the Former Soviet Empire. Studies of Communism in Transition*, London: Edward Elgar.

Fox, Annette Baker (1959). *The Power of Small States. Diplomacy in World War II*, Chicago: University of Chicago Press.

Fox, Annette Baker (1977). *The Politics of Attraction*, New York: Columbia University Press.

Friedrich, Carl J. and Zbigniew K. Brzezinski (1956). *Totalitarian Dictatorship and Autocracy*, Cambridge: Harvard University Press.

Fure, Odd-Bjørn (1996). *Mellomkrigstid. Norsk utenrikspolitikks historie*, Bind 3, Oslo: Universitetsforlaget.

Furman, Dmitrij (1995). 'Vneshnepoliticheskiye oryentiry Rossii', *Svobodnaja Mysl'* (8).

Gannon, J. Martin and Associates (1994). *Understanding Global Cultures – Metaphorical Journeys through 17 Countries*, Thousand Oaks, CA: Sage.

Gatley, Stephan, Ronnie Lessem and Yochanan Altman (1996). *Comparative Management*, London: McGraw-Hill.

Geipel, Gary, L. (1995). 'Germany and the Burden of Choice', *Current History* (94 – Nov.).

Ghauri, Berez and Jean-Claude Usunier (1996). 'Negotiating with Eastern and Central Europeans', in Berez Ghauri and Jean-Claude Usunier (eds), *International Business Negotiations*, Oxford, Elsevier: Pergamon, 335–52.

Gilpin, Robert (1981). *War and Change in International Politics*, Cambridge: Cambridge University Press.

Glaser, Charles (1997). 'The Security Dilemma Revisited', *World Politics*, 50 (1): 171–201.

Glassner, M.I. (1993). *Political Geography*, New York: John Wiley and Sons.

Glenn, Edmund S., D. Witmeyer and K.A. Stevenson (1977). 'Cultural Styles of Persuasion', *International Journal of Intercultural Relations*, 1 (3 – Autumn): 52–65.

Goble, Paul A.(1993). 'Russia and Its Neighbours', *Foreign Policy* (Spring).

Goble, Paul (1997). 'The Spirit of Vilnius', *RFE/RL Newsline* (8 Sept.).

Goble, Paul (1997a). 'Drawing Borders Geographic and Political', *RFE/RL Newsline* (23 Oct.).

Goble, Paul (1997b). 'Returning to the Baltics', *RFE/RL Newsline* (7 Nov.).

Goble, Paul (1998). 'One Country, Two Foreign Policies', *End note, RFE/RL Newsline* (188) (5 Jan.).

Godzimirski, Jakub M. (1993). 'Baltyckie perspektywy', *Polska w Europie* (10).

Godzimirski, Jakub M. (1996). 'Soviet Roots of Russia's Policy towards the "Near Abroad"', in Jakub M. Godzimirski (ed.), *Russia and Europe*, NUPI Report 210, Oslo: Norwegian Institute of International Affairs.

Goldmann, Kjell and Kristina Boréus (1990). 'Etik och politik: Kärnvapen och internationalism', *Statsvetenskaplig Tidskrift* (2).

Graham, J.L. (1983). 'The Influence of Culture on the Process of Business Negotiations', *Journal of International Business Studies*, 16 (1): 81–96.

Gray, Colin S. (1996). 'The Continued Primacy of Geography', *Orbis*, 40 (2).

Grekov, Igor B. (1975). *Vostochnaja Evropa i upadok Zolotoj Ordy* (Eastern Europe and the Decline of the Golden Horde), Moskva: Nauka.

Grenville, J.A.S. (1974). *The Major International Treaties 1914–1973. A History and Guide with Texts*, London: Methuen.

Griffin, Trenholme J. and W. Daggart (1990). *The Global Negotiator*, New York: Harper Collins.

Gromak, V. (1992). 'Komu ugrozhayet Kaliningradskaya oblast?', *Krasnaya Zvezda* (19 June).

Gromak, Valeriy (1994). 'Yantarnyy bereg – osobyy oboronitelnyy rayon Rossii', *Krasnaya Zvezda* (19 March).

Gudykunst, William and Stella Ting-Toomey (1988). *Culture and Interpersonal Communications*, Beverly Hills, CA: Sage.

Gustafsson, Bengt (1996). Statement by the Chief of Defence. Stockholm: Kungl. Krigsvetenskapsakademien (13 Nov.).

Gylys, Povilas (1994). 'Litva ne pretenduyet na kaliningradskiye zemli', an interview with Povilas Gylis, *Izvestiya* (26 March).

Gylys, Povilas (1996). 'The Baltic Dimension of European Integration: The Lithuanian Perspective', Presentation given at the Institute of East–West Studies Conference, Riga, 24–5 August.

Gylys, Povilas and Ole Norrback (1996). *Joint Statement*, Vilnius, 14 April, retrieved from gopher://marvin.nc3a.nato.int:70/00/partners/lithuania/mfa/baco/badoc.doc

Haab, Mare (1997). 'Between Russia and the West – How much security for Estonia?', Second draft paper (January).

Haab, Mare and Peeter Vares (1996). 'The Future of European Security as Viewed in Estonia', in Anders Orrenius and Lars Truedson (eds), *Visions of European Security – Focal Point Sweden and Northern Europe*, Stockholm: The Olof Palme International Centre, 148–61.

Hækkerup, Hans (1996). 'A Multinational Force Culture', *Enjeux atlantiques* (13 – June).

Hækkerup, Hans (1997a). 'From Adazi to Tuzla', Speech by Danish Minister of Defence. Conference: 'St Petersburg, the Baltic Sea and European Security', St Petersburg, 26 April 1996. *Danish Foreign Policy Yearbook 1997*, Copenhagen: DUPI, 135–9.

Hækkerup, Hans (1997b). *Østersøen i det nye Europa: Danmarks militære østsamarbejde*, Oslo: DNAK, Det sikkerhetspolitiske bibliotek (8).

Haftendorn, Helga (1996). 'Gulliver in the Centre of Europe', in Bertel Heurlin (ed.), *Germany in Europe in the Nineties*, London, New York: St Martin's Press.

Hall, Edward T. (1976). *Beyond Culture*, New York: Doubleday.

Hall, Edward T. and Mildred R. Hall (1990). *Understanding Cultural Differences*, Yarmouth, ME: Intercultural Press.

Hall, John A. (ed.) (1986). *States in History*, Oxford: Basil Blackwell.

Hall, Wendy (1995). *Managing Cultures*, Chichester: Wiley.

Hampden-Turner, Charles (1994). *Corporate Culture*, London: Piatkus.

Hampden-Turner, Charles and Fons Trompenaars (1993). *The Seven Cultures of Capitalism*, New York: Doubleday.

Handel, Michael (1981). *Weak States in the International System*, London: Frank Cass.

Hansen, Birthe (1996). 'Dansk Baltikumpolitik 1989–1995', in *Dansk Udenrigspolitik Årbog 1995*, Copenhagen: Dansk Udenrigspolitisk Institut, 35–65.

Hansen, Birthe (1998). 'The Baltic States and Security Strategies Available', in Birthe Hansen and Bertel Heurlin (eds), *The Baltic States in World Politics*, New York: St Martin's Press, 86–111.

Hansen, Erik (1996). 'Coping with It: St Petersburg and Kaliningrad Facing Reform. The Norbalt Living Condition Project', *FAFO-Report* (201), Oslo: FAFO, Institute for Applied Social Science.

Harris, Philip R. and Robert T. Moran (1979). *Managing Cultural Differences*, Houston, TX: Gulf.

Heisler, M.O. (1992). 'Migration, International Relations and the New Europe', *International Migration Review*, 26, 2 (Summer): 596–622.

Helveg Petersen, Niels (1996). 'Security Cooperation and Integration in the Baltic Region. The Role of the European Union: Soft Security', Copenhagen, mimeo.

Helveg Petersen, Niels (1997). 'Speech by Danish Minister for Foreign Affairs. Seminar, 7 October, 1996. The Role of the Organization for Security and Cooperation in Europe (OSCE) in European Security Architecture', *Danish Foreign Policy Yearbook 1997*, Copenhagen: DUPI, 143–7.

Herd, Graeme P. (1997). 'Baltic Security Politics', *Security Dialogue*, 28 (2): 251–3.

Herz, John H. (1959 [1951]). *Political Realism and Political Idealism. A Study in Theories and Realities*, Chicago, IL: University of Chicago Press.

Heurlin, Bertel (1995). 'Security Problems in the Baltic Region in the 1990s.

The Baltic Region and the New Security Dynamics and Challenges', in Pertti Joenniemi and Carl-Einar Stålvant (eds), *Baltic Sea Politics: Achievements and Challenges*, Stockholm: The Nordic Council, 55–75.

Heurlin, Bertel (1996). 'The Baltic Sea Region and New Security Challenges', in Bertel Heurlin (ed.), *Security Problems in the New Europe*, Copenhagen: Copenhagen Political Studies Press, 68–90.

Hill, Fiona, Pamela Jewett and Sergei Grigoriev (1994). *Back in the USSR*, Harvard: John F. Kennedy School of Government.

Hjelm Wallén, Lena (1996). *Common Security in the Post-Cold War – A Swedish View*, Stockholm, Ministry for Foreign Affairs, mimeo.

Hofstede, Geert (1991). *Cultures and Organizations*, London: McGraw-Hill.

Hofstede, Geert (1996). 'Images of Europe: Past, Present and Future', in Pat Joynt and Malcolm Warner (eds), *Managing Across Cultures: Issues and Perspectives*, London: International Thomson Business Press, 147–65.

Holm, Hans-Henrik (1997). 'Denmark's Active Internationalism: Advocating International Norms with Domestic Constraints', *Danish Foreign Policy Yearbook 1997*, Copenhagen: DUPI, 52–80.

Holst, Johan Jørgen (1967). *Norsk sikkerhetspolitikk i strategisk perspektiv. Bind I: Analyse*, Oslo: Norsk Utenrikspolitisk Institutt.

Horowitz, D.L. (1985). *Ethnic Groups in Conflict*, Berkeley and Los Angeles: University of California Press.

Hsu, Francis L.K. (1981). *Americans and Chinese – Passage to Differences*, 3rd edition, Honolulu: University of Hawaii Press.

Hubel, Helmut (1994). 'The Baltic Dimension of European Unification', in Kaisa Lähteenmäki (ed.), *Dimensions of Cooperation and Conflict in the Baltic Sea Rim*, Tampere: Tampere Peace Research Institute, TAPRI Research Report no. 58: 57–67.

Hubel, Helmut (1996). 'Die schwierige Partnerschaft mit Rußland' (The Difficult Partnership with Russia), in Karl Kaiser and Joachim Krause (eds), *Deutschlands neue Außenpolitik*, vol. 3: Interessen und Strategien, Munich: Oldenbourg: 137–41.

Hubel, Helmut (1997). 'Regionale Konflikte nach dem Ost-West-Antagonismus', *Zeitschrift für Politikwissenschaft*, 7 (2): 405–21.

Huitfeldt, Tønne and Gullow Gjeseth (1996). 'Nordisk og baltisk sikkerhet', *Den norske atlanterhavskomites skriftserie* (193). Oslo: The Norwegian Atlantic Committee.

Huntington, Samuel P. (1993). 'The Clash of Civilizations?', *Foreign Affairs*, 72 (3 – Summer).

Huntington, Samuel P. (1996). *The Clash of Civilizations and the Remaking of World Order*, New York: Simon & Schuster.

Huth, Paul (1988). 'Extended Deterrence and the Outbreak of War', *American Political Science Review*, 82: 423–42.

Huth, Paul and Bruce Russett (1984). 'What Makes Deterrence Work? Cases from 1900 to 1980', *World Politics*, 36 (4): 496–526.

Ilnicki, Marek and Andrzej Karkoszka *et al.* (1991). 'Security and Politico-Military Stability in the Baltic Region', Warszawa: *PISM Occasional Papers* (21).

Ilves, Toomas Hendrik (1997a). Remarks by Toomas Hendrik Ilves, Estonian

Minister of Foreign Affairs, at Columbia University, New York, 31 March, retrieved from http://www.vm.ee/speeches/1997/0331colu.html

Ilves, Toomas Hendrik (1997b). Remarks by Toomas Hendrik Ilves, Estonian Minister of Foreign Affairs, to the Danish Defence Commission, Tallinn, 14 April, retrieved from http://www.vm.ee/speeches/1997/0414taan.html

'Interesy Bezopasnosti Rossii i Evropy na Baltike' (1995). (Security Interests of Russia and Europe in the Baltic Sea), *Mezhdunarodnaya Zhizn'* (6): 18–22.

Jackson, R.H. (1990). *Quasi-states: Sovereignty, International Relations and the Third World*, Cambridge: Cambridge University Press.

Jæger, Øyvind (1997). 'Securitising Russia. Discursive Practices of the Baltic States', *COPRI Working Papers* (10).

Jakobson, Max (1961). *The Diplomacy of the Winter War*, Cambridge, MA: Harvard University Press.

Jakobson, Max (1968), *Finnish Neutrality. A Study of Finnish Foreign Policy Since the Second World War*, London: Hugh Evelyn.

Järve, Priit (ed.) (1997). *Vene noored Eestis: sotsioloogiline mosaiik*, Tast Ülikool, Tallinn: Kirjastus Avita.

Jenkins, D. (1968). *The Progress Machine*, London: Robert Hole.

Jepperson, Ronald L., Alexander Wendt and Peter J. Katzenstein (1996). 'Norms, Identity, and Culture in National Security', in Peter J. Katzenstein (ed.), *The Culture of National Security. Norms and Identity in World Politics*, New York: Columbia University Press, 33–75.

Joenniemi, Pertti (ed.) (1993). *Cooperation in the Baltic Sea Region*, London: Taylor & Francis.

Joenniemi, Pertti (1995). 'Security in the Baltic Sea region; the Contest between Different Agendas', Paper at the 13th Nordic Peace Research Conference, Lohusalo, Estonia, 29 June–2 July, mimeo.

Joenniemi, Pertti (1996). 'Kaliningrad: A Region in Search for a Past and a Future', Travemünde: Ostsee-Akademie.

Joenniemi, Pertti (ed.) (1997). *Neo-Nationalism or Regionality. The Restructuring of Political Space Around the Baltic Rim*, København: NORDREFO/Nordiska Institutet för Regionalpolitisk Forskning.

Joenniemi, Pertti (1997). 'Kaliningrad: a Double Periphery?', *COPRI Working papers* (17), Copenhagen: Copenhagen Peace Research Institute.

Joenniemi, Pertti and Carl-Einar Stålvant (1995). 'The Region', in Pertti Joenniemi and Carl-Einar Stålvant (eds), *Baltic Sea Politics: Achievement and Challenges*, Stockholm: Nordic Council.

Judt, Tony (1996). *A Grand Illusion? An Essay on Europe*, Harmondsworth: Penguin.

Jung, Carl G. (1921). *Psychological Types*, Princeton, NJ: Princeton University Press.

Jurgaitiene, Kornelija and Ole Wæver (1996). 'Lithuania', in Hans Mouritzen, Ole Wæver and Håkan Wiberg (eds), *European Integration and National Adaptations. A Theoretical Inquiry*, Commack, NY: Nova Science Publishers, 185–229.

Kamiñski, Antoni *et al.* (1993). *Raport o stanie panstwa – aspekty zewnetrzne*, Warszawa: Polski Instytut Spraw Miedzynarodowych PISM.

Kamiñski, Bartlomiej, Zhen-kun Wang and L. Alan Winters (1996). 'Foreign

Trade in the Transition: The International Environment and Domestic Policy', *Studies of Economies in Transformation*, no. 20, Washington, DC: World Bank.

Karpinski, Jakub (1996). 'Poland and Lithuania Look Toward a Common Future', *Transitions*, 3 (6): 15–17, 56.

Katzenstein, Peter J. (1977). 'Conclusion: Domestic Structures and Strategies of Foreign Economic Policy', *International Organization*, 31 (4 – Autumn): 879–920.

Katzenstein, Peter J. (1984). *Corporatism and Change. Austria, Switzerland and the Politics of Industry*, Ithaca, NY: Cornell University Press.

Katzenstein, Peter J. (1985). *Small States in World Markets. Industrial Policy in Europe*, Ithaca, NY: Cornell University Press.

Katzenstein, Peter J. (ed.) (1996). *The Culture of National Security. Norms and Identity in World Politics*, New York: Columbia University Press.

Kennedy, Paul (1987). *The Rise and Fall of Great Powers*, New York: Random House.

Keohane, Robert O. (1993). 'Institutional Theory and the Realist Challenge After the Cold War', in David A. Baldwin (ed.), *Neorealism and Neoliberalism*, New York: Columbia University Press: 269–300.

Keohane, Robert O. and Joseph S. Nye (1977). *Power and Interdependence. World Politics in Transition*, Boston: Little, Brown & Co.

Keohane, Robert O., Joseph S. Nye and Stanley Hoffmann (eds) (1993). *After the Cold War. International Institutions and State Strategies in Europe*, Cambridge, MA: Harvard University Press.

Khalilzad, Zalmay and Ian. J. Brzezinski (1993). 'Extending the Democratic Zone of Peace to Eastern Europe', *The Polish Quarterly of International Affairs*, 2 (3).

Kimura, Hiroshi (1996). 'The Russian Way of Negotiating', *International Negotiation*, 1 (3): 365–89.

Kirch, Aksel and Marika Kirch (1995). 'Search for Security in Estonia: New Identity Architecture', *Security Dialogue*, 26 (4).

Kivinen, Olli (1997). 'Ruotsi ja Tanska väärässä', *Helsingin Sanomat*, 11 September, A2.

Klyamkin, Igor and Tatjana Kutkovets (1996). 'Komu v Rossii nuzjna imperija?', *Segodnja* (1 Feb.).

Knudsen, Olav F. (1988). 'Of Lambs and Lions: Relations Between Great Powers and Their Smaller Neighbors', *Cooperation and Conflict*, 23 (4): 111–22.

Knudsen, Olav F. (1996a). 'Norway' in Axel Krohn (ed.), *The Baltic Sea Region – National and International Security Perspectives*, Baden-Baden: Nomos, 116–28.

Knudsen, Olav F. (1996b). 'Bound to Fail? Regional Security Cooperation in the Baltic Sea Area and Northeast Asia', *NUPI Working Paper No. 566* (December).

Knudsen, Olav F. (1998a). 'The Nordic–Baltic Region before Madrid: Diagnostic Statements Assessing Security', in Hans Henrik Holm and Georg Sørensen (eds), *And Now What? The International System After the Cold War. Essays in Honour of Nikolaj Petersen*, Århus: Politika, 124–48.

Knudsen, Olav F. (1998b). 'Cooperative Security in the Baltic Sea Region', *Chaillot Papers*, Paris: Institute for Security Studies, Western European Union.

Knudsen, Olav F. and Iver B. Neumann (1995). 'Subregional Security Co-operation in the Baltic Sea Area: An Exploratory Study', *NUPI Report* (189), Oslo: Norwegian Institute of International Affairs (March).

Kolankiewicz, George (1994). 'Consensus and Competition in the Eastern Enlargement of the European Union', *International Affairs*, 70 (3 – July): 477–95.

Kolecka, Beata (1996). 'Stosunki z państwami baltyckimi', in Barbara Wizimirska (ed.), *Rocznik polskiej polityki zagranicznej 1996*, MSZ.

Kolstoe, Paal (1995). *Russians in the Former Soviet Republics*, Bloomington and Indianapolis: Indiana University Press.

Koopmann, Werner (1997). 'Das Baltikum als Handelspartner und Investititionsstandort', *Wirtschaft zwischen Nord- und Ostsee* (Aug.), Kiel: Industrie- und Handelskammer zu Kiel.

Kozyrev, Andrey (1995). *Preobrazheniye*, Moscow.

Kozyreva, Anna (1994). 'Kaliningrad ili Kenigsberg? Kaliningradskaya oblast – voprosy toponimiki i problemy politiki', *Rossiyskaya Gazeta* (3 Dec.).

Krasner, Stephen (1977). 'US Commercial and Monetary Policy: Unravelling the Paradox of External Strength and Internal Weakness', *International Organization*, 31 (4 –Autumn): 635–71.

Krasner, Stephen (1978). *Defending the National Interest. Raw Materials Investment and U.S. Foreign Policy*, Princeton, NJ: Princeton University Press.

Krause, Keith and Michael C. Williams (1997). 'From Strategy to Security: Foundations of Critical Security Studies', in Keith Krause and Michael C. Williams (ed.), *Critical Security Studies*, Minneapolis, MN: University of Minnesota Press, 33–59.

Krohn, Axel (ed.) (1996). *The Baltic Sea Region. National and International Security Perspectives*, Demokratie, Sicherheit, Frieden, vol. 105. Baden-Baden: Nomos Verlag.

Krohn, Axel (1996). 'Germany', in Axel Krohn (ed.), *The Baltic Sea Region. National and International Security Perspectives*, Baden-Baden: Nomos Verlag.

Kukk, Mare (1994). 'Ostseerat: Mitten im Teich', *Nordeuropa-Forum* (1): 20–27.

Kukk, Mare and Sverre Jervell, Perti Joenniemi (eds) (1992). *The Baltic Sea Area – A Region in the Making*, Oslo: Europaprogrammet.

Küng, Andres (1990). *(S) och Baltikum: En bakgrund till Sten Andersson-affären hösten 1989*, Stockholm: Timbro.

Kurth, James (1995). 'Germany and the Re-emergence of Mitteleuropa', *Current History* (94 – Nov.).

Kuzniar, Roman (1993). 'The Geostrategic Factors Conditioning Poland's Security', *The Polish Quarterly of International Affairs*, 2 (1).

Lake, David A. and Patrick M. Morgan (eds) (1997). *Regional Orders: Building Security in a New World*, University Park, PA: The Pennsylvania State University Press.

Lakoff, George and Mark Johnson (1980). *Metaphors We Live By*, Chicago, IL: University of Chicago Press.

Lambsdorff, Otto Graf (1997). 'Eine stabile Instabilität' (A Stable Instability), *Internationale Politik* (Bonn), 52 (4): 41–6.

Lamentowicz, Wojtek (1997). 'Russia and East-Central Europe. Strategic Options', in: Baranovsky, Vladimir (ed.), *Russia and Europe. The Emerging Security Agenda*, Oxford: Oxford University Press for SIPRI.

Lange, Peer H. (1993). 'Das Gebiet Kaliningrad – Wegscheide für Russlands Politische Strategie', *Europa Archiv* 10.

Lange, Peer H. (1997). 'In wichtiger Transmissionsrolle für eine strukturierende Ostpolitik der EU', *Das Parlament* (32 – 1 Aug.).

Latawski, Paul (1993). 'The Polish Road to NATO: Problems and Prospects', *The Polish Quarterly of International Affairs*, 2 (3).

Lebow, Richard Ned (1998), 'Beyond Parsimony: Rethinking Theories of Coercive Bargaining', *European Journal of International Relations*, 4 (1): 31–66.

Lejinš, Atis and Daiana Bleiere (eds) (1996), *The Baltic States: Search for Security*, Riga: Latvian Institute of International Affairs.

Lejinš, Atis (1997). 'The Quest for Baltic Unity: Chimera or Reality?', in Atis Lejinš and Zaneta Ozolina (eds), *Small States in a Turbulent Environment. The Baltic Perspective*, Riga: Latvian Institute of International Relations, 147–83.

Lepskiy, Yuriy (1994). 'Sosedy v evropeyskom dome, Rossiya i Litva o probleme voyennogo tranzita v Kaliningradskuyu oblast', *Trud* (15 Sep.).

Lessem, Ronnie and Fred Neubauer (1994). *European Management Systems*, London: McGraw Hill.

Lewis, Ralph (1993). 'A Jungian Guide to Competences', *Journal of Managerial Psychology*, 8 (1): 29–32.

Lewis, Richard D. (1996). *When Cultures Collide*, London, Nicholas Brealey.

Libak, Anna (1997). 'Baltisk ingemandsland', *Weekendavisen* (4–10 July): 12.

Lieven, Anatol (1993). *The Baltic Revolution. Estonia, Latvia, Lithuania and the Path to Independence*, New Haven, CT: Yale University Press.

Link, Arthur S. (1963). *Woodrow Wilson and the Progressive Era. 1910–1917*, New York: Harper Torchbooks.

Lipponen, Paavo (1997). 'Introductory Statement in Parliament on the Council of State's Report on Security and Defence Policy 17 March 1997', Helsinki, mimeo.

Lofgren, Joan (1997). 'A Different Kind of Union', *Transitions*, 4 (6): 46–52.

Luik, Jüri (1994). 'Security in the Baltic Sea Region – A Guarantee of Stability in Europe', Address by Jüri Luik, Minister of Foreign Affairs of the Republic of Estonia at the Swedish Institute of International Affairs, Stockholm, 2 March, retrieved from http://www.vm.ee/speeches/1994/94mar2.html

Luttwak, Edward N. (1976). *The Grand Strategy of the Roman Empire*, Baltimore and London: The Johns Hopkins University Press.

March, R.M. (1988). *The Japanese Negotiator – Subtlety and Strategy Beyond Western Logic*, New York: Harper & Row.

Marczak, Jozef and Jacek Pawlowski (1995). *O obronie militarnej Polski przelomu XX–XXI wieku*, Warszawa: Wydawnictwo Bellona.

Maslov, Igor (1997). 'The Baltic Aspect to NATO Enlargement. Post-Soviet States' Membership Seen by Moscow as Challenge to Russia's Interests', *Nezavisimaya Gazeta* (16 April).

Mathisen, Trygve (1971). *The Functions of Small States in the Strategies of the Great Powers*, Oslo: Universitetsforlaget.

Matochkin, Yuriy (1994). 'Chto delat s zapadnym forpochtom Rossii: ukreplyat' ili razvivat'?', *Nezavisimaya Gazeta* (27 Aug.).

Mearsheimer, John (1990). 'Back to the Future', *International Security*, 15 (1): 5–56.

Migranjan, Andranik (1994). 'Rossija i blizjneje zarubezje: Vsio prostranstvo byvsjego SSSR javljajetsja sferoj zjiznennykh interesov Rossii', *Nezavisimaja Gazeta* (18 Jan.).

Miles, Lee and John Redmond (1996). 'Enlarging the European Union. The Erosion of Federalism?', *Cooperation and Conflict*, 31 (3 – September).

Miloz, Czeslaw (1993). 'Swing Shift in the Baltics', *New York Review of Books*, 40 (18): 12–16.

Miniotaite, Grazina (1997). 'Lithuania: Towards the European Security Community?'. Paper presented to the 37th Annual Convention of the International Studies Association, Toronto, 18–22 March.

Ministry for Foreign Affairs (1995). *Security in a Changing World. Guidelines for Finland's Security Policy. Report by the Council of State to the Parliament 6 June 1995*, Helsinki: Ministry for Foreign Affairs.

Ministry of Foreign Affairs (1996). *Action programme of the Government of the Republic of Lithuania for 1997–2000*, retrieved from gopher://marvin. nc3a.nato.int:70/00/partners/lithuania/mfa/action/1219viln

Ministry of Foreign Affairs (1997). 'Borders and Border control', Estonian Ministry of Foreign Affairs, Tallinn, retrieved from http://www.vm.ee/ features/ eu/iiipillar/ border.html

Ministry of Defence (1997a). *The BALTBAT Project', Documentation from the Danish Ministry of Defence*, Copenhagen: Ministry of Defence, February.

Ministry of Defence (1997b). 'Danish Defence Cooperation with Partners', Ministry of Defence, Copenhagen: Ministry of Defence, March, mimeo.

Modelski, George (1978). 'Long Cycles of Global Politics and the Nation State', *Comparative Studies in Society and History*, 20: 214–38.

Möttölä, Kari (1997). 'Security Around the Baltic Rim: Concepts, Actors and Processes', paper presented at the OSCE seminar on 'Regional Security and Cooperation', 2–4 June, Vienna.

Möttölä, Kari (1998). 'A Security Space In-Between: The Baltic Sea Region, States and Europe'. Paper prepared for the 39th Annual Convention of the International Studies Association, Minneapolis, MN, 17–21 March.

Mouritzen, Hans (1988). *Finlandization: Towards a General Theory of Adaptive Politics*, Aldershot, UK: Avebury.

Mouritzen, Hans (1997). 'Denmark in the Post-Cold War Era: The Salient Action Spheres', *Danish Foreign Policy Yearbook 1997*, Copenhagen: DUPI, 33–51.

Nahaylo, Bohdan and Victor Svoboda (1990). *Soviet Disunion: a History of the Nationalities Problem in the USSR*, New York: The Free Press.

Nakamura, Hajime (1964). *Ways of Thinking of Eastern Peoples: India, China, Tibet, Japan*, Honolulu, Hawaii: East–West Center Press.

Naval Forces Special Issue (1996). 'Roles, Mission and Structure of the German Navy'.

Neumann, Iver B. (1996). 'Ny giv for nordisk samarbeid' in Iver B. Neumann and Ståle Ulriksen (eds), *Sikkerhetspolitikk. Norge i makttriangelet mellom EU, Russland og USA*, Oslo: Tano.

Neumann, Iver B. and Ståle Ulriksen (eds) (1996). *Sikkerhetspolitik. Norge i makttriangelet mellom EU, Russland og USA*, Oslo: Tano.

Neumann, Iver B. (1996). 'Russland og en geopolitikk renset for objektive faktorer', *Den norske Atlanterhavskomités skriftserie*, Oslo: Den norske Atlanterhavskomité.

Neumann, Iver B. (1997). 'The Geopolitics of Delineating "Russia" and "Europe": The Creation of the "Other" in European and Russian Tradition', in Ola Tunander, Pavel Baev and Victoria Ingrid Einagel (eds), *Geopolitics in Post-Wall Europe*, London: Sage.

Nielsen-Stokkebye, Bernd (1997). 'Eine Politik der Verleumdungen', *Frankfurter Allgemeine Zeitung*, 18 February, p. 14.

Nilsson (Dahl), Ann-Sofie (1991). *Den Moraliska Stormakten*, Stockholm: Timbro.

Nisnevich, B. (1995). 'Vladimir Shumeyko o sudbe Kalinigradskoy oblasti', *Kalinigradskaya pravda* (1 Aug.).

Norton, B.G. (1991). *Towards Unity Among Environmentalists*, New York: Oxford University Press.

'Noviy Oblik Baltiyskogo Flota' (1997). (The New Image of the Baltic Fleet), *Krasnaya Zvezda* (18 December).

Nudler, Oscar (1990). 'On Conflicts and Metaphors: Towards an Extended Rationality', in John W. Burton (ed.), *Conflict: Human Needs Theory*, London: St Martin's Press, 177–201.

Ohmae, Kenichi (1995). *The End of the Nation-State. The Rise of Regional Economics*, London: Harper Collins.

Oldberg, Ingmar (1995). 'Kaliningrad områdets framtid: Kasern, handelsplats eller stridsäpple', *Internasjonal Politikk*, 53 (3).

Öövel, Andrus (1995). Remarks by Andrus Öövel, Minister of Defence of the Republic of Estonia at the Meeting of Defence Ministers of Northern Countries, Bornholm, 23 May, retrieved from gopher://marvin.nc3a.nato.int:70/00/partners/estonia/mod/transcripts/1995/est2205

Opinion 96 – svenskarnas syn på samhället, säkerhetspolitiken och försvaret (1996), Stockholm: Styrelsen för psykologiskt försvar.

Orrenius, Anders and Lars Truedson (eds), *Visions of European Security – Focal Point Sweden and Northern Europe*, Stockholm: The Olof Palme International Centre.

Park, Andrus (1995). 'Russia and Estonian Security Dilemmas', in *Proceedings of the Estonian Academy of Sciences, Humanities and Social Sciences*, 44 (3).

Parsons, Talcott (1951). *The Social System*, New York : The Free Press.

Parsons, Talcott and Edward A. Shils (1951). *Towards a General Theory of Action*, Cambridge, MA: Harvard University Press.

Partem, Michael G. (1983). 'The Buffer System in International Relations', *Journal of Conflict Resolution*, 27 (1): 3–26.

Patai, Raphael (1973). *The Arab Mind*, New York: Charles Scribner's Sons.

Peabody, Dean (1985). *National Characteristics*, Cambridge: Cambridge University Press.

Peristiany, J. (ed.) (1965). *Honour and Shame. The Values of Mediterranean Society*, London: Weidenfeld & Nicolson.

Persson, Göran (1996). Address by the Prime Minister of Sweden at the Foreign Policy Association, New York, 25 September.

Petersen, Nikolaj (1994). 'Denmark and the New Germany. Cooperation or Adaptation', Copenhagen: Institut for Statskundskab.

Pishchev, Nikolay (1997). 'NATO: Myths and Reality', *Krasnaya Zvezda* (5 Jan.).

Plotnikov, Nikolay (1994). 'Baltiyskiy flot sokhranilsya vopreki vsem problemam', *Nezavisimaya Gazeta* (17 Aug.).

Polmar, Norman (1983). *Guide to the Soviet Navy*, Annapolis, MD: Naval Institute Press.

Poulsen-Hanssen, Per (1997). 'NATO, the EU and the Baltic Sea Region', in Bo Huldt and Ulrika Johannssen (eds), *1st Annual Stockholm Conference on Baltic Sea Security and Cooperation: Conference Papers*, Stockholm: Utrikes- politiska institutet.

Pushkov, Aleksey, (1995). 'Nato Enlargement: A Russian Perspective', *Strategic Forum* (34) National Defense University, Institute for National Strategic Studies.

Quester, G. H. (1990). 'Finlandization as a Problem or an Opportunity', *Annals of the American Academy of Political and Social Science*, 512 (November): 33–45.

Rahr, Alexander and Joachim Krause (1995). 'Russia's New Foreign Policy', *Arbeitspapiere zur Internationalen Politik* (91). Bonn: Forschungsinstitut der Deutschen Gesellschaft für Auswärtige Politik.

Rakowska-Harmstone, Teresa (1994). 'Russia's "Monroe Doctrine". Peace- keeping, Peacemaking, or Imperial Outreach?' in Maureen Appel Molot and Harald von Riekhoff (eds), *Canada Among Nations*, Carleton, Canada: Carleton University Press.

Razuvayev, Vladimir(1997). 'V Rossii vsegda budyt opasat'sya NATO', *Nezavisimaya Gazeta* (24 Jan.).

Reisinger, William M., Arthur H. Miller, Vicki L. Hesli and Kristen H. Maher (1994). 'Political Values in Russia, Ukraine and Lithuania: Sources and Implications for Democracy', *British Journal of Political Science*, 24: 183–223.

Reiter, Dan, 1994. 'Learning, Realism and Alliances: The Weight of the Shadow of the Past', *World Politics*, 46 (4): 490–526.

Remnick, David (1997). 'Can Russia Change?', *Foreign Affairs*, 76 (January/ February): 35–49.

Rice, Condoleezza (1991). 'The Evolution of Soviet Grand Strategy', in Paul Kennedy (ed.), *Grand Strategies in War and Peace*, New Haven and London: Yale University Press.

Riekhoff, Harald von and Hanspeter Neuhold (eds) (1993). *Unequal Partners: A Comparative Analysis of Relations between Austria and the Federal Republic of Germany, and Between Canada and the U.S.*, Boulder, CO: Westview Press.

Riste, Olav (1965). *The Neutral Ally. Norway's Relations with Belligerent Powers in the First World War*, Oslo/London: Universitetsforlaget/Allen & Unwin.

Robelek, Marian and Antoni Kamiński *et al.* (1994). *Bezpieczenstwo Polski w zmieniajacej sie Europie*, Warszawa-Torun: Wydawnictwo A. Marszalek.

Roder, Philip G. (1997). 'From Hierarchy to Hegemony: The Post-Soviet Security Complex', in David A. Lake and Patrick M. Morgan (eds), *Regional Orders. Building Security in a New World*, University Park, PA: The Pennsyl- vania State University Press, 219–44.

Rodionov, Igor (1992). 'Approaches to Russian Military Doctrine', speech given at the General Staff Academy's Military-Science Conference from 27–30

May 1992; reprinted in *Voyennaya Mysl'* (July 1992 Special Edition).

Rodionov, Igor (1996a). 'What Kind Of Defense Does Russia Need?', *Nezavisimoye Voyennoye Obozreniye* (28 Nov.).

Rodionov, Igor (1996b). 'Prevent the Appearance of New Division Lines in Europe – text of I. Rodionov's speech at his meeting with NATO Ministers of Defence in Bergen in Sept. 1996', *RIA Novosti, Military News Bulletin*, V (10).

Rognes, Jorn K. (1994). 'Norway', in M. Afzalur Rahim and Albert A. Blum (eds), *Global Perspectives on Organizational Conflict*, Westport, CT: Praeger, 67–86.

Rose, Richard and William Maley (1994). *Conflict and Compromise in the Baltic States. What Do the Peoples There Think?* Glasgow: University of Strathclyde. Studies in Public Policy no. 231.

Rosenau, James N. (1990). *Turbulence in World Politics. A Theory of Change and Continuity*, Princeton, NJ: Princeton University Press.

Rosenau, James N. and Mary Durfee (1995). *Thinking Theory Thoroughly. Coherent Approaches to an Incoherent World*, Boulder, CO: Westview.

'Rossiya i Pribaltika' (1997) (Russia and the Baltic states), Report of the Council on Foreign and Defence Policy, *Nezavisimaya Gazeta* (28 Oct.)

Rothstein, Robert L. (1968). *Alliances and Small Powers*, New York: Columbia University Press.

Ruggie, John Gerard (1997). 'Consolidating the European Pillar: The Key to NATO's Future', *The Washington Quarterly*, 20 (1).

Rühle, M. and N. Williams (1995). 'NATO Enlargement and the European Union', *The World Today* (May).

Russett, Bruce (1993). *Grasping the Democratic Peace. Principles of a Post-Cold War World*, Princeton, NJ: Princeton University Press.

Russett, Bruce and Harvey Starr (1992). *World Politics. The Menu for Choice*, New York: Freeman, 4th ed.

Ruus, Jüri (1996). 'Hanseatic Security. The Baltic Perspective', in *Mare Balticum '96*, Lübeck – Travemünde: Ostsee Akademie, 43–56.

Saffrais, Guylaine (1998). 'Lente intégration des Russes dans les pays baltes', *Le Monde diplomatique* (February), 10.

Sarjusz-Wolski, Marek (1996). 'Forteca na mieliznie', *Zycie Warszawy* (7 May).

Saudargas, Algirdas (1997). Address at the XIVth Conference in Prague, retrieved from gopher://marvin.nc3a.nato.int:70/00/partners/lithuania/mfa/fact/fact13.txt

Schmidt, Burkard (1997). 'NATO à la francaise', *Blätter für deutsche und internationale Politik*, 5: 567–76.

Schmidt, Peter (1996). 'Deutsche Sicherheitspolitik im Rahmen von EU, WEU und NATO', *Aussenpolitik* (III): 211–22.

Schneider, Klaus (1995). 'Partnerschafts- und Kooperationsabkommen mit der Europäischen Union – Russische Föderation und Ukraine' (Partnership and Cooperation Agreements with the EU – Russian Federation and Ukraine), in Werner Weidenfeld (ed.), *Demokratie und Marktwirtschaft in Osteuropa*, Gütersloh: Bertelsmann Foundation: 437–65.

Sergounin, Alexander (1997). *Russia and the Evolving Security Environment in the Baltic Sea Area*, Nizhny Novgorod: University of Nizhny Novgorod, Department of Political Science.

Sergounin, Alexander (1997a). 'Post-Communist Security Thinking in Russia: Changing Paradigms', *COPRI Working Papers* (4).

Sergounin, Alexander A. (1997b). 'In Search of a New Strategy in the Baltic/ Nordic Area', in Vladimir Baranovsky, (ed.), *Russia and Europe. The Emerging Security Agenda*, Oxford: Oxford University Press for SIPRI.

Shakhrai, Sergey (1994). 'Kaliningrad–Kenigsberg–Krulevec ... Kak ukrepit' zapadnyy forpost Rossii', *Nezavisimaya Gazeta* (26 June).

Shedadi, Kamal S. (1997). 'Clash of Principles: Self-Determination, State Sovereignty, and Ethnic Conflict', in Sohail H. Hashmi (ed.), *State Sovereignty. Change and Persistence in International Relations*, University Park, PA: The Pennsylvania State University Press, 131–50.

Sherr, James (1995). 'Russia, Geopolitics and Crime', Conflict Studies Research Centre, R.M.A. Sandhurst, F49, (February).

Shidlovskiy, P. (1994). 'Skazki u pogranichnogo stolba, O pravakh Rossii na Kaliningradskuyu oblast', Sankt Petersburgskiye vedomosti (3 Sept.).

Singer, Max and Aaron Wildavsky (1993). *The Real World Order: Zones of Peace/Zones of Turmoil*, Chatham, NJ: Chatham House Publishers.

Skrzydlo, Andrzej (1994). 'Euroregions with Polish Participation as a Form of Transfrontier Cooperation', *The Polish Quarterly of International Affairs*, 3 (3).

Sloss, Leon and M. Scott Davis (1987). 'The Soviet Union: the Pursuit of Power and Influence through Negotiation', in Hans Binnendijk (ed.), *National Negotiating Styles*, Washington, DC: Foreign Service Institute, US Department of State, 17–44.

Smith, Graham, Aadne Aasland and Richard Mole (1994). 'Statehood, Ethnic Relations and Citizenship', in Graham Smith (ed.), *The Baltic States. The National Self-determination of Estonia, Latvia, Lithuania*, New York: St Martins Press.

Smith, Hedrick (1976). *The Russians*, New York: Quadrangle/New York Times Book Co.

Smoker, Paul and Linda Groff (1996). 'Spirituality, Religion, Culture and Peace: Exploring the Foundations for Inner–Outer Peace in the Twenty-First Century', *International Journal of Peace Studies* (1 – January): 57–113.

Sniderman, P.M., J.F. Fletcher, P.H. Russell and P.E. Tetlock (1996). *The Clash of Rights*, New Haven, CT: Yale University Press.

Snyder, Glenn H. (1984). 'The Security Dilemma in Alliance Politics', *World Politics* 36 (4): 461–95.

Snyder, Jack (1991). *Myths of Empire. Domestic Politics and International Ambition*, Ithaca and London: Cornell University Press.

Solana, Javier (1997). Statement by the Secretary General at NATO's Summit Meeting, in *The Madrid Summit: Official Texts* (Press Info., Madrid, 8 July 1997).

Sorokin, Yevgeniy (1997). 'Polzuchaya anneksiya Kaliningradskogo anklava', *Nezavisimoye Voyennoye Obozreniye* (1 March).

SOU (1994). *Om kriget kommit ...*, Stockholm: Statens Offentliga Utredningar (SOU, 1994: 11).

Spector, Bertram (1995). 'Creativity Heuristics for Impasse Resolution: Reframing Intractable Negotiations', *Annals of the American Academy* (542): 81–99.

Sperling, J. and E. Kirchner (1997). *Recasting the European Order: Security Architectures and Economic Cooperation*, Manchester: Manchester University Press.

Steen, Anton (1997). 'Baltikum i internasjonal politikk: forbilder og samarbeid', *Internasjonal Politikk*, 55 (1): 79–92.

Stein, Arthur A. (1990). *Why Nations Cooperate. Circumstance and Choice in International Relations*, Ithaca, NY: Cornell University Press.

Stephan, Walter G. and Marina Abalakina-Paap (1996). 'Russia and the West – Intercultural Relations', in Dan Landis and Rabi S. Bhagat (eds), *Handbook of Intercultural Training*, 2nd Edition, Thousand Oaks, CA: Sage, 366–82.

Stewart, Edward C. and Milton J. Bennett (1991). *American Cultural Patterns: a Cross-Cultural Perspective*, Yarmouth, ME: Intercultural Press.

Stranga, Aivars (1996). 'Russia and the Security of the Baltic States: 1991–1996', in Atis Lejiņš and Daiana Bleiere (eds), *The Baltic States: Search for Security*, Riga: Latvian Institute of International Affairs, 141–85.

Stranga, Aivars (1997). 'Baltic–Russian Relations: 1995–Beginning of 1997', in Atis Lejiņš and Zaneta Ozolina (eds), *Small States in a Turbulent Environment*, Riga: Latvian Institute of International Affairs, 184–237.

'Study on NATO Enlargement' (1995). Brussels: NATO Office of Information and Press (September).

Suhrke, Astri (1973). 'Gratuity or Tyranny: The Korean Alliances', *World Politics*, 25 (4): 508–32.

SVOP (1994). 'Strategiya dlya Rossii (2) Sojuz po vneshney i oboronnoy politikie', *Nezavisimaya Gazeta* (27 May).

Taina, Anneli (1997). 'Säkerhetsutvecklingen i Europa och Finlands försvar'. Statement by the Minister of Defence to Parliament, 17 March, SRR 1/1997, Helsinki.

Thakur, Ramesh (1991). 'The Elusive Essence of Size: Australia, New Zealand, and Small States in International Relations' in Richard Higgott and J.L. Richardson (eds), *International Relations: Global and Australian Perspectives on an Evolving Discipline*, Canberra Studies in World Affairs, no. 30, Canberra: Australian National University, 241–87.

The Baltic Times (1997a). 'Laying Regional Defence Foundations' (10–16 April): 3.

The Baltic Times (1997b). 'Baltic Militaries Look for Answers' (3–9 April): 7.

The Military Balance, 1997–98 (1997). *International Institute for Strategic Studies*, Oxford: Oxford University Press.

Timmermann, Heinz (1996). 'Die Europäische Union und Rußland – Dimensionen der Partnerschaft' (The European Union and Russia – Dimensions of a Partnership), *Integration* (Bonn) 19 (4): 195–207.

'Totalförsvar i förnyelse' (1996). Government's Whitepaper 1996/87: 4. Stockholm: Ministry of Defence.

Tregubova, Elena (1994). 'Germaniya nie pretenduyet na byvshiy Kenigsberg', *Segodnya* (24 Sept.).

Trenin, Dmitriy, and Mikhail Borodin (1992). 'Vtoroy shans Rossii v Vostochnoy Prussii', *Novoye Vremya* (13).

Trenin, Dmitry (1997a). 'Baltiyskaya Kontseptsiya Rossii' (Russia's Baltic Concept), *Nezavisimaya Gazeta* (11 March).

Trenin, Dmitry (1997b). *Baltiysky Shans. Strany Baltii, Rossiya i Zapad v Skladyvaushcheys'a Bolshoi Evrope* (A Baltic Chance: The Baltic States, Russia and the West in the Emerging Great Europe), Moscow: Carnegie Endowment for International Peace.

Triandis, Harry C. (1995). *Individualism and Collectivism*, Boulder, CO: Westview Press.

Trompenaars, Fons (1993). *Riding the Waves of Culture*, London: Nicholas Brealey.

Tsedilina, Yelena (1996). 'The Military Factor in Russia's Policy for CIS', *Nezavisimoye Voyennoye Obozreniye* (26 Sept.).

Tunander, Ola (1992). 'The Strategic Significance of the Nordic–Baltic Region', in Mare Kukk, Sverre Jervell and Pertti Joenniemi (eds), *The Baltic Sea Area – A Region in the Making*, Oslo: Europaprogrammet.

Tunander, Ola, Pavel Baev and Victoria Ingrid Einagel (eds) (1997). *Geopolitics in Post-Wall Europe. Security, Territory and Identity*, London: Sage.

Udgaard, Nils Morten (1997). 'Baltikum avdekker Nordens svakhet', *Aftenposten* (10 November).

Ulmanis, Guntis (1996a). 'Latvia – Part of the European Strategic Area', Address given at reception for Ambassadors in Riga, 3 May, retrieved from gopher://marvin.nc3a.nato.int:70/00/partners/latvia/mfa/speeches/lat030 5.96

Ulmanis, Guntis (1996b). Statement by the President of Latvia, Riga, 20 May, retrieved from gopher://marvin.nc3a.nato.int:70/00/partners/latvia/mfa/stat/lat2005.96

Usunier, Jean-Claude (1992). *Commerce entre cultures*, vol. 1, Paris: Presses Universitaires de France.

Værnø, Grethe (1993). *Lille Norden, hva nå?*, Oslo: Europaprogrammet/ Cappelen.

Værnø, Grethe (ed.) (1990). *Dialog Norge–Sverige – Fra arvefiende til sambo*, Stockholm: Atlantis.

Van Dyke, Vernon (1985). *Human Rights, Ethnicity, and Discrimination*, Westport, CT: Greenwood Press.

van Ham, Peter (ed.) (1995). *The Baltic States: Security and Defence after Independence*, Chaillot Papers (19), Paris: The Institute for Security Studies, Western European Union (June).

Van Horne, W.A. (ed.) (1997). *Global Convulsions: Race, Ethnicity, and Nationalism at the End of the Twentieth Century*, Albany, NY: State University of New York Press.

van Staden, Alfred (1995). 'Small State Strategies in Alliances: The Case of the Netherlands', *Cooperation and Conflict*, 30: 31–51.

Vares, Peeter (1993). 'Dimensions and Orientations in the Foreign and Security Policies of the Baltic States', in *New Actors on the International Arena: The Foreign Policies of the Baltic Countries*, Tampere: Tampere Peace Research Institute, 3–32.

Vares, Peeter (1994). 'Russia and the Baltic States: Are there Common Security Perspectives?' in *Common Security in Northern Europe after the Cold War. The Baltic Sea Region and the Barents Sea Region*, Stockholm: The Olof Palme International Center, 139–47.

Vares, Peeter and Olga Zhuryari (1995). 'Estonian Foreign Policy', *Nationalities Papers*, 23 (1): 61–6.

Vares, Peeter and Olga Zhuryari (eds) (1996). *Estonia and Russia, Estonians and Russians. A dialogue*, Tallinn: The Institute of International and Social Studies, Stockholm: The Olof Palme International Centre.

Väyrynen, Raimo (1971). 'On the Definition of Small Power Status', *Cooperation and Conflict*, 6: 191–201.

Väyrynen, Raimo (1984). 'Small States in Different Theoretical Traditions of International Relations Research', in Otmar Höll (ed.), *Small States in Europe and Dependence*, The Laxenburg Papers, Vienna: Wilhelm Braumuller.

Väyrynen, Raimo (1998). 'Towards a Security Community in the Baltic Sea Region?', in Georg Sørensen and Hans-Henrik Holm (eds), *And Now What? International Politics after the Cold War. Essays in Honor of Nikolaj Petersen*, Aarhus: Politica, 149–74.

Velliste, Trivimi (1993a). Speech by Trivimi Velliste, Minister of Foreign Affairs of the Republic of Estonia at the NUPI-CSIS Conference on Baltic and Nordic Security, Oslo, 21 September, retrieved from http://www.vm.ee/speeches/1993/93sept21.html

Velliste, Trivimi (1993b). Remarks by Trivimi Velliste, Minister of Foreign Affairs of Estonia at the NACC Foreign Minister's meeting, Brussels, 2 December, retrieved from http://www.vm.ee/speeches/1993/93dec3.html

Vigor, R.H. (1975). *The Soviet View of War, Peace, and Neutrality*, London and Boston: Routledge & Kegan Paul.

Visuri, Pekka (1992). 'The Changing Political and Military Status of the Baltic Region', in Mare Kukk, Sverre Jervell and Pertti Joenniemi (eds), *The Baltic Sea Area – A Region in the Making*, Oslo: Europaprogrammet.

Vital, David (1967). *The Inequality of States*, Oxford: Clarendon Press.

Vital, David (1971). *The Survival of Small States. Studies in Small Power/Great Power Conflict*, London: Oxford University Press.

Vushkarnik, Anton (1997). 'Problemy Otnosheniy Rossii so Stranami Baltii (1990–1996)' (Problems of Russia's Relations with the Baltic States, 1990–1996), *Reports of the Institute of Europe*, Moscow: Institute of Europe (36).

Wæver, Ole and Morten Kelstrup (1993). 'Europe and its Nations: Political and Cultural Identities', in Ole Wæver, Barry Buzan, Morten Kelstrup and Pierre Lemaitre (eds), *Identity, Migration and the New Security Agenda in Europe*, London: Pinter Publishers.

Walker, Gregg B. (1990). 'Cultural Orientations of Arguments in International Disputes – Negotiating the Law of the Sea', in F. Korzenny and S. Ting-Toomey (eds), *Communicating for Peace, Diplomacy and Negotiation*, Newbury Park, CA: Sage, 96–117.

Walt, Stephen M. (1987). *The Origins of Alliances*, Ithaca, NY: Cornell University Press.

Waltz, Kenneth N. (1975). 'Theory of International Relations', in Fred I. Greenstein and Nelson W. Polsby (eds), *Handbook of Political Science, Vol. 8. International Politics*, Reading, MA: Addison-Wesley, 1–86.

Waltz, Kenneth N. (1979). *Theory of International Politics*, Reading, MA: Addison Wesley.

Waltz, Kenneth N. (1993). 'The New World Order', *Millennium Journal of International Studies*, 22 (2): 187–95.

Watson, D.M. (1980). *Proxemic Behaviour*, The Hague: Mouton.

Wedge, Bryant and Cyril Muromcew (1963). *A View from the East: a Study of Psychological Factors in Soviet Disarmament Positions*, Princeton, NJ: Institute for the Study of National Behavior.

Wellmann, Christian (ed.) (1992). *The Baltic Sea Region: Conflict or Cooperation?*, Kiel: Kiel Peace Research Series.

Wellmann, Christian (1996). 'Russia's Kaliningrad Exclave at the Crossroads: The Interrelation between Economic Development and Security Policies', *Cooperation and Conflict*, 31 (2): 161–83.

Werner, Jann (1994). 'Common Security in the Baltic Sea Region: The View from the German Länder', *Common Security in Northern Europe after the Cold War, a report from the Olof Palme International Centre Seminar*, Stockholm, 18–20 March.

Wight, Martin (1991). *International Theory: The Three Traditions*, Gabriele Wight and Brian Porter (eds), Leicester and London: Leicester University Press (Royal Institute of International Affairs).

Williams, Michael C. (1997). 'The Institutions of Security. Elements of a Theory of Security Organizations', *Cooperation and Conflict*, 32 (3): 287–307.

Yemelyanenko, Vladimir (1994). 'Pridnestrovskiy sindrom', *Moskovskiye novosti* (5).

Zaccor, A.L. (1993). 'The Baltic States and Kaliningrad. A Briefing', Fort Leavenworth, KS, and Sandhurst: Foreign Military Studies Office and Conflict Studies Research Centre.

Zagorski, Andrei (1997). 'Rußlands Erwartungen an Deutschland' (Russia's Expectations From Germany), in *Aus Politik und Zeitgeschichte. Beilage zur Wochenzeitung 'Das Parlament'* (1–2), 3 January: 46–53.

Zamfirescu, Elena (1996). 'Mapping Central Europe', *Clingendael Paper* (May).

Zelikow, P. (1996). 'NATO, European Security and Transatlantic Relations: The Masque of Institutions', *Survival*, 38 (1 – Spring): 6–18.

Zhirinovski, Vladimir (1993). *O sud'bakh Rossii. Chast' II. Posledny brosok na jug*, Moscow: Rajt.

Zhuryari Olga (1994). 'The Baltic Countries and Russia (1990–1993): Doomed to Good-Neighborliness?', in *The Foreign Policies of the Baltic Countries: Basic Issues*, Riga: Centre of Baltic–Nordic History and Political Studies, TAPRI, 75–86.

Index